Also by Paddy Ashdown

The Cruel Victory: The French Resistance, D-Day and the Battle for the Vercors 1944

A Brilliant Little Operation: The Cockleshell Heroes and the Most Courageous Raid of World War II

A Fortunate Life: The Autobiography of Paddy Ashdown

Swords and Ploughshares: Bringing Peace to the Twenty-First Century

The Ashdown Diaries (two volumes)

Beyond Westminster

Citizens' Britain

Game of Spies: The Secret Agent, the Traitor and the Nazi

PADDY ASHDOWN

IN COLLABORATION WITH SYLVIE YOUNG

NEIN!

STANDING UP TO HITLER

1935–1944

WILLIAM
COLLINS

William Collins
An imprint of HarperCollins*Publishers*
1 London Bridge Street
London SE1 9GF
WilliamCollinsBooks.com

First published in Great Britain by William Collins in 2018

1

A catalogue record for this book is
available from the British Library

ISBN 978-0-00-825704-0

Printed and bound in Great Britain by
CPI Group (UK) Ltd, Croydon

MIX
Paper from
responsible sources
FSC™ C007454

This book is produced from independently certified FSC paper
to ensure responsible forest management

For more information visit: www.harpercollins.co.uk/green

To Hans Oster, *preux chevalier*

Contents

List of Illustrations

Carl Goerdeler. *(Papers of Arthur Primrose Young, Modern Records Centre, University of Warwick: MSS.242/X/GO/3)*
Wilhelm Canaris. *(Popperfoto/Getty Images)*
Ludwig Beck. *(Ullstein bild Dtl: Getty Images)*
Henning von Tresckow. *(Ullstein bild Dtl: Getty Images)*
Hans Oster. *(AfZ: NL Hans Bernd Gisevius/6.7)*
Erwin von Lahousen. *(ÖNB)*
Hans Bernd Gisevius. *(SZ Photo/Süddeutsche Zeitung)*
Robert Vansittart. *(Scherl/Süddeutsche Zeitung Photo)*
Stewart Menzies and his wife Pamela. *(Evening Standard/Stringer/Hulton Archive: Getty Images)*
Neville Chamberlain on his return from Munich, September 1938. *(Keystone/Stringer/Hulton Archive: Getty Images)*
Paul Thümmel, Agent A54. *(UtCon Collection/Alamy Stock Photo)*
Madeleine Bihet-Richou.
Ursula Hamburger ('Sonja').
Ursula with her children, Nina, Micha and Peter Beurton. *(Courtesy of Michael Hamburger and Peter Beurton)*
Leon 'Len' Beurton. *(Courtesy of Peter Beurton)*
Halina Szymańska. *(Courtesy of Marysia Akehurst)*
Alexander Foote. *(CRIA/Jay Robert Nash Collection)*
Rachel Duebendorfer. *(The National Archives, ref. KV2/1619)*
Allen Dulles. *(NARA 306-PS-59-17740)*
Rudolf Roessler. *(CRIA/Jay Robert Nash Collection)*
Sándor Radó with his Geopress staff.
Sándor and Helene Radó with their two sons, June 1941. *(Bundesarchiv, Berlin-Lichterfelde)*
'De Favoriet', the Jelineks' shop in The Hague, c. 1939.
Bernhard Mayr von Baldegg, Alfred Rosenberg and Max Waibel.

Defenceless under the night
Our world in stupor lies;
Yet, dotted everywhere,
Ironic points of light
Flash out wherever the just
Exchange their messages:
May I, composed like them
Of Eros and of dust,
Beleaguered by the same
Negation and despair,
Show an affirming flame.

From W.H. Auden, 'September 1, 1939'

'The only salvation for the honest man is the conviction that the wicked are prepared for any evil … It is worse than blindness to trust a man who has hell in his heart and chaos in his head. If nothing awaits you but disaster and suffering, at least make the choice that is noble and honourable and that will provide some consolation and comfort if things turn out poorly.'

Baron vom Stein, urging Friedrich Wilhelm III
to oppose Napoleon in 1808

Introduction

This book is about those at the very top of Hitler's Germany who tried to prevent the Second World War, made repeated attempts to kill him, did all they could to ensure his defeat, worked for an early peace with the Western Allies, and ultimately died terribly for their cause.

Most of my books have been about individual events, or people. The canvas of this one, by contrast, encompasses every sector of German society during the war; international statesmanship – or lack of it – in capitals from Berlin, to London, to Washington, to Moscow; battles fought from the shores of the Volga to the shadow of the Pyrenees; and spy rings plying their trade in Geneva, Zürich, Paris, Amsterdam, Istanbul and beyond.

Now that I have written it, I am a little surprised to find that a work I thought would tell the history of the Second World War through different eyes turns out also to be a story on the subject to which I return again and again: how human beings behave when we are faced with the challenges of war – and especially how, when confronted by great evil and personal jeopardy, we decide between submission and resistance: between loyalty and betrayal.

Is it ever possible to be both traitor and patriot? Is it treachery to betray your state if to do otherwise is to betray your humanity? Even if treachery changes nothing, must you still risk being a traitor in the face of great evil, if that is the only way to lighten the guilt that will fall on your children and your future countrymen? How do people make these choices? How do they behave after they have made them?

Dietrich Bonhoeffer – himself one of those murdered for his role in the anti-Hitler resistance – said: 'Responsible action takes place in the sphere of relativity, completely shrouded in the twilight that the historical situation casts upon good and evil. It takes place in the midst of the countless perspectives from which every phenomenon is seen. Responsible action must decide not just between right and wrong, but between right and right and wrong and wrong.'

So it is, exactly, here. There are no blacks and whites, just choices between blacker blacks and whiter whites. There are no triumphal personal qualities, and no triumphant outcomes. Just flawed individuals who, at a time of what Bonhoeffer referred to as 'moral twilight', felt compelled to do the right thing as they saw it. That is a lesser triumph than we might wish for in dangerous times, but it was then – and is now – probably the only triumph we can reasonably expect.

This story is, at its heart, a tragedy. Like all great tragedies it involves personal flaws, the misjudgements of the mighty, and a malevolent fate. There is individual pity and suffering, and a deal of personal stupidity, here.

But – and herein lies the history – since these were human beings of consequence, their personal decisions affected lives and events far beyond their circle and their time.

The two central historical questions posed by this book are stark: did the Second World War have to happen? And if it did, did it have to end with a peace which enslaved Eastern Europe?

My purpose is not to provide definitive answers, but rather to present some facts which are not generally known – or at least not taken account of – and place these against the conventional view of the origins, progress and outcomes of World War II.

In reading this book you may be struck, as I was in writing it, by the similarities between what happened in the build-up to World War II and the age in which we now live. Then as now, nationalism and protectionism were on the rise, and democracies were seen to have failed; people hungered for the government of strong men; those who suffered most from the pain of economic collapse felt alienated and turned towards simplistic solutions and strident voices; public institutions, conventional politics and the old establishments were everywhere mistrusted and dis-believed; compromise was out of fashion; the centre collapsed in favour of the extremes; the normal order of things didn't function; change – even revolution – was more appealing than the status quo, and 'fake news' built around the convincing untruth carried more weight in the public discourse than rational arguments and provable facts.

Painting a lie on the side of a bus and driving it around the country would have seemed perfectly normal in those days.

Nevertheless, I have found myself inspired in writing this story. It has proved to me that, even in such terrible times, there were some who were prepared to stand up against the age, even when their cause was hopeless, and even at the cost of their lives.

I hope that you will find that inspiration here, too.

Main Dramatis Personae

Anulow, Leonid Abramovitsch – Alias 'Kolja' – Soviet 'Rezident' in Switzerland before Radó

Attolico, Bernardo – Italian ambassador in Berlin

Bartik, Major Josef – Head of Czech intelligence 1938

Beck, General Ludwig – Chief of staff of the German army until dismissed by Hitler in 1938. The army leader of the anti-Hitler plot

Bell, George – Anglican theologian and bishop of Chichester

Beneš, Edvard – Czech president 1935–38

Beurton, Leon Charles – Known as Len. Friend of Alexander Foote. Radio operator Dora Ring

Bihet-Richou, Madeleine – Lover of Erwin Lahousen. French secret services

Blomberg, Field Marshal Werner von – Commander-in-chief of the German army until dismissed by Hitler in 1938

Bock, Field Marshal Fedor von – Von Tresckow's uncle. Commander of Army Group Centre

Bolli, Margrit – Alias 'Rosy'. *Rote Drei* radio operator

Bonhoeffer, Dietrich – Theologian, German pastor and key plotter

Bonhoeffer, Dr Karl – Father of Dietrich. Took part in the September 1938 plot

Bosch, Robert – German industrialist. Founder of the Bosch industrial empire. Supporter of Goerdeler

Brauchitsch, Field Marshal Walther von – Commander-in-chief of the German army up to the defeat at Moscow in 1941

Cadogan, Sir Alexander – Head of the British Foreign Office

Canaris, Erika – Wife of Wilhelm

Canaris, Wilhelm – Head of the German Abwehr until his dismissal in 1944

Chojnacki, Captain Sczcęsny – Polish intelligence spy-master based in Switzerland

Ciano, Galeazzo – Italian foreign minister

Colvin, Ian – Central European correspondent of the London *News Chronicle*. Arranged von Kleist-Schmenzin's visit to Britain in 1938

Daladier, Édouard – French prime minister

Dansey, Sir Claude – Deputy head of MI6 and founder of the 'Z Organisation'. Known as 'Colonel Z'

Dohnányi, Hans von – Lawyer in the Abwehr and a key conspirator

Donovan, Major General William 'Wild Bill' – Head of the US intelligence agency (OSS)

Duebendorfer, Rachel – Alias 'Sissy'. 'Dora Ring' agent

Dulles, Allen – OSS representative in Bern

Eden, Anthony – British foreign secretary

Farrell, Victor – MI6 head in Geneva

Fellgiebel, General Fritz Erich (known as Erich) – Chief of the German army's Signal Establishment and a key plotter

Foote, Alexander – Alias 'Jim'. Radio operator, 'Dora Ring'

Franck, Aloïs – Paul Thümmel's Czech spy-handler

François-Poncet, André – French ambassador in Berlin at the time of Munich

Fritsch, Colonel General Werner von – Commander-in-chief of the German army until his dismissal on trumped-up charges of homosexuality in January 1938

Gabčik, Josef – Operation Anthropoid Czech agent

Gersdorff, Rudolf-Christoph von – Henning von Tresckow's staff officer; volunteered to assassinate Hitler by suicide bombing on 21 March 1943

Gibson, Colonel Harold 'Gibby' – Head of the MI6 station in Prague

Gisevius, Hans Bernd – The 'eternal plotter' in the Abwehr. Key early conspirator and Canaris's conduit to Halina Szymańska

Goerdeler, Anneliese – Carl Goerdeler's wife

Goerdeler, Carl – Key early plotter. Ex-mayor of Leipzig

Groscurth, Lieutenant Colonel Helmuth – Canaris's liaison officer with the army at Zossen

Guisan, General André – Head of the Swiss army

Haeften, Lieutenant Werner von – Von Stauffenberg's adjutant

Halder, Colonel General Franz – German chief of staff under von Brauchitsch

Halifax, Lord Edward – British foreign secretary under Chamberlain and a key appeaser

Hamburger, Ursula – *Née* Kuczynski. Code name 'Sonja'. Soviet spy who arrived in Switzerland in 1936

Hamel, Olga and Edmond – 'Dora Ring' radio operators

Hassell, Ulrich von – German ambassador in Italy before the war. Liaison between Beck and Goerdeler

Hausamann, Captain Hans – Founder of the Büro Ha, a private intelligence bureau in Switzerland

Heinz, Lieutenant-Colonel Friedrich – Leader of the commando who were to kill Hitler in 1938

Henderson, Sir Nevile – British ambassador in Berlin before 1939

Hoare, Sir Samuel, MP – One of Chamberlain's leading appeasement supporters

Hohenlohe von Langenberg, Prince Maximilian Egon – Freelance spy. Friend of Dulles, Canaris and Himmler

Jelinek, Charles and Antoinette – Owners of 'De Favoriet' bric-à-brac shop in The Hague

Keitel, Field Marshal Wilhelm – Chief of the German armed forces high command

Kleist-Schmenzin, Ewald von – German emissary of the opposition to Hitler; saw Churchill in London in August 1938

Kluge, Field Marshal Günther von – Commander of Army Group Centre. Reluctant plotter

Kordt, Erich – Head of Ribbentrop's office in Berlin

Kordt, Theo – Brother of Erich. Official at the German embassy in London

Kubiš, Jan – Operation Anthropoid Czech agent

Lahousen, Major General Erwin von – Head of the Austrian Abwehr and then senior officer in the German Abwehr. Close to Canaris and a key plotter. Lover of Madeleine Bihet-Richou

Manstein, Field Marshal Erich von – Commander of Army Group South and mastermind of the Kursk offensive

March, Juan – Mallorcan businessman and prime mover in Spain – contact of Canaris and MI6

Masson, Roger – Head of Swiss intelligence

Mayr von Baldegg, Captain Bernhard – Staff member of Swiss army intelligence; Waibel's deputy head

Menzies, Sir Stewart – Head of MI6

Mertz von Quirnheim, Colonel Albrecht – Friend of Stauffenberg; involved in the 20 July 1944 plot

Moltke, Count Helmuth von – Founder of the 'Kreisau Circle'

Morávec, Colonel František – Head of the Czech intelligence service

Morávek, Václav – Resistance leader in Prague

Mueller, Josef – Canaris's spy in the Vatican

Navarre, Henri – Madeleine Bihet-Richou's French intelligence 'handler'

Niemöller, Martin – Anti-Hitler Lutheran pastor

Olbricht, General Friedrich – Key plotter. Involved in the 20 July coup

Oster, Colonel Hans – 'Managing director' of the attempted 1938 coup. Head of Z Section in the Tirpitzufer

Pannwitz, Heinz – SD officer in charge of finding the 'Dora Ring'

Payne Best, Captain Sigismund – MI6 officer captured at Venlo

Puenter, Dr Otto – 'Dora' agent – also in touch with MI6

Radó, Sándor – Head of the 'Dora' spy network

Ribbentrop, Joachim von – German ambassador to London and later Hitler's foreign minister

Rivet, Colonel Louis – Head of French military intelligence (SR)

Roessler, Rudolf – Codename 'Lucy'. Private purveyor of intelligence in Switzerland

Sas, Gijsbertus Jacobus – Dutch military attaché in Berlin; contact of Oster and Waibel

Schacht, Hjalmar – German minister of economics and president of the Reichsbank

Schellenberg, Walter – Heydrich's protégé and mastermind of Venlo

Schlabrendorff, Fabian von – German lawyer. Liaison between Tresckow in Russia and Beck in Berlin

Schneider, Christian – Alias 'Taylor'. Swiss businessman. Cut-out supplying information from Roessler to the Dora Ring

Schulenburg, Friedrich-Werner von der – Pre-war ambassador to Moscow and senior resistant

Schulte, Edouard – German businessman and one of Chojnacki's agents

Sedláček, Karel – Alias 'Charles Simpson'. Czech intelligence officer in Bern

Stauffenberg, Colonel Claus Schenk, Graf von – Architect and perpetrator of the 20 July 1944 bomb plot

Stevens, Major Richard – MI6 officer captured at Venlo

Suñer, Serrano – Spanish foreign minister

Szymańska, Halina – Wife of the Polish military attaché in Berlin before the war. Channel for Canaris to pass information to Menzies

Thümmel, Paul – Many aliases. MI6 agent A54. Important spy in the early part of the war

Timoshenko, Marshal Semyon – Commander of Soviet forces at Moscow, Stalingrad and Kursk

Tresckow, Henning von – Chief of staff of Army Group Centre; a key plotter

Trott zu Solz, Adam von – German lawyer, diplomat and active resister

Vanden Heuvel, Count Frederick – Head of MI6 in Bern after 1941

Vansittart, Sir Robert – Head of the pre-war British Foreign Office

Waibel, Captain Max – Swiss intelligence officer

Weizsäcker, Ernst von – Head of the German Foreign Office and key plotter

Wilson, Sir Horace – Personal adviser to Chamberlain. Appeasement supporter

Witzleben, General Erwin von – Commander of the Berlin garrison and de facto leader of the September 1938 coup

Young, A.P. – One of Vansittart's 'spies' in contact with Goerdeler

Zaharoff, Basil – Director of Vickers and notorious arms dealer

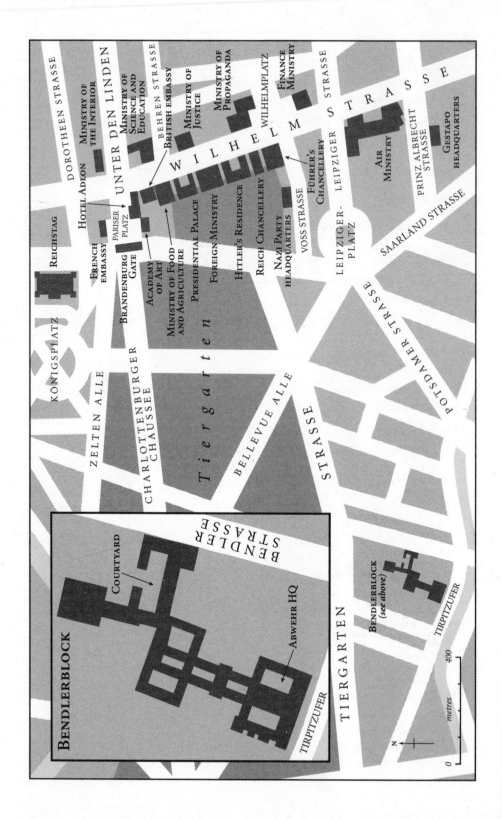

Prologue

To the millions whose votes helped make Adolf Hitler chancellor of Germany, he was the hero who would rescue them from the humiliations of the Versailles Treaty and the shaming chaos that followed.

John Maynard Keynes, who attended the 1919 peace conference, condemned Versailles afterwards in unforgiving and uncannily prophetic terms: 'If we aim at the impoverishment of Central Europe, vengeance, I dare say, will not limp. Nothing can then delay for very long the forces of Reaction and the despairing convulsions of Revolution, before which the horrors of the late German war will fade into nothing, and which will destroy, whoever is victor, the civilisation and the progress of our generation.'

Keynes was not the only person to understand that in the punitive conditions imposed by Versailles lay the seeds of another explosion of German militarism. Others referred to it as 'the peace built on quicksand'.

Under Clause 231 of the Treaty, the 'War Guilt' clause, Germany was deprived of all her colonies, 80 per cent of her pre-war fleet, almost half her iron production, 16 per cent of coal output, 13 per cent of her territory (including the great German-speaking port of Danzig) and more than a tenth of her population. To add to these humiliations, the victorious Allies also planted a deadly economic time bomb beneath what was left of the German economy. This took the form of war reparations amounting to some $US32 billion, to be paid largely in shipments of coal and steel.

In 1922, when Germany inevitably defaulted, French and Belgian troops occupied the centre of German coal and steel production in the Ruhr valley. Faced with the collapse of the domestic economy, the German government sought refuge in printing money, with the inevitable consequence of explosive runaway inflation. In 1921 a US dollar was worth 75

German marks. Two years later, each dollar was valued at 4.2 trillion marks. By November 1923, a life's savings of 100,000 marks would barely buy a loaf of bread.

In the months immediately following the Armistice, an armed uprising inspired by Lenin and the Russian Revolution ended in 1919 with the removal of the kaiser and elections for Germany's first democratic government, christened the Weimar Republic after the city in which its first Assembly took place. It all began in a blaze of hope, but soon descended into squabbling and dysfunctionality. Unstable, riven with shifting coalitions, burdened with war reparations, incapable of meeting the challenges of the global depression, the new government, along with politicians of every stripe and hue, soon became objects of derision and even hatred. Compromise was seen as failure, easy slogans replaced rational policies, the elite were regarded with suspicion, and the establishment was deluged with accusations of corruption and profiteering.

A new myth – that of the 'stab in the back' – began to be promulgated by the German right. This blamed 'the politicians' for the defeat of 1918 and the Versailles humiliations that followed. It was claimed that the German army was undefeated, but had been betrayed by the politicians in Berlin who signed the Armistice. It was not long before the Jews were added into the mix, which swiftly mutated into an international conspiracy aimed at the destruction of Germany and its people. The 'stab in the back' legend became so deeply imbedded in the German pre-war psyche that it would restrain Hitler's domestic opponents, and influence the Allies' terms for peace, right up until the end of the coming war.

Between 1924 and 1929 the German economy stabilised, thanks in large measure to US loans. A period of great artistic renaissance followed. Berlin, reverberating to the talents of Thomas Mann, Bertolt Brecht, Max Reinhardt, Marlene Dietrich and the artists and architects of the Bauhaus movement, became the cultural capital of the world.

No sooner was hope reborn than it was broken again on the wheel of a second economic crisis, this time brought about by the Wall Street crash of October 1929. By 1932, with unemployment standing at six million, those, including dependants, directly affected by loss of work amounted to 20 per cent of the German population.

Revolt was once again in the air. Running battles broke out in the streets between communists and Hitler's stormtroopers. A German commentator on these years wrote, 'In [these] times, principles are cheap and perfidy, calculation and fear reign supreme.'

These were perfect hothouse conditions for the growth of the most radical forms of extremism. Driven by a mystic and misshapen belief in the moral rebirth of Germany, unencumbered by doubt, unheeding of convention, fed on hate, armoured with conspiracies and slogans and led by a messianic leader who combined charisma with an astonishing ability to move the masses, the Nazi Party's time had come. In the 1928 elections, the National Socialist Democratic Party – known by its shortened version, 'Nazi' – was no more than a tiny fringe party winning only 2.6 per cent of the vote. Just four years later, in July 1932, Hitler's party secured 13.7 million votes, making it, with 37 per cent of the national vote, by far the largest party in the German Reichstag. A second national election in November of that year saw a drop in the Nazi vote. Nevertheless, after a period of parliamentary stalemate, the ageing German president Paul von Hindenburg appointed Hitler chancellor in 1933, believing that this was the best means to control him. 'We've engaged him for ourselves,' said former chancellor Franz von Papen, one of the grandest of the grandees in German politics. 'Within two months we will have pushed Hitler so far into the corner that he'll squeak.'

By these miscalculations the nation of Beethoven and Schiller, of Goethe and Schubert, was given over, lock, stock and barrel to the most primitive, destructive and primeval force for barbarism that Europe had seen since the Dark Ages.

While most of the elite saw Hitler as a harmless eccentric who they could control and who would not last for long, many ordinary Germans, even those who did not vote for him, believed that he might represent a new start and should be given a chance – after all, many argued, things couldn't get worse, could they?

All of them had misjudged their man.

Adolf Hitler was remarkable in many ways. He was always thinking the unthinkable; always proposing the objectionable; always choosing to shock, rather than to comfort; always rejecting the constraints of convention; always preferring myth and mission to reality; always taking people by surprise with his undiluted radicalism; always trusting his own inner voice in preference to facts and other people's opinions. 'I confront everything with a tremendous ice-cold lack of bias,' he once declared. Because a thing should be, it would be – that was Hitler's doctrine. On the altar of this absolutism, bolstered by his much-vaunted 'triumph of the will', Hitler would lay waste to half of Europe.

But it was not these manic qualities which made Adolf Hitler different. What distinguished him from the many other fascist leaders of his age, and from the myriad self-declared prophets of history, was his genius for political action – he was a mythmaker with a practical understanding of power and how to use it to achieve his ends.

It was this, more than anything else, which caused friend and foe alike to look upon him with a wonder which produced adulation, fear and intrigued curiosity, depending on where you stood in relation to his power.

Foreign capitals, blindly hoping to 'tame the beast' who would not be tamed, proposed the usual well-tried European inducements of agreements, pacts, bribes and appeasements in the vain hope of containing the uncontainable. The whole of Europe was mesmerised – paralysed too – by what had happened in Berlin. A German observer in Paris noted among the French 'a feeling as if a volcano has opened up in their immediate vicinity, the eruption of which may devastate their fields and cities any day. Consequently they are watching its slightest stirrings with astonishment and dread. A natural phenomenon which they are forced to confront … helplessly. Today Germany is again the great international star that appears in every newspaper, in every cinema, fascinating the masses with a mixture of fear and reluctant admiration … Germany [under Hitler] is the great, tragic, uncanny, dangerous adventurer.'

Inside Germany, it did not take long for those who disagreed with Hitler to find out that things could get worse – very much worse.

The first underground opposition to the Nazis grew out of a combination of political groupings which had stood against him in the elections – chiefly the communists and the Social Democrats.

Tainted by their association with the failures of the Weimar Republic, and in the case of the communists by their refusal to join an alliance against Hitler during the economic crises of 1930–33, Hitler's democratic opponents were easily outmanoeuvred and broken by his ruthless pursuit of power.

Like so many others at home and abroad, Germany's conventional parties failed to recognise the uniqueness of Hitler's demonic nature, and presumed that his revolution was just another episode in the normal rhythms of the democratic cycle. 'Harsh rulers don't last long,' said the chairman of the last great Social Democratic Party rally in Berlin in 1933.

A terrible price would soon be paid for this apathy.

On 22 March 1933, just seven weeks after Hitler became chancellor, the first concentration camp opened its gates to admit two hundred political prisoners to an old gunpowder and munitions factory which SS leader Heinrich Himmler had chosen at Dachau, sixteen kilometres from Munich. The camp, with its gates bearing the infamous legend 'Arbeit macht frei' – Work will make you free – would remain a byword for torture, every kind of inhumanity and mass extermination, until it was overrun by American troops in the last year of the war. By the end of 1933, 20,000 of Hitler's political opponents were either in jail or doing their best to survive under the most brutal conditions in Dachau and other concentration camps, now popping up across Germany.

Despite violent anti-communist purges, which started very soon after Hitler became chancellor, communist cells began to reseed themselves in factories and workplaces. Mostly these numbered no more than six or eight people, connected by a sophisticated courier system to other cells, the identities of whose members they often did not know. These networks extended into other European countries, where they were especially active in German émigré communities. In due course, after a brief period of quiescence during the Nazi–Soviet Non-Aggression Pact, and despite being energetically pursued by Hitler's secret state police, the Gestapo, the German communist underground network would turn to sabotaging the war effort and spying, not least through the great Russian wartime spy network which operated throughout occupied Europe, nicknamed by Himmler's security structures *die Rote Kapelle* (the Red Orchestra).*

What was left of Hitler's political opposition went underground. Among the German resistance's early supporters were numerous activists in the social democrat cause and many in the trade union movement.

Opposition to Hitler was not confined to the workers. Although some German industrialists and financiers, such as Alfred Krupp, found good commercial reasons to support Hitler, a number of others, like the great engineering industrialist Robert Bosch in Stuttgart, courageously provided active succour to the opposition.

With the communists, liberals and social democrats forced underground, it was left to some elements of the German Church to nurture popular opposition to National Socialism. The Barmen synod of May 1934 in Wuppertal brought together Lutherans who openly condemned the materialism and ungodliness of National Socialism, attracting tens of

---

* Literally 'the Red Chapel'. In this usage the word '*Kapelle*' is meant to indicate that it is a secret organisation. The translation of '*Kapelle*' as 'orchestra' is capricious and confusing. 'Ring' would have been better.

thousands from all over Germany to an open-air demonstration at which they voiced their opposition to what was happening. In the St Annen-Kirche in the Berlin suburb of Dahlem, the middle class thronged to hear 'the fighting pastor' Martin Niemöller preach his incendiary sermons against all the Nazis stood for. In southern German cities like Nuremberg, Stuttgart and Munich, Christians marched in the streets in support of Lutheran bishop Theophil Wurm and his colleague Hans Meiser, bishop of Munich, both of whom had been placed under house arrest for inciting public disturbance. An anti-Nazi tract written by Helmut Kern, a Lutheran pastor from Nuremberg, sold 750,000 copies in short order – the highest circulation for a religious tract since those of Luther himself.

Hitler, despite his by-now unchallenged dominion over the instruments of the German state, shrank from open warfare with the mass ranks of the German Churches, Protestant and Catholic. But he tried every other means to suppress the dissent. Niemöller was arrested and sent to a concentration camp, from which he did not emerge until the war was over. Troublesome pastors were conscripted *en masse* into the army, the Church's work with the young was curtailed, teaching permits were withheld for those lecturing in theology at German universities, and permission was refused for the publication of all pamphlets except those acceptable to the Nazi regime. Hitler's supporters even managed to infiltrate the Church elections of July 1933 to such an extent that he was able to enforce the anti-Semitic 'Aryan Law', removing all pastors who were 'tainted' by descent from Jewish or half-Jewish forebears.

On 14 March 1937, Pope Pius XI issued a powerful encyclical attacking the new wave of 'heathenism' in such strong terms that it became a call to arms against the Nazis. What followed was an open and violent counter-attack on the monasteries, led by Hitler's minister of propaganda Joseph Goebbels. In a purge reminiscent of Henry VIII, some were commandeered for military bases, others were banned from accepting new entrants or holding religious processions. Between 1933 and 1945 thousands of brave pastors and friars were to be found among the inmates of the concentration camps, where many of them lost their lives as martyrs for their beliefs.

Although Hitler was finally able to stem 'the mischief-making of the Church', religion and religious activists, including the great pastor, theologian and spy Dietrich Bonhoeffer, played a huge part in providing the inspiration, moral underpinning and manpower for the anti-Hitler resistance.

Scattered amongst these organised and semi-organised structures of the German resistance were a number of individuals who, as the excesses and horrors of Nazism became more and more evident, started to wage their own private and lonely struggles against the Nazi state. Among these were the Württemberg carpenter Georg Elser, who, acting entirely alone, missed assassinating Hitler with a bomb by a hair's breadth because of fog at Munich airport; Otto and Elise Hampel, who distributed over two hundred anti-Hitler messages around Berlin and died under the guillotine as a result, and the students of the White Rose Circle who, led by their tutor, met the same fate for distributing pamphlets around Munich.

These remarkable individuals – Auden's 'ironic points of light' – ignited brief beacons of moral courage in the darkness. But they did not – could not – alter the course of the war.

As they, and many we do not know of, changed their stance from supporting Hitler to actively opposing him, others in the most senior echelons of the Nazi state were tracing similar paths towards their own individual epiphanies.

Chief among these were three men: a civilian who could have been chancellor in Hitler's place; a general who many believed was destined to lead his armies; and the head of his foreign intelligence service.

1

Carl Goerdeler

Late-evening sunlight streamed through the Palladian windows of the dining room of the National Liberal Club in London. It fell on a damask tablecloth laid with silver and porcelain in a secluded alcove set slightly apart from the other tables. The wooden panels all around glowed a deep mahogany, and the air resonated with the low murmur of diners enjoying themselves, despite the stern gaze of William Gladstone's twice-life-size statue at the far end of the room.

The six men at the alcove table were not cheerful. They were sombre, quiet-voiced, and listening carefully to one of their number, an imposing figure with boyish good looks, startling light-grey eyes, heavy eyebrows and a forceful personality. The fifty-two-year-old Carl Goerdeler was a serious man who was used to being taken seriously. Ex-lord mayor of the great German city of Leipzig, until recently a key official in the government of Adolf Hitler and a sometime candidate for chancellor of Germany, Goerdeler was a dinner guest whom it was easier to listen to than to converse with.

Born on 31 July 1884 in the west Prussian town of Schneidemuehl, Carl Friedrich Goerdeler, the son of a district judge, had been a brilliant student at school, a brilliant law graduate at Tübingen University, and by all accounts a brilliant practising lawyer before finding his metier as an economist and senior official in German local government. He soon proved a talented and effective administrator, whose grasp of economics, incorruptible personality and ability to charm were quickly recognised. In 1912, at the age of just twenty-eight, Goerdeler was unanimously elected as principal assistant (effectively deputy) to the mayor of the Rhenish town of Solingen in western Germany. His military service on Germany's Eastern Front in the First World War ended with a period as the administrator of a large swathe of territory in present-day Lithuania and Belarus which had been occupied by Germany under the terms of the Brest-Litovsk Treaty of

1918. Here he added a reputation for humanity and compassion to his other recognised virtues.

The Armistice in November 1918 changed everything for Goerdeler, and for Germany. Like most Germans, he felt that his country's emasculation in the Versailles settlement inflicted a deep shame and injustice on his Fatherland. It was in these post-war years that Goerdeler the nationalist and patriot began to take form. The brutal amputation of Danzig from the 'motherland', in order to give newly-enlarged Poland a corridor to the sea, especially offended his sensitivities, both as a German and as a Prussian. He maintained a vocal opposition to this Versailles humiliation long after most other civil and military leaders had accepted the necessity to move on. This was as admirably fearless as it was tactically stupid. It was also an early example of a stubborn refusal to compromise when Goerdeler considered his cause just, which would become a *leitmotif* of his life until the very end.

By now Goerdeler's political views had solidified. He was by upbringing a devout Lutheran, and by political conviction a conservative with an attraction to constitutional monarchism. He was authoritarian, patriotic, consumed by a belief in the power of political ideals and democracy (but only to the point where these did not interfere with efficient government). Economically, he believed in financial rectitude; in his dealings with others he was punctilious, in his personal habits he was frugal, and in his personal life he was guided by an unyielding moral code which even extended to refusing entry into his family home to those who had been divorced. One of his friends, and a future fellow plotter against Hitler, wrote: 'Goerdeler was a clear-headed, decent, straightforward kind of man who had very little or nothing about him which was sombre, unresolved or enigmatic. He therefore assumed his fellow human beings needed only enlightenment and well-meaning moral instruction to overcome the error of their ways.'

These qualities would have made Carl Goerdeler a great man in any stable age, but they rendered him a hopelessly naïve utopian in the cruel age of turbulence and revolution in which he had to live his life.

After a period as the deputy mayor of Königsberg on the Baltic coast during the 1920s, Goerdeler was elected Oberbürgermeister (lord mayor) of Leipzig in 1930, just two months before his forty-sixth birthday. Now he was a big figure on the national stage. At the time he took over the Leipzig administration, Germany was midway through its second great economic convulsion, following the hyper-inflation of the early 1920s. In

Carl Goerdeler

December 1931, with unemployment rocketing, Goerdeler accepted an invitation from President Hindenburg to join his government as Reichskommissar (State Commissioner) for price control. His deft handling of this delicate role earned him widespread acclaim. When Hindenburg's chancellor, Heinrich Brüning, resigned in May 1932, Goerdeler was widely thought of as his successor. But the political turmoil which ensued did not produce a man of rectitude and order – it produced instead Adolf Hitler, who became chancellor of Germany on 30 January 1933.

Goerdeler did not at first oppose Hitler. He saw the new chancellor as potentially an enlightened dictator, who with the right advice could be a force for good and for order after the upheavals and failures of the Weimar years.

It did not take long for the scales to fall from the lord mayor of Leipzig's eyes.

On 1 April 1933, when the city's Jewish businesses were threatened by Nazi stormtroopers of the Sturmabteilung (SA) during Hitler's 'day of national boycott', it required an appearance by the mayor in full ceremonial dress, backed by the police, to save the situation from descending into violence and calamity. There followed several instances when Goerdeler had to intervene personally to save Jewish enterprises from the consequences of Hitler's policy of sequestrating Jewish assets and businesses in order to 'Aryanise' the German economy.

There was worse – much worse – to come. On 30 June 1934 Hitler launched the internal putsch which history has come to know as the Night of the Long Knives. The ostensible purpose of this act of national bloodletting was to exterminate the paramilitary SA, which Hitler saw as a growing threat to his power. But the killings extended into a general orgy of score-settling with enemies of the Nazi regime. Among the eighty-five killed were the army general who was Hitler's immediate predecessor as chancellor, the personal secretary of another chancellor, and several Catholic political leaders. It was now plain to all that Hitler's government was prepared to behave illegally, unscrupulously, murderously, and completely without reference to either moral or legal codes. This was a turning point for many.

But not, despite all his moral rectitude, for Carl Goerdeler.

On 5 November 1934, barely four months after the Night of the Long Knives, Goerdeler accepted an offer from Hitler to become, for the second time, Germany's commissioner for price control. His decision to serve Hitler at this time was one he would find difficult to explain later. Why did he do it? The answer provides keys to two of the most puzzling paradoxes of Goerdeler's complex personality. Alongside an all-consuming conviction of what was right and wrong, including a willingness to accept any personal sacrifice rather than to submit, he also possessed an almost childlike ignorance about the true nature of evil. Because of this, despite his worldly wisdom in matters of politics, government and the economy, he completely overestimated his ability to persuade bad men to do good things, by talking sensibly to them.

The truth was that Goerdeler accepted Hitler's post because he believed he could change him. His chosen weapons for doing this were a stream of long (in some cases very long) memoranda and papers on the economy, directed at the chancellor. These were read either skimpily or not at all. Following a succession of turf battles and disagreements on public policy-making, the inevitable rupture between the two men occurred in 1936, when Goerdeler lost all power and influence in Hitler's circle.

This was the moment for which the lord mayor's Nazi enemies in Leipzig had been waiting.

In early November that year, the Oberbürgermeister was invited to speak at the German-Finnish Chamber of Commerce in Helsinki. At the time Goerdeler was under attack by the local Leipzig Nazi leader because of his refusal to remove the statue of Felix Mendelssohn, the great German-Jewish composer, from its position outside the city's concert hall. Pointing out the statue to a visitor, the Oberbürgermeister complained: 'There is one of my problems. They [the Brownshirts] are after me to remove that monument. But if they ever touch it I am finished here.' To his daughter Marianne he seems to have indicated that what really affronted him was an outrageous attack not so much on a Jew, as on German culture: 'All of us listened to Mendelssohn's songs with great pleasure and sang them as well. To deny Mendelssohn is nothing, but an absurd, cowardly act.'

Before leaving for Helsinki, Goerdeler extracted promises from Hitler and Himmler that they would personally ensure the safety of the statue in his absence. Nevertheless, the local Nazis pulled it down while he was away. Returning to Leipzig in a fury, Goerdeler issued an ultimatum that the missing statue should be replaced forthwith. When it wasn't, in typical Goerdeler style, he resigned. It should be noted that his resignation was far more a protest against the loss of his authority than against anti-Semitism, for his position on the Jews at this time was at best ambivalent. Even so, for this act of principle against tyranny and of protest against an outrage to German culture, Carl Goerdeler became an overnight hero to many across Germany who saw him as having sacrificed his public career rather than lend his name to a shameful deed.

As the bearer of all that was good and great about German culture, order and respect for the law, Goerdeler, who never liked to be without a mission for long, now decided that personal responsibility and conscience demanded that he should henceforth dedicate his superhuman energy, ability and moral purpose to a single end – the removal of Adolf Hitler.

His first task was to warn the world about the true nature of the German dictator and the threat that he posed. But how? Goerdeler was, after all, not only without a job, but also without a passport, which had been confiscated by a local Gauleiter.

What he needed for his new mission was money, and his passport back.

The money came from Robert Bosch, the head of the Bosch industrial empire and leader of a small group of Stuttgart democrats who were hostile to Hitler. Bosch appointed Goerdeler (who had already turned down a post with Alfred Krupp, a man of very different political views) as financial and international adviser to his firm, so providing him with both a reason to go abroad and a comfortable salary to live on.

Goerdeler got his passport back from an unexpected source – Hermann Göring. Göring, who was in charge of the German rearmament programme at the time, was becoming increasingly concerned about the possibility of a future war. Cleverly playing on this (and probably also on Göring's desire to build up his own private information network) Goerdeler proposed that he should undertake a foreign tour, and report back on opinion in Western capitals. Göring jumped at the idea, arranging for the return of Goerdeler's passport and instructing his new emissary as they parted that he should always remember on his travels to conduct himself 'as a patriot'.

The would-be wanderer left Berlin on 3 June 1937, at the beginning of a series of foreign trips which over the next two years would take him to Belgium, Britain (twice), Holland, France (twice), Canada, the USA, Switzerland (twice), Italy, Yugoslavia, Romania, Bulgaria, Algeria, Libya, Egypt, Palestine, Syria and Turkey.

His message was always the same. Hitler was evil; his government had done evil things, and would do many more; he had neither moral restraint nor human scruple; his aim was war, and if he was left unchallenged, war would be inevitable. The only way to avoid this was for the Western powers to be firm in opposing him – 'call black, black and white, white' as he put it. Any equivocation or appeasement would be regarded by Hitler as weakness, and would further inflame his megalomania. If standing firm against Hitler was the policy of the Western powers, Goerdeler promised, he and his friends would get rid of him from inside Germany – even at risk of their lives.

It must have been startling for the quiet English gentlemen sitting around the dining table in the comforting normality of the National Liberal Club in Whitehall to realise that they were being warned of an impending putsch designed to remove Hitler and change the government of Germany.

Standing in the darkness on the pavement outside the club after they had waved their guest goodbye in a London taxi, one of the company said to their host, 'He has decided with commendable courage to go forth and fearlessly condemn the Hitler regime, regardless of what the personal consequences may be'.

Goerdeler's fellow diners that night were not in themselves in any way remarkable. They consisted of an ex-World War I fighter pilot, an industrialist, a renowned German educationalist and a middle-ranking civil servant. They had been brought together for the occasion by Arthur Primrose Young. Young (he preferred to be known as 'A.P', in preference to anything which included Primrose) was a senior industrialist and a member of a small group who acted as occasional gatherers of intelligence for Sir Robert Vansittart, permanent under secretary at the Foreign Office and close adviser to Anthony Eden, the foreign secretary. Every word that was said that night would be reported back. Vansittart was the invisible seventh diner at the table on this ordinary July evening in 1937.

Most permanent under secretaries at the British Foreign Office are unobtrusive, background men, whose voices are seldom heard. But Sir Robert Vansittart – widely known in Whitehall as 'Van' – was different. Knowledgeable, clever and very well informed, he was so influential over Eden that the foreign secretary was often maliciously referred to behind his back as 'His Master's Voice' – the point of the barb being that 'Van' was the foreign secretary's master, not the other way round.

Vansittart was, in short, anything but quiet and unobtrusive. His frequently-voiced concerns about the rise of Hitler were so contrary to the appeasement policy of His Majesty's Government of the time that one of prime minister Neville Chamberlain's close advisers referred to him as 'an alarmist, [who] hampered all attempts of the Government to make friendly contact with the dictator states'.

A few days later, Goerdeler had a meeting with Vansittart, no doubt as a result of Young's report on the National Liberal Club dinner. Afterwards, Van wrote a memorandum to Eden for circulation to the cabinet. In it he underlined Goerdeler's warnings, referring to the visiting German as 'an impressive, wise and weighty man [who by coming to Britain is] putting his neck in a halter'.

Vansittart's minute got no further than Eden's desk. It did not accord with the prevailing government policy of appeasement, and would therefore, the foreign secretary judged, not be welcomed by his cabinet colleagues.

The minute still exists in Van's private papers. On it, in Vansittart's hand, are written the words: 'Suppressed by Eden'.

2

Ludwig Beck

If there was a soldier in the German army who embodied the antithesis of all that Hitler and the Nazi Party stood for, it was Ludwig Beck.

And yet, he was not one of life's natural rebels. He was too intellectual, too thoughtful, too careful, too considered and too punctilious (that word again) to be a great plotter – and far too straightforward to be a successful conspirator.

And that was his problem. Like Carl Goerdeler, Ludwig Beck was a man made for a different age than the one in which he found himself.

Also like Goerdeler, Beck at first welcomed the arrival of Hitler and the Nazis on the German scene. In the autumn of 1930 he famously defended young officers in his unit who were court-martialled for being members of the Nazi Party, contrary to the rules of the time which prohibited army officers from political activity. When the Nazis seized power in 1933, Beck, whose Lutheran faith had incorporated a degree of anti-Semitism since the days of Luther himself, announced, 'I have wished for years for the political revolution, and now my wishes have come true. It is the first ray of hope since 1918.'

Ludwig August Theodor Beck was born the son of a gifted metallurgical engineer on 29 June 1880 in Biebrich, then a small village on the opposite bank of the Rhine from Mainz. As a middle-class Prussian brought up in the long afterglow of the victories of the Franco-Prussian War and the ensuing unification of Germany, and living little more than a stone's throw from Frankfurt, where the treaty which sealed these triumphs was signed, the young Beck's career would probably have been decided from the moment he was born – he was to be a soldier.

What followed was an education in the classic Prussian military tradition. This produced officers of high professional ability, who regarded a commitment to their country as synonymous with loyalty to their regiment and to the brotherhood of their fellow officers. For these men the

Prussian military code, characterised by the motto *Üb Immer Treu und Redlichkeit** (Always practise loyalty and sincerity), was more than a slogan – it was a way of life that they were sworn to follow and protect. Later this sense of loyalty and brotherly solidarity among the officer corps would protect even plotters against the German state from discovery by the security services.

Ludwig Beck's moral compass, founded on *Üb Immer Treu und Redlichkeit*, was different from that of Carl Goerdeler – but its pull was no less strong.

Tall, angular, thin, Beck's physical appearance closely mirrored his personality. He had the look of an ascetic, with what one colleague described as 'facial skin so tight as to seem ghoulish, especially on the rare occasions when he smiled'. Another noted his 'tense, sensitive, finely chiselled face with slightly sunken, rather sad eyes'. To his contemporaries Beck seemed a solitary figure, set slightly apart from the crowd, as though close human contact was strange and uncongenial to him. A committed and practising Lutheran, for Beck, austerity, rectitude and restraint were the guiding principles of his life and the cornerstone of his religious beliefs.

Beck the young officer was no moustachioed, boneheaded Prussian militarist of the sort beloved of cartoonists and popular legend. He was what was known in the Germany of the time as an 'educated officer'. Like Frederick the Great he was keen on music, and played the violin well. Widely read, knowledgeable and engaged in all aspects of German cultural life, he was fluent in English, an admirer of French culture and, unlike most in the Prussian officer class, engaged freely with politicians. Intellectually disciplined, he was widely recognised as a man of refinement and integrity; in later life he would earn the nickname 'the philosopher general'.

But Ludwig Beck had his flaws too – they were the flaws which can often weaken the soldier who has more intellect than is needed for the job. He was a man of thought rather than of action, who weighed every step so carefully that he could sometimes miss the fleeting opportunity whose lightning exploitation is the true test of the great commander. One contemporary put it more prosaically: 'Everyone who knew him, knew he

---

* The motto is taken from a song of this title that from 1797 to 1945 was played every hour by the bells of Potsdam's Garrison Church, the burial place of Frederick the Great. The words, by the eighteenth-century poet Ludwig Hölty, were set to the tune of Papageno's song 'Ein Mädchen oder Weibchen' from Mozart's opera *The Magic Flute*. The motto became closely associated with Prussian values and the creed of Freemasonry.

Ludwig Beck

could not be persuaded into a cavalry charge.' Men looked up to Beck not
for his battle-readiness, but for his deep spiritual and intellectual qualities,
and for his unshakeable integrity.

By the time the First World War came, Ludwig Beck was an experienced thirty-four-year-old professional soldier, widely regarded as a man
on the way up. He spent most of the first three years of the war as a staff
officer on the Western Front, earning a reputation for diligence and an
extraordinary capacity for hard work. He worked such long hours at the
front that he was forced to give up his beloved violin. In May 1916 he took
a few days' leave from the front to marry Amalie Pagenstecher, the daughter of a Bremen merchant and, at twenty-three, twelve years Beck's junior.
Nine months later the couple had a daughter, Gertrud. Then, in November
1917, tragedy struck when Amalie suddenly died. Beck arranged for
Gertrud's care and swiftly returned to his duties at the front line. After the
war ended he took over his daughter's upbringing himself, throwing
himself into the task with typical dedication and energy.

A period commanding an artillery regiment in present-day Baden-
Württemberg followed, before Beck was posted to the Department of the
Army in Berlin in 1931. He arrived in the capital just in time to have a
ringside seat for the final stages of the collapse of the Weimar Republic,
and the rise of Adolf Hitler.

Beck's job was to lead a team tasked with producing the German army's new operations manual, the *Truppenführung*, which first appeared in 1933. A modified version of this widely acclaimed work is still in use in the German Federal Army of today. In 1932 Beck was promoted to lieutenant general, and in 1933, the year Hitler became chancellor, he was made head of the army department. By this time the army department had effectively become the German general staff, despite an explicit prohibition against the creation of such an organisation in the Versailles Treaty. Beck threw himself into his new task with his usual ferocious energy. He rose each morning at 5.30 and rode from six to eight, before being driven to army headquarters on Bendlerstrasse at 8.30. He worked in his office overlooking the courtyard from 9 a.m. until seven in the evening, when he returned home to dine. After dinner he did paperwork for a further three hours, before retiring to bed punctually at midnight.

These long hours were not spent only on military matters. By this stage of his life Beck was fully engaged in his second great love – politics.

It did not take him long to realise that his hope that Hitler would be a necessary and passing evil after the chaos of the Weimar years was to be confounded. Like Goerdeler and many others, Beck and his army colleagues were horrified by the lawlessness and bloodletting of the Night of the Long Knives, especially when one of the army's own, Hitler's predecessor as chancellor, General Kurt von Schleicher, and his wife were cold-bloodedly murdered in their home.

Three weeks later, an attempted putsch by Austrian Nazis to overthrow their government, in which Hitler's hand was clearly visible, failed disastrously.

To Beck, who had close contacts in the German Foreign Office, the failed coup confirmed what he had feared for some time: that the long-term consequence – and probably intent – of Hitler's foreign policy was war. Shortly afterwards, he wrote a memo to his superiors warning that premature foreign adventures would ultimately result in a 'humiliating retreat'.

Beck, however, went further than predictions. Basing his arguments on religious and moral convictions similar to those of Goerdeler, he asserted, in a way that foreshadows the Nuremberg trials of more than a decade later, that legitimate action by the state and its servants in the army had to be based on morality. To prevent modern conflict becoming total war, he wrote, what was needed was 'a policy with moral bases which knows to retain its supremacy on the foundation of a new moral idealism in the state itself and in its relations with other nations'. It goes without saying that if such a moral context for state policy and action was what Beck hoped for, he must have known that it could never be found in Hitler and his associates.

On 2 August 1934, a month after the Night of the Long Knives, the death occurred of the eighty-six-year-old President Paul von Hindenburg, the only person whose status and position could act as a counterbalance to Hitler's growing command of the German state. A little over two weeks later, in a referendum called the day before the old president's death, 89.9 per cent of Germans voted to combine the offices of president and chancellor, conferring absolute power on Adolf Hitler. All civil servants and members of the armed forces were now required to attend mass rallies and swear an oath of personal allegiance to Hitler (rather than, as previously to 'the People and Fatherland'): 'I swear by God this sacred oath, that I will render unconditional obedience to Adolf Hitler, the Führer of the German Reich and people, Supreme Commander of the Armed Forces, and will be ready as a brave soldier to risk my life for this oath.' Beck, who claimed to have been unaware of the full form of the oath until he arrived at the ceremony, declared to a friend afterwards, 'This the blackest day of my life.' Later, in a classic Beck afterthought, he confided to another, Hans Bernd Gisevius, that he 'could never rid himself of the awful thought that at the time he should not, perhaps, have given his oath'.

Very few felt as Beck did. The average officer in the Wehrmacht was delighted by the new mood of militarism in Germany, by the respect the army appeared to receive from Hitler and by the physical consequence of this: increased budgets for the latest arms and equipment, and a massive expansion in numbers. True, some were concerned that the flood of new recruits – especially members of the Hitler Youth, for whom the notion of *Üb Immer Treu und Redlichkeit* was as alien as it was quaint – would alter the nature of the German army. Most officers consoled themselves with the thought that the army would change the newcomers before they changed the army; and anyway, since the man to whom they had just sworn absolute fealty clearly needed them, what had they to fear?

Beck was one of very few who understood that the imposition of Hitler's *Führerprinzip* (the leader principle), with its demand for absolute obedience, meant the destruction of the normal checks and balances of a democratic state. His answer to this threat was for the army, as Germany's strongest and most revered institution, to play its role as the essential counterweight needed to keep the state on a safe course. In a normal democratic state, he suggested, military action was tasked and constrained by the political leaders. But if this balance was broken or dysfunctional, the roles should be reversed, and it should become the responsibility of the army to set its own limits for the politicians. 'It is not what we do,' he wrote to one of his subordinates in 1935, 'but how we do it which is so bad. [It is a] policy of violence and perfidy.' National confidence in Germany's most illustrious arm, its military, depended, Beck asserted, on the army's refusal to allow itself to be used as the tool of a foreign policy built on naked adventurism. The army, in short, had a duty to act as the emergency brake on political folly or evil.

Beck was now on territory which was dangerously close to rebellion. Writing to his superior Werner von Fritsch in January 1937, he insisted, 'All hope is placed in the army. The Wehrmacht will never permit adventure – for able and clever men are its head. Total responsibility rests [on us] for future developments. There is no escaping that.'

It did not take long for Beck to be cruelly disabused of these elaborate niceties.

Hitler's long-term intentions had for some time been strongly hinted at for those with ears to hear. As early as May 1935, Beck, as chief of staff, had been ordered to start planning for Operation Schulung, an 'imaginary' invasion of Czechoslovakia. In the first months of 1937, responding to the mood in Hitler's Chancellery, Beck began considering how he would implement an order to bring Austria into the German fold.

On 5 November 1937, Hitler finally made plain what had so far only been implied. In a long monologue delivered at a secret meeting with his key military leaders, the chancellor announced that his intention was indeed to go to war with his neighbours: 'The first German objective ... should be to overthrow Austria and Czechoslovakia simultaneously ... the descent upon the Czechs [should be carried out] with lightning speed [and might take place] as early as 1938.' Hitler stressed that he was not predicting a short conflict – his long-term aim, he warned, was to acquire more 'living space' (*Lebensraum*) for Germany's population by 1943.

Any hope that the army would act as Beck's hoped-for 'emergency brake' on what was now plainly revealed as Hitler's headlong dash to war vanished in the early months of 1938, when the German army suffered a double blow to both its prestige and its power. It began with a carefully engineered 'scandal' which on 27 January ended the career of the then minister of war and commander-in-chief, Field Marshal Werner von Blomberg. Eight days later the head of the army, Colonel General Fritsch, the man to whom Beck had written a few weeks earlier asserting that the army would never permit 'adventure', was forced to resign because of an alleged, but entirely manufactured, homosexual encounter with a male prostitute in a backstreet close to a Berlin railway station. The army, in which Beck had invested 'all hope', stood silently by and uttered not a squeak of protest at these public crucifixions of two of its most respected officers, or at the step-by-step emasculation of its power and position which ensued. On 4 February, Hitler, seeing this weakness, seized direct personal control of Germany's military machine, declaring, 'I exercise henceforth immediate command over the entire armed forces.'

Following the Fritsch affair and Hitler's takeover of the army, whispered talk began to circulate about the possibilities of taking direct action. Carl Goerdeler lobbied some generals to initiate a coup d'état by using the army to seize Gestapo headquarters. But Ludwig Beck had not yet crossed the Rubicon. Asked at a meeting about this time if he had any comment on the recent events, he responded that the question was improper: 'Mutiny and revolution are words which will not be found in a German soldier's dictionary.'

Despite all the evidence to the contrary, Beck, still failing to understand the true nature of Hitler's demonic will, continued to believe that he could divert the coming war by persuasion and legal means.

Again, he was soon proved wrong.

Hitler swiftly consolidated his mastery of the German machine by appointing his most loyal acolyte, Wilhelm Keitel, as chief of the newly created high command of the armed forces, and Joachim von Ribbentrop as his new foreign minister. Then, following the annexation of Austria in March, he convened a secret meeting with his generals on 30 May, and proclaimed: 'It is my unalterable decision to smash Czechoslovakia by military action in the near future.'

For Beck, this was the last straw. In a minute to his superior, Field Marshal Walther von Brauchitsch, he wrote: 'The Führer's remarks demonstrate once again the total insufficiency of the existing military hierarchy at the highest level … If the lever is not applied here soon … the future fate … [of] peace and war and with it the fate of Germany … can only be seen in the blackest colours.'

Now at last Ludwig Beck understood that all attempts to alter Hitler's 'unalterable resolve' were in vain. If war was to be prevented, the time had come, the philosopher general concluded, to pass from protests to the preparation of coups and assassinations.

3

Wilhelm Canaris

At a little before eight o'clock on the morning of 2 January 1935, a slight and rather unprepossessing man with sad china-blue eyes and prematurely white hair for a forty-eight-year-old walked through the front door of Tirpitzufer 72–76, an imposing five-storey granite building a kilometre or so from Hitler's Chancellery. Standing by the small concierge's kiosk just inside the front door, a casual observer not in the know (the visitor's presence that day was a state secret) would not have marked the small figure down as anyone of particular importance. True, his admiral's uniform and his complexion, ruddy with the lash of salt breezes, told of a life at sea. But senior military figures were two a penny in Berlin these days. This man's dress looked 'shop-soiled and old', and his bearing far from military, so that the observer might have imagined that he was perhaps retired, rather than someone at the very top of Chancellor Hitler's hierarchy. 'He gave the impression of a civilian, rather than a senior German officer,' said one commentator.

The admiral walked up a flight of steps set between two fluted Doric pillars and across the glistening tiled floor of the Tirpitzufer entrance hall to a creaky lift with a reputation for breaking down, positioned to one side of a balustraded stairway sweeping down from the first floor. He entered the lift and, pressing the button for the third floor, was duly deposited in front of a pair of heavy oak doors which led through an outer office to an empty, high-ceilinged room, which echoed to his footsteps. Looking around, the newcomer would have noted to himself, with the habit of a man used to taking over other people's jobs, that his predecessor had taken all the furniture.

Wilhelm Canaris's journey to his new post as head of the Abwehr,* Germany's principal foreign intelligence service, had been a long and

---

* Its full title was the Amtsgruppe Auslandsnachrichten und Abwehr.

romantic one. It had taken an inexperienced young naval officer and made him into what a contemporary described as 'one of the most interesting phenomena of the period … a combination of disinterested idealism and of shrewdness such as is particularly rare in Germany. In Germany one very seldom finds the cleverness of a snake and the purity of a dove combined in a single personality.'

Born to a wealthy industrialist near Dortmund on 1 January 1887, Wilhelm Franz Canaris was a few years younger than both Ludwig Beck and Carl Goerdeler. According to family legend he was a descendant of the nineteenth-century Greek admiral, liberation hero and politician Constantine Kanaris. Canaris liked to repeat this story in preference to the truth, which was that his ancestors were the Canarisi family from the area around Lake Como in northern Italy, who took their winemaking skills to the Mosel region of Germany in the late seventeenth century. There was indeed something not quite German – something more of the south – about Wilhelm Canaris. In later life he would express a dislike of cold northern climes, and a preference for the warmth, charm and easy living of the south. His personality too seemed more in tune with the sinuosity and subtlety of the Mediterranean than with the eternal search for logic, resolution and mastery of the Atlantic races.

A pious Protestant all his life, he was nevertheless fascinated by the spiritualism and rituals of the Catholic Church, and believed in the super-natural. Moral precepts played an established part in his life – though not as clearly defined a part as with Goerdeler or Beck. Canaris's compass, unlike theirs, gave him a firm general direction of travel built on strong principles. But when it came to the application of these, he was serpentine, flexible and full of ruses and devices. A few meanderings here and there were of little consequence, provided his basic moral foundation remained uncompromised. His character was founded on a deep strain of ambiva-lence. One observer commented, 'Canaris had a profound sense of adven-ture, including the adventure of evil itself.' His was a mind capable of coping with paradox, and, in the right circumstances, he did not find it difficult to accept that ends could justify means, provided they were care-fully chosen and judiciously applied.

One other unusual feature marked Canaris's personality. He never looked back. What had gone had gone, and was of no consequence. The only thing that mattered to him was what was ahead.

Wilhelm Canaris had a gentle disposition. 'He hated violence in itself,' a friend noted. '[He] was repelled by war … [and had] an exaggerated love

Wilhelm Canaris

for animals. "Anyone who does not love dogs, I judge out of hand to be an evil man," he once announced … I never witnessed in Canaris a trace of crudity or brutality … only sudden revelations of his deep-seated humanity.' Another of his contemporaries noted that he was, in all his dealings and whatever the provocation, invariably 'a kind person'. His wife Erika described him as a man of 'tender emotions'.

Politically, Canaris was a natural conservative. But his views were moderately held, and tempered always with an instinct for humanity and an internationalist world view. Later on, possibly under the influence of Goerdeler, he believed that after the war there should be a United States of Europe led by a triumvirate of Britain, France and Germany.

Physically, he was small and slight. Frequently mocked for his lack of stature by his classmates, he left school to enlist in the Imperial German Navy at the age of eighteen, later claiming that his choice of this career was due to his famous (but entirely unrelated) Greek 'ancestor'.

The young Wilhelm Canaris first came to prominence in Germany (and Britain) as a result of a First World War game of hide-and-seek played out along the west coast of South America between the Royal Navy light cruiser HMS *Glasgow* and the German light cruiser *Dresden*, on which

Canaris was a junior officer. On 14 March 1915 the *Glasgow* finally found the *Dresden* sheltering in a bay on an isolated island in Chilean waters. Following negotiations between the two warships, in which Canaris (who spoke excellent English and had a reputation for exquisite manners) was involved, the *Dresden*'s captain, realising he was cornered, opened her sea-cocks, scuttled his ship and surrendered his German crew to internment. Canaris, who also spoke perfect Spanish (he was said to be fluent in six languages) did not remain behind bars for long. On 4 August 1915 he escaped captivity and made his way disguised as a peasant by train, foot, boat and horseback over the Andes to Buenos Aires. From there, assuming the identity of a Chilean widower, 'Señor Reed Rosas', young Lieutenant Canaris took a slow boat home through, among other places, Falmouth (where he assisted British immigration officials with information on a fellow traveller). He finally arrived back in Germany on 30 September 1915.

Towards the end of that year, the slight figure of 'Señor Reed Rosas' turned up again, this time in Madrid, where he took out a lease on a flat not far from the German embassy. Wilhelm Canaris, alias Reed Rosas, alias 'Carl', codename 'Kika' (a childhood nickname which means 'peeker'), was on a spying mission for his country.

Despite suffering recurrent bouts of malaria, exacerbated by the excessively hot summers and bleak winters of Madrid, Canaris found that his posting to Spain was the start of a love affair with the Iberian peninsula and its people that would last the rest of his life. 'I like Italians, just as I like Greeks and Spaniards,' he told a friend. 'If a Spaniard gives me his word of honour, I place confidence in it. I am much more cautious towards the Greeks and especially the Italians. In Italy sincerity is often camouflaged behind different colours, like the slices on a Neapolitan cake.'

Ordered home through Italy, Canaris, still masquerading as Señor Rosas, and accompanied by a Spanish priest also travelling under a false identity, left Spain for France on 21 February 1916. Both men claimed to be travelling to Switzerland to take the cure for tuberculosis (an illness it was easy for Canaris to feign because of his malaria). After crossing the French–Italian border without difficulty, the pair headed for Domodossola on the Swiss–Italian border, thirty kilometres north of the Italian lakes.

By now, however, the French and the British had alerted the Italian border guards to look out for a Chilean passport in the name of Reed Rosas. The fugitives were arrested on 24 February, and summarily thrown into jail. An extensive period of interrogation in the none-too-gentle hands of Italian counter-intelligence followed, during which Canaris took to biting his lip so that he could convincingly spit blood to back up his claim to tuberculosis. Soon German and Chilean diplomatic wheels began to turn in Madrid. Under pressure from the Chilean government, the Italian authorities agreed not to hang the pair, and bundled them on board a freighter bound for Cartagena. On 15 March, Canaris arrived back in Madrid, emaciated, convulsed with shivering and racked with a roaring malarial fever.

The experience of being arrested, jailed, very nearly hanged and struck down with malaria ought to have put him off spying forever. But it didn't. Over the next year he made the contacts and put together the spy networks in Spain and Portugal that would form the foundation of his later work on the Iberian peninsula during the 1930s and 40s.

He swiftly became a familiar of the shadowy demi-monde of spies, corrupt officials, bankers, money-launderers, arms traders, adventurers, and all the hangers-on who circle like scavengers around rotten meat in the neutral spaces of any conflict. Among these were two men who would be of special interest to him in the future. The first was Basil Zaharoff, a director of the British engineering company Vickers Armstrong, an occasional British agent and one of the world's most notorious arms salesmen. The second was a Mallorcan fisherman and tobacco-smuggler called Juan March. March, whose fingers were in almost every dubious Iberian pie and who ended his life a very rich man because of it, was one of Canaris's most important agents. According to rumour and the voluminous files held on him in the British National Archives, he also performed the same function for the British Secret Intelligence Service (SIS, also known as MI6), a fact of which both sides were probably very well aware.

In late 1916, with his work in Spain finished, Canaris made a second attempt to get back to Germany, finally reaching safe territory on 9 October 1916, when he was landed from the German submarine U-35 at the Croatian port of Cattaro.

On his return to Germany he was awarded the Iron Cross First Class and immediately posted back to regular service, commanding a succession of U-Boats in the Mediterranean and sinking several Allied ships before the war ended.

After such a war, what could the thirty-one-year-old Canaris do next for adventure? He began casting around to find a stage on which he could use his talents and his love of conspiracy. Politics was the obvious answer,

and there was more than enough of it to go round in the chaos and revolution of post-Versailles Germany. In the early post-war years Canaris was
deeply involved in combating the threat of communism, which at the time
seemed poised to overwhelm Germany. He was an early activist in the
formation of the anti-communist Freikorps paramilitary units which
roamed the country. In this role he almost certainly had dealings with his
old Iberian adversary Basil Zaharoff, who was at the time busy selling
weapons from his German factories to anyone who would buy them.

In the post-Bismarck German constitutional settlement, the army's
position was almost that of a state within a state. High-level politics and
high-level military command occupied a deeply enmeshed common space
at the pinnacle of the German state, and often flowed into each other in a
way unknown in most other European democracies. Although still only a
very minor player, this was the space in which Wilhelm Canaris had now
arrived, and the space in which he would, with only brief exceptions,
spend the rest of his life.

But the young naval lieutenant's hyperactivity in 1919 was not confined
to politics and conspiracies. He was also pursuing romance.

His first love had been an English girl, Edith Hill, the daughter of a
wealthy northern industrialist to whom Canaris, a lifelong anglophile, had
become more or less engaged. At the outbreak of war, however, Miss Hill
terminated the relationship on the grounds that it would be improper to
marry a citizen of her nation's enemy. Around 1917, probably after his
well-publicised escape from South America, he met and fell in love with
Erika Waag, also the daughter of an industrialist. When peace came, he
assiduously tracked her down and, three days after finding her, proposed.
They married in 1919, and went on to have two daughters. The marriage
was not on the whole a contented one. Erika's passion for music and the
arts, and Wilhelm's for politics and plotting, did not always sit easily
together. Canaris was never likely to be the kind of man who would submit
himself to uxorious domesticity.

In June 1923, doubtless in an attempt to keep him away from more
political mischief, Canaris was posted to the cadet-training ship the *Berlin*,
a superannuated pre-war cruiser which should have been despatched long
ago to the breaker's yard. He found his fellow officers boorish, the job
monotonous, and his enforced exclusion from intrigue unbearable.
Depression – always quite close to the surface of the Canaris personality
– set in. He believed his naval career was over, and toyed with
resignation.

The one bright spot in his life on the *Berlin* was a slim, fresh-faced, fair-haired young man with an artistic temperament and a high-pitched voice (he was nicknamed 'Billy Goat'). Despite the age difference between Canaris and Reinhard Heydrich, there was much which brought the two men together. Heydrich was teased by his fellow cadets because of his effeminate appearance, just as Canaris had been teased for his short stature. Both men were outsiders. Neither found the upper-class overlay of life in the German navy either comfortable or congenial. Observers noted the 'father and son' relationship that developed between the two. On some occasions young cadet Heydrich, an accomplished violinist, would visit the Canaris home, where he accompanied Erika on the piano, while her husband, complete with chef's hat, cooked his favourite dish, saddle of wild boar in a croute made of crumbled black bread and red wine. In the years to come, after Heydrich, then the head of Himmler's Sicherheitsdienst (SD), had himself married, the Canarises and the Heydrichs would twice choose to live as neighbours in the same street.

After the war, Heydrich's wife Lina described the relationship between the two couples: 'Mrs Canaris played the violin and so soon we came to see each other frequently, and this social intercourse … was not to be interrupted until the death of my husband … We used to see each other on our birthday parties; the two men went hunting together; no festivities in our houses passed without our taking part in them … We had a picture of the *Dresden* in the Battle of the Falkland Isles. It was a present from Canaris; he had painted it himself.'

It seems that the relationship between the two couples was actually rather more complex than Lina Heydrich's post-war description makes it seem. By the time they were next-door neighbours in the area around Berlin's Schlachtensee lake there was already an atmosphere of wariness between the two men, neither of whom was averse to using his wife or his private contacts to keep an eye on the other. On one occasion Erika Canaris was invited to her next-door neighbours' for an afternoon coffee party. She did not want to go, but Canaris insisted 'for appearances' sake'. At the event, Lina Heydrich, who was well aware that the Canaris's daughter Eva had been severely incapacitated by meningitis, insisted that, in line with Hitler's new policy of racial purification, 'We have to kill all disabled children.' In any normal relationship, this would have caused a permanent rupture between the two families. Instead, the neighbours' habit of regular, if guarded, social contact seems to have continued uninterrupted. One of his anti-Hitler co-conspirators would later comment on Canaris's puzzling habit of socialising with even the most extreme Nazis: 'Canaris considered them to be thugs and crooks, but he had no objection to observing them. It was like living in some well-written crime story.'

Canaris's 'penal servitude' on his cadet-training ship did not last long. In the spring of 1924, to his huge relief, he exchanged naval uniform for civilian clothes and went undercover again, this time in Japan, where he was engaged in a secret joint enterprise with the Japanese for the construction of the U-Boats Germany was prohibited from having under the terms of Versailles. But the project was stillborn when German defence policy changed from trying to deceive the Royal Navy about the building of illicit U-Boats to cooperating with it, in the hope of achieving some relaxation of the Versailles straitjacket.

Canaris was brought back to a Berlin desk job, which he hated with a passion that left him with a lifetime aversion to staff work, bureaucracies and all sedentary jobs. One of his superiors of this time noted perceptively, 'His troubled soul is appeased only by the most difficult and unusual of tasks.'

True to form, a Berlin desk job did not hold Wilhelm Canaris, now thirty-seven, for long. By the end of 1924, despite government jitters, he was once again deep in backstreet dealings with right-wing bankers and his old spy networks in Spain, creating a series of front companies to cover another attempt at secret ship- and U-Boat-building, this time in Spain and Greece. It was not long before Canaris, assisted by his Mallorcan fisherman friend Juan March, had woven a powerful network of influence in Spain which included Argentine venture capitalists, German industrialists, Spanish shipbuilders, film-makers, bankers, the chief of the Spanish secret police, corrupt officials, government ministers, right-wing members of the Spanish aristocracy, and even the royal family. Inevitably, Canaris's old adversary-cum-partner, the king of arms dealers, Basil Zaharoff, got to hear what was going on, and tipped off the British.

It was not only the British who now moved against Canaris. Thanks to his right-wing activities, he had made powerful enemies at home. Their chance came when one of Canaris's front companies, the film-making enterprise Phoebus, went bankrupt. In the ensuing hullabaloo, his attempts to bypass the Versailles Treaty were exposed, along with his right-wing links. An embarrassment to the navy at home and abroad, he was hurriedly withdrawn from Spain and given a posting away from the public eye on another elderly training ship, the *Schlesien*, on which he served initially as first officer and then, from 30 September 1932, as captain.

It was in this post that, at Hitler's review of the fleet in 1933, Canaris first met the new German chancellor. Hermann Göring too paid a visit to the *Schlesien* that year, but it was far less successful. The future head of the Luftwaffe, who was violently and incessantly seasick, took exception to being the butt of some rather laboured inter-service jokes at his expense from one of the *Schlesien*'s officers. Canaris had to discipline the officer to save his own career, after which the threat quickly passed.

The next crisis was more serious. Canaris liked to be in command, not under it – he was famous for his tetchy and truculent relations with his senior officers. In the late summer of 1934 his immediate superior complained to the head of the navy, Admiral Raeder, about Canaris's behaviour. Raeder, who had already had to deal with the fallout from his difficult subordinate's escapades in Spain and elsewhere, decided that enough was enough, and banished the troublemaker to command an isolated Napoleonic naval fortress at Swinemünde on the Baltic coast. Here Canaris whiled away his time cantering his horse along the deserted beach and waiting for something to come along.

In due course it did. In the last weeks of 1934, after an internal struggle between the army and the navy as to who should fill a vacancy at the head of the Abwehr, Canaris got the job. The fact that he was well known to be on very bad terms with Raeder may have helped. Although the Abwehr was officially the German foreign intelligence service, it was organisationally attached to the army general staff, making Canaris, though a senior naval officer, effectively an 'adopted son' of what was known at the time as the Reichswehr (the German army). Appointing Canaris, the Führer, an avid devotee of British spy novels, said, 'What I want is something like the British Secret Service – an order, doing its work with passion.'

What Hitler saw in the forty-seven-year-old rear admiral (Canaris was promoted on his appointment) was a master right-wing conspirator who could be put to his service. What he didn't see was the subtly independent spirit, sustained by a strong moral code and firm principles, that was hidden below.

The event which marked the greatest single service Wilhelm Canaris rendered his master during his early years as Abwehr chief began on 25 July 1936.

Returning that evening from Wilhelm Furtwängler's triumphant production of Wagner's *Die Walküre* at Bayreuth's Festspiel opera house, Hitler was handed a personal letter from a largely unknown forty-three-year-old Spanish colonel called Francisco Franco Bahamonde. Franco, as he soon became known, was trapped in Morocco with 30,000 troops, unable to transport them over the Straits of Gibraltar to the Spanish mainland, where they were desperately needed to stem the advance of Republican forces threatening Seville, because of an embargo enforced by the Spanish navy. What he needed – and desperately – was aircraft to fly him and his men to the beleaguered Spanish city. He had appealed to Mussolini for help, but was refused. He now turned to Hitler.

Though the hour was late, Hitler called in Göring and the armed forces' commander-in-chief, Werner von Blomberg. At the conclusion of discussions which ended in the early hours of the following morning, Hitler decided to throw his weight behind Franco. It now fell to Canaris to deliver the aid his master had promised. The one-time spy was in his element, using his old contacts in the Spanish government and secret police.

Twenty Junkers 52 transports (ten more than Franco had asked for) and six Heinkel 51 fighters, some flown by British pilots, were swiftly chartered through London – probably with the help of Basil Zaharoff – and despatched to Tetouan airfield in northern Morocco. This was followed by a massive build-up of military aid and arms from Berlin, including the deployment of the German Condor Legion, whose destruction of the defenceless little town of Guernica by bombers in April 1937 was to prove a harbinger of the fate of so many innocent towns and cities across Europe in the years to come. Canaris's intervention tipped the balance of the Spanish Civil War in Franco's favour. On 28 March 1939, Franco occupied Madrid. Three days later he was able finally to declare the victory that put an end to Spain's long and bloody years of conflict.

Hitler's gamble had paid off – he had now extended his influence to the westernmost limit of Europe. It had paid off for Canaris, too, who had achieved unrivalled influence and leverage with the Spanish dictator and his new government. Spain had become the Abwehr chief's private playground and refuge – Franco even gave him a villa for his private use as a mark of his gratitude.

Like Ludwig Beck and Carl Goerdeler, Wilhelm Canaris had at first welcomed Hitler as a necessary evil to put Germany back on its feet. Also like his two soon-to-be fellow conspirators, he would become horrified by the blood, conflict and criminality of Hitler's behaviour in power. But Canaris's journey from naïve belief in Hitler to understanding the threat he posed to all that he himself stood for was a slow one – for which history has often criticised him.

The turning point in Canaris's loyalty to his Führer finally came with the Fritsch affair in January 1938. This was the moment when it became evident to Canaris, as to so many of his fellow Germans, that Hitler's demonic will would not be restrained by the norms of accepted behaviour, by the constraints of the law, or by the limits of democratic government. 'If you are looking for one specific event that shook Canaris's allegiance to Hitler, then there [in the Fritsch affair] you have it,' commented his predecessor as chief of the Abwehr. Canaris's subordinates in the Abwehr noted the change too: 'Hitler's criminal procedure against ... Fritsch had a [profound] effect upon the Wehrmacht and the Abwehr. The result ... split ... opinion ... The systematic organisation ... among Hitler's opponents began at this point. The final decision to work for the regime's overthrow ... by the [Canaris] group was ... made [at this time],' one reported after the war.

From this watershed onwards all the formidable energy and cunning of this part Hamlet, part moral mystic, part German patriot, part conspirator at the court of Cesare Borgia, would be directed towards undermining and frustrating his master, Adolf Hitler.

4

Madeleine and Paul

The couple, he magnificent in the red-lined grey cape and gold-trimmed shako of a lieutenant colonel in the Austrian army, and she radiant in a spring dress, seemed like kingfishers flashing along a muddy river as they pushed their way through the tide of humanity pressing – panicking – to find a place on the train to Switzerland.

He led her to the platform and they said their goodbyes as lovers do when they are uncertain whether they will ever see each other again. Then he took her into a carriage, found her a seat amidst the crush, and left.

Three days previously, on 12 March 1938, she had watched the German troops marching into Vienna under brilliant skies. She had felt the tramp of their boots in the pit of her stomach, and heard their chants: 'Today Vienna; tomorrow Prague; later Paris.' And Madeleine Bihet-Richou, thirty-six years old, daughter of a French government official, native of Toulouse, divorcee, mother of a son, teacher of French in Vienna and for the last four years the lover of Erwin Lahousen Edler von Vivremont, the head of the Austrian Abwehr, had been frightened.

As Madeleine watched Hitler's troops streaming into Vienna that day, her lover was with Wilhelm Canaris in Abwehr headquarters not far away. The admiral had dashed to the city by plane ahead of the forward troops in order to seize documents in Lahousen's files. It would have been embarrassing, to say the least, if these had fallen into the hands of SS chief Heinrich Himmler, for they revealed the extent of cooperation between Canaris and his Austrian counterpart, which had included warnings and plans of the coming German invasion. With the German takeover imminent, Canaris asked Lahousen to gather as many of his most trusted colleagues as possible and join him in the Tirpitzufer in Berlin, adding, 'Above all, don't bring in any Nazis to our Berlin headquarters, bring me true Austrians, not thugs.'

Lahousen decided that it would be too dangerous to take Madeleine with him to Berlin – and too dangerous to leave her in Vienna without his protection. She would have to return to France and await events.

On the day of the invasion, Lahousen asked her to take a message to the French military attaché, Colonel Roger Salland, whom he had warned the previous night of the forthcoming German assault. She was to tell her countryman that Lahousen would have to 'break off all contact with his French friend'. Salland was surprised to receive this message, and on questioning Madeleine he was even more surprised – and interested – to hear of her relationship with the chief of the Austrian Abwehr, who was now to take up a senior post in the German Abwehr in Berlin.

The weather over the three days of the *Anschluss* seemed to mock the tumult and terror of the times. A high-pressure zone centred near Vienna brought frosty champagne mornings, sparkling blue skies, balmy days and evenings that made the blood sing. The cherry trees in the city's Hainburger Weg and Stadtpark hung heavy with blossom, as Jews were rounded up and gangs of uniformed paramilitaries hunted down their prey.

With Vienna reeling under the chaos of the German invasion, the two lovers prepared for their enforced separation. Lahousen, tall, athletic and, at forty, four years older than Madeleine, warned her that all those trying to flee were being robbed by the SS gangs roaming Austria; she should leave her valuables in his safekeeping, save for the few Austrian schillings she would need for the journey. The couple also agreed a plain-language code system they could use to keep in touch by telephone, letter and postcard. Finally he bought her a ticket to Switzerland, and they waited for the trains to start running again.

On the morning before her departure, making her way to the French embassy on a last visit, Madeleine was caught up in a vast crowd gathered in Heldenplatz and heard Hitler announce the end of Austria with the triumphant words, 'The oldest eastern province of the German people shall be, from this point on, the newest bastion of the German Reich.' Two hundred thousand voices hurled repeated *Heil Hitler*s back at the diminutive figure standing above them, alone on the balcony of the Hofburg Palace. Madeleine noted that among the women in the crowd were 'several vulgar uneducated harridans wearing luxurious furs which a few days previously would have been the property of Jews'. She was glad she was leaving, even if it meant leaving her lover behind.

As Lahousen had predicted, the journey from Vienna's Südbahnhof station to Switzerland was neither quick nor easy. At two in the morning

Madeleine's train, overcrowded well beyond its normal capacity, clanked to a stop at Salzburg station, where armed SS soldiers lined the platform. By the light of torches, the luggage in the baggage wagon was pillaged. Two young men with SS armbands and pistols entered Madeleine's carriage, demanding papers. A Jew sitting opposite her had the contents of his wallet minutely examined before being left in peace; an Italian singer, mistaken for a Jew because of his olive skin, was badly man-handled, and an old man reduced to a state of quivering panic by the threats and insults.

Their indignities over, the passengers were allowed to continue their journey to the German–Swiss border crossing at Feldkirch, where they arrived at eight in the morning to find their train once again surrounded by a cordon of armed SS guards. Ordered onto the platform with their hand baggage, they were subjected to another, even more violent and intrusive, search.

'Where is your money?' an SS man demanded of Madeleine after rifling energetically through every item in her suitcase.

'I knew you would steal everything,' she replied coolly, 'so I left my money in safe hands.' For her cheek, she was forced to stand naked while her clothes were inspected. Many passengers, especially Jews, were arrested and taken away.

Finally the train was allowed to cross over the Rhine into Switzerland. In due course it reached Basel, whose cavernous, high-arched station hall, lit by blue stained-glass windows, was about to become the first refuge of freedom and safety for thousands fleeing their homelands in terror.

Madeleine arrived in Paris ten days later. The peace and order of the city seemed somehow unreal after the turbulence and violence of Vienna.

Four months later, on a July holiday in La Rochelle, Madeleine received an unexpected message from a certain Colonel Louis Rivet, who, though she did not know it at the time, was the head of French military intelli-gence. Would she be prepared to meet one of his representatives at a place of her choosing in the near future? A rendezvous was fixed at a hotel in Angoulême, where, sitting on the terrace in the summer sunshine, Madeleine Bihet-Richou was formally recruited to spy for her country. Her job was to pass on the information she received from her lover to her French intelligence 'handling officer', Captain Henri Navarre.

A few days before meeting Navarre, Madeleine had received a postcard from Lahousen. It was postmarked Madrid: 'The time is coming. When can I write to you again? May God protect you and yours.'

And so it was that a line of communication which would over time develop into one of the most valuable spy channels of World War II was opened up between Erwin Lahousen, now a senior officer at Abwehr headquarters in the Tirpitzufer, and Hitler's enemies. What would follow over the next two years was a stream of information which would prove extremely useful to the Allies and harmful to Hitler's cause. It was information of a very specific and precise nature, including dates, names, plans and places, all passed in a professional manner from Erwin to Madeleine, not as part of their love affair, but under its cover. Speaking after the war, Madeleine said: 'He knew nothing explicitly about the true nature of my secret mission [as a French spy]. I thought it preferable to say nothing which might trouble his conscience; we both understood that there were some things which were better left unsaid.' Lahousen, however, knew well enough that she was working for French intelligence, and that the information he gave her would be passed on to the West, as he admitted in the full report on his activities which he provided to the Allies after the war.

So, if Lahousen knew the true destination of the information he was giving Madeleine, did Wilhelm Canaris know it too? That Lahousen sent Madeleine to the French attaché with her 'non-message' immediately after spending a whole day with Canaris, and accepting his invitation to go to Berlin, seems unlikely to be just a coincidence. To this should be added the fact that Canaris and Lahousen were very close, and also very professional. Each was to depend for his very life on the integrity and judgement of the other in the years to come. Given these factors, it seems safe to presume that Canaris knew perfectly well what his subordinate was doing – and that he approved of it.

Erwin Lahousen and the Austrian Abwehr were not the only people to know of the German invasion of Austria before it happened.

Two hundred and fifty kilometres north-west of Vienna, Czech intelligence in Prague were also aware of what was about to happen, thanks to German codes which had been passed to them by an Abwehr officer four months previously.

It had all begun on 8 February 1936, when a man of medium height in his mid-thirties, with a Prussian haircut, prominent eyes surrounded by smile lines, brown hair and slightly bowed legs, boarded the night train from Dresden to the Czechoslovak town of Brück, fifteen kilometres south of the Czech–German border. The following morning he breakfasted in the station buffet, posted a letter in a local postbox, and returned to Dresden on the next train.

So began the career of one of World War II's most remarkable spies.

It is often possible to gauge the importance of a spy by the number of his or her aliases. Over the next seven years this man would be known as 'R.V.', 'F.M.', 'Agent A54', 'Voral', 'Josef Koehler', 'François', 'René', 'Dr Holm', 'Dr Steinberg', both 'Eva' and 'Peter' 'Teman', 'Jochen Breitner', 'Emil Schwarz', 'Karl', 'Petr Tooman' and 'Traitor X'. Indeed, so elusive was he that his true identity was only established beyond doubt after the war. We now know him as Paul Thümmel, one-time master baker, founder member of the Nazi Party, holder of the party's golden badge, friend of Himmler, and in 1936 a member of Wilhelm Canaris's Abwehr station in Dresden, which was charged with spying on Czechoslovakia.

Two days after Thümmel posted his letter, an unmarked blue envelope arrived in the office of Major Josef Bartik of the Czechoslovak intelligence service in Victory Square, Prague. It was postmarked 'Brück', and hand-addressed in German to the Ministry of National Defence, Intelligence Section.

When Bartik opened the envelope he found the kind of offer a spy chief can only dream of:

> The author of this letter offers his services to the Czech Intelligence
> Service …

After this greeting, the writer, who wrote in badly-spelt German and signed himself 'F.M.', listed the kind of intelligence to which he had access: German intelligence requirements for 1935 and 1936; details of German infantry, armour, air force, police, Gestapo and customs units; the new organisation table of all German intelligence and security structures; the names and addresses of all the senior personnel in the Gestapo, Abwehr and civil service; and the names and codenames of German intelligence officers working on Czechoslovakia, together with their agents, wireless networks and codes. Bartik concluded from this list that the would-be spy clearly had access to information well beyond the reach of a normal junior member of the Abwehr.

Having laid out his wares, 'F.M.' set his terms:

1. You shall never know my name
2. I will never meet you on Czech territory

3. If measures have to be taken as a result of the information I give you must use it with extreme care and avoid making the Germans suspicious of me

4. I want 15,000 marks in German currency in old notes, 4,000 marks of which should reach me within three weeks, as I have a debt to pay off.

He ended his letter in a way which left no doubt that he was a professional in the business of spying:

> I shall await your reply, poste restante, each time in a different town of Saxony and Bavaria. Your reply to this letter will determine whether I pass my information to you, or offer it to French Intelligence. I also expect to receive, with your reply, an advance to buy a camera and settle other expenses. My offer is genuine and you need have no fear that your money will be wasted. I ask you to reply … by 14 February at the latest. This does not give you much time, but I am at present in Saxony, near the frontier.

On the face of it, this was a sensational offer – almost too good to be true. And that was the problem. 'F.M.' was what is known in the spying trade as a 'walk in', and they are often used as bait for a trap.

Major Bartik was a cautious man – and he had good reason to be. He had already used just such a ploy to fool Canaris into paying huge sums for totally worthless intelligence. This coup resulted in the Abwehr chief christening his Czech opponent, not without a degree of admiration, 'the limping devil' because of his effectiveness and a rolling gait caused by a First World War leg wound. Not long previously, moreover, one of Bartik's officers had been kidnapped by the Germans at a meeting with an agent close to the Czech–German border. By the time Bartik finally got his man back, he had been so badly tortured by the Gestapo that he had to be confined to a mental institution for the rest of his life.

Bartik's reply to F.M. was guarded:

> Sir, Your communication interests me. Although you give no guarantees, I enclose the advance you asked for. The money is yours even if you fail to supply the information promised in your letter. The total sum will be paid within three weeks if you permit us to examine the material. Please reply to the following address: Karl Schimek, Prague XIX Dostalova 16.

Thus began the cautious minuet played out between spy-master and potential spy, as each tries to assess the balance of advantage and risk involved in a relationship. Finally, after much to-ing and fro-ing, Bartik agreed to meet F.M. at 8.30 on the evening of Saturday, 4 April at a deserted steam mill set amongst trees, fifty metres on the Czech side of the frontier with Germany and close to the village of Vejprty.

It was a cold night, with low cloud and misty rain blown along on a boisterous breeze. The wind buffeted a loose flap on the corrugated-iron roof of the mill, making it bang loudly. The street lamps hanging on wires in the middle of the village roads swung in wild circles, sending strange shadows lurching out in all directions. Two of Bartik's men, armed with pistols, stood in a deep pool of blackness on one side of the mill, and a little way back, tucked discreetly in a copse of trees, were three cars containing Bartik and half a dozen of his men armed with automatics. The Vejprty church clock struck 8.30. Somewhere a dog barked, and very shortly afterwards a shape emerged from the trees and started up the road. He was sturdily built, walked with the gait of a young man, but cautiously, wore dark clothes and a beret, and carried a haversack.

Bartik's two watchers left the shadows, and in a few paces had joined the man on the road.

'*Grüss Gott*,' said the stranger in a low voice.

'Give the password,' was the sharp retort.

'*Altvater*.'

Bartik's men escorted their charge to the Czech intelligence chief sitting in his car, its engine purring quietly amongst the trees. Safely ensconced in the back seat, the night traveller took several documents from his haversack and handed them to Bartik to examine under the feeble illumination of the car's roof-light. The papers mostly dealt with the organisational structure of the Abwehr offices in Dresden, Munich and Breslau. But they also included some interesting local Gestapo reports. Bartik sent one of the waiting cars with the documents to the police station in Louny, seventy kilometres distant, where they were carefully photographed. Meanwhile, Bartik himself drove his new charge to an army barracks twenty kilometres away at Komotau for further debriefing. Over the next three hours Thümmel was closely questioned about his background, identity and motives. On the face of it, his story sounded convincing. He claimed to be 'Jochen Breitner', a former draughtsman and photographer who worked as a civilian in the Dresden Abwehr office, and said he was offering his services as a spy because he needed the money to marry a girl working as a clerk in the same office. It was his girl, he added, who had access to documents of interest because of her work in the Abwehr registry. His interrogators were impressed by 'Breitner's' quick-wittedness, and swiftly concluded that they were dealing with the genuine article, a trained intelligence agent, not an agent provocateur. Bartik assigned his new agent the codename by which he would be known – 'A54'. As the first streaks of dawn began to lighten the sky, the Czech spy chief dropped his new recruit back at the old steam mill and watched as he vanished into the trees in the direction of the German frontier.

Bartik's haul from his new recruit that night was not high-grade. But it was interesting, for it indicated not just Thümmel's seriousness, but also his access. Over the next months Thümmel proved himself a reliable, professional and productive source. One piece of information he gave Bartik in this period was of special value to the Czechs – full details of the network of spies, secret radios and codes which Canaris's men were setting up amongst the German-speaking population of Czech Sudetenland. Thanks to deciphered messages from this source, Bartik was able to warn the Czech government a week or so before the *Anschluss* that SS regiments were gathering on the Austrian border, preparing to march on Vienna. Apart from this, Thümmel's 'intelligence product' for the next year was in the main low-level, low-grade and local, consistent with his apparent position as a medium-level officer in one of Canaris's many Abwehr out-stations across Germany.

But then, suddenly, around the middle of 1938, with the Czech crisis deepening and the world edging towards war, the quality of Thümmel's intelligence began to change dramatically. In May he told Bartik that the Germans were preparing a campaign of sabotage and disruption leading to a coup in the Sudetenland by the end of that month. It is very probable that these reports from Thümmel were the basis for an urgent message sent by Group Captain Graham Christie, one of Sir Robert Vansittart's secret informants who operated from Prague, who reported that 'Both SIS in Prague and Czech military intelligence report German troop man-oeuvres on the border which ... [point] to an early invasion.' What followed was a scurry of intense diplomatic activity aimed at averting the coming 'invasion'. The British ambassador in Berlin warned the head of the German Foreign Office of the gravity of the situation, and reinforced the message in a personal interview with Ribbentrop. Using a most un-Foreign-Office-like double negative, he told the German foreign minister that if Czechoslovakia was attacked, 'His Majesty's Government could not guarantee [not] … to become themselves involved'.

In fact the whole thing was an elaborate hoax. There was no German invasion planned for May. Hitler was not yet ready.

There is only one likely explanation for this seemingly bizarre prologue to the coming Czechoslovak crisis – Paul Thümmel had been used by Canaris, or someone very close to him at the top of the Abwehr, to pass false information in order to alert the wider world to Hitler's plans to invade the Sudetenland in the near future. There is no evidence that Czech intelligence's confidence in their new agent was shaken by the false alarm he had caused in May 1938 – probably because it served Czechoslovakia's purposes too, and because they realised that it was intended to do so.

Hitler, however, was furious at being pre-empted, and at the diplomatic furore that ensued.

Now things began to move from elaborate charade to true high drama. Over June and July 1938 Thümmel provided Bartik with the secret order from Hitler instructing his generals to be ready for Operation Green – the invasion of Czechoslovakia – by 1 October. In early September Thümmel followed this with the full details of the invasion plan, including troop deployments, invasion points and other important information.

By now Bartik must have known that A54 was far, far more than just a low-level Abwehr draughtsman/photographer in Dresden. Paul Thümmel was needy, vain and greedy. But he was also a high-level spy with direct access to the most senior levels of the Tirpitzufer in Berlin.

5

Germany in the Shadow of War

By 1938 Goerdeler, Beck and Canaris, together with other Berlin conspirators, were gathering regularly under the cover of the prestigious Free Society for Scholarly Entertainment, colloquially known as the *Mittwochgesellschaft* (Wednesday Society) after the day of the week on which it met. Slowly the ad hoc resistance network against Hitler was becoming a formal structure gathered around the three men who would be its initial driving force.

Carl Goerdeler was the movement's Thomas More: formidably intelligent, spiritually resolute, unshakeably optimistic and driven by a burning sense of mission and the conviction that reason always triumphs over evil. But the superiority of his intelligence made him insensitive to others, brittle in personal relationships, uncomfortable in his certainties and annoyingly didactic (his colleagues called him '*Pfaf*', German slang for preacher). His utopianism rendered him completely devoid of the worldly wisdom and darker political skills necessary to deal with a tyrant, especially one so pathologically barren of moral values as Adolf Hitler.

If Goerdeler was More, then Canaris was Talleyrand, but with charm in place of a repugnant personality, and a powerful moral compass where Talleyrand had none. His subtle, flexible spirit was quite capable of operating simultaneously at two contradictory levels without losing its way; the perfect mind for a spy chief. Canaris preferred the tangential rather than the direct route for dealing with Hitler, delivering little successes to his master, the better subtly to confound his grander megalomaniac designs.

The third member of this trio, 'the philosopher general' Ludwig Beck, was a soldier's soldier in the tradition of Frederick the Great. He admitted no contradiction between his profession and a life sustained by the values of the Enlightenment. He was the man everyone trusted and everyone looked up to – but for his moral and intellectual qualities, not his soldiering ones.

Post-war opinion has often mistakenly believed that Hitler led a united nation into war. This is far from the truth. By the mid-1930s most Germans supported what Hitler had done through his much-vaunted 'triumph of the will' to restore German pride, redress the humiliations of Versailles and bring order to the chaos of the Weimar years. They wanted him to continue making Germany strong again, but not – definitely not – at the price of another war. Public support for Hitler's policy of toughness with Germany's neighbours was in large measure due to the fact that he successfully portrayed himself in each of the pre-war crises as the peacemaker, not the warmonger. The popular mood in Germany was in favour of the new chancellor, but it was also deeply fearful, and strongly opposed to another war.

Among the institutions of the German state, the picture was rather more mixed.

Obviously those around Hitler knew of his plans for war. Most, such as Himmler and Ribbentrop, supported the Führer. But some, like Göring, were more cautious. Others, such as the minister of economics and president of the Reichsbank Hjalmar Schacht, hovered in the outer circles of the resistance, without ever quite allowing themselves to be drawn fully in.

In 1938, after a spell as ambassador to London, Joachim von Ribbentrop was appointed as Hitler's new foreign minister. In both jobs he acted as the faithful echo to his master's opinions and demands. The German Foreign Office over which he presided was, by contrast, a hotbed of active resistance to the Führer and his plans. One of the most prominent of the Foreign Office conspirators was Ernst von Weizsäcker. The father of a future German president, von Weizsäcker believed that Hitler's foreign policy would inevitably lead to war. Like Canaris, Weizsäcker had served as a naval officer in the First World War. Now, as state secretary, he was the most senior Foreign Office official under Ribbentrop. Also like Canaris, Weizsäcker chose, at least initially, to oppose Hitler by indirect means, through what he described as 'feigned cooperation', while conspiring 'with the potential enemy for the purpose of ensuring peace'. A number of more junior Foreign Office officials shared von Weizsäcker's views, but were more direct in their opposition, and more deeply engaged in the resistance cause. These included Oxford-educated Adam von Trott zu Solz and the brothers Kordt, one of whom, Erich, held a senior position in Ribbentrop's Berlin office, while the other, Theo, served in the German embassy in London.

When it came to the German armed forces, the Luftwaffe, being the newest arm and therefore unencumbered with traditions, was in the main loyal to Hitler, and played no part in the resistance. The navy, the Kriegsmarine, with the exception of Canaris, preferred to steer well clear of politics.

It was in the German army that the resistance found its leading figures. These came mostly from the senior ranks and those who had belonged to the professional army before the war. Drawn in large measure from the old aristocracy and trained in the Prussian tradition, the army was an institution like no other in the German state. Sustained by its aristocratic roots, it had – at least in its own eyes – a degree of independence from the government of the day. This included, in extremis, the presumed right to unilateral action as the guardian and physical expression of the German nation. In normal times the army's leaders enjoyed a large degree of autonomy in the conduct of their operations, and an entitlement to be consulted and listened to when it came to foreign policy and statecraft. Underpinning all this was the Prussian officer code *Üb Immer Treu und Redlichkeit*.

Hitler had offended against all these values and beliefs. He was an uncouth parvenu who lacked manners, education, culture and any of the attributes of refinement which army officers so valued in themselves. He demanded allegiance to himself, not the state. He first shamed and then sacked a head of the army (Fritsch), and used the opportunity to take personal command. He had led an assault on the values of decency, and unleashed his supporters and secret police to commit appalling violence against German citizens. Worst of all, he was marching Germany to a war which most senior military figures believed would end in defeat and disaster.

The problem for the generals, however, was that the army (known as the Reichswehr before the Fritsch crisis and the Heer afterwards*) was no longer the same organisation as the one in which they had grown up.

The army's unwillingness to protest at the horrors of the Night of the Long Knives – even though one of its most senior brethren had been amongst the murdered – and its quiet acquiescence during Beck's 'blackest day', when all the generals meekly lined up to take the oath of allegiance to Hitler, had weakened both its influence and its self-respect. The army's leaders may have been trained to take bold decisions in battle, but their indecisiveness and hesitancy on the field of politics was – and would

---

* The term Wehrmacht was used for the entire armed forces.

continue to be – a fatal brake on their ability to halt or change what all of them believed was a coming catastrophe. A British politician described the Wehrmacht leadership in 1938 as 'a race of carnivorous sheep'. Even allowing for the fact that this was an easy criticism to make when you did not have to risk your life to oppose your government, there was much truth in the cruel epithet.

The composition of the Wehrmacht was also different from its predecessor. The old professional army, along with the traditional comradeship of its officer corps, had been diluted and submerged under the vast expansion of the army's numbers. The flood of new equipment, much of it of world-beating quality, along with the attention, promotions, medals – and even in some cases money and estates – which Hitler showered on the Wehrmacht and its senior officers, sapped the army's will to do what it knew it should to stop the headlong rush to war.

Nevertheless, pre-war opposition to Hitler remained strong amongst the most senior ranks of the Wehrmacht, even to the point of contemplating a coup to remove him. In 1938, those who supported Ludwig Beck's view that if Hitler could not be stopped, he would have to be removed, included the commander-in-chief of the Wehrmacht, General Walther von Brauchitsch, and the majority of his senior generals, especially in the Reserve Army* based around Berlin.

Although active resistance to Hitler was variably scattered across most German institutions, its highest concentration was in the Abwehr, and particularly in the Tirpitzufer building (nicknamed the *Fuchsbau*, or Fox's Lair), which was part of a large Berlin administrative complex called the Bendlerblock. This also housed the Naval Warfare Command and the headquarters of both the Wehrmacht and the Reserve Army. Though physically connected to the Bendlerblock, the closed enclave of Abwehr headquarters was in every other way a world apart. Here Wilhelm Canaris gathered together as many as he could of those who, like him, opposed Hitler. They formed such a tight-knit group that the Tirpitzufer was sometimes referred to in Berlin circles as 'Canaris Familie GmBH' (The Canaris Clan Inc.). Among those closest to the Abwehr chief were Hans Bernd Gisevius, a lawyer of formidable physical proportions whom his friends christened the 'eternal plotter'; Hans von Dohnányi, a gifted young judge who was the son of the famous composer Ernst von Dohnányi and

* Known as the Ersatzheer, this had the responsibility of training soldiers to reinforce first-line divisions. Sometimes referred to as 'the Replacement Army'.

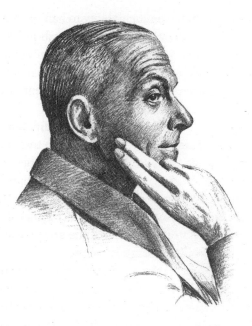

Hans Oster

brother-in-law of Dietrich Bonhoeffer; and the impetuous, fanatical Hitler hater and member of Pastor Niemöller's congregation, Colonel Hans Oster. Sleek, fearless, cunning and a gifted amateur cello player, Oster, who made a habit of referring to Hitler as 'the Swine', was described by one contemporary as 'an elegant cavalry officer of the old school, handsome, gallant with the ladies and contemptuous of the national socialist leaders. He was all for striking when the iron was hot; but the admiral had a more hesitant nature.'

Canaris encouraged his senior lieutenants to do as he did, and recruit those sympathetic to the cause. His often-repeated instruction when it came to new recruits was 'Being anti-Nazi is more important than any other quality.' He also went out of his way to use the Abwehr as a refuge for Jews, placing them in posts outside Germany beyond the reach of the Gestapo, and claiming when challenged that they were essential to the Abwehr's work in gathering foreign intelligence.

In the middle of the 1930s, the Abwehr over which Canaris presided as what one colleague referred to as the '*grande éminence grise*' was probably the best foreign-intelligence service in the world. The French Deuxième Bureau, one of the most proficient interwar spy services in Europe, went through a series of convulsive reorganisations in the early 1930s which sapped its effectiveness. Britain's MI6 was going through a difficult period too, after much of its network of intelligence stations across the Continent had been blown. A whole new British spy network was being constructed in great secrecy, and without the knowledge of anyone apart from the MI6 chief Sir Hugh Sinclair and his closest advisers. This was known, rather melodramatically, as the 'Z Organisation', after its creator 'Colonel Z', otherwise known as Claude Edward Marjoribanks Dansey. The Russian spy agencies, meanwhile, though still capable of effective work, were hobbled by the repeated waves of Stalin's purges.

Canaris's value to Hitler lay in the priceless information he was able to bring his chief, including, crucially, both the military plans and the political intentions of his foreign enemies. Britain and France, with their many high-level admirers of Hitler and their public policies of appeasement, were rich sources of information for Canaris's Abwehr. Before the war Canaris boasted to Juan March (or was it a threat, given March's dealings with the British?): 'I have penetrated the [British] Naval Intelligence Division and MI6. So if any German, however important or discreet, felt tempted to work with the British, be sure I should find out.' According to his own claim, Canaris had one very high-level source close enough to the British cabinet to enable him to assure Hitler in early 1936 that if Germany marched into the Versailles-protected demilitarised zone of the Rhineland, Britain would not energetically oppose this.

The Abwehr chief himself set the tone of his organisation from his Spartan office on the third floor of the Tirpitzufer. At one end of a room of modest proportions was Canaris's desk, behind which were three full-length windows and a glazed door leading onto a small balcony looking over the Landwehr Canal. The desk was unadorned except for a routine scatter of papers, a model of his old cruiser the *Dresden*, and a small paperweight in the shape of the three monkeys – 'See no evil, speak no evil, hear no evil.' Otherwise the room was largely empty save for two or three chairs, a bookshelf full of books, many of them on music and the arts, and an iron camp bed on which Canaris would from time to time take a nap. Only three photographs hung on his walls – one of Franco, one of a handsome young Hungarian hussar, and one of his beloved dachshund Seppl, which took pride of place on the wall immediately opposite his desk.

The house near Berlin's Schlachtensee in which Canaris lived with his wife Erika, their daughters Eva and Brigitte, a Polish cook, a Moroccan former prisoner of war who acted as the family servant, and two dachs-hunds, was frugal by the standards of high officials in Hitler's Reich. It had six bedrooms but no grand reception rooms, a modest garden amongst trees and a shared fence with the Heydrichs next door.

Canaris's style of management was relaxed. One of his senior colleagues described it as 'passive leadership … under the pretence of the greatest apparent activity'. The Tirpitzufer was the only government building in Berlin where the familiar second-person pronoun '*du*' was in common usage rather than the more formal '*Sie*'. Canaris (known affectionately as 'old white head' and 'the little sailor') was not a micro-manager. He set broad tasks, and then let his section chiefs get on with it. He hated bureaucracy, and often caused his subordinates despair by his inability to read and clear documents in a timely fashion. Erwin Lahousen wrote:

> Canaris was the most difficult superior I have [ever] encountered. Contradictory in his instructions, given to whims, not always just [but] always mysterious, he had … intellectual and above all human qualities which raised him far above the military rubber stamps and marionettes that most of his colleagues and superiors were … He was not at all a technical expert in his work, rather he was a great dilettante. The underground circles that he … gathered around himself were as colourful and heterogeneous as his own personality. Men of all classes and professions, people whose horizons were broad and narrow, idealists and political adventurers, sober rationalists and imaginative mystics, conservative noblemen and Freemasons, theosophists, half-Jews or Jews, Germans and non-Germans … men and women – all of them united only [by their affection for him] and … by their resistance to Hitler and his system. This circle was by no means directed by secret orders. Rather it was an intellectual circle constantly influenced by slight or direct hints … which he guided by active intervention only in rare cases. Only a few initiates received concrete instructions, and even these were not always clear.

'Old white head' was also trusted and, it seems, genuinely loved by the more junior members of the Abwehr: 'Admiral Canaris was absolutely trustworthy, clever, extremely gifted, honest, talented above [the] average and a person of sterling character,' wrote one of his subordinates after the war. 'He was well fitted for his position from a personal point of view. The things he [was] able to do for the Abwehr in the face of every obstacle could have been accomplished by no one else.'

But if Canaris was relaxed in his management style, he was utterly precise when it came to the standards he demanded of the Abwehr. His motto, borrowed from Germany's great World War I spy chief Walter Nikolai, was '*Le service de renseignements est l'apanage des gentilhommes. Si il est confié à d'autres, il s'écroule*' (The profession of spying should only be conferred upon gentlemen. If others get involved, disaster follows). He also discouraged an obsessional approach to the job: 'An intelligence officer worthy of his profession,' he once said to his staff, 'should be in bed by ten. After that, all is nonsense and stupidity.' While women spies were useful, in Canaris's Abwehr any officer who slept with one would be dismissed. He made it clear to his officers that their job was exclusively to gather intelligence, and did not include assassination, torture, blackmail or coercion – such unpleasant things should be left to others. An ability to lie, on the other hand, was a prerequisite. 'Lying is our trade,' he instructed. 'Lying is an art. If you cannot lie, there is no place for you in the Abwehr.' The great theologian Dietrich Bonhoeffer, whose role as the 'pastor' of the resistance is often underestimated, famously gave this pragmatic philosophy theological underpinning by proclaiming that God required a lie if this was the only way to protect a deeper truth against evil.

The Abwehr expanded explosively under Canaris's leadership, growing from 150 staff when he took it over in early 1935, to 1,000 in 1937. By 1943 it had surged in size to 30,000, with an annual budget in today's terms of close to £100 million. The organisation was based around four 'operational sections': Section I, dealing with secret intelligence; Section II, sabotage and disruption; Section III, counter-intelligence; and a foreign department which took responsibility for overseas relations, including political and military evaluation. There was also an 'administration' section called 'Section Z'. On the surface this dealt with mundane administrative matters such as archives, legal affairs, personnel and technical equipment. But Section Z, commanded by the Hitler-hating Hans Oster, was also the home of 'the Abwehr within the Abwehr' – a special and highly secret cell whose job it was to frustrate Hitler's plans and undermine, first his march to war, and later, as things developed, his chances of victory. Known as 'the Oster circle' and 'the Civilians' – because of Oster's habit of wearing civilian clothes (despite Canaris's disapproval) and the culture of informality within his unit – Section Z was treated with some suspicion, even hostility, inside the Abwehr. In time it would become the nerve-centre of the entire high-level German conspiracy against Hitler.

One further addition hugely extended the power and reach of Canaris's organisation. Though operating under a separate command, a military unit called the Brandenburg Division was attached to and tasked by the Abwehr. The 'Brandenburgers', as they were called, were arguably the first ever special forces unit. Unlike British special forces units, which in the early years of the war were used for pinprick raids, they were deployed, like special forces today, exclusively on strategic tasks. Multilingual, multinational (they included many Russian and Caucasian troops), highly mobile and superbly trained and equipped, their job was to operate behind enemy lines ahead of an invading force, disrupting communications and sabotaging bridges and command structures, in much the same way as Britain's SAS did in the latter stages of the war in Europe.

As 1937 drew to a close, Hitler's successful occupation of the Rhineland without, as Canaris had predicted, any serious international opposition or criticism, emboldened the Führer to annex Austria. Again, there was little reaction from Britain beyond a diplomatic shrug of resignation. Surely this would now be enough, London hoped, to satisfy the German dictator's appetite. That was certainly prime minister Neville Chamberlain's view. Writing to his sister Ida at about this time, he commented that if Hitler was appeased, then sooner or later he would become 'sated, indolent and quiescent'.

But of course the opposite was the truth. Hitler's generals understood what the rest of the world should have known: that victories do not satiate a tyrant's appetite, they sharpen it. As Carl Goerdeler put it, presciently, 'You know, a dictator must always be bringing along for breakfast a new kill if he is to thrive and survive. This time it is Austria. Next it will be Czechoslovakia, and so on and on.'

In April 1938 Goerdeler returned, accompanied by his wife and daughter, to London, where in two meetings with Vansittart he explained Hitler's secret plans for the invasion of Czechoslovakia, and expatiated at length on the hostility of the Wehrmacht's generals towards the Führer. But, following the line set by Chamberlain, Vansittart dismissed this as 'treasonable talk'. There was also supposed to be a meeting between Goerdeler and Churchill, but this fell through at the last minute due to a misunderstanding over time and place.

Hitler's secret instruction to his generals in November 1937 that they should prepare for an attack on Czechoslovakia in the following year now began to dominate the work of the planners in Berlin. Amongst the generals, however, there was consternation. This would be bound to lead to war, and that could ultimately end only in catastrophe for Germany. There was a united view that this time Hitler must be diverted; if this proved impossible, he should be removed – if necessary by force. Canaris issued instructions that Abwehr reports to Hitler should exaggerate the strength of the Czech defences, and stress the probability that Britain, France and Russia would go to war if Hitler attacked. On 30 May 1938 Ludwig Beck warned Hitler, 'the campaign against Czechoslovakia can be very successful, but Germany will lose the war'. He followed this up on 3 June by sending the Führer a courageous memo opposing the planned invasion on military grounds. On 16 July he sent another, even more forthright, memo warning that an attack on Czechoslovakia would involve war with Britain and France. Finally, on 18 August, six weeks before the planned invasion, Beck resigned his post as chief of the army general staff and accepted a posting to command the German First Army on the Western Front. From his new position he opened up a secret and traitorous dialogue with foreign contacts in Basel.

It was around this time that Beck, Canaris, Goerdeler and their fellow conspirators concluded that the only way to stop the coming war was to send secret emissaries to European capitals – especially London and Paris. As Canaris put it to his friend Ewald von Kleist-Schmenzin, 'England must lend us a sea-anchor if we are to ride out this storm.'

6

The Emissaries

Suddenly they came upon a clearing bathed in sunshine. They stopped at the edge, astounded by the light. It seemed to them a symbol of hope, in contrast to the close-hemmed gloom of the trees and the heaviness of their spirits.

The day, 6 August 1938, was stiflingly hot and humid, even by the standards of a Baltic summer. It was evening now, and an offshore breeze blew softly through the stands of silver birch, causing their leaves to shiver and dance in the failing light.

The three men – two Germans and an Englishman – had been walking for nearly two hours. Their conversation had been earnest and conducted in confidential tones, despite their being out in the open and away from prying eyes and ears.

A few days earlier, Carl Goerdeler had sent a message to a mutual contact in Britain asking for an urgent meeting. Sir Robert Vansittart – now, after Anthony Eden's resignation over appeasement, chief adviser to the new British foreign secretary Lord Halifax – decided that the man to go and see him should be A.P. Young, the host of Goerdeler's dinner at the National Liberal Club almost a year earlier.

That afternoon, after a brief stay in Berlin, Young arrived at the station of the Baltic seaside resort of Rauschen-Düne. Stepping out onto the platform in a swirl of steam, sand and dust, he spotted the imposing, heavily-built figure of Goerdeler standing discreetly in the shade of the station awning. The two men walked the short distance to Goerdeler's summer holiday house, a substantial, steep-roofed chalet-style building with shuttered windows set amongst trees and rhododendron bushes. A family supper with Goerdeler's much-loved brother Fritz, his wife Anneliese and the couple's two teenage sons followed. Afterwards, at Goerdeler's suggestion, the three men set off for an evening walk through the woods, beyond the reach of possible Gestapo eavesdroppers.

Goerdeler's message was sombre. Hitler was determined on war, and would march on Czechoslovakia within weeks. The German dictator had concluded that Britain and France were weak, and bluffing. They would, he was certain, not react if he occupied the German-speaking Czech Sudetenland. He would get away with it, just as he had done over his recent annexation of Austria.

Goerdeler had good news, too. The German public did not want war. Hitler's closest advisers, from Himmler to Göring, were also against it, and with the economy in dire straits and army reservists only recently called up, Germany was not yet ready for conflict. The generals too were opposed. The message Goerdeler asked Young to transmit to London was that it was Hitler who was bluffing. If Britain stood up to him, then a powerful group, led by Goerdeler himself and including many of Germany's top industrialists, a significant number of its Foreign Office officials and all of its most senior generals, would remove the dictator in a putsch, and replace him with a government which was ready to move away from the path to war. 'A revolution is no place for children,' Goerdeler added darkly, making it clear that the planned coup would be a violent one, if that was what was needed. This was the turning point, Goerdeler insisted. The German opposition to Hitler was ready to act, if Britain and France would do so too.

On his way back to London on 9 August, Young wrote an extensive report on his conversations for Vansittart, who passed it on to both prime minister Chamberlain and foreign secretary Halifax.

Six days after Young's return to London, at 7.15 a.m. on 17 August, a large black saloon carrying the insignia of German Army Supreme Headquarters cruised past the imposing monumental façade of Berlin's newly-constructed Tempelhof Airport. It swung into a side entrance which was already open and waiting for its arrival. It did not stop for checks of papers or personnel, but swept on, bypassing customs and immigration, to the steps of the Hansa Airlines 0800 flight from Berlin, via Amsterdam, to London. The Junkers 52 was parked under the airport's huge semi-circular cantilevered roof, waiting for its passengers to arrive. Two men got out of the limousine, one in the full uniform and regalia of a Wehrmacht general, the other a middle-aged civilian with a cadaverous frame, a receding hairline, and an ascetic face with hard, gimlet-grey eyes which matched his suit. A close observer might have noted from their body language that there was an unusual closeness between the two, for they were in fact uncle and nephew. The general accompanied his charge to the aircraft steps. The captain, in uniform and cap, welcomed the older

Ewald von Kleist-Schmenzin

man with a salute, led him up the steps and settled him into his seat before the other passengers boarded. His task over, the general returned to his car, which swung round and sped away.

The subject of all this preferential treatment was a Prussian landowner called Ewald von Kleist-Schmenzin, and he too was a secret envoy. A long-time and vocal opponent of the Nazis, who had narrowly escaped being murdered on the Night of the Long Knives and was closely watched by the Gestapo, Kleist-Schmenzin was not travelling under his own name, but under a false identity provided for him, complete with documents and sterling currency, by Admiral Wilhelm Canaris.

Von Kleist-Schmenzin's mission to London had been well prepared. His task, like that of Goerdeler, was to warn the highest echelons of the British government of Hitler's imminent plans to invade the Sudetenland, and to inform them on behalf of Hitler's most senior generals of the putsch they were preparing to launch if Britain would commit to defending Czechoslovakia. Kleist-Schmenzin had received his instructions a few days before his departure from Ludwig Beck: 'Bring me certain proof that England will fight if Czechoslovakia is attacked and I will make an end of this regime.'

The Gestapo may not have been aware of Kleist-Schmenzin's travel plans. But London was.

On the day before his departure, the appeasement-supporting British ambassador to Berlin, Sir Nevile Henderson, sent a coded telegram to Whitehall reporting that Kleist-Schmenzin would be travelling to the British capital claiming to represent the 'moderates of the German Staff'. Henderson advised: 'It would be unwise for [him] to be seen in official quarters.'

What the ambassador did not know was that he was already too late to block the secret visitor's access to senior officials in London.

Two days before his departure Kleist-Schmenzin had asked for a meeting with the Central European correspondent of London's *News Chronicle*, the well-informed and well-connected Ian Colvin. It was not their first encounter. Three months previously the two men had met in Berlin's fashionable Casino Club. Colvin would write of that meeting: 'For the first time, I heard spoken in a whisper the name of the man who was protecting them [the resistance] and furthering their efforts: the name of Canaris.' During their earlier discussion Kleist-Schmenzin had asked Colvin's advice about how to reach senior British politicians, explaining that Canaris was looking for a means to make direct high-level contact with them, but did not want to go through the normal intelligence channels. 'I must warn you against the British Secret Service for several reasons,' Canaris had said. 'Should you work for them it will most probably be brought to my notice, as I think I have penetrated here and there. They will want to send messages about you in cipher and from time to time we can break a cipher. Your names would appear in files and registers. That is bad too. It would be difficult to overlook such activities in the long run. It has also been my experience that the British Secret Service will reward you badly – if it is a matter of money, let me tell you, they do not reward services well, and if they have the least suspicion, they will not hesitate to betray you to me or to my colleagues of [Himmler's] Reich Security Service.'

This time, Colvin's meeting with von Kleist-Schmenzin took place not in a well-known Berlin club, but in a dimly-lit backstreet bar in Bendlerstrasse, close to army headquarters. The German had something important to say 'in a few short sentences, any one of which would have been enough to send him to instant execution'. Kleist-Schmenzin informed Colvin of the purpose of his forthcoming visit to the British capital: 'The Admiral [Canaris] wants someone to go to London … We have an offer to make to the British and a warning to give them.' That night Colvin wrote from the Adlon Hotel to his fellow journalist and friend, Winston Churchill's son Randolph: 'A friend of mine will be staying at the Park Lane Hotel from the 18th to the 23rd. I think it essential he should meet your father. Please put nothing about him in your column or mention him to any of your colleagues. The visitor will have information of great interest to your father.'

On his arrival at Croydon Aerodrome, Kleist-Schmenzin was observed to board a coach for London, where he booked into the Park Lane Hotel. The following afternoon the German visitor, describing himself as 'a conservative, a Prussian and a Christian', met Sir Robert Vansittart for tea – '[But not] I need hardly add … at the Foreign Office,' Vansittart was careful to explain in his subsequent report.

The Foreign Office mandarin was impressed with Kleist-Schmenzin: 'He spoke with the utmost frankness and sincerity … [He] has come out of Germany with a rope around his neck, staking his last chance of life on preventing [the war],' he reported, adding: 'Of all the Germans I saw, Kleist had the stuff in him for a revolution against Hitler.'

Over tea, Kleist-Schmenzin told Vansittart that war was now 'a complete certainty' unless Britain acted. 'Hitler has made up his mind … the mine is to be exploded [after 27 September] … All [the generals] … without exception … are dead against the war. But they will not have the power to stop it unless they get encouragement from outside. We are no longer in danger of war, but in the presence of the certainty of it … [But if Britain acted to defend Czechoslovakia] it would be the prelude to the end of the [Hitler] regime. [His army friends were unanimous] … they had taken the risk and he had taken the risk of coming out of Germany at this crucial moment … but they alone could do nothing [if Britain did nothing].'

The following day, 19 August, Kleist-Schmenzin was driven south through the ripening fields and orchards of Kent to Chartwell House, where Winston Churchill, out of government, was struggling to catch up on a missed deadline for his magnum opus, *A History of the English-Speaking Peoples*. The two met that afternoon in the room Churchill had set aside for important visitors. It was a space that would have been very familiar to a Prussian with an ancient lineage, with its heavy dark-oak carved furniture and Gothic-style beamed ceiling hung with a banner bearing the Churchill coat of arms. In one corner, where the sunlight streamed through a south-facing latticed window, was a table cluttered with family photographs. Close by, two comfortable chairs were drawn up in front of an Elizabethan fireplace. Churchill's son Randolph sat to one side on an upright chair, taking notes in shorthand.

'Kleist started by saying that he thought an attack on Czechoslovakia was imminent and was most likely to occur … [before] the end of September,' Randolph scribbled. 'The generals are for peace … and … if only they could receive a little encouragement they might refuse to march … Particularly was it necessary to do all that was possible to encourage the generals who alone had the power to stop war … In the event of the generals deciding to insist on peace, there would be a new system of government within forty-eight hours … [which would] end the fear of war.'

Winston Churchill understood very well what Kleist-Schmenzin was telling him. He would later write: 'There can be no doubt of the existence of a plot … and of serious measures taken to make it effective.'

Kleist-Schmenzin seems to have asked Churchill for a personal assurance he could take to Ludwig Beck in Berlin that Britain would act militarily if Hitler attacked Czechoslovakia, for at one point Churchill broke off the conversation to ring Halifax. The foreign secretary agreed the outlines of a letter which Churchill could secretly send to Kleist-Schmenzin in the near future, to 're-assure his friends' that Britain would defend the Czechs.

Travelling back to London through the failing light of an English summer's evening, with Churchill's promise ringing in his ears, Ewald von Kleist-Schmenzin must have felt that his dangerous trip had been worth it – he had what Beck and his friends in Germany had asked him to get: a clear commitment that London would act if Hitler moved against Czechoslovakia. Now they could get on with planning the coup to remove the dictator and prevent the coming war.

The next day, Churchill sent the record of his meeting to prime minister Chamberlain, foreign secretary Halifax, Halifax's predecessor Anthony Eden, and shortly afterwards to the French prime minister, Édouard Daladier.

Chamberlain was again dismissive. In a note to Halifax he wrote that Kleist-Schmenzin and his friends 'remind me of the Jacobites at the Court of France in King William's time and I think we must discount a good deal of what he says'. But a double negative in the last sentence of the prime minister's minute seems to betray some uncertainty: 'Nevertheless I confess to some feeling of uneasiness and I don't feel sure that we ought not to do something … Inform [Sir Nevile] Henderson … and tell him … to make some warning gesture.'

A few days later a diplomat at the British embassy in Berlin discreetly slipped an unaddressed envelope to Ian Colvin, who passed it on to Kleist-Schmenzin in the backstreet bar in Bendlerstrasse where the two men had met before the German emissary's departure for London.

Inside the envelope a letter from Churchill read:

My Dear Sir,

I have welcomed you here as one who is ready to run risks to preserve the peace of Europe … I am sure that the crossing of the frontier of Czecho-slovakia … will bring about a renewal of the world war. I am as certain as I was at the end of July 1914 that England will march with France and … the United States … the spectacle of an armed attack by Germany upon a small neighbour … will rouse the whole British Empire and compel the gravest decisions.

Do not, I pray be misled upon this point. Such a war, once started, would be fought out like the last, to the bitter end …

As I feel you should have some definite message to take back to your friends in Germany … I believe that a peaceful solution of the Czecho-slovak problem would pave the way for the true reunion of our countries on the basis of the greatness and the freedom of both.

In time to come, Churchill's brief note would fall into the wrong hands, and become a death warrant for Ewald von Kleist-Schmenzin and many of his colleagues.

Three weeks after Kleist-Schmenzin's visit to London, on Monday, 5 September, a young woman also checked in at Tempelhof ostensibly on a short visit to the British capital. Her luggage was light, but her mind bore a very important message. This was not the first text too secret to be written down which Susanne Simonis, the European correspondent for the *Deutsche Allgemeine Zeitung*, had memorised for her cousin Erich Kordt, the head of foreign minister Ribbentrop's personal office – but it was the most important. For this was a piece of secret information to be passed to the very top of the British government by Kordt's brother Theo, a senior diplomat at the German embassy in London – and it had the potential to avoid a world war. The message was that a high-level 'conspiracy against Hitler exists in Germany and that a firm and unmistakable attitude by Britain and France would give the conspirators their opportunity [to remove the Führer] on the day that the German mobilization [for the invasion of Czechoslovakia] is announced'.

The day after Simonis's arrival in London, Theo Kordt was smuggled into 10 Downing Street by the 'secret' door which leads from Horse Guards Parade into the prime minister's garden. From there he was led up to the office of Chamberlain's personal emissary to Hitler, Sir Horace Wilson. Wilson, who was also a convinced appeaser, listened attentively to Kordt's message, and his assurance that if Britain and France stood up to Hitler on Czechoslovakia, the Wehrmacht would depose him at the instant he ordered the invasion. Wilson, who had met Kordt previously and trusted him, was impressed, and asked the German diplomat to return the following day to meet the foreign secretary, Halifax.

After listening to Kordt's message the following evening, Halifax said he would do his best to ensure that the prime minister was informed – and perhaps some other cabinet colleagues too. Kordt was experienced enough to know that this was the kind of politeness the English use to cover lack of enthusiasm. He was shown back to the Downing Street garden door, and walked out onto Horse Guards Parade and into the London night puzzled and worried by Halifax's muted response. And well he might have been. For Halifax could not tell his visitor that his master, Neville Chamberlain, had already decided not to resist Hitler's demands for the Sudetenland, but to yield to them. 'We could not be as candid with you as you were with us,' Halifax was later to tell Kordt – long after the damage was done.

On Sunday, 11 September, four days after Kordt's second backdoor visit to Downing Street, Vansittart's secret emissary A.P. Young flew to Switzerland for another meeting with Carl Goerdeler in Zürich, once again at the German's urgent request. The two met in the St Gotthard Hotel and strolled to Zürich's Belvoir Park, where they spent two hours walking in the autumn sunshine among the flowerbeds and carefully manicured lawns, discussing the coming war and how it could now be stopped only by a combination of strong British and French action, backed by a coup to remove Hitler. At Zürich station that evening, as the world teetered towards the brink of war, Goerdeler waved goodbye to Young with the words, 'Remember always that we shall win the *last* battle.'

7

'All Our Lovely Plans'

In the early hours of Wednesday, 28 September 1938 an armed raiding party, nicknamed 'Commando Heinz' after its leader, gathered in the Hohenzollerndamm headquarters of the Wehrmacht's Third Army Corps, responsible for the defence of Berlin. The unit consisted of fifty or sixty assorted desperadoes, ranging from Abwehr and Wehrmacht officers, to armed civilians and civil servants, to student leaders. Under the command of an ex-Nazi thug and serial revolutionary called Friedrich Wilhelm Heinz, they were ready for action and equipped with weapons supplied on the instructions of Admiral Canaris. 'The silence of pre-dawn Berlin,' a commentator wrote later, 'was broken by the click-click-click of ammunition being loaded into [the magazines of] carbines and automatic weapons.'

Commando Heinz's orders were to arrest Adolf Hitler at the moment he gave the order to invade Czechoslovakia at two o'clock that afternoon, and take him to a nearby hospital. There the dictator would be seen by the psychiatrist Dr Karl Bonhoeffer, the father of the great theologian, who would declare the Führer insane and commit him to a lunatic asylum. But some in the group did not intend to let Hitler get that far. They had secretly sworn to kill him in the confusion of the arrest.

The conspirators' task was, on the face of it, not a difficult one. Only fifteen SS soldiers guarded Hitler in his Chancellery at any one time. The great double doors of the building would be secretly unlocked from the inside by one of the Foreign Office conspirators so as to give the raiding party easy access. There were plenty of reinforcements ready to come to the raiders' assistance if required. In the Foreign Office and the Interior Ministry, anti-Nazi diplomats and officials had been issued with arms, and were ready to play their part. Other reserve forces made up of small groups of officers were waiting in private houses and apartments across the German capital, like the group holed up in the ornate white-stuccoed art-nouveau block of flats at Eisenacher Strasse 118, close to the government quarter. One of the plotters told his brother over dinner that evening, 'Tonight Hitler will be arrested.'

There were good reasons for this confidence. Among those backing the putsch were the chief of the German staff and his predecessor, the commander-in-chief of the Wehrmacht, the political and operational leaders of the criminal police, the commander of the Berlin military district and one of his subordinates, the state secretary of the Foreign Office and his chief of ministerial office, the president of the Reichsbank, a senior official in the German embassy in London, another in the Department of Justice, and Hitler's personal interpreter.*

The plot had been meticulously prepared.

Two weeks earlier, on 14 September, after several days spent carrying out a detailed reconnaissance of all the key sites, there was a full paper rehearsal of the coup plans, which incorporated the seizure of key Berlin police stations, an armed takeover of the state wireless transmitters, telephone installations and repeater stations, and the occupation of Hitler's Chancellery and key ministries. When the exercise ended, General Erwin von Witzleben, the commander of the Berlin garrison and the coup's de facto leader, declared that all preparations had been completed. They were ready. The moment Hitler gave the order to invade the Sudetenland, they would make their move.

But in all his careful preparations, Erwin von Witzleben had missed one crucial factor – the British prime minister.

On the evening of 14 September, as the coup rehearsal concluded in Berlin, Neville Chamberlain, in London, suddenly stunned everyone, including his own cabinet and Hitler (who was 'flabbergasted'), by announcing that he would fly to the Führer's mountain retreat at Berchtesgaden in the Bavarian Alps for talks the following day.

It is important at this point to record the precise sequence of events.

As a result of the messages from Goerdeler in early August and mid-September, and of the visit of Kleist-Schmenzin to London in mid-August, we can presume that the British government must have

---

* Respectively: Generals Franz Halder and Ludwig Beck; General Walther von Brauchitsch; Graf Wolf von Heldorf, Graf Fritz-Dietlof von der Schulenberg and Arthur Nebe; General Erwin von Witzleben and Walter Brockdorff-Ahlefeldt; Ernst von Weizsäcker and Erich Kordt; Hjalmar Schacht; Theo Kordt; Hans von Dohnányi; and Paul Schmidt.

Erwin von Witzleben

known of the existence of the plot against Hitler, although we cannot be certain that this knowledge extended to No. 10 and the prime minister. However, after Theo Kordt's backdoor visit to No. 10 and his discussion with Halifax on the evening of 7 September, no such uncertainty is possible. From this moment onwards No. 10 knew of the plot, and it is overwhelmingly likely that the prime minister knew of it too. It is a matter of record that, at least from the end of August, Neville Chamberlain and his closest advisers had been secretly considering a personal last-minute appeal to Hitler. But the fact that this took place – stunning everyone, including the cabinet – just eight days after the Kordt visit raises the strong suspicion that the British prime minister's sudden visit to Berchtesgaden was, if only in part, designed to pre-empt the coming coup so as to give Chamberlain the peacemaker his time upon the stage.

Whatever the truth of this, Chamberlain's unexpected flight in a specially chartered aircraft (it was his first time on a plane) to join Hitler at Berchtesgaden left the plotters crestfallen and discomfited. They had no option but to put their plans on ice and wait for developments.

In the talks that followed, Chamberlain privately conceded the Sudetenland to Hitler, subject to a plebiscite in the disputed territory and a number of other weak safeguards. Afterwards the British prime minister gave his impressions of the meeting and of Hitler in a letter to his sister, which concluded: 'I thought I saw in his face … that here was a man who could be relied upon when he had given his word.' Returning to London, Chamberlain met with the French and persuaded them to help pressure the Czechs into accepting the deal, despite the fact that it would effectively dismember their country. Eventually, the Czech president Edvard Beneš had no option but to cave in.

If Chamberlain expected a welcome from his cabinet on his return from Berchtesgaden, he did not get one. Their meeting of 17 September was fractious, and treated the prime minister's 'peace deal' with deep scepticism. Even Halifax, Chamberlain's right-hand man in the business of appeasement, expressed his opposition: 'Hitler has given us nothing and is dictating terms as if he had won a war,' he said. Duff Cooper, the First Lord of the Admiralty, was even blunter, warning the cabinet of the 'danger of being accused of truckling to dictators and offending our best friends'. Britain should, he said, 'make it plain that we would rather fight than agree to an abject surrender'.

But Chamberlain would not be diverted. Still determined to push through his peace plan, on 22 September he flew back to see Hitler at Bad Godesberg, near Bonn, expecting to sign the final agreement that would settle the Czech crisis.

He had another shock waiting for him. Instead of signing the deal, Hitler upped his demands with a new set of conditions for 'peace', accompanied by an ultimatum requiring the full and unconditional withdrawal of Czech forces from the Sudetenland by 1 October. Chamberlain was forced to fly home that evening crestfallen and empty-handed.

On 26 September the prime minister's adviser Horace Wilson was despatched back to Berlin as Chamberlain's 'personal envoy'. His instructions were to deliver two messages. The first was the carrot: there should be a meeting between the Germans and the Czechs 'with a view to settling by agreement the way in which the territory [of the Sudetenland] could be handed over'. The second, and more important, part of Wilson's message was the stick: if Hitler rejected this course of action and invaded, then he should be clear that France's treaty obligations to Czechoslovakia meant she would have to defend her ally with force, and Britain would join her.

Wilson met Hitler at 5 p.m. that day. The Führer, preparing for a big speech in the evening, was in a foul temper. As soon as he heard Chamberlain's proposal for more talks he flew into a towering rage, shrieking that there would be no talks unless the Czechs first accepted his terms as outlined at Bad Godesberg. He followed this outburst by issuing another ultimatum – now he must have the Czechs' answer by 2 p.m. on 28 September – just two days away.

The Führer abruptly terminated the meeting before Chamberlain's envoy had the opportunity to deliver the crucial second part of the prime minister's message, containing the threat of a British and French response in kind if Hitler chose the path of military action instead of talks.

The Berlin conspirators were delighted with this outcome. Now, at last, there was a precise date and time for the coup, and it was a mere two days away. 'Finally we have clear proof that Hitler wants war, no matter what. Now [if he invades] there can be no going back,' Hans Oster commented to a friend. The carefully laid plans to remove Adolf Hitler were reinstated, and the key coup plotters began moving into position.

On the morning of the next day, 27 September, there were the first signs of a stronger British line: the Royal Navy was ordered to move to battle stations. Hitler, taken aback, said to Göring, 'The English fleet might shoot after all.'

At midday Wilson, at Chamberlain's insistence, returned to see the Führer, this time finally giving the strong warning that the prime minister had asked him to deliver the previous day: if Hitler attacked, France would act and Britain would follow.

According to insiders in Berlin, Hitler had already started to wobble. At 9 a.m. Carl Goerdeler sent an urgent telegram to Vansittart: 'Don't give away another foot. Hitler is in a most uncomfortable position ...'

But then the rollercoaster lurched again.

Whatever 'tough' message was meant by the mobilisation of the British fleet and the warning Wilson delivered to Hitler, what the British prime minister said in his now infamous BBC broadcast to the nation at 6.15 that evening could not have been read by the German leader as anything other than a signal that Britain would not act if Czechoslovakia was invaded:

How horrible, fantastic, incredible it is that we should be digging
trenches and trying on gas-masks here because of a quarrel in a far-away
country between people of whom we know nothing. It seems still more
impossible that a quarrel that has already been settled in principle
should be the subject of war ... However much we may sympathise with
a small nation confronted by a big and powerful neighbour, we cannot
in all circumstances undertake to involve the whole British Empire in

war simply on her account. If we have to fight it must be on larger issues than that.

All eyes now focused on Hitler's deadline – 2 p.m. the following day. The coup plotters and their forces were on hairtrigger alert, and the world held its breath.

The morning hours of 28 September ticked past in much scurrying to and fro between the various groups of plotters in their secret locations across Berlin. Von Witzleben calmed one of his colleagues who tried to persuade him to launch early: 'It won't be long now.' At 11 a.m. Erich Kordt got a call from his brother Theo at the German embassy in London informing him, on apparently good information, that Britain would indeed declare war if Hitler launched his armies at 2 p.m.

What Theo Kordt did not know, however, was that an hour earlier, at 10 a.m., Chamberlain had rung the British ambassador in Rome and instructed him to get a message to Mussolini asking the Italian dictator to intervene 'in the last useful hours to save peace and civilization'. The ambassador swiftly passed the message on to Il Duce. At 11 a.m., as Erich Kordt was being assured that Britain was ready to go to war at two o'clock that afternoon, Mussolini, who had been something of a bystander up to now, was ringing the Italian ambassador in Berlin, Bernardo Attolico: 'Go to the Führer and tell him, considering that I will be by his side, whatever may happen, that I advise him to delay the start of hostilities for twenty-four hours. In the meantime I intend to study what can be done to resolve the problem.'

Shortly afterwards a second message from No. 10 arrived at the British embassy in Rome instructing the ambassador to get a message to the Italians 'suggesting Mussolini supports Chamberlain's proposal for a conference in Germany involving Italy, Germany, France and Britain to solve the Sudetenland problem'. A little later a telegram arrived in Downing Street from the ambassador in Rome saying that Mussolini had agreed to Chamberlain's proposal, and would recommend it to Hitler.

As all this was going on, a constant stream of visitors flowed in and out of Hitler's Chancellery. At 11.15 the French ambassador, the luxuriantly moustachioed André François-Poncet, speaking on behalf of both Paris and London and unaware of what had been happening between London and Rome, urged Hitler to accept Chamberlain's proposal for more talks. Twenty-five minutes later a portly, stooped figure emerged from a taxi. Bald, bespectacled, sweating, breathless and without his hat, ambassador

Attolico scurried in through the Chancellery doors, bearing the message from Mussolini. Hitler broke off from seeing François-Poncet to meet the new arrival. 'Il Duce informs you,' Attolico said, his high-pitched voice rising several notes from the tension, 'that whatever you decide, Führer, Fascist Italy stands behind you. Il Duce is, however of the opinion that it would be wise to accept the British proposal and begs you to refrain from mobilisation.' Finally, with just two hours to go to the 2 p.m. deadline, Hitler, the man whose reputation had been built on 'the triumph of the will', backed down, announcing that, instead of invading Czechoslovakia, he would accept talks at Munich.

Chamberlain heard the news in the House of Commons at a little before 4.20 that afternoon, and immediately announced he would go to Munich the following day. There was a moment of stunned silence, and then the Commons chamber erupted with shouts of elation and joy.

And so there was no order to invade, no launching of armies, and no trigger for a coup. It was over.

A senior army general involved in the aborted coup said later, 'I had already passed the order to Witzleben to start the coup when the information reached us that Chamberlain and Daladier were coming to Munich and therefore I had to withdraw the order ... the coup d'état was to have been justified before the people by saying that Hitler was provoking a war and that, without a violent coup d'état war could not be prevented. Now that was no longer possible.' Another asked sharply, 'What can troops possibly do against a leader this victorious?'

Though they would try again many times in the coming years to replicate the coup of 1938, this was the best chance the conspirators would get to remove Hitler – and, thanks to the British prime minister, they had lost it.

French ambassador François-Poncet, as famous for his merciless eye as he was for his magnificent moustaches, described Chamberlain arriving at Munich on 30 September: 'Grey, stooped, with bushy eyebrows, blotched skin and chapped hands – he seemed typical of a grand Englishman from a bygone age.'

As all the world knows, what followed was the Munich agreement which gifted the Sudetenland to Hitler without a shot being fired.

Chamberlain returned in triumph to Croydon Aerodrome, with a flutter of paper in his hand, announcing 'peace for our time'. In the House of Commons and across Britain that day there was cheering and jubilation. But not from Winston Churchill, who denounced Chamberlain's deal as 'the first foretaste of a bitter cup' to shouts of abuse from all sides of the Commons chamber. For a Britain dangerously underprepared for war, there was a substantial upside to Munich – the country now had more time to get ready. But the cost to national prestige, standing and influence was huge. And the consequence of now having to deal with a Hitler magnified in size to his own people, and in his own sense of destiny, would be very great.

The French prime minister Édouard Daladier understood perhaps better than Chamberlain what had happened. Waving to cheering crowds on his return to Paris, he was heard to mutter under his breath. '*Ah, les cons. S'ils savaient!*'*

Hitler celebrated a triumph too, though it was not the one he had wanted. He was initially furious at the outcome of Munich, flying into a rage and shouting that Chamberlain had tricked him out of the military victory over the whole of Czechoslovakia that he wanted so badly. But he soon realised that the British prime minister had delivered him victory enough for the moment. The rest of Czechoslovakia could come later.

As the Commons debated in London, German troops marched through jubilant crowds into the Czech Sudetenland. They were followed four days later by the Führer standing in the front of an open-topped Mercedes, his right arm stretched out ramrod-straight in the Nazi salute, which the crowd returned with cheers, children bearing flowers and a forest of extended arms. Czechoslovakia, brought into existence by the Versailles Treaty, would over the next years lose 70 per cent of its iron, steel and electricity production, a third of its people, and enough weapons and ammunition from its arsenals and armaments factories to equip half the Wehrmacht.

Two days later, on 5 October, Churchill pronounced a final accusatory obsequy in the House of Commons over the dismembered remains of Hitler's prey: 'Silent, mournful, abandoned, broken, Czechoslovakia recedes into the darkness … terrible words have for the time being been pronounced against the Western democracies: "Thou art weighed in the balance and found wanting."'

On 4 November, five weeks after Munich, members of Churchill's Epping Constituency Conservative Association moved a motion of no confidence in their MP. Churchill survived by the skin of his teeth, thanks to what he later described as 'the speech of my life'. Thus was Hitler denied

---

* The polite English translation would be, 'Ah, the bloody idiots. If they only knew!'

a double victory: one at Munich which gave him the Sudetenland; and one at Epping, where fate came within a hair's breadth of removing his most capable adversary in the coming conflict.

The Abwehr's 'eternal plotter' Hans Bernd Gisevius, who had been amongst the most active of the conspirators right from the start, commented bitterly after the war: 'Peace for our time? Let us put it a bit more realistically. Chamberlain saved Hitler.'

In a letter to an American friend, Carl Goerdeler wrote: 'The Munich agreement was just sheer capitulation by France and England ... By refusing to take a small risk, Chamberlain has made a war inevitable. Both the British and French nations will now have to defend their freedom with arms in hand ...'

In his memoirs written after the war, Erich Kordt recorded: 'Never since 1933 was there such a good chance to free Germany and the world.'

On the evening the Munich agreement was signed, the key Berlin plotters gathered in the grand house of the commander of the Berlin garrison, Erwin von Witzleben. In the words of one of those present, 'all our lovely plans' were unceremoniously burnt in Witzleben's baronial fireplace.

One general wept, and the world, unchecked, marched on to war.

8

March Madness

It did not take long for London to understand the opportunities that had been lost at Munich by its failure to act on the warnings it had received of Hitler's intentions towards Czechoslovakia.

A late-1938 MI6 analysis concluded that the German generals 'strove unremittingly and courageously to restrain Hitler'. Even the strongly pro-appeasement British ambassador in Berlin, Sir Nevile Henderson, found himself unable to gloss what had happened in his customary diplomatic language. 'By keeping the peace, we have saved Hitler and his regime,' he wrote to foreign secretary Halifax a week after Munich was signed. In December 1938 the British chargé d'affaires in Berlin noted that 'authoritative circles' in London now hoped that a revolt would remove Hitler, the man Chamberlain's flight to Munich had rescued from removal just two months previously.

But the damage was done.

The West's surrender to Hitler's demands at Munich caused a catastrophic decline of morale and will amongst the September plotters. Carl Goerdeler, who had spent the week of the Czech crisis in Switzerland, on the shores of Lake Constance, waiting for the call to take up his post as the new chancellor of Germany, wrote to a friend predicting that war was now inevitable. The majority of those closely involved in the plot considered that they had risked their lives to rid the world of a war-obsessed tyrant, only to be abandoned by those they had most trusted among the Western powers. The word 'betrayal' was on many lips.

The truth was that there had been a shameful failure of communication between the Berlin plotters and the governments of France and, perhaps especially, of Britain. There were several factors which produced this 'dialogue of the deaf' in which the last, best chance of avoiding the coming war was lost.

Chief among these was Chamberlain's conviction that Hitler would be amenable to reason, and that appeasement (in the 1930s the word meant putting peace first, and did not carry the pejorative overtones it does today) was the way to persuade him to back away from war. This, added to the sense of personal responsibility Chamberlain felt for ensuring the peace of his age, created a deadly cocktail in which hubris and sense of mission combined to distort the British prime minister's judgement and reduce his capacity to take measured, thought-through actions.

Chamberlain's appeasement, however, was not based only on a naïvely utopian view of Hitler's true nature. It was also firmly founded on what had been, with the terrible exception of the Great War, British foreign policy for the past hundred years. It is important to remember that Chamberlain's analysis was shared by the majority of British political and public opinion of the day – especially among the generals: 'Of our top military and air people whom I questioned on the subject, I don't think I found one who did not think that appeasement was right,' wrote Sir Alexander Cadogan, who succeeded Sir Robert Vansittart as head of the Foreign Office in 1938.

It was Churchill and those closest to him, along with the Labour Party and the Liberals, who were regarded as being out of step with reality and with history, not Chamberlain.

Since the post-Napoleonic settlement, Britain's strategy had been to stay out of military engagements on the European mainland. Successive British governments were, in the main, sniffily indifferent to what the Europeans did on their continent, so long as they did not threaten the wider peace or interfere in the process of building and maintaining the British Empire. The Europeans could have the Continent, was London's unspoken motto, provided Britain could have the sea. Chamberlain's 'betrayal' of Czechoslovakia was thus fully consistent with Britain's traditional policy of managing the European peace not through armies, but through constantly-shifting diplomatic alliances designed to preserve the balance of power established at the Congress of Vienna in 1815. What matter if this policy earned Britain the French insult 'Albion perfide' – so long as it kept her powerful, prosperous, peaceful, and out of the wars that convulsed Europe in the nineteenth century. In the view of the appeasers in 1938, it was the abandonment of this policy in 1914 that had caused such ghastly consequences for the generation that had fought in the First World War, and who now governed Britain. It was to this traditional policy that the country should now return, they insisted, so that the terrible blood sacrifice which was the inevitable consequence of modern total war should never again be allowed to happen. When Hitler hinted, in a 'peace speech' to the Reichstag on 21 May 1935, that he favoured a broad settlement based on 'leaving Europe to the Europeans and letting Britain have the sea', he was skilfully playing both to Britain's traditional foreign policy and to popular and official British sentiment.

It was for this reason that when Goerdeler and his plotters started appearing in Whitehall in 1937 and 1938 with their warnings of an approaching apocalypse, they were seen not as good men seeking to save the world from tyranny, but as meddlers and interferers in a policy which everyone believed in, and which had proved its worth over the previous hundred years. If it is the case, as seems likely, that Chamberlain's hurried first flight to Bad Godesberg on 15 September 1938 was intended, at least in part to forestall the plot Goerdeler and his friends had been hatching, then in all probability what would have been on his mind was 'Better the devil you know, than the conspirators you don't.'

Herein also lay the last major ingredient of the tragically missed opportunity of September 1938. Goerdeler and his fellow plotters knew and understood the exceptional nature of the demonic power they were seeking to remove. Chamberlain and the British, on the other hand, saw Hitler as just the latest in the long line of Continental tyrants behaving badly, as Continental tyrants always had, from Napoleon to Bismarck to Kaiser Wilhelm II. Worse still, the 1938 plotters were, in the British government's eyes, yet another bunch of conservative Prussian landowners, monarchists and militarists with no attachment to democracy. Their primary aim, like that of Hitler, was to recover the lands Germany had lost under the Versailles settlement. What Chamberlain, Halifax and Henderson did not see was that, whatever the democratic deficiencies of the September plotters, they were nevertheless motivated by conventional religious and European values of morality, which were totally absent from the character and actions of Adolf Hitler. The plotters understood the unique moral bankruptcy of the Hitler phenomenon. Chamberlain and his government, it seems, did not.

Behind the September plotters' complaints about the moral failures of Britain and France during the Czech crisis lay a crucial failure of their own – one which was fatally to hobble them right through to 1944. They wanted to be rid of Hitler, but they were never prepared to take the initiative to do so. They shied away from triggering events themselves, and depended on others to do this for them (in the case of the Czech crisis, the trigger was Hitler's order to mobilise). They were actors in the wings, always waiting for a cue to come onto the stage which never came. Eventually, as successive 'ripe moments' for their 'lovely plans' came and went, waiting became a kind of strategy in itself – until finally an impetuous, headstrong young man strode into their midst in 1944 and shook them from their torpor.

In the immediate aftermath of Munich, most of the plotters slunk away into the shadows to wait and watch for the next propitious moment to strike. Goerdeler spent the end of September and the first week of October writing a series of long, impatient and rather self-righteous memos to London and Washington – including his first proposition for a united Europe as a solution to the rising threat of European nationalism. In the middle of October he called Vansittart's 'agent' A.P. Young to a meeting at a private address in Zürich. There he passed on some useful intelligence, including the information that Hitler had sent Canaris to persuade Franco into an alliance aimed at capturing Gibraltar and sealing off the Mediterranean from the British.

A further meeting between Young and Goerdeler took place on 4 December, this time in a hotel room in Zürich. On this occasion Goerdeler, using two fingers and a typewriter borrowed from the hotel, laboriously typed out ten paragraphs of a suggested 'Heads of Agreement between Great Britain and Germany'. Despite the fact that nearly all his recommendations had already been incorporated in Foreign Office forward papers, his proposals were roundly rejected by the mandarins of King Charles's Street, who, having been proved wrong about Goerdeler's warnings about the Sudetenland, were now finding his preachy style irksome and patronising.

It was not just the British who were put off by Goerdeler's didacticism. Hans Bernd Gisevius wrote at this time that Goerdeler's 'finest virtue was also his gravest weakness. The passion for justice burned so fiercely in him that he forgot all moderation. He preached and preached and preached, until … people … lost all patience with him.'

On 10 December 1938, Sir Alexander Cadogan reflected the same weariness with the German emissary in his diary: 'had a message from G [Goerdeler] outlining a plan of [an army] revolution in Germany to take place before the end of the month. G wants a message from us … He had already sent us a "programme" which we couldn't subscribe to – too much like *Mein Kampf* – and that rather put me off him. But he may want something merely to show his fellow conspirators that we shan't fall upon a divided Germany and would want to work with any decent regime that may come out of this mess ... I don't believe much in this,' he concluded, but added a wary codicil: 'but if there is anything in it, it's the biggest thing for centuries'.

Along with his recommendations for British policy, Goerdeler also included a report predicting, among other things, that Hitler would soon turn his attention to Holland, Belgium and Switzerland. Over the next year, Goerdeler's use to the British changed from being an occasional (and by now mostly unwanted) diplomatic adviser on Germany, to a primary source of intelligence on Hitler's plans and intentions.

Madeleine Bihet-Richou was not able to enjoy autumn in Paris for long after her narrow escape from Vienna. In the last days of September her French intelligence handler, Henri Navarre, asked her to return to Berlin, where a job had been arranged for her at the French Institute. She was now able to continue her affair with Lahousen, who was by this time installed as one of Canaris's closest advisers in the Tirpitzufer. At the end of October the two lovers were taking advantage of a brilliant late-autumn day to pay a visit to the Berlin Zoo. Admiring the giraffes, Lahousen said in a quiet voice that Hitler had just ordered plans to be drawn up for the takeover of the remains of Czechoslovakia in the middle of March the following year.

'This time,' he added, 'if France and Britain react, it will be war.'

Madeleine rushed, first to the French embassy to send a brief coded telegram to Navarre in Paris, and then to the Anhalter station in Potsdamer Platz, where she caught a train to the French capital to report personally on what she had learned. She met Navarre and Louis Rivet, the chief of French military intelligence, at a restaurant on the Rond-point des Champs-Élysées and gave them the whole story. A report was sent to French foreign minister Georges Bonnet, who responded that if Hitler went ahead with his plan, France could only react if Britain did – and Britain showed no signs of wanting to.

Rivet, conscious that he now had a very high-level source in Madeleine, instructed his new spy that she was never again to visit the French embassy in Berlin. In future she should pass her information by telephone to the French military attaché in the city, using a secret number which she should dial only from public phoneboxes.

On the evening of 8 November, not long after Madeleine's return to the German capital, she was strolling with Lahousen down Kleiststrasse when he mentioned the assassination the previous day of a German diplomat in

Paris by a Polish Jew. 'The government,' he told her, 'has secretly ordered a "spontaneous wave" of reprisals to be launched by paramilitaries against the Jews, under cover of which their private wealth will be pillaged and Jewish synagogues will be burnt. Fire engines will be pre-positioned around the synagogues – not to stop them burning, but to save neighbouring buildings.'

The following night, Germany was convulsed and the world shocked by yet another outrage against the Jews. *Kristallnacht* was so named because of the carpets of broken glass which littered German streets after violent nationwide attacks on Jews and their property. Over a thousand synagogues were set on fire, many of them being totally destroyed; more than 7,500 Jewish businesses were demolished; at least ninety-one Jews were killed, and 30,000 arrested and incarcerated in Dachau, Buchenwald and Sachsenhausen. For Carl Goerdeler, himself not immune to a degree of anti-Semitism, this was a turning point. 'The shame and bitterness of the most patriotic went so far as to make them be ashamed before the world of the name German which we loved and of which we were so proud … For many who hesitated there was now no possibility of reconciliation with this regime of violence,' wrote one witness after the war.

Some of the September plotters went further, actively helping the Jews to escape the mobs and the Gestapo. Canaris was later thanked by Jewish leaders for what he did that night to save members of their community. Hans Oster offered to smuggle his Jewish neighbours out of harm's way:

In the afternoon of 9th November 1938 our neighbour, the wife of Colonel, later General Hans Oster, called on us to offer the shelter of their home to my father, who was a lawyer aged 58. The news of the arrest of Jewish men had spread to both our families. The Osters and our family lived on the same floor of a Berlin apartment block. There were two staircases, one for tradesmen and one for us. Mrs Oster proposed that if the Gestapo called at the front door, my father could easily slip across to their flat by the back door.

Afterwards, Canaris, Oster and the Abwehr lawyer Hans von Dohnányi set up a secret organisation to smuggle Jews out of Germany, often by recruiting them into the Abwehr and then sending them abroad as Abwehr 'agents'. The son of Canaris's pastor recalled one among many recorded examples of Canaris and the Abwehr helping Jews to escape:

Thirteen Jewish men who had married non-Jewish women ... were deported to different camps ... all of them were released thanks to the combined efforts of Canaris and his staff ... the Admiral succeeded in organising their transport in a closed train compartment to Madrid, where they came under Franco's protection. Canaris used his connections to put thirteen of them up in private homes in Madrid before some of them were flown to England. Most ... joined the British military.

On New Year's Day 1939, with international tension rising again over Czechoslovakia, Canaris appointed Erwin Lahousen as the head of Section II of the Abwehr (sabotage and disruption), and gave him two sets of orders. One was designed for official consumption; the other was 'unofficial', and described Lahousen's real task, which Canaris ordered should be to form 'a secret organisation within Abwehr II and the Brandenburg Regiment, with the purpose of bringing together all anti-Nazi forces and preparing them for illegal acts ... against the system ... With the successful incorporation of Czechoslovakia into ... the Third Reich ... the way to war with Poland has been opened for Hitler and his clique of criminals. I am convinced that the other great Powers will not be caught this time by the political ... tricks of this pathological liar. War will result in a catastrophe ... [not just] for Germany [but also] for all mankind ... if there were victory for the Nazi system.'

With her lover busy out of Berlin taking over his new organisation, Madeleine Bihet-Richou used the opportunity for a swift visit to Paris. There she received training in the use of secret ink, and underwent a deep-level interrogation about her relationship with Lahousen and his possible motives in talking to her so openly.

The early months of 1939 were full of intense diplomatic manoeuvring as everyone waited for Hitler's next play. On 20 February, Spain, under substantial German and Italian pressure, agreed 'in principle' to join Hitler's Anti-Comintern pact, insisting, however, that it should do so secretly. Five days later, to even up the balance and keep everyone on their toes, Franco signed an agreement with France that Madrid would stay neutral. Most small states in Europe, inferring from the Czech crisis that the *Pax Britannica* of the nineteenth century was now a dead letter, began negotiating bilateral non-aggression pacts with Hitler. The British government for its part resolved that, since it was no longer able to honour guarantees, it should avoid giving any. Meanwhile, after a government study into how France could defend itself against air attack had concluded that it couldn't, French foreign minister Bonnet decided that the best protection for his country lay not in anti-aircraft batteries, but in a piece of paper declaring lasting friendship between Paris and Berlin. In all this scurry of diplomatic to-ings and fro-ings, one assumption was commonly held by all: that, given Hitler's high-octane, high-volume and high-frequency warnings of the communist threat to Europe (accompanied by insults to match), the one pact that was out of the question was an alliance between Hitler and Stalin. In February, however, both Canaris and Churchill simultaneously picked up tremors that all was not as it seemed, and that there were signs of a growing rapprochement between Berlin and Moscow. Unaware of this, the Bank of England, at the government's behest, offered the German Reichsbank a huge loan designed to encourage Hitler to make his next move for 'Lebensraum' east towards the Ukraine and Russia, rather than west.

In the spring of 1939, the shadow-boxing suddenly turned into the real thing.

In early March Lahousen told Paris, through Madeleine, that German armour and troops were concentrating near the Bohemia–Moravia border, where they would be within swift striking distance of Prague. A little later he followed this up by providing Madeleine with the complete German plan for the invasion of what remained of Czechoslovakia. What Hans Bernd Gisevius was to call 'the March madness' had begun.

At 7 a.m. on 11 March, at Paul Thümmel's request the Abwehr spy met his Czech handler in the station buffet of the Czech market town of Turnov. 'The final decision has been taken in Berlin,' Thümmel reported. 'On 15 March Czechoslovakia will no longer exist.' Thümmel was swiftly bundled into a car and driven to Prague, where in a Czech intelligence safe house he outlined in detail, complete with supporting documents, the German plan of attack on Czechoslovakia. He also handed over an original Gestapo document which contained orders for all Czech intelligence officers to be rounded up after the invasion and submitted to 'interrogation with great severity'. Thümmel's information was rushed to Colonel František Morávec, the head of the Czech intelligence service, who instructed that the German spy should be given six emergency 'accommodation' addresses through which he could keep in contact if the Czech government was forced to go into exile. Two of these were in The Hague, two in London, one in Sweden and one in Zürich. As he left to return to

Germany, Thümmel turned to Morávec: 'Good luck, Colonel. This is not goodbye, but *auf Wiedersehen*.'

The Czech spy chief passed Thümmel's information to the pro-German Czech foreign minister, who dismissed it as alarmist: 'If such events were in store, I, as Foreign Minister, would be the first to know ... In future do not bring such upsetting reports which could spread alarm and disturb the peace.'

This view was shared by the British ambassador in Berlin, Nevile Henderson, who sent a telegram to London anticipating 'in the immediate future, a period of relative calm'. He backed this up with a report a week later, on 9 March, predicting that if the remains of Czechoslovakia were to be 'absorbed' into the German Reich, it would not happen for 'a year or two'. The following day, the MP Sir Samuel Hoare, one of Chamberlain's close supporters, made a speech to his constituents in Chelsea confidently predicting that Europe could now look forward to a 'Golden Age' of peace, prosperity and stability.

František Morávec did not share this Panglossian view. He arranged a swift meeting with Colonel Harold 'Gibby' Gibson, the head of the MI6 station in Prague, and asked for help. As a result, at around one o'clock on the afternoon of 14 March, a DC Douglas aircraft belonging to KLM made an unscheduled stop at Ruzyně airfield, twelve kilometres east of the Czech capital. There it was loaded with eleven men of the Czech intelligence service and numerous boxes of files. At 5.15 p.m. the plane took off for Rotterdam, where after dropping off one of its passengers, Aloïs Franck, who had orders to establish himself in The Hague, it continued its journey to Croydon Aerodrome outside London.

At dawn the following day, German armoured units stormed over the Sudetenland frontier and occupied Prague. By this time Thümmel's files, codes and contacts were safely in London. From now on, the ultimate destination of his priceless intelligence would be the British government, and in due course its great wartime prime minister, Winston Churchill.

9

The March to War

Up to the final act in the destruction of Czechoslovakia, Hitler had always defended his aggressions under the pretence of protecting the rights of self-determination of German-speaking people, claiming that they were 'under foreign occupation' as a result of Versailles. With the occupation of Prague, he finally crossed the Rubicon by launching a naked assault for which there was nothing but the very flimsiest attempt at justification. This was a genuine watershed moment, and ought to have been a trigger for the plotters to act. But the Führer had deliberately kept his plans close to his chest, revealing them to his officer corps only at the last moment.

In the days following the assault on Prague, Ludwig Beck met with General Franz Halder, his successor as head of the Army High Command (the Oberkommando des Heeres – OKH) at his secluded mansion on Berlin's tree-lined Goethestrasse. They agreed that Hitler was determined on war, and that he must be got rid of by force. But they couldn't agree on when or how. Halder thought they should wait until war was imminent. Beck warned that a putsch would be more difficult once hostilities started, and was irked by his successor's caution: 'As an experienced rider, Halder must have known that one had first to throw one's heart over the obstacle,' he commented tartly afterwards. The two men parted company, divided in their opinions and on strained terms.

Despite these disagreements at the top, elsewhere in army circles there were some attempts to reassemble and strengthen the resistance networks scattered by Munich and the failure of the September 1938 coup. These steps included sending Erwin Lahousen to Stockholm, ostensibly to secure assurances from Swedish firms that they would continue to deliver iron ore to Germany if war broke out. The other, hidden purpose of his visit was to bring back a British-made bomb for use in any early plan to kill Hitler.

Despite these scurryings after the event, the truth was that the September plotters had been caught scattered and flatfooted by Hitler's swift occupation of Prague, and once again had to be content with grumbling in private while lauding Hitler's victory in public. Another opportunity had been lost; they would have to fall back once more on preparing and waiting.

Waiting seemed to be Neville Chamberlain's policy too – that is, waiting and hoping for Hitler's appetite to be satiated. Speaking in the House of Commons on the day after the Führer's triumphal entry into Prague he said, more in sorrow than in anger, 'It is natural that I should bitterly regret what has occurred … [but] do not let us … be deflected from our course. The aim of the Government is now, as it has always been, to substitute the method of discussion, for the method of force in the settlement of differences.'

Wilhelm Canaris's 'eternal plotter' Hans Bernd Gisevius was determined on a more active course. Taking the early steps which would eventually lead him down the path of full-scale treason, he made a series of trips to Basel in Switzerland to meet representatives of the Western powers. 'We wanted to establish closer connections with the British and French, and it no longer seemed advisable to do this in Berlin,' he commented after the war. On 23 March he, Hjalmar Schacht and Goerdeler met 'a person of considerable influence in London and Paris political circles' near the Château d'Ouchy in Lausanne. The Germans asked for an urgent warning to be passed to London and Paris that Hitler was now intent on an invasion of Poland in the early autumn.

It is tempting to think that it was this warning which finally alerted Neville Chamberlain to the coming threat, for eight days later, on 31 March 1939, he announced a hardening of British policy in the House of Commons: 'In the event of any action which clearly threatened Polish independence … His Majesty's Government would feel themselves bound at once to lend the Polish Government all support in their power … The French Government have authorised me to make it plain that they stand in the same position in this matter as do His Majesty's Government.' A week later, on 6 April, during a visit to London by the Polish foreign minister, Chamberlain's statement of intent was widened into a formal Anglo–Polish military alliance, reinforced by British promises to help other smaller European nations with rearmament. The immediate effect was to make the Poles more intransigent in talks on the future of Danzig, which were by this time under way.

According to Canaris, Hitler, taken aback by this unexpected stiffening of British backs, flew into a rage, banged his fist on the table and shouted, 'Now I will mix for them a witches' brew!' It was another watershed moment. Hitler, who had hoped for an arrangement with Britain against Russia, now concluded that Britain could not be persuaded to support his plans, and would have to be defeated before he could look eastward for *Lebensraum* through the conquest of the Ukraine and Russia.

Three days after Chamberlain's announcement, on 3 April the Führer issued a secret directive to his generals to start planning for the invasion of Poland, ordering that what was to be known as Operation White 'must be ready to be launched from 1 September onwards'. That evening Lahousen relayed the information to Madeleine Bihet-Richou, who passed it on to Paris without delay.

During the next three months, hardly a day passed in London when the city was not playing host to clandestine visitors from Berlin bearing calamitous warnings. Carl Goerdeler was the first, in mid-March. In May he was back again, at the start of an international tour that took him to Libya, Egypt, Palestine, Syria, Turkey and Switzerland. He was one of no fewer than five key anti-Hitler plotters* who visited the British capital during May and June 1939, all with the same message for Vansittart (now serving as the government's chief diplomatic adviser) and the Foreign Office: Hitler was secretly working for a deal with Stalin. To one of these bearers of bad news the great Van replied, 'Keep calm, it is *we* who will sign the deal with Russia.'

Goerdeler claimed that during his May visit he also met with Churchill, but there is no record of this in Churchill's diaries or papers, or in the Chartwell visitors' book. In June 1939, Canaris and Oster tried to persuade Ewald von Kleist-Schmenzin to pay another visit to London, as a follow-up to his attempt to warn of the impending Czech crisis in September 1938: 'What have we to offer?' the Prussian responded. 'I am not going to London with empty hands.' Eventually they persuaded one of the German general staff to make the journey. He met the British service chiefs, but achieved nothing.

All Europe was now making dispositions for war.

Over the summer, Soviet intelligence agents in Germany started setting up the great spy network *die Rote Kapelle*, which in time would reach into every corner of occupied Europe.

---

* The others were Fabian von Schlabrendorff, Theo and Erich Kordt, and Lieutenant Colonel Count Gerhard von Schwerin, who was sent by the German general staff.

British intelligence too was about its spying business. In early May, MI6 issued a false British passport in the name of Charles Simpson to one of František Morávec's Czech intelligence officers, Karel Sedláček, who had operated undercover as a journalist in Zürich since 1934. Sedláček's task was to be Paul Thümmel's 'postman'. He was to organise the safe reception of Thümmel's secret letters to the Zürich accommodation address Morávec had given him on the eve of the German invasion of Czechoslovakia, and to ensure that these were quickly and safely passed on to London.

Aloïs Franck, the Czech intelligence officer dropped off in The Hague as his colleagues fled Prague for London, was also equipped with a false British identity as the Dutch representative of a coal-importing firm, Foster & Co., from Bristol. Franck's orders were to act as Thümmel's contact in the city, using a Jewish couple called Charles and Antoinette Jelinek. The Jelineks ran a bric-à-brac shop, 'De Favoriet', on the ground floor of an old lattice-windowed, redbrick, step-gabled merchant's house in a narrow, cobbled backstreet of The Hague* – another of the accommo-dation addresses Morávec had given Thümmel for his secret messages.

On 2 April 1939, just two weeks after the German occupation of Prague, the first return card from Thümmel, postmarked Dresden, arrived at De Favoriet. It contained no information – its purpose was simply to say that Agent A54 was back in touch.

London communicated with Thümmel through messages in invisible ink on what appeared to be an innocuous postcard. These were sent through the diplomatic bag to the British embassy in The Hague, which passed them to Franck, who passed them to a German refugee, who passed them to a nun, who smuggled them in her habit to Aachen, from where they completed their journey to Thümmel through the German postal system.

In the first days of June a second postcard from Thümmel, now using the codename 'Carl Voral', arrived in Zürich and was collected by Sedláček, who forwarded it to London in the Czech diplomatic bag. It read: 'Dear Uncle, I think I am in love. I have met a girl …' Between the lines of the visible text, another message, written in milk, appeared when the paper

---

* The building is still there, at Noordeinde 148. It is now a restaurant called 'Het Heden' (The Future). During the war it was owned by a Mrs Jansen, who also operated another accommodation address for Thümmel at her home. Thanks to Mike Van der Heijden for his help in finding this address and the history attached to it. See *Het Koninkrijk der Nederlanden in de Tweede Wereldoorlog – Deel 2 – Neutraal.*

was gently heated: 'I will be in The Hague shortly. Would like to meet you or your deputy. Place: Hotel des Indes. Name: Lustig. Date: June 15. Carl.' At the meeting which followed, Thümmel explained that he was now working in the Tirpitzufer in Berlin, and told Franck that the plan for Operation White – the German invasion of Poland – was now almost ready. It would involve nine Panzer divisions, and the target date for its launch had been fixed as no later than 1 September 1939. Morávec, in London, passed the information on to the British, who in turn passed it on – in a form sufficiently bowdlerised to conceal its source – to the Poles, who were alarmed, and to the French, who were sceptical.

As Thümmel was handing over Hitler's plans for the invasion of Poland, a twenty-five-year-old junior diplomat at the British embassy in Berlin was sent to the German Foreign Ministry to complain about a consignment of German arms that had been ordered and paid for by London, but had not yet been delivered. 'My dear fellow,' his German counterpart replied, in a languorous upper-class drawl, 'you will be very lucky if you get these now … at least not in the form that you were expecting them!'

The weather in The Hague on 3 August 1939 was brilliant and swelteringly hot. As evening fell, a brisk offshore breeze set the great sails turning on the windmills that stood like sentinels on the flat land around the city. Shortly after dusk, just as the street lights came on, a burly figure appeared in the arched doorway of De Favoriet. '*Grüss Gott*,' he said, smiling at Aloïs Franck, who was waiting for him in the dimly-lit, high-vaulted space of the Jelineks' shop. Without another word, the new arrival walked through to a back room, empty save for a table, a chair, a typewriter and neat stacks of white cardboard boxes marked with stencils proclaiming 'Gloves – Made in Czechoslovakia'.

Paul Thümmel, alias Agent A54, sat down and began typing, hesitantly and with two fingers, for he was not used to a typewriter:

> Nazi leaders think that France and England will not intervene in the
> event of a clash with Poland and that support for Poland will be limited
> to the supply of war materials and financial aid … If France does decide
> to fight … she will not be attacked … The Germans will take up
> defensive positions behind their 'Western Wall' lines of defence …

As Thümmel worked, occasionally pulling on a cigarette burning in an ashtray beside him, the stack of typed A4 pages by his typewriter grew. At around 2 a.m., with the room thick with the fug of cigarette smoke, his ashtray full of butt-ends and a sizeable pile of paper by his typewriter, he pushed back his chair and proclaimed his work finished. A final cigarette, a glass of schnapps, a few words with Franck about their next meeting, and Thümmel left as swiftly as he had come, into the night.

The following morning, Thümmel's report was taken to the British embassy in The Hague and sent to London by diplomatic bag. It was voluminous, detailed and, in intelligence terms, a goldmine. It contained, among other things, the entire detailed battle plan for the invasion of Poland, including a sketch map showing the invasion routes, the details of the two army groups that were to spearhead the attack, and the names of the German commanders involved down to divisional level. It also provided a complete list of Polish agents working for the Abwehr, along with a curious and seemingly puzzling piece of extra information: Hitler had ordered Canaris to provide SS chief Heinrich Himmler with 150 Polish army uniforms and firearms from the infiltration equipment store used by the special forces of the Brandenburg Regiment. Quizzed about this, Thümmel presumed that the uniforms were needed for some kind of manufactured 'incident' involving an act of fake 'aggression by Polish troops'. This was important information, not just for its own sake, but also because it showed that A54 had access, if not to Canaris himself, then to someone very close to him. In the event, Canaris deftly used the rivalries in Hitler's administration to divert Himmler from getting his hands on the Abwehr's Polish uniforms, scoring a small but satisfying bureaucratic victory. But since Himmler then managed to get the uniforms from another source, this had no effect at all on the progress of events, which were by now moving at increasing speed towards their ineluctable conclusion.

Not long after Thümmel's second meeting with Franck, Madeleine Bihet-Richou heard news from Paris that her son Pierre was critically ill with pneumonia. As she said a hurried goodbye to Lahousen, he whispered to her that a plot to eliminate Hitler had been prepared, but there was hesitation amongst the plotters because of the overwhelming popularity of the Führer. Madeleine packed a small overnight bag so as not to give the impression that she was fleeing Berlin for good with the clouds of war gathering, and took the first train to Paris. She arrived just in time to get Pierre into hospital for an emergency operation.

Lahousen's whispered farewell message was accurate. Throughout June, July and August there had been regular secret plotters' meetings, involving, among others, Goerdeler, Oster, Canaris, Beck, von Witzleben and the senior Foreign Office official and previous ambassador to Rome, Ulrich von Hassell, who, using an English parliamentary phrase, christened the group of resisters 'His Majesty's Most Loyal Opposition'. There was unanimous agreement that Hitler must go, but, as before, none at all about when and how the deed was to be done.

On 22 August Hitler called his generals to Berchtesgaden. Leaning on a grand piano and holding his notes in his left hand, he informed his audience that the pact with Stalin being secretly negotiated by Ribbentrop was imminent. As soon as it was signed, he would strike Poland. The target date was Saturday, 26 August. Canaris, propped against a pillar at the back of the room, and against Hitler's specific instructions, took notes of the meeting. He reported to his Abwehr officers afterwards that the Führer had declared: 'Poland is now right where I want her ... Our opponents are little worms [who will not move against us]. I saw them in Munich. [My chief concern is that] ... at the last minute, some bastard will produce a mediation plan.'

The following day, 23 August, to the astonishment of all – especially in London, where the government believed that it was about to conclude its own agreement with Stalin – Hitler, with appropriate flourish, unveiled the Soviet–German Non-Aggression Pact. It contained a secret protocol stipulating that Poland and Eastern Europe were to be divided up and parcelled out in two packages – one for Führer Adolf Hitler, and the other for 'Uncle' Joseph Stalin.

As the world reverberated to Hitler's astonishing diplomatic coup, Madeleine Bihet-Richou in Paris began to receive the first of a stream of postcards from Lahousen. Each was sent from a different location close to the Siegfried Line, which protected Germany's western border. Using the secret code the two had devised between them, Lahousen informed Madeleine about Hitler's Berchtesgaden meeting and the new launch date for Operation White, the invasion of Poland: Saturday, 26 August 1939.

On 25 August, the day before Hitler's projected start date for the attack, Carl Goerdeler flew to Stockholm, ostensibly on business for Robert Bosch, but in reality to set up a secret channel to London which could be used if war broke out. The main conduits for this were two Swedish bankers, Jacob and Marcus Wallenberg, who used their Enskilda Bank in the Swedish capital to communicate with London.

Now began a wild scramble to prevent the coming catastrophe, through diplomatic means in the West and by means of Hitler's assassination in Berlin.

On the morning Goerdeler flew to Stockholm expecting war, Hitler called in British ambassador Nevile Henderson and announced that he wanted to make a 'big proposal' for peace. Henderson arrived in the Chancellery at 1.30 p.m., to be told by Hitler that 'under the condition that, during a lengthy period, Germany's colonial demands would be fulfilled through peaceful negotiations, and under the further condition that Germany's relations to Italy [sic] and the Soviet Union would not be prejudiced, he would not only guarantee the existence of the British Empire, but promise German assistance whenever and wherever it would be required'. It was a feint designed to hoodwink London into believing that the danger of war had passed. No sooner had Henderson left than Hitler called one of his adjutants and instructed him to issue the order that the attack on Poland was to be launched at 5 a.m. the following day. Then the Führer sent a message to the French ambassador, calling him to the Chancellery at 5.30. Hitler's aim in seeing the Frenchman was to sow further confusion by asking him to seek Paris's views on his 'big proposal' for peace.

Things started to go wrong for Hitler's plans at around 3.30 p.m., when, following an urgent request, he agreed to see the Italian ambassador. Attolico, his voice again an octave higher than normal, said, 'I must unfortunately inform you that Italy, without the supply of the necessary raw materials, cannot enter the war.' Mussolini had picked up word of a new Anglo–Polish treaty which was just about to be signed, and had suddenly been overtaken with another attack of cold feet.

The meeting which followed with the French ambassador was short and perfunctory, ending at 6.15 p.m. As soon as the French emissary was safely out of the building, Hitler promptly rescinded the order he had given only four hours earlier to launch the attack on Poland.

What Hitler did not know, any more than he knew that his last-minute hesitation on Czechoslovakia a year previously had saved his life, was that history had almost precisely repeated itself.

A few days earlier, Hans Oster had instructed Friedrich Heinz, the man in charge of the commando raiding party in the September 1938 coup attempt, to be ready to carry out the same operation to capture and kill the Führer at very short notice. Over the following days, all the 'lovely plans' which had been burnt in General von Witzleben's fireplace on the evening of Munich were painstakingly reconstructed. The intention was to launch a coup at the moment Hitler gave the order to attack Poland.

As Hitler was seeing his succession of ambassadors on the afternoon of 25 August, Hans Bernd Gisevius, accompanied by Georg Thomas, the general in charge of German army logistics and armaments, and Reichsbank president Hjalmar Schacht, were on their way to pick up Canaris from the Tirpitzufer. Their intention was to drive to army head-quarters at Zossen, thirty kilometres south of Berlin. There they would confront army commander-in-chief Walther von Brauchitsch and Ludwig Beck's successor as chief of staff, Franz Halder, and demand that they choose between joining them in arresting Hitler that afternoon, or being exposed as members of the coup that had sought to remove him in September the previous year. Arriving at the Tirpitzufer, the three plotters were met by Oster, who, 'shaking his head' and 'laughing heartily', told them that Hitler had once again changed plan, and the coup was off. Gisevius wanted to continue with the putsch anyway, but none of the others would join him. There was jubilation. All present thought war had been conclusively avoided.

They ought to have known better.

Over the next three days, Hitler's will returned. The first inkling of this was uncovered by Max Waibel, a Swiss intelligence officer with very good high-level contacts in Berlin (probably Oster), who signalled his head-quarters on the afternoon of 27 August, reporting that the new launch date for Hitler's attack on Poland was to be 1 September. Given the close rela-tions between Swiss intelligence and MI6 at the time, it seems certain that this message reached London and Paris either that day, or the one following.

Finally, on 31 August, after some further diplomatic shadow-boxing designed to conceal his intentions, the Führer again gave the order to launch the attack on Poland at dawn the following day.

A few minutes after eight o'clock that evening, a small group of German SS troops dressed in Polish uniforms 'seized' the German wireless station at Gleiwitz, close to the Polish frontier, broadcasting some violently anti-German messages before withdrawing and leaving behind several of their dead. In fact the 'dead Polish attackers' were pro-Polish German Silesians captured the previous day. Along with several prisoners from Dachau, the captured men had been first dressed in Polish uniforms, then killed with lethal injections, and finally shot and disfigured to prevent identification. Their corpses were left scattered around Gleiwitz as 'Polish casualties' of the 'attack'.

At dawn the following morning, on the pretence of retaliating for the previous night's provocations, Hitler launched five Panzer divisions in a massive two-pronged attack supported by aircraft and tanks. Their orders were to wipe Poland off the map. Two days later, the world was at war.

Bumping into Hans Bernd Gisevius in a Tirpitzufer corridor on the day war was declared, Wilhelm Canaris growled, '*Finis Germaniae*' – thus ends Germany.

10

Switzerland

In war, neutral countries always become hotbeds for espionage.

In World War II, these neutral spaces were Spain, Turkey and Switzerland. The greatest of these, in spying terms, was Switzerland, which after the fall of France in June 1940 became a tiny enclave of freedom at the heart of the Axis behemoth.

It was through Switzerland, more than any other neutral country, that the German resistance probed for an early peace with the Allies and passed them, especially via Hans Oster, crucial intelligence on Hitler's battle plans.

The invasion of Poland started a flood of secret agents and intelligence organisations taking refuge in the Swiss Federation. As the countries of Western Europe fell to Hitler's stormtroopers, many more made their way to this small, isolated redoubt of freedom to ply their trade.

The Swiss government, for obvious reasons, had a strong interest in knowing what was going on around their encircled state. Almost all the major combatants in the war, including those which would in due course have governments-in-exile in London, had legations and consulates scattered across Switzerland. These housed, as the Swiss well knew, not just diplomats, but also nests of spy-masters running agents into their home countries, and especially into Germany. The Swiss response to all this spying in their country was to adopt a policy of benign ignorance. Provided it was not so blatant as to cause a diplomatic protest which could endanger Switzerland's neutrality, and provided the Swiss got a fair share of any intelligence which affected their own security, they didn't much care. The best way to get intelligence on Hitler's intentions towards Switzerland, they argued, was to use others to get it for them as the price for being permitted to operate from the Swiss Republic.

There was one exception to this rule: the Soviet Union. Russia, being communist and revolutionary, was not at all welcome in this Alpine fortress of stability and energetic free-market capitalism. Russian spying from Switzerland had to be conducted by entirely secret and hidden networks, which the Soviets started constructing through agents infiltrated into Switzerland some time before the war started. When the Swiss occasionally uncovered these secret Russian networks, they mostly let them run, under discreet surveillance to see where the espionage trail would lead. In cases where, because of diplomatic complaints, they had to roll up a Russian network, the penalties imposed by Swiss courts for Soviet spying on Swiss territory tended to be minor and symbolic, provided the activity concerned was directed at one of the other combatant powers, and not at Switzerland itself. The Swiss authorities were, on the whole, rather restrained in applying the ultimate penalty for spying, which at the time was death.*

This generally tolerant policy towards foreign spying on Swiss territory was applied variably. The Swiss themselves had a capable intelligence service, especially when it came to signals interception and counter-intelligence.

Their dealings with other intelligence services based in the country were driven exclusively by Swiss interest. Their closest working relationship was with Britain's SIS, and their most distant one with the Germans – or at least those Germans loyal to Hitler. This was not because the Swiss liked the British any better than the Germans – after all, the greater part of Switzerland is German-speaking. It was because Hitler had plans to invade Switzerland (Operation Tannenbaum), and London did not. If they wanted to see what Hitler was planning, one of the best ways to do so was through the eyes of British spies. The other key window on German intentions was, of course, through German resisters like Ludwig Beck, who established contact with 'foreign powers' through Basel in 1938, or Hans Bernd Gisevius, who visited Lausanne in 1939 immediately after 'the rape of Prague', in order to send the message to London that Poland was next.

In September 1939, as the war began, MI6's Claude Dansey – 'Colonel Z' – moved his 'Z Organisation' to Paris and Zürich, where under the false front of an import/export business 'Colonel Z' and his spies occupied a whole floor of a block of apartments called Schloss am Mythenquai, on the eastern shore of the Zürichsee. It was a strange choice to make as the head-

---

* In all, 865 people (more than half of them Swiss nationals) were tried in Swiss courts for espionage between 1939 and 1945. The number of death sentences passed was only thirty-three – less than 4 per cent of those tried.

quarters of an intelligence organisation, for it was very far from secure. 'Colonel Z' had to insist that his staff did not refer to him by his rank, in a vain attempt not to attract too much attention. Eventually Dansey and his team of five officers were given cover in the visa section of the British consulate in Zürich, from where they directed the Z Organisation's Europe-wide networks. Colonel Z himself was not a man for keeping records. But one of his maps with notes does survive, and is reproduced on the inside front cover of the official history of MI6. It shows that the range of Z networks, many run from Switzerland, stretched into every corner of Europe and the Middle East, from the Vichy administration in the south of France, north to Paris, further north to Stockholm, east to Stuttgart, Hamburg and Berlin, south to Milan, Turin and Genoa, across the Mediterranean to North Africa, and south-east to Hungary and Turkey.

In November 1939 Dansey was recalled to London, leaving his deputy, the bibulous Andrew King, to run the organisation. In 1940, MI6 in Switzerland moved its headquarters from Zürich to the British legation in Bern. In addition to its main office in Bern, MI6 also had four substations in the British consulates around Switzerland, one of which was in Geneva, where the British spies had their headquarters on the first floor of an ornate block of lakefront offices at 41, quai Wilson.

Germany, which had 150,000 of its citizens living in Switzerland, had two separate intelligence organisations operating in the Swiss Confederation: Canaris's Abwehr, and Heinrich Himmler's powerful Reich security HQ, the Reichssicherheitshauptamt (RSHA), which combined the Gestapo and the SD. There was no love lost between the two. Each tracked the other closely, the SD hunting for signs of treachery and the Abwehr for any SD activity which might expose their anti-Hitler operations. German intelligence operations, like those of the British, centred on their legation in Bern and their consulates scattered around Switzerland, especially in Zürich.

Although the United States did not enter the war until December 1941, Washington was active in the spying business in Switzerland even before 1939. US intelligence's Swiss 'representative' in these years was an American banker called Royall Tyler,* who had a part-time interest in archaeology and used his financial support for Byzantine excavations in southern Europe and his involvement with relief agencies in Italy as a

---

* Tyler had been a US intelligence officer in World War I, an adviser to the Reparation Commission in the 1920s, and held a senior post in the League of Nations in the 1930s.

cover to build a broad network of sources, one of whom was the German aristocrat and general 'spy for hire', Prince Maximilian Egon zu Hohenlohe Langenburg.

Of the other national intelligence services operating in Switzerland, three were of particular note: the French, the Czech and the Polish.

The French intelligence service,* like those of other countries, was based in their national legation in Bern. Under the terms of the armistice in 1940, the French service was officially disbanded. In secret, however, it simply moved to French-controlled Vichy, where it operated clandestinely until November 1942, when the Germans finally completed their occupation of all France. Thereafter the control of French intelligence activities lay mostly with General de Gaulle's government-in-exile in Algiers and London. Although the French did have some good sources in Germany and Italy, their main effort was directed towards occupied France and the French resistance.

The Czech intelligence service established itself in Zürich in 1934, and, even before the war, shared much of its intelligence product with the Swiss. Headed during the war years by Paul Thümmel's 'postman' Karel Sedláček, the Czech station ('Kazi'), also based in its Bern legation, had a direct wireless link with František Morávec and the Czech government-in-exile in London.

The British insisted that all information gathered by the intelligence services of the governments-in-exile in London had to be shared with them. They also demanded that – for reasons, they claimed, of cypher security – coded traffic from the London governments-in-exile could only be sent using codes provided by MI6. This 'security measure' had the convenient by-product of giving London the ability to read the messages its allies were sending to and from the British capital.

There was only one exception to this rule – the Poles. It is probable that the best spies in World War II were Polish. German counter-intelligence certainly thought so, describing the star Polish intelligence officer in Switzerland as outshining his British colleagues as 'the sun outshone the moon'. The reason the Poles did not have to submit to using British codes was because on 16 August 1939, just a fortnight before the start of the Second World War, the Polish intelligence service delivered a perfect working copy of the German 'Enigma' coding machine to British intelli-

---

* Commanded by Commandant Gaston Pourchot, who by D-Day headed a team of 243 agents. His intelligence network was called 'Bruno'.

gence, where it was received with a 'triumphant welcome'. The British agreement to allow the Poles to use their own codes was, however, less generous than it appeared. The Bletchley Park codebreakers soon broke the Polish cyphers, enabling MI6 to read their 'traffic' anyway.

The Poles' star wartime spy-master in Switzerland was the Polish deputy consul in Bern, Captain Szczęsny Chojnacki, cover name 'Jacek Lubiewa', alias 'Darek'. Chojnacki – the 'sun' to the British intelligence 'moon' – ran a network of agents into Germany, some of them at the very top of Hitler's high command. This ring, codenamed 'Jerzy', was, according to one expert, 'probably the biggest anti-Nazi information-gathering group in Continental Europe at the time'.

Intelligence officers love the company of other intelligence officers. This is partly because gossip is their stock in trade, and partly because only another intelligence officer knows the true nature of the strange, misshapen world their profession requires them to inhabit. World War II Switzerland was so crowded with spies and the hangers-on of spies that they almost tripped over each other in the street. Cooperation and exchange were the two principles on which this intelligence bazaar operated: mutual back-scratching, under-the-counter bartering and 'I'll-show-you-mine-if-you-show-me-yours' were the order of the day. Each rival organisation fraternised with each other, used each other and exploited each other as much as it could get away with. The head of Swiss intelligence, Roger Masson, was, for instance, one of Colonel Z's contacts from before the war. But he was also in direct clandestine contact with Canaris through Hans Bernd Gisevius. When, in his reports to his government-in-exile in London, Szczęsny Chojnacki quoted 'Source 501', he was referring not to a foreign agent, but to Gaston Pourchot, the head of the French intelligence service in Switzerland; his 'Source 555' is thought to have been the Swiss intelligence head Roger Masson. The Belgian, Dutch and Yugoslav military attachés were also on Chojnacki's comprehensive list of contacts. Karel Sedláček, similarly, had a close working and intelligence-sharing relationship with MI6 and with Swiss intelligence. And so on, all round the circus.

It was inevitable that, in a Switzerland made rich on its ability to trade and exchange, this unregulated free market in secrets would soon give rise to the freelance independent intelligence broker.

By far the most successful of these was a German Protestant pacifist called Rudolf Roessler, codename 'Lucy' (said to refer to the fact that he lived in Lucerne). Roessler, a bespectacled émigré of modest stature, was forty-one years old at the start of the war and, like the best spies, grey, quiet and unobtrusive. In 1921 he founded a literary society in Munich which numbered amongst its members Thomas Mann, Hermann Hesse and Stefan Zweig. In 1928, at the height of the Weimar Republic's cultural flowering, Roessler, now a publisher and art critic of some note, left Munich for Berlin, where he soon established a reputation among the artistic community as the leader of a powerful new theatre movement, the Bühnenvolksbund, and editor-in-chief of its influential publishing house. Soon, however, he fell foul of the Nazi Party for his liberal views and publications. When trumped-up charges were brought against him in 1934 he fled to Lucerne, where, with the help of his wife and Swiss friends, he set up a publishing house, Vita Nova Verlag. It was under cover of this business that Roessler began to construct his 'Lucy' spy network, which included anti-Nazis in the highest levels of German government and society. Throughout the war and for several years afterwards, Roessler strenuously refused to reveal the identities of his Lucy Ring agents. Post-war historians and those active in the espionage business have speculated mightily in an attempt to unravel the secrets of Rudolf Roessler's extraordinary access, coming up with all manner of bizarre theories.

Three years before his death on 11 December 1958, Roessler finally revealed his sources to a trusted friend. According to this testimony, his spies in Berlin included Carl Goerdeler, Hans Bernd Gisevius, and most probably Hans Oster. His other sources are thought to have included the head and deputy head of communications at German High Command; the chief of intelligence, Army Group Centre (which would play a crucial part in Hitler's Russian campaign); and the chief of intelligence evaluation, Army Group South-East (Athens).*

No one has ever been able to work out how Roessler managed to obtain such high-grade access without either intelligence training or any intelligence background. True, he had been a member of Berlin's exclusive Herren Club, which in pre-war years overflowed with members of the German establishment. Nevertheless, how he achieved such high-level access remains a puzzle to this day. This leads to the possibility that it was not Roessler who recruited senior members of the German resistance as sources, but they who sought him out for use as a channel which they could use to pass information to the Allies.

---

* Respectively General Erich Fellgiebel and Lieutenant General Fritz Thiele; Colonel Rudolf von Gersdorff; and Colonel Fritz Boetzel.

As for personal motives, Rudolf Roessler's were, it seems, exclusively mercenary. 'I seem to detect a professional touch in the assiduity with which Roessler … screwed [money out of his customers],' said a colleague in the spying business after the war. If this was so, Roessler was onto a very good thing indeed. His contacts among the anti-Hitler resistance in Germany made him an intelligence purveyor of great interest (and reward) to almost everybody who was anybody in World War II Swiss spying circles. His intelligence 'clients' included, at the start of the war, the British, the Czechs, the Yugoslavs, the anti-Hitler Germans and no fewer than three of the main players in Swiss intelligence.

By the time the war started there were already well-established channels by which those who resisted Hitler inside Germany could – and did – pass priceless, war-changing secrets through Switzerland to the Allies.

11

Halina

Halina Szymańska was not a woman who frightened easily. But this was news of the very worst sort. It was the third week of September 1939, and she was travelling east amidst a swollen river of humanity trying to escape the German onslaught on her Polish homeland.

Halina and her three daughters, Ewa, aged eleven, eight-year-old Anna (known as Hanka) and five-year-old Maria (Marysia) had been on their traditional summer holiday at Lichawa, the country estate of a cousin, at the outbreak of war. Her husband, the popular young German-educated Polish military attaché to Berlin, Lieutenant Colonel Antoni Szymański, had had to stay in the German capital because of the deepening crisis.

Immediately the war started Halina, accompanied by her girls, left for her parents' house in a suburb of Warsaw close to the airport. Around the end of the second week of September, Halina heard that her uncle, Józef Szymański, had been captured, tortured and executed by the Germans. With Warsaw squeezed in the pincer grip of two German columns converging on the city, and the airport a target for clouds of Stuka dive-bombers, screaming out of the sky like angry hornets, Halina decided it was time to take her family to a safer place.

Joining forces with the wife of the Polish cultural attaché in Berlin, she hired a horse and cart and, with her friend, their five children and the family maid, set off east. It was not an easy journey amidst the press of desperate humanity trying to do the same thing. Rain showers driven on a boisterous wind lashed the miserable column as it tramped east, turning earth roads into mud. Halina's party were robbed on the journey. A little later their horse bolted during a strafing raid by German aircraft, over-turning their cart, throwing little Marysia into a water-filled ditch and scattering their possessions to the four winds. Nevertheless, with every step they took east, Halina Szymańska felt a little safer, as the columns of smoke rising from burning Warsaw diminished behind them.

And then, this morning, 17 September 1939, the word spread like fire down from the front of the column: the Russians, greedy for their share of spoils in the dismemberment of Poland, had just invaded from the east.

Trapped between the Russians in front, the Germans behind and the Stukas above, there was nothing for it but to turn the cart around and head back to Lichawa.

Arriving in Lublin, and desperate for news of her husband, Halina took the risk of stopping a German officer, because she thought he 'looked a decent kind of person'. She chose well. The officer, Lieutenant Colonel Hartwig, was the head of the Lublin Abwehr station, and he had recently been instructed by Wilhelm Canaris to help prominent Poles in danger of being hunted down and executed by Reinhard Heydrich's Einsatzgruppen.

Colonel Hartwig asked Halina to name three people she knew in Berlin. The first two, men of her husband's rank, drew a blank. Then she mentioned Canaris's name. The colonel, surprised, snapped immediately to attention.

Halina and the girls were driven under escort in a German car to relatives in Poznań. There was fear in the household when the black Mercedes with German plates drew up at the gates of the suburban villa, until Halina emerged with the children and reassured them.

Canaris was duly informed. He remembered Halina well from diplomatic receptions in the brighter days before the war, for she was a striking woman – tall, self-possessed, rarely without a hat and known around Berlin as an elegant and cultivated hostess. He would see her, he decided, on his next visit to Poland.

A few days later, around 20 September, Halina was told that Canaris would shortly be in Poznań with a group of foreign diplomats visiting the site of the Battle of the Bzura River, the decisive conflict which effectively ended the September campaign. Canaris asked if Halina would meet him at the German consulate in the city.

The bloodbath which followed Hitler's assault on Poland had a profound effect on Wilhelm Canaris. He had not experienced war up close and personal before. This was very different from two cruisers lobbing shells at each other from twenty kilometres' distance. In that war there was honour, and death, when it came, came swiftly and was swiftly swallowed by the sea.

But this was a war without honour, or compassion, or – so far as Canaris could tell – any trace of humanity. Its aftermath lay strewn in bloody, accusatory heaps of broken bodies and twisted limbs for all to see for days afterwards. The German invasion of Poland had not been a military battle. It had been the merciless crushing of an entire nation and its people. Polish cities had been unrelentingly terror-bombed. Polish prisoners, nearly a thousand of them, had been summarily shot or forcibly drowned. The Polish intelligentsia had been ruthlessly hunted down and executed by Heydrich's Einsatzgruppen. Polish women and girls had been raped as a sideshow to mass executions. It took 10,000 railway wagons to transport the plunder from Poland and its people back to Germany. And he, Wilhelm Canaris, the man who cooked dinner in a chef's hat while his wife played Schubert, the man who had set firm moral limits on the actions of his Abwehr, had been part of it. It was his Brandenburger special forces who had paved the way for these horrors, who had made them possible – or at least easier. He could not even claim ignorance of what would follow. On 8 September, a week after the initial assault on Poland, his 'friend' and next-door neighbour Reinhard Heydrich had warned explicitly enough: 'We will spare the common folk. But the aristocrats, priests and Jews must be killed. After moving into Warsaw I shall arrange with the army how to squeeze them all out.'

In the days that followed the invasion, Canaris spent most of his time not in the Tirpitzufer, but drawn back again and again to the Polish battle-field, as though he was forcing himself to witness and rewitness the horrors as an act of penance. According to a co-conspirator, the diplomat Ulrich von Hassell, he was 'completely shattered … [after seeing] the results … especially in devastated Warsaw'. The sight of the burning city brought him close to tears. Another Abwehr man reported him spending days being driven aimlessly through the streets of the Polish capital, muttering, 'How terrible! … Our children's children will have to bear the blame for this.' To his wife Erika he said, 'If there is any justice, and I believe there is, we will go through the same things [as the Poles]. And then God save us … We are all guilty – all – and we will all have to pay for it.'

Canaris sought consolation and contrition in little acts of personal mercy towards refugees and victims of the horrors he had helped unleash. He issued orders to all Abwehr outstations in Poland to escort prominent Poles to safety. He used Abwehr resources to find a rabbi friend of the US consul general in Berlin, and sent the frightened fugitive safely on his way to New York. He arranged for the rescue of the Ukrainian archbishop of Kraków and the bishop of Przemyśl. The bishop's nephew even gave him 'a cashbox containing US$46,000 and 40 gold ducats for safekeeping'.

It was in this context that Canaris met Halina Szymańska at the German consulate in Poznań. She was cool, poised and brisk. She wanted nothing except safe passage for her and her children to return to her parents' house in Warsaw. Canaris shook his head. 'Humanity will not forget for a thousand years what Hitler has done in Poland,' he said, insisting that she must leave the country as soon as possible and take refuge in a neutral state. Switzerland would be best, he thought, since her husband had recently received a new posting there as Poland's military attaché. When Halina asked how he knew this, Canaris explained that he had lunched with Colonel Szymański a week before the attack on Poland at a restaurant on Berlin's Schlachtensee, and had warned him of the coming invasion. That afternoon Szymański, a fervent Polish patriot, had, Canaris thought, left the German capital for Warsaw. He promised that if Halina accepted his offer, he would ensure that she and her girls were safely delivered to Switzerland. There they could wait for the colonel to join them.*

But first her papers would have to be put in order and certain arrangements would have to be made, which, Canaris explained, could take some time. Frightened that Halina and her children, as prominent Poles, might be at risk from Heydrich's death squads in Poznań, Canaris ordered an Abwehr officer to stay with them until they could leave.

During the next two months, Halina and the girls waited in the villa in Poznań. The period was not without drama. Five-year-old Marysia contracted severe appendicitis and had to be operated on by German doctors in the military hospital in Poznań. The beds around her were filled with wounded German and Polish soldiers.

Finally, in early December they were picked up in an official car and taken to Berlin. Passing through the devastated countryside of her homeland, teeming with desperate people and littered with the blackened shells of burnt homes, Halina worried that, travelling in a German car, she would be taken for a collaborator.

In Berlin, Canaris arranged for the family to be accommodated in the safety of the Spanish ambassador's residence until the final stage of their journey could be arranged. They remained there for a week, paying daily

---

* In fact Szymański, determined to join his regiment, travelled to Copenhagen, and then through Helsinki to Lvov, where he arrived just in time to be captured by the Russians, who incarcerated him first in Starobjelsk PoW camp and then in the Lubjanka prison in Moscow, from which, following British pressure, he was released after Operation Barbarossa.

visits to their old apartment to pack up such valuables and clothes as they could carry with them.

Around the second week of December, Erika Canaris escorted the little family to Berlin's Anhalter station. Here, in the cavernous space beneath the arched roof, filled with smoke and swarming with a melee of soldiers, she gave the Szymański children Christmas gifts and escorted them all to a private carriage. They travelled through the night, always escorted by an Abwehr officer. Nevertheless, with only Polish documents, Halina felt vulnerable to any sudden document check, and instructed the girls to speak only in German and to refer to her as 'Aunt'. After a long, nerve-racking journey, the train arrived at the German–Swiss border at dawn the following day. They were met by an official Abwehr car and driven over the border at Basel, where their escort saw them safely through the German and Swiss frontier formalities and, after kissing Halina's hand and offering her some money (which she refused), bade them goodbye and left.

Halina's first act was to ring the Polish embassy in Bern. As luck would have it, she was put straight through to the deputy consul, Sczcęsny Chojnacki, whom she had known before the war. She had no idea at the time of Chojnacki's double role as an intelligence officer.

The little family were duly installed in a first-floor apartment* in a quiet street just a kilometre from the British legation in Bern.

Not long before Christmas, Chojnacki and Halina made a trip to Paris, where she was formally recruited as a spy for Poland and Britain, and encouraged to maintain her contact with Canaris. She was paid a salary from British funds and given a cover job as a cipher clerk at the Polish legation, entitling her to a diplomatic passport so that she could travel freely. The British provided her with a forged French identity card issued on 5 June 1940 in the name of 'Madame Marie Clénat' of Lyon. London also agreed to her demand that after the war she and her family would get British passports, and her daughters would receive a free education in a British public school.

Halina's new life as a spy had begun. In due course she would accumulate a number of additional codenames, aliases and false identities. She was known on MI6's books as 'Agent Z5/1', by Polish intelligence as 'Krzywda' and 'Madame Czarnocka', and by the Abwehr as 'Hans'.

---

* At Sonnenhofweg 10 (information supplied to the author by Marysia Fabian-Akehurst).

One evening, a few days after her return from Paris, Halina answered a knock on the door to find Wilhelm Canaris standing on her doorstep. He was in civilian clothes, and travelling under a false identity. He asked after the girls and Halina's family, promising to use Abwehr channels to get letters through to her mother and father in Warsaw. Then the two got down to business, speaking for two hours, during which the Abwehr chief expressed some highly critical opinions about the German conduct of the war and Hitler's future intentions. 'I don't suppose you could call Canaris an indiscreet man, but he could be very outspoken,' she said later. Canaris, suspecting correctly that he was talking through Halina to those at the very top of Britain's war command, was at pains to say that the British should on no account do a deal with Hitler. They should fight on, confident that they had friends at the very highest levels in Berlin. As he left, he promised to be in touch again soon.

True to his word, sometime in late January 1940 Halina received a message through the Abwehr office in Bern proposing a rendezvous with Canaris at a hotel in Milan. Travelling on her diplomatic passport, she took the train to Milan and met the Abwehr chief for dinner. 'All his talk was of high politics, but you could sense from this what was imminent. He would not have told me purely military matters – small treasons such as agents deal in. When he spoke it was of the Reich and Russia and Great Britain and America,' she reported later, adding confirmation that for Canaris she was a one-way channel only: 'The Admiral never asked me to find out anything for him from the Allies, although he must have known that I was in touch with my own countrymen in Bern and through them with the British.'

MI6, too, was clear that the admiral knew very well that he was speaking through Halina to London. 'Canaris knew that anything he told this Polish lady would be reported, she being a patriotic Pole, straight to Polish intelligence, who would of course pass it on to us,' commented Nicholas Elliott, a future MI6 station chief in Bern, after the war. Those close to Canaris in the Tirpitzufer also knew of his contacts with Halina, and what they meant. Erwin Lahousen regarded Halina as 'a very wise [and] politically educated woman who Canaris looked up regularly when he was in Switzerland [and who he used] … to maintain direct contact, via Switzerland, with the Allied intelligence services'. This high opinion was shared by Halina's MI6 contacts, one of whom described her as 'a very attractive and formidable personality'.

At the end of their dinner in Milan, Canaris warned Halina that their meetings would be infrequent, and perhaps – for him – increasingly dangerous. He would send one of his best and most reliable men, Hans Bernd Gisevius, to Switzerland to act as their channel of communication. But, Canaris stipulated, though they would communicate through a third party, Halina should realise that she was dealing directly and personally only with him. She knew that this too was not a message for her, but for her spy-masters in London.

In February 1940 an ungainly figure with a large, moon-shaped face, enlivened by watchful eyes which peered out from behind wire-rimmed glasses, started paying occasional visits to the German vice-consul's office in Zürich, with its bay window overhanging the narrow cobbled Kirchgasse.

Not long after the newcomer's arrival in the city, Halina Szymańska issued stern instructions to her daughters that if they saw a pair of galoshes outside the sitting-room door, they should on no account enter. Little Marysia found the strange items of footwear which soon began barring her access to her mother so enormous that she could comfortably put both her feet in one of them – which was not surprising, for they were made to fit the feet of the outsize, six-foot-four-inch frame of Hans Bernd Gisevius. Clever, but with a tendency to recklessness, Gisevius was vividly portrayed in a post-war description: 'A man of towering height, he looked like a caricature of a senior Prussian civil servant. He was so ostentatious in his behaviour that few chose to believe that this strange creature was a bona fide secret agent. Some thought him a buffoon, others an imposter putting on an elaborate act. Many believed he was a dyed-in-the-wool Nazi trying to hoodwink the Swiss and the Allies.'

In the same month that Gisevius began visiting Switzerland as Wilhelm Canaris's personal contact with Halina Szymańska, Sir Stewart Menzies, the newly appointed head of MI6, sent Count Frederick Vanden Heuvel (known as 'Fanny'), one of his most trusted officers, to take over the MI6 station in Bern. Among Vanden Heuvel's main tasks would be to manage relations with Halina, and to ensure that the information which Canaris passed through her reached London quickly and safely. It did not take long for 'Fanny' Vanden Heuvel to confirm what Halina claimed, that through the Gisevius link she was 'first and foremost acting as an intermediary for "Theodor" [the codename for Canaris in MI6]'. In all, Gisevius was to furnish MI6 with no fewer than twenty-five high-grade reports on Hitler's intentions between August 1940 and December 1942. Many of these came directly from Canaris himself, through Halina.

Thus, just four months after the war started, Sir Stewart Menzies, the head of MI6 at Broadway Buildings in London, and Wilhelm Canaris, his opposite number in the Tirpitzufer in Berlin, had established a secure, personal and reliable means of communication, beyond the prying eyes of their political masters.

12

Sitzkrieg

'This war implies the end of Germany and of ourselves,' Wilhelm Canaris told his Tirpitzufer colleagues in the days after war had been declared. '[If Germany loses, it will be a] terrible misfortune and catastrophe. But even greater than that catastrophe would be the triumph of this [Nazi] system. To prevent this by all possible means is the ultimate aim and purpose of our struggle.'

Canaris's view of what needed to be done had changed as a result of what he had witnessed in Poland. The horrors of that battlefield, magnified no doubt by a sense of personal guilt and the need for expiation, moved him from opposing Hitler chiefly through subtle means, to becoming a full participant in plotting his assassination. He started to compile a personal file listing all the Polish executions, and flew into a temper with his Abwehr officers on the ground if they failed to get the information he needed.

Even before the conquest of Poland had been completed, Canaris began reaching out to the generals and re-energising the scattered remnants of the September 1938 coup. 'He was whipping things up in these days,' noted one of the generals in his diary.

In the first ten days of the Polish campaign, there was a brief attempt to organise a putsch. An anti-Nazi general, recalled from retirement to command an army group on the Western Front, undertook to invite Hitler to his headquarters in Cologne, where he would be arrested and 'neutralised'. Sir George Ogilvie-Forbes, one of the last British diplomats to evacuate the British embassy in Berlin, was secretly informed of the impending coup. But Hitler, suspicious of the general involved, turned down the invitation and the plot collapsed.

As news of atrocities on the Polish front started to reach a wider circle in Berlin, Carl Goerdeler and Ludwig Beck started testing the ground for yet another attempt at a revolt. For many key figures in the army, the

Wehrmacht's – albeit chiefly passive – complicity with Heydrich's death squads in Poland was a turning point, as was the cynical carving up of Poland with Stalin's Soviet Union, which had brought 'the advance of Bolshevism … right up to our borders'.

All of these nascent moves towards action were suppressed by one discomforting fact.

The deafening silence and inactivity of the Western Allies.

Many of the generals had predicted that if Hitler's attack on Poland in the east precipitated a war, then France would immediately take advantage of the vacuum and attack from the west. Canaris had even deployed a screen of Abwehr stations along the length of what the British now called the Siegfried Line and the Germans knew as the Westwall, a line of as-yet-uncompleted fortifications designed to defend Germany against just such a possibility. But Canaris's stations reported nothing but calm and silence.

As the Polish ally for which it went to war bled out her life blood, the French army, true to the anti-war slogan of earlier that year, 'Why die for Danzig?', stayed snug, secure and quiescent in the bunkers of the Maginot Line. London and Paris watched, but did not act, despite having 110 divisions facing only twenty-three German ones on the Western Front.

This period has been christened the *Sitzkrieg* (the Sitting or Phony War). But it was not phony for the Polish units fighting hopeless battles against the full might of German armour storming across their country, or for the hundreds of thousands of refugees fleeing for their lives from Heydrich's murder squads, Luftwaffe bombing and the advancing Russians. This was a phony war only because the West made it so by doing nothing and allowing Hitler free rein to wreak his havoc in the east. It was not as though they did not know what was happening in Poland. They knew well enough – and ignored it. Or worse. On 20 September, just three weeks after the invasion of Poland and with the slaughter in full swing, Sir Nevile Henderson, newly returned to London after the start of the war, wrote his valedictory despatch:

> It would be idle to deny the great achievements of the man who restored to the German nation its self-respect and its disciplined orderliness. The tyrannical methods which were employed within Germany itself to obtain this result were detestable, but were Germany's own concern. Many of Herr Hitler's social reforms, in spite of their complete disregard of personal liberty of thought, word or deed, were on highly advanced

democratic lines ... above all, the organisation of the labour camps ...
are typical examples of a benevolent dictatorship. Nor can the appeal of
Nazism, with its slogans so attractive to a not over-discerning youth, be
ignored. Much of its legislation in this respect will survive in a newer
and better world, in which Germany's amazing power of organisation
and the great contributions which she has made in the past to the
sciences, music, literature and the higher aims of civilisation and
humanity will again play a leading part.

Amongst ordinary German people, who knew nothing of the Polish
horrors, this kind of moral elasticity, reinforced by Western inertia, only
served to heighten the mood of celebration for the triumph of German
arms and the leadership of the Führer. They hoped – and believed – that,
with the Versailles humiliations reversed, there would now be room for a
peace with honour. Against this backdrop, and without any evidence of
the public turning against the Führer, the reawakening of resistance to
Hitler stuttered to a halt.

Once again it was Hitler himself who gave the plotters the stimulus they
needed.

Germany's central position as the fulcrum of Europe meant that since
the time of Frederick the Great (and probably right back to the age of the
Goths) it had had only two viable expansionist strategies to choose from.
It could either combine with the West against the East, or with the East
against the West. Britain's rise to the status of a mercantile superpower
during the nineteenth century further refined this German strategic
choice into one between a land-based strategy with Russia against the
West, or a sea-based strategy with Britain and France against the East.
Stalin believed that the only rational explanation for why the great world
powers like Britain and France were pursuing policies of supine appeasement was because there was a deep-seated Anglo–French–German
conspiracy eventually to combine their forces against Russia. There were
many in Britain and France who, in terror at the threat of Bolshevism, saw
things in this way as well. Hitler himself, up to the invasion of Poland,
hoped it might be so. True, the Nazi–Soviet Pact signed ten days before the
start of the war seemed to point in the opposite direction. But many saw
this as no more than a temporary arrangement to facilitate the carving up
of Poland. Furthermore, they argued, with Hitler and Stalin now eyeball
to eyeball across a common frontier, the pact would be unlikely to last very
long. For the moment, London and Paris considered that, unless provoked,

the ravenous beast would be too busy dealing with his prey in the east to have the time or resources, at least for the moment, to turn west.

They were wrong.

Less than two weeks after the invasion of Poland, Hitler confided to one of his adjutants that he had taken the decision to launch a full-scale attack on the West by, at the latest, the end of the autumn. He confirmed this decision a week later to Field Marshal Wilhelm Keitel, the head of the armed forces. On 27 September he ordered his most senior generals to start planning for the assault westwards. When they protested, they were curtly told that they had doubted his plans before, and been proved wrong. Their job now was to obey orders, not question them. The generals produced a string of reasons why such an early assault on the West was militarily impossible: the troops were too tired; the logistics and ammunition were exhausted; winter was coming; the air force would be stronger in the spring; and the supply lines were all facing in the wrong direction after the Polish campaign. But the Führer angrily overrode these as excuses.

The plotters now had their new trigger for action. If the war could be confined to Poland, they reasoned, it could soon be closed down in favour of a negotiated peace. But once it widened to the West it would become global and unstoppable. Led by Canaris and Beck, they embarked on a strategy to frustrate Hitler's planned attack on the West if they could, and to remove him by a coup if they couldn't.

By the end of September, Canaris had completed a tour of all military headquarters on Germany's Western Front. His ostensible reason for this round of visits was to gather opinions on a western assault, but he used this as a cover to sound out some key commanders on the possibility of a coup. Walther von Brauchitsch, the commander-in-chief of the army, met his chief of staff Franz Halder for an in-depth discussion of the situation on 14 October. They considered three options: carry out Hitler's demands; drag their feet as much as possible to delay operations; or, as the official record of their meeting euphemistically puts it, 'fundamental changes' – code for eliminating Hitler. Von Brauchitsch as ever, opted for delay.

But Hitler simply outflanked all attempts at procrastination by insisting that the attack on the West was 'unalterable', and would be launched during the third week of November. On 27 October, following the Allies' inevitable rejection of his 'peace proposals', which were based on a demand for the acceptance of his Polish gains, the Führer brought the target date for the westward assault forward to 12 November 1939.

Meanwhile, with Canaris's encouragement, Hans Oster started recruiting a new band of plotters to his secret Abwehr department in charge of anti-Hitler activity. Contact was made once again with Carl Goerdeler, who during this period of forced inactivity seems to have gone through some kind of psychological crisis. In Goerdeler's attempts to break the inertia by doing something, he began cooking up more and more fantastic schemes to stop the impending catastrophe. These included trying to persuade Hitler to send him to London and Paris as a peacemaker. Other civilian groups outside the main circle of plotters gathered in secret conclaves to discuss even wilder plans, such as the return of the German monarchy.

Canaris, meanwhile, started to create a network of contacts and liaison officers with other ministries in Berlin, especially with Ribbentrop's state secretary at the Foreign Office, Ernst von Weiszäcker.

Everyone knew, however, that nothing serious could happen without the army. And so, for the first time, genuine coordination began to be established between the army and the civil resistance, led by Goerdeler. The fact that the army's headquarters were at Zossen, thirty kilometres south of Berlin, made this difficult. In an attempt to overcome this problem, Canaris sent one of his most trusted young officers, Lieutenant Colonel Helmuth Groscurth, to Zossen to act as his liaison link with the army chiefs.

Ultimately, however, it all depended on the two generals at the top, army commander-in-chief von Brauchitsch and his chief of staff, Halder. Finally, on the evening of 31 October, with the attack on the West just two weeks away, Halder informed Groscurth that he would support a coup, revealing, with tears in his eyes, that 'for weeks on end he had been going to see Hitler with a pistol in his pocket to gun him down'.

That evening, at a meeting at Ludwig Beck's mansion in Goethestrasse, Oster and Erich Kordt of the Foreign Office had a long discussion with Beck outlining their plans. As with the September 1938 'Czechoslovak' coup, the new putsch was to be triggered at the moment Hitler gave the order to march on the West. Then he would be killed.

The next morning (1 November) Kordt paid a visit to the Tirpitzufer, where he found Oster in a mood of resignation: 'Who will throw the bomb that will liberate our generals from their scruples?' he despaired. Kordt replied, simply, that he would; he had come to Oster's office to tell him just that. But he needed the explosives. Oster, astonished, promised to have them ready for him in ten days' time, on 11 November, the day before Hitler's target date for the invasion of the West.

After Kordt left his office, Oster called in Erwin Lahousen.

'Lahousen, you know me and I know you. You know what this criminal [Hitler] has in mind and you know the methods of these bandits … We want to render this mad beast harmless. You must procure us explosives and time fuses, can you do that?'

'Does the admiral know of this affair?' Lahousen asked cautiously.

'No. It is really better that you do not discuss it with him. It would oppress him, and the old chap is already quite harried enough without this.'

'Do you already have the man to carry it out?'

'Yes, the man is at hand.'

'Can the person in question also manage time-clock fuses?'

'No, that must be first taught to him.'

The coup planning now began to gather pace. As with the failed September 1938 attempt, the centre of Berlin was to be occupied. Beck and Goerdeler (the latter just back from a visit to see the Wallenbergs in Stockholm) were told to be ready to form a new government, with Goerdeler as chancellor and Beck as head of the army. Preparations were made for the execution of Hitler, Göring, Himmler, Ribbentrop and Heydrich. All post, telegraph, broadcasting and police facilities were to be occupied. Elections were to be held and negotiations for an armistice leading to a full peace agreement initiated.

On 5 November, with a week to go before Hitler's planned launch date for the Western invasion, Brauchitsch decided on one last attempt to dissuade the Führer from his plans. Hitler, sensing what was coming, did not let his commander-in-chief get beyond the first few words before flying into a terrible rage. Shouting about death sentences for undisciplined troops who didn't obey orders, he stormed out, slamming the door behind him and leaving Brauchitsch 'chalky white … his face twisted'. Returning to his headquarters, the deeply shaken commander-in-chief said, 'It is not possible to avert the western offensive. I simply cannot do it.' Brauchitsch and Halder began to speculate that Hitler's outburst about 'death sentences' meant the coup may have been betrayed. Halder, in a panic, ordered that all the newly-reassembled coup documents should again be destroyed (not all were, with consequences that would later prove fatal).

Shortly afterwards, Hitler's orders to launch the western offensive arrived in Zossen. This was supposed to be the trigger to instigate the putsch. But it became instead the prompt for von Brauchitsch to do an immediate and very unsoldierly about-turn. Arguing that, since the orders had been given, the attack could not now be stopped, he added, 'I myself won't do anything, but I won't stop anyone else from acting.' Halder, the man who, just a week previously, had admitted to 'going to see Hitler with a pistol in his pocket to gun him down', followed his commander-in-chief into swift retreat, telling Groscurth to inform Canaris that, because the order to attack had now been given, 'the forces we were counting on are no longer bound to us'. When Groscurth protested that, on the contrary, Beck, Goerdeler and Canaris were still ready to launch the putsch, Halder responded sharply, 'Then let the admiral take care of it himself.'

The entire edifice of the coup now began to collapse, as individual army commanders followed Halder in expressing doubts that it could succeed.

The unravelling process accelerated on 7 November, when Hitler announced the first of a series of delays in the date for the launch of the assault on the West. The reason given to his generals was that the Führer had just received a joint peace appeal from the king of the Belgians and the queen of the Netherlands, and a few days would have to be left for decency's sake before the attack could be launched. But many clung to the hope that the real reason was that Hitler was at last listening to their warnings. Those plotters who were already getting cold feet now had a further argument for procrastination.

Matters were, however, about to be taken out of their hands by a lone thirty-six-year-old Württemberg carpenter.

Unlike the high-level opponents to Hitler at this stage of the war, Georg Elser had always opposed the Nazis. He never voted for them, and refused either to give the Hitler salute or to join friends listening to his speeches. Elser's was not a plot assembled with others. It was all his own. He concluded, alone, and as far back as 1938, that it was his personal duty to rid his country of this evil. 'I had to do it because, for his whole life, Hitler has meant the downfall of Germany,' he said – simply and without artifice or complication.

He obtained the explosives entirely through his own means, and tested them in an orchard near his home. He designed his bomb without anyone's help, using a timer from the movements of a clock he was given in lieu of wages from a failing clock factory at which he had briefly worked. Without discussion with anyone, he took the decision to kill Hitler as he was addressing the annual 8 November rally held in Munich to celebrate the 1923 Bürgerbräukeller putsch, which had started the Nazis' rise to power.

In August 1939 Elser travelled by train, alone, to Munich, and spent three months preparing his attack. He became a regular visitor to the

Bürgerbräukeller, smuggling himself into the hall where Hitler habitually spoke just before it closed and allowing himself to be locked in over thirty to thirty-five nights. During these long hours of darkness he worked, a lonely figure in the small circle of light provided by a torch muffled with a blue handkerchief, to excavate a secret cavity behind the speaker's rostrum. Four days before the rally he planted his bomb in the pillar, camouflaged the recess with a false panel he had made himself, and set the clock ticking. His task completed, he celebrated, as he recalled later, by going 'to the Isartorplatz where at the kiosk I drank two cups of coffee' – alone.

Elser's planning was perfect, and his device worked flawlessly, exploding with massive force at 9.20 p.m., the precise moment when, according to the original schedule, Hitler was due to be making his speech, just feet away.

Elser had meticulously prepared and planned for everything. But he could not plan for the weather. There was fog in Munich that night, and Hitler's plane was grounded. He had to be in Berlin the following morning for a meeting on his revised plans for the assault on the West. In order to catch his train from Munich station he cut his speech short and left the hall at 9.07, thirteen minutes before Elser's bomb went off.

And so it was that a lone anarchist carpenter came closer to assassinating Hitler than all the plans and all the preparations and all the rehearsals and all the generals and all the spies and all the high officials and all the diplomats and all the experts in Berlin put together. Ironically, the failure of Georg Elser's bid to kill Hitler with a bomb led to the collapse of Erich Kordt's attempt, planned for three days later, to do the same thing. Security around the Führer was tightened to such a level that even the implacably determined Hans Oster concluded that the attempt should not be made.

The procrastination of the generals in this shambolic affair confirmed what Oster had already concluded – that they could not be relied on any more. He was already setting up his own, even more dangerous, personal 'second front' to defeat Hitler.

Hans Bernd Gisevius, writing after the war, described what Oster was doing at this time: 'Oster … had formed a circle around himself … he utilised the potentialities of the Abwehr so cannily that he was able to establish a whole network of confidential agents … Oster seemed to be organising an intelligence service of his own, within the counter-intelligence service … One of the most important of his activities was to install his own confidential agents in the most diverse positions.'

Oster did not confine himself simply to organising. Triggered by Hitler's earlier Führer Directive No. 6, a secret instruction issued on 9 October 1939 which ordered that the assault on the West should begin with 'an attack … on the northern flank … through the Luxemburg/Belgium/ Holland area', he had already decided to take his own unilateral action.

Oster got wind of the plan to start the western assault with an invasion of the Low Countries on 8 October, the day before it was announced. That evening, after a period sunk in thought in the back seat of his car while being driven to his modest apartment in the Wilmersdorf suburb of Berlin, he suddenly asked his long-standing personal driver Franz Leidig to first drop him off at the home of the Dutch military attaché in Berlin, Gijsbertus Jacobus Sas (known as 'Bert'), a close friend since the 1936 Berlin Olympics. Emerging an hour or so later, having warned Sas of Hitler's plan to attack his country, Oster climbed back into his car, announcing to Leidig, 'There is no turning back for me. It is far easier to take a pistol and kill someone, it is far easier to charge into a hail of machine-gun fire … than it is to do what I have done. If things should ever come to this pass, then please be the friend, even after my death, who knows how it was and what moved me to do these things, that others might never understand or undertake themselves.'

Oster had concluded that if a military defeat was the only way to create the circumstances in which the generals would act, he had better organise one. 'One may say I am a traitor to my country,' he said to Sas during their meeting. 'But actually I am not that. I regard myself as a better German than all those who follow Hitler. It is my duty to free Germany and thereby the world of this plague.'

By warning the Dutch of Hitler's intention to attack the West in a few days' time, and of the plan to make the first thrust through the lowlands of Belgium, Holland and Luxembourg, Oster was giving information to the enemy which could have cost many German lives. Driven by patriotism, he had become a traitor. He had crossed the Rubicon, and could never now retrace his steps.

It cannot be a coincidence that, at the same time in early October 1939 that Hans Oster was passing state secrets to 'Bert' Sas, Max Waibel, the Swiss military intelligence officer responsible for spying on Germany, was also recruiting Sas and his Belgian military attaché colleague in Berlin, Colonel Georges Goethals, to the Swiss-run 'Viking Line' of spies. This spy ring would in the future prove a crucial source of information on Hitler's plans, especially those relating to the possible invasion of Switzerland. It has always been a puzzle quite how the Viking Line continued to provide the Swiss with priceless intelligence even after Holland and Belgium had been submerged under German occupation and both Sas and Goethals had lost their jobs. We now know that it was because the real original source of the Viking Line intelligence was not Sas or Goethals, but Oster himself. That night in early October when Oster crossed his Rubicon he was not just passing secrets to the Dutch and the Belgians, he was also establishing a line of communication to Swiss intelligence and those among the international community in Switzerland, including the British, with whom the Swiss shared their secrets.

Hans Oster was not the only source of intelligence on Hitler's plans for an attack west reaching the British and Dutch in October 1939. Carl Goerdeler, encouraged by one of the generals, was also using his Wallenberg channel in Stockholm to inform London and The Hague of the planned date for the assault.

Meanwhile, Wilhelm Canaris too seems to have concluded that the generals could not be relied on: '[Canaris] has given up all hope of resistance from the generals and thinks it would be useless to try anything else along this line,' Oster commented to a German Foreign Office colleague around this time. To another he said, 'The old man has completely lost his nerve.'

In fact, Canaris had decided to change tack. Instead of trying to deflect the Führer through the generals, he began doing what Oster was already doing: frustrating Hitler by warning the West of his plans, while at the same time attempting to arrange a separate peace before the conflict widened into a global war.

To achieve this, Canaris started to construct his own independent channels to reach out to Western capitals. It seems probable that his efforts to get Halina Szymańska and her family set up in Switzerland at the end of 1939 were part of this. But Halina was only one part of the Abwehr chief's private network which provided him with secret lines of contact with the West. Another was the formidable Countess Elena Alexandra Theotokis. Canaris had first met the countess in Athens in October 1935, when he negotiated a secret arms deal with her politician husband, the future Greek foreign and prime minister Ioannis Theotokis. Senior members of the Abwehr knew of the countess – she was described as 'a very clever Greek, Jewish or half Jewish woman … she lived at the time in Corfu. Canaris met her often in Rome or Venice … she was connected with the British Intelligence Service'. MI6 records show that Theotokis (the British knew her as Helen) was communicating with them as early as 15 October 1941. There is evidence to support the fact that Halina Szymańska and Countess Theotokis were just two amongst a rabbit warren of personal lines of contact which Canaris set up to communicate directly to Menzies and MI6. One close student of Canaris wrote after the war: 'He planted trusted personal contacts in several key capitals … to serve the purposes of the resistance by providing information to the Western Allies.'

At around this time, Canaris issued instructions to his Abwehr stations in Switzerland, the Vatican, Spain and Finland to maintain close contacts, if necessary through third parties, with the British.

While Hans Oster, Carl Goerdeler and Wilhelm Canaris were busy passing secrets to the enemy, Madeleine Bihet-Richou was on her way to Budapest.

Not long after the war started, following some weeks of silence Madeleine finally received a postcard from Erwin Lahousen, sent from the Hungarian capital. Once again the content of the card appeared innocuous to the casual observer. But, meeting Madeleine for lunch at their favourite rendezvous, the restaurant on the Rond-point des Champs-Élysées, her French intelligence handlers, Louis Rivet and Henri Navarre, concluded that it was in fact an invitation. They suggested that Madeleine should go to Budapest, where they would set her up in her own travel agency as cover for further meetings with Lahousen. In mid-October 1939, Madeleine, equipped with the appropriate visas and documentation and escorted by an undercover member of the French Deuxième Bureau, boarded a train for the thirty-hour journey from Paris to Budapest via Milan, Venice, Trieste and Lake Balaton. Arriving in the Hungarian capital she installed herself in the Carlton Hotel and set about finding a property for her 'travel agency'. She eventually chose a small corner shop on Váci Utca, one of the main shopping thoroughfares on the Pest side of the river, not far from Abwehr headquarters. Not long after she arrived, she was visited by a member of the Budapest Abwehr station who instructed her that if she wished to deliver any messages to Lahousen, she should leave them with him and he would pass them through the Abwehr courier service to their destination.

British and Allied intelligence must by now have been very well aware of the impending danger of an assault on the West on or around 12 November.

But then, the day after Georg Elser's unsuccessful attempt to kill the Führer, and three days before the proposed date for the opening of

Germany's assault westwards, an event took place in the small Dutch frontier town of Venlo which rocked MI6 to its foundations and caused a crisis of confidence in its German sources that would last until almost the end of the war.

In a brilliant intelligence ploy, a young SD officer close to Heydrich called Walter Schellenberg, posing, complete with monocle and the full range of Prussian bombast, as 'Hauptmann Schämmel', succeeded in persuading two MI6 officers, Captain Sigismund Payne Best and Major Richard Stevens, that he represented disgruntled German generals who wanted to depose Hitler and negotiate a peace with Britain. It was what spies call a 'coat trail' – and it was a perfectly tailored one because it played precisely, as Schellenberg well understood, to what the British already knew, or thought they knew – that there were indeed senior German officers who wanted to be rid of Hitler, and that separate peace feelers were indeed being pursued in the Vatican (and, as it happens, but with no connection to the plotters, in Sweden).

After a series of meetings 'Hauptmann Schämmel' suggested a rendezvous with the dissident German officers on 9 November 1939, the day after Georg Elser's bomb exploded. The meeting, he suggested, should be held in the Café Backus in Venlo, a border town on the Dutch side of the frontier with Germany. For the British this was an offer just too tempting to resist.

It was, of course, an ambush.

At 4 p.m. the two British spies drove up to the Café Backus, just thirty metres from the German border. Before they even had time to get out of their car, a German assault team led by SD officer Alfred Naujocks roared over the border to kidnap them. In the wild shoot-out that ensued, one Dutchman was killed and the two MI6 officers, together with their driver, were bundled across the border into Germany.

It was a disaster for MI6, which as a result of the Venlo scandal had to close down its entire operation in Holland. Under interrogation the two MI6 officers gave the Germans not only details of their spy rings in the Low Countries, but also large quantities of valuable intelligence on the organisation of MI6 and British intelligence in London. Their capture was also, but much later, to have a deadly effect on Canaris and one of MI6's most important agents.

Canaris was furious when he heard: 'This *Schweinerei* [mess, or scandal] is Heydrich's doing,' he exploded, adding prophetically that Schellenberg, now a rising star in Himmler's entourage, was 'a person we should be wary of having anything to do with'. He gave instructions to his staff to keep him closely informed on the interrogation of the two British MI6 officers.

The Abwehr chief had good reason to be nervous. His next-door neighbour Heydrich was by now becoming deeply suspicious about what was going on in the Abwehr, and hoped that the Venlo operation would, among other things, uncover treachery in the Tirpitzufer.

It didn't.

But Venlo delivered something perhaps even more damaging to Canaris and his fellow plotters.

The incident had a searing effect on MI6 – and especially on Stewart Menzies, who only three days before had taken over at the organisation on the unexpected death of its previous head, Hugh Sinclair. MI6 now began to see a Venlo around every corner. When Hitler did not attack westwards on 12 November, as MI6 had been warned, they presumed that this was because, as at Venlo, they had been 'played'. For some time all intelligence being passed by Oster, Canaris, Paul Thümmel and Madeleine Bihet-Richou was treated by MI6 with the utmost suspicion as German misinformation. As a result, crucial warnings would be ignored and many opportunities lost in the months to come.

Worse still, the fact that the Chamberlain government was conducting secret peace talks with the Germans came to light as a result of Venlo. Winston Churchill castigated the prime minister for his duplicity in encouraging the nation to supreme effort for war, while secretly negotiating a shameful deal to end it. Venlo and its political aftermath made Churchill deeply opposed to doing deals with the German resistance for the rest of the war.

Churchill's refusal to consider anything but outright war and outright victory was one of his most heroic characteristics, and it inspired a nation on the threshold of defeat to follow him.

And that, though the plotters did not yet realise it, would be the long-term legacy of Venlo.

With Chamberlain still in power and the world not yet across the threshold of global conflict, the future might still be changed by putsches, espionage and secret diplomacy. Once Winston Churchill entered Downing Street, the space for such subtleties would be crushed in the struggle between two titanic wills, each of them determined only on outright victory.

13

Warnings and Premonitions

On 25 November 1939, two weeks after Hitler's first target date for the invasion of the West, Paul Thümmel turned up again at the Jelineks' shop De Favoriet in The Hague. He was not expected. The letter he had sent a month previously warning of his visit was at the time lying unnoticed in a pile of correspondence in MI6's registry in London, having been on a roundabout journey involving a Czech spy in Stockholm, an MI6 accommodation address in London, and a short period being examined with intent in the offices of the British censor.

This time, Agent A54 was not in his usual rush. Thümmel had managed (probably with Canaris's help) to get himself transferred to the Abwehr office in Munster, and had been ordered to spy out the land on the Dutch side of the German border ahead of the coming invasion – so he had a good excuse to be in The Hague for a week or so. In all he spent three days in De Favoriet being debriefed, first by his Czech handler Aloïs Franck, and then by another unnamed intelligence officer (probably from MI6) who flew out from London specially to speak to him. On this visit, most of A54's intelligence, which it seems safe to conclude came either from Canaris or from Oster, was related to counter-espionage, and included information on German agents working in Britain and the details of German operations against other Allied spy networks in Czechoslovakia.

Two pieces of strategic intelligence were, however, of wider note.

Following Hitler's postponement of the western invasion, Thümmel predicted that, because of the approach of winter, there would now not be a western thrust until after the spring of the following year. The plans for the attack were being constantly revised, he reported. He promised to tell them in good time what these contained, using codewords for the countries to be targeted – 'Hilda' for Holland, 'Bobby' for Belgium, 'Emile' for England, 'Franz' for France.

Finally, A54 reported that Hitler was developing a new, unmanned weapon to use on London. He described it as a 'sort of aerial torpedo which, after being fired behaved like an aeroplane. So far the trajectory is not very accurate.'

During these three days in De Favoriet it came to light that Thümmel was also in close contact with the local resistance in Prague. This ought to have sent loud alarm bells ringing in the heads of his British and Czech handlers. Agent A54 had proved an extremely important spy, with access to the very top of the Abwehr. His reports were of such strategic importance that they had the potential to change the course of the next stage of the war. Involvement in the minor-scale activities of the local Czech resistance could only make A54 vulnerable to betrayal. This was a dangerous indulgence which London should have stopped. But it didn't.

Thümmel's intelligence that Hitler's 12 November postponement of the attack on the West would be followed by further postponements through the winter proved correct. Between the autumn of 1939 and the spring of 1940, the Führer put back the date for the grand assault no fewer than twenty-nine times. Paradoxically, the repeated delays – many of them because of the generals' insistence that they weren't ready – resulted in improvements to the plan, without which the eventual invasion might well have been much less successful.

Apart from winter and military foot-dragging, there was a third reason for the delay. Thanks largely to Wilhelm Canaris, the focus of Hitler's attention had temporarily shifted from the west to the north.

On 14 December 1939, Canaris's spies brought him solid evidence that the British cabinet was planning a seaborne assault ('Plan R4') on the Narvik area of northern Norway, with the aim of cutting off German supplies of iron ore. Hitler, determined to pre-empt this, ordered his planners to put the Western invasion on temporary hold, and begin planning for Operation Weserübung, the invasion and conquest of Denmark and Norway.

In fact it was all a typical Canaris double – or in this case triple – play. At the same time as delivering to his master a considerable intelligence 'plum' in the form of the British cabinet plans, he was deliberately exaggerating the strength of Swedish defences. His purpose was to discourage the Führer from also attacking Norway's neighbour, where the German resistance had by now established an important channel of communication to London, not least through Goerdeler and the Wallenberg brothers' Enskilda Bank in Stockholm.

With Hitler's attention fixed firmly on the north, Canaris shifted his focus to the south, and the Vatican. Over the last months of 1939 and the early months of 1940 he did all he could to negotiate his own separate peace deal with London through the offices of Pope Pius XII, whom he had known personally when he and the Holy Father, then the papal nuncio in Germany, had been horseriding companions in the pre-war years.

The key interlocutor for Canaris in these manoeuvres, codenamed by the Tirpitzufer 'Operation X', was an Abwehr agent called Dr Josef Mueller, alias 'Ochensepp'. Mueller, a committed Catholic, often flew to and from his meetings in the Vatican in a small private plane which he piloted himself, carrying his secret documents in a briefcase hidden under the aircraft's instrument panel. London's side in the negotiations was represented by the British minister to the Holy See, Sir Francis d'Arcy Osborne. So far as we know, Osborne never met Mueller. The two men conducted their negotiations by exchanging documents through the pope (referred to as 'Chief') and his German private secretary Robert Leiber (known as 'Gregor'). Neither Pope Pius nor his private secretary took any active part in the negotiations, though Leiber did from time to time act as a lobbyist for the German plotters, doing all he could to persuade the British of their sincerity of intent.

Despite a rickety start, real progress was made towards an understanding on which a peace could be constructed. Knowledge of the Vatican discussions was very tightly controlled in the British capital. Beyond Chamberlain, Halifax, the king and the very small number of FCO officials directly involved, the rest of the cabinet were ignorant of the whole process, as were Churchill and Vansittart.

Documents which have come to light since the war reveal that the German side undertook to remove Hitler, and the British promised not to take any military advantage of the period of internal chaos that would follow, provided only that the action to remove the Führer was taken before any widening of the war towards the West. Once an assault on the West was launched, the terms of the agreement would immediately become null and void. When Hitler had been removed, a peace would be negotiated between the Allies and the new German government. This would be based on Germany retaining the Sudetenland and Austria but withdrawing from Poland, and on an undertaking that Germany's pre-Versailles eastern borders would be the subject of further consideration.

Army chief of staff Franz Halder was briefed on the deal, and welcomed it. But when he informed his superior, Walter Brauchitsch, of what had been happening, the army commander-in-chief exploded, 'You should not have brought this to me – it is simply high treason! Under no circumstances can I share in such doings. In war no contact with a foreign power is permissible to a soldier.' Halder responded coolly, 'If you are bent on arresting someone, you'd better arrest me.'

It was of course inevitable, given the number of those in the know on the German side in the latter stages of these negotiations, that Heydrich, whose SD spies in the Vatican included a Benedictine monk, would eventually hear of the treasonous dealings. To make matters worse, Heydrich's men had broken the Vatican codes and could now read for themselves what was happening. London soon picked up on the danger of the widening circle of knowledge and began to get cold feet, warning d'Arcy Osborne to watch out for spies amongst his Vatican interlocutors. Osborne replied tartly, 'The German seminarists are dressed from head to toe in the brightest possible scarlet, which does not easily conduce to the work of secret agents.'

With Heydrich on a hunting expedition and London fearful of another Venlo, everyone retreated to safe ground. Mueller was withdrawn, the process ran out of steam, and another chance for peace – almost the last one – was lost.

Heydrich's investigations too ran into the sand, not least because, following a protest from Canaris, Himmler ordered him to drop the matter. Heydrich submitted to Himmler's orders, but gave instructions that files should be created to collect information on what would in due course be known within the SD as *die Schwarze Kapelle* ('the Black Orchestra'), a title intended to connote that this was an internal anti-Hitler spy ring, as opposed to *die Rote Kapelle* (the Red Orchestra), which was Soviet-inspired and -run.

A second and parallel secret attempt to find a way to peace took place at Ouchy in Switzerland during February 1940. This involved multiple moving parts, including foreign secretary Halifax; a British traveller and amateur diplomat; a former German chancellor; Ulrich von Hassell's son-in-law; and FCO officials sent out by Chamberlain, who was now eager to encourage those he had previously dismissed as mere 'Jacobins'. But the Ouchy talks, too, led to nothing, in part again because of British post-Venlo fears that it was all a trick.

Back in Germany, meanwhile, during the early months of 1940 changes were taking place amongst the once again scattered and disparate elements of the resistance.

Thanks in large measure to the failure of the coup attempt in November

1939, there was a general view among some younger officers in the Wehrmacht that the 'old men' could not be relied on for action. It was time for a new generation to give dynamism and leadership to the anti-Hitler resistance. These 'young Turks' also saw the act of resistance as opening the way to an era of reform and renewal which would decisively break with Germany's past. They were more radical, more action-oriented, less hidebound by tradition and far less respectful of hierarchy and Prussian values than their elders. In the words of the German Foreign Office's Adam von Trott zu Solz, one of the leaders of this group, the resistance needed to 'avoid any hint of being reactionary, of gentlemen's clubs or of militarism'.

Two resistance groupings began to emerge from this process, one military and one civil.

In the more unified military circles of the resistance, the colonels would become more prominent and the generals less so. In mid-April a group of 'new faces', including Erwin Lahousen, Hans von Dohnányi and Brandenburg Regiment commander Friedrich Heinz, gathered in Hans Oster's office in the Tirpitzufer to discuss how the explosives and detonators might be obtained for a bomb to kill Hitler before the western assault could be launched. But the plan foundered due to lack of access to the Führer. This illuminated what was, at this juncture, the young Turks' problem. They had the will, but not the access, while their seniors had the access, but not the will. Later that month Carl Goerdeler once again discussed the possibility of a coup with Halder, but the army chief of staff refused to countenance any action on the grounds that, now that Britain and France had declared war, it would be treason.

In parallel with the military resistance groups – and with considerable overlap between them – a number of heterogeneous civilian resistance organisations also began to come together around this time. The most prominent of these was what has come to be known as the 'Kreisau Circle', after their meeting place on the Kreisau estate of Count Helmuth James von Moltke, a descendant of the legendary victor of the Franco-Prussian War in the nineteenth century. Although there were many in this new group who were not aristocrats, the preponderance of members with 'von' in their names gave rise to the Kreisau Circle being known – not least, in due course, by the Gestapo – as the 'Counts' group'.* The Kreisau organi-

---

* Its members included, among others, Peter Yorck von Wartenburg, Adam von Trott zu Solz, Count Fritz-Dietlof von der Schulenberg, Julius Leber, Adolf Reichwein, Paulus van Husen and Carl Dietrich von Trotha.

sation, comprising mainly young intellectual idealists, was opposed to all forms of anti-Semitism. Eclectic in its make-up, it included men and – unusually – a few women from a wide variety of backgrounds, including devout Catholics and Protestants, government officials (especially from the Foreign Office), professionals, landowners, socialists, pacifists and conservatives. Their main activity was not to mount coups, but to plan the structure and constitution of post-war Germany. Their proposals, which bear remarkable resemblance to the shape of Germany today, included a strong element of governmental decentralisation with substantial power being transferred to the provinces (*Bundesländer* in present-day Germany), a heavy stress on local community structures and self-government, social reform and industrial partnership.

Other civilian groups included the so-called 'Freiburg Circle' of economists, whose work laid the basis for what would in future be known as the German 'social market economy'. One right-wing group produced a draft constitution in 1940 whose authoritarian and statist provisions were strongly opposed by more progressive voices, for instance in the Kreisau Circle.

Behind all this ferment of ideas, discussions and plans stood the substantial, uncompromising figure of Carl Goerdeler. Always pushing for action and fostering confidence among the faint-hearted, frequently disagreeing with conclusions he didn't like and constantly proselytising his own ideas, Goerdeler, for all his flaws, was still regarded as the towering moral force behind the civilian resistance. He also acted, with Hans Oster, as an essential bridge to Ludwig Beck and the older military leaders, with whom Goerdeler remained closely connected.

It was at this time that Goerdeler, his mind again racing ahead to what would come after the war, returned to his work on a series of papers which he had begun in 1939 on the shape of post-war Germany and his dream of a united Europe. Arguably the most important of these was entitled 'The Aim', a ninety-nine-page memorandum, that he would finish in early 1941, which stressed the importance of individual freedom and self-governance within a system of government based on the rule of law.

The German resistance to Hitler had now resolved into three distinct elements. The civilians, who knew the Germany they wanted to create after Hitler had been removed, but didn't have the means to remove him. The generals, who had the means to remove him, but couldn't bring themselves to do it. And a third, small group, including Hans Oster, Wilhelm

Canaris and Erwin Lahousen, who had concluded that since the generals would only become brave once Hitler had endured a defeat, they had better set about arranging one. If this entailed betraying the German state and jeopardising the lives of German soldiers, then, given the scale of the evil they were fighting, they considered themselves justified in taking this risk.

In early January 1940, after another long period of silence, Madeleine Bihet-Richou received a card from Erwin Lahousen, postmarked Rome. It was phrased in coded language, but Henri Navarre, Madeleine's Deuxième Bureau case officer in Paris, knew very well what it meant. Lahousen wanted to see her in Rome; she should go there immediately. Early on 8 January 1940 Madeleine, having taken the train from Budapest through Trieste, arrived in Rome and booked herself into the luxurious Savoy Hotel, an ex-palazzo on the Via Ludovisi, two kilometres from the Forum. As cover, her intelligence controllers arranged for French Railways to commission an article from her on the Italian railway system.

Madeleine waited in Rome for Lahousen for a month, spinning out her work on the article she was supposed to be writing. But it was all in vain. Eventually, in late February, Lahousen sent her a telegram saying he was in Budapest. She took the first train to the Hungarian capital, where on 27 February she was finally reunited with Lahousen in a small café on the Pest bank of the Danube. During their meeting, which lasted until the early hours of the following morning, Lahousen told her that ten days earlier Hitler had ordered that Operation Weserübung, the assault on Norway, was now to start with an attack on Denmark which should take place in the first days of April, just five weeks away.

Madeleine reported all this back to Paris, only to receive a message shortly afterwards that the French government, Venlo no doubt fresh in their minds, regarded her intelligence as 'implausible', and probably deliberate misinformation planted by Lahousen, who, they now concluded, was working for the other side. Madeleine, infuriated, took the first train to Paris to protest, declaring that if her reports were not to be taken seriously she would not return to Budapest. At this her French handlers retreated, and over the inevitable splendid lunch in the restaurant on the Rond-point des Champs-Élysées, managed to persuade her to go back to the Hungarian capital, where she arrived on 19 March.

It is difficult to see what happened next as anything other than a planned and coordinated attempt by those at the top of the Abwehr, and especially Canaris, Lahousen and Oster, to warn the West, by all the channels available to them, of when, how and where Hitler planned to launch his attacks on the remaining free countries of western Europe.

On 21 February a letter from Paul Thümmel, passed through Karel Sedláček in Zürich, arrived in London. The secret-ink passages concealed between the lines of a seemingly innocent letter from a nephew to his uncle read: 'The build-up continues for air attacks on England … consumption of petrol will be cut by half … all private cars have been confiscated … all leave has been suspended … a new Stuka plane is under construction … they are preparing an offensive on the West. They will probably cross the Franco–Belgian border near the Channel. Belgium will be invaded.'

On 25 March, four weeks after Madeleine's meeting with Lahousen in Budapest, a second letter from Thümmel, again passed through Sedláček in Zürich, arrived in London. The secret-writing message gave the outlines of the planned German attack on France: 'Main … attack to be launched in the centre, through the Ardennes, the Panzer units to cross the Meuse north of Sedan and drive towards the Channel. A feint [will be made] by the right wing to bring Allied units into Belgium – the genuine attack force will, by heading north-west, entrap them.' London took the intelligence seriously, commenting, 'A54 is an agent at whose words armies march.' But Paris again rejected the reports as more Venlo-style misinformation.

In mid-March, Hans Oster's contacts in the Swiss-run Viking Line 'supplied [Max Waibel] with [Germany's] plan for the invasion of Scandinavia. On April 30 [they] informed us about the beginning of the campaign in the West and on 1 May about the campaign against Russia. The informer is well placed at a high level in the Abwehr.'

Two weeks later, at the end of March, Francis d'Arcy Osborne in the Vatican reported to London that he too had been warned that Hitler was considering an attack on Norway.

Sometime in early April, Halina Szymańska, reporting on a meeting with either Gisevius or with Canaris himself, confirmed to London that Hitler's attack on France (codenamed Operation Yellow) would come, not as was expected with a frontal assault on the carefully prepared defences of the Maginot Line, but through Belgium and the supposedly tank-hostile Ardennes forest.

On 2 April Hans Oster told his friend the Berlin-based Dutch military attaché 'Bert' Sas that the invasion of Norway was imminent, asking him to forward the intelligence to the Norwegians and the Danes, and to ensure 'above all' that it reached the British. Sas duly passed the information on to the Norwegian legation in Berlin, who judged it too incredible to send on to Oslo.* A few days later the Danes acknowledged receipt of Oster's information with thanks. Sadly, Sas's Dutch intelligence colleagues omitted to inform the British, who remained in the dark.

At about the same time, a Swedish diplomat made a special visit to Oslo to warn the Norwegians that, according to the Swedish military attaché in Berlin, they would shortly be attacked by Hitler, and should take urgent action to protect their ports. He too, for his pains, was 'frightfully snubbed and told not to talk nonsense' by his Norwegian opposite number. Returning to Stockholm, the Swedish diplomat decided to use a more public means to sound the alarm, and gave the story to the Stockholm correspondent of the London *Daily Telegraph*, which published it, unnoticed and unremarked, on its back page.

On 6 April the Swedes also informed Lord Halifax in London of the forthcoming attack on Denmark and Norway.

In the afternoon of 8 April, survivors picked up by the Norwegian navy from a German merchantman, the *Rio de Janeiro*, which had been torpedoed by a British submarine, the Polish-manned *Orzeł* (Eagle), arrived in Oslo. Finding that the shipwrecked mariners were all young men, all armed and all in battle dress, Oslo finally realised that a German invasion was imminent. But it was too late. Canaris's Brandenburgers had already infiltrated the Norwegian capital. At dawn the following morning, 9 April 1940, Denmark came under attack, while the German navy launched a simultaneous assault on Narvik in the north. After a sharp battle, in which the Royal Navy sank ten German destroyers, Oslo fell. Narvik was occupied before the British could get there, and Norway started its long, bitter period of occupation by German troops.

Now, all eyes swung to the Western Front.

In the days immediately following the attack on Norway, Henri Navarre sent Madeleine Bihet-Richou a handsome letter of apology for doubting Lahousen's warnings of Operation Weserübung. Very soon afterwards, Lahousen began sending a further series of postcards, couched in the

---

* Ulrich Stang, a Norwegian diplomat at the legation, was well known to be strongly pro-Nazi, which may be another reason the information was not forwarded.

plain-language code the two had agreed, to Madeleine in Budapest. Each was postmarked from a different place. One, sent in mid-April, informed her that Berlin was now making active preparations for an attack through the Low Countries into France.

Paul Thümmel, who was by this time recognised in British circles as SIS's most important agent in Europe, sent, in all, fourteen reports between April and December 1940 on the coming invasion of the Low Countries and France. This, he said, would be followed by an attack on Britain, preceded by heavy bombing. Nearly all of these reports were regarded as of such importance that they were circulated to the foreign secretary, 10 Downing Street and very probably the king.

In the last days of April, Canaris, Beck and Oster made one final, desperate and risky attempt to inform Western capitals what was about to happen. They asked Josef Mueller, the Abwehr agent who had tried to negotiate a peace deal through Pope Pius's offices earlier in the year, to return to the Vatican, seek out a reliable diplomat and pass on the date for Operation Yellow, the attack on France. Mueller, though travelling under an alias and with a false rank, was very conscious of Heydrich's spies in the Vatican, and did not stay long in Rome. But he did manage to get the message to the Belgian minister to the Holy See. Passing through Venice on his way back to Berlin, some sixth sense for self-preservation caused Mueller to inveigle a friendly Italian frontier official, whom he had previously cultivated with cigars and chocolates, into parting company for a few moments with his official rubber stamp. Using this, Mueller altered the record of his entry date by a few days.

What Mueller did not know was that Heydrich's men had broken the Belgian diplomatic code. Shortly after Mueller arrived back in the Tirpitzufer, Canaris called him to his office and showed him the German decrypt of a telegram sent to Brussels by his Belgian diplomat contact in the Vatican:

> From His Excellency the Belgian Minister, the Holy See.
> To Foreign Minister, Brussels.
> An officer of the German General Staff visiting Rome today reports the invasion of Belgium and Holland may be expected with certainty on or soon after May 10th.

Mueller later remarked that he caught a whiff of the firing squad at this moment. Fortunately his foresight in arranging the falsified exit date-stamp at the Italian frontier saved him from interrogation by Heydrich's SD.

On that same day, 1 May, Erwin Lahousen posted a letter to Madeleine Bihet-Richou containing a dried sprig of lily of the valley and giving dawn on 10 May as the time Hitler had ordained for the launch of the attack on the Low Countries and France.

As Lahousen was posting his letter, a telegram was being delivered to the Jelineks' shop in The Hague. It read: 'Delivery of the merchandise on May 12 is impossible. Letter follows. Karl.' It was of course from Paul Thümmel, who had previously agreed with Aloïs Franck, his Czech handler, that if he got to know the start date for the German assault on the West he would send a telegram in which he would add two days to the actual date. Franck telegrammed London that the attack would commence on 10 May. Then he packed his bags and left for the British capital.

At 9.30 on the evening of 9 May, Hans Oster contacted 'Bert' Sas to tell him that the codeword that would launch the invasion the following morning was 'Danzig'. Sas immediately sent word to his Belgian military attaché colleague Georges Goethals. Then he turned his mind to how to warn The Hague. In view of the urgency he decided not to send a coded telegram, as this would take time to decipher. Instead he took the risk of making a phone call on an open line. Finally reaching the lieutenant on duty in the Dutch Ministry of War, Sas, keeping his call as cryptic as possible to confuse eavesdroppers, said, 'Tomorrow morning at dawn. You know what I mean ...' The lieutenant did, and put Sas straight through to the senior officer on duty, who in response to the dramatic news blurted out, 'Will the Germans really attack tomorrow?' Sas, furious at the breach of security, angrily confirmed that they would. But his superior in The Hague, noting that the Germans had not cut their telephone lines, concluded that it was another deception, and refused to inform the commander of Dutch forces. The Belgians also declined to act on the warning.

Not long after Oster had warned Sas of what was about to happen, radio-monitoring stations across Western Europe picked up the word 'Danzig', which had been broadcast on all German military wavelengths. Shortly afterwards, Hitler's attack on the West, preceded by the unleashing of mayhem behind the lines by Canaris's Brandenburgers, surged forward, following almost precisely the plan which had already been passed from many sources to London, Brussels and Paris.

Despite this, the French were still surprised to find the Maginot Line outflanked by the German assault through the Ardennes, and the British were still shocked when the Wehrmacht feint into Belgium ended with the British forces retreating in disarray to Dunkirk.

On 10 May, as the German attack gathered pace, a three-day debate in the House of Commons on the failure of the previous month's Narvik operation ended with Neville Chamberlain being thrown out of Downing Street and Winston Churchill being installed in his place.

14

Felix and Sealion

Wilhelm Canaris greatly admired Winston Churchill.

He insisted on receiving Churchill's speeches from the Abwehr monitoring service on the day they were made, and took the forbidden texts home to his house near the Schlachtensee, where, with the Heydrichs just next door, he read them out with approval to his wife Erika. 'They are lucky over there to have a statesman to lead them, we have only a guttersnipe here who bawls across the fence,' he declared. Here at last was what Canaris and his resistance colleagues had waited for – a British leader with backbone. What he could not have realised at the time was that Churchill's backbone would turn out to be one of Canaris's greatest problems.

'He [Canaris] had the same initials and would refer to him [Churchill] as the great WC, whereas he was the small WC,' observed one of Canaris's close friends after the war, adding that when Churchill did something of which the Abwehr chief approved he would exclaim in mock despair, 'What can I do against the great WC? I am only the little WC.'

Was there a direct line of communication between the two men? Canaris always claimed so, but in terms too vague to indicate that the contact was more than indirect – or even metaphorical. Asked by a writer after the war how it was that he had been so well informed about Hitler's invasion plans, Churchill walked over to his bookshelf and silently pointed to a biography of the Abwehr chief displaying the single word 'Canaris' on its spine. There are scraps of evidence here and there which might suggest something concrete, but they are thin and circumstantial. Churchill, for instance, admitted after the war to knowing of Hitler's decision to postpone the invasion of the south coast of England after the Battle of Britain even before this was known by the Führer's generals, or could have been known to Churchill as a result of Bletchley Park decrypts.

What is more certain is that, although he would not have known their names, Churchill would have been aware that MI6 had excellent sources on Hitler's intentions through agents such as A54 (Paul Thümmel) and Z5/1 (Halina Szymańska). He probably also knew that, in the case of Szymańska at least, MI6 believed that the original source of her intelligence was Canaris himself. In the 'darkest hour' of the new prime minister's tenure, after the fall of France, when Britain stood entirely alone and mercies were few and far between, it must have been of some small comfort to Churchill that the head of the German Abwehr was, though tenuously and within tightly constrained limits, on his side.

The triumphant sweep of Hitler's armoured columns through the disintegrating French army, and an armistice which France's generals were forced to sign in the very railway carriage where the Germans had agreed to surrender in 1918, brought a catastrophic end to both men's best plans. The British prime minister now had to lead a country that stood completely alone and without the ally on which it had placed all its strategic hopes. Canaris and his plotters, who had looked to a defeat to provide the necessary circumstances for a coup, now had to face a Hitler who, in rejecting the pessimism of his generals, had become the master of Europe and a near god to his people. The senior generals who led the army had now been wrong in 1936 (rearmament), wrong twice more in 1938 (Austria and Czechoslovakia), wrong again in 1939 (Poland), and catastrophically wrong in their pessimism over Hitler's invasion of Western Europe in 1940. The effect of this accumulation of errors of judgement on the self-confidence of generals like Brauchitsch and Halder should not be underestimated, for it was this more than anything else that would emasculate their ability to act decisively in the face of the challenges to come. Once again the plotters were left with no option but to slink away into the shadows and hope for something to come along.

Canaris mournfully noted at this time that the active members of the resistance had 'shrunk to fewer than the five fingers on one hand'.

SD reports confirmed that Germany in 1940 was united as never before, with opposition groups scattered, few and confined mostly to sporadic leafleting. There were, however, some notable exceptions. Lack of broad support meant that large-scale plans for a coup were impossible. Instead, the more determined plotters fell back on individual assassination attempts. One group in the Kreisau Circle tried to form a 'commando unit' to kill Hitler, but failed to get the numbers necessary to carry out the attempt. Two Wehrmacht officers in Paris planned to have Hitler assassinated by sharpshooters during his triumphal victory parade down the Champs-Élysées. But the parade was cancelled for security reasons. One of these would-be assassins went on to plan a second attempt, this time with a hand-grenade attack on the Führer when he visited his unit's headquarters on the Western Front. But the Führer never came.

In the summer of 1940, despite Hitler's triumphs, civilian discontents began to gather and grow again, largely as a reaction to the inactivity of the Wehrmacht leaders, whose string of military successes had dulled their political judgement. Carl Goerdeler and others saw, as their military counterparts did not, that the avalanche of victories would end up exhausting the country's reserves, emboldening Hitler to errors and enlarging the scale of the catastrophe that would eventually descend on Germany and its people. A great calumny was put about after the Second World War that opposition to Hitler only began to emerge after his defeat was inevitable. Nothing more gives the lie to this claim than the remarkable moral courage and acuity of Goerdeler and his civilian resisters, who even at the height of Hitler's power and popularity risked their lives to insist that he was leading their country to a disaster which they had a duty to oppose. In the conclusion of a paper written for army officers in the immediate aftermath of the conquest of France, Goerdeler used the famous words of Baron vom Stein in 1808, urging Friedrich Wilhelm III to oppose Napoleon: 'The only salvation for the honest man is the conviction that the wicked are prepared for any evil … It is worse than blindness to trust a man who has hell in his heart and chaos in his head. If nothing awaits you but disaster and suffering, at least make the choice that is noble and honourable and that will provide some consolation and comfort if things turn out poorly.'

Stein's words would prove prophetic. Goerdeler intended them in 1940 as a clarion call for action. By the end they would become, for him and many others, the only remaining comfort in the face of bottomless despair.

Meanwhile, after conquering Western Europe, the Führer now had to decide where he would go for his 'next kill for breakfast'.

Hitler's greatest flaw as a strategist was impatience.

Following a brief delay after the triumph of his conquest of France, he turned the main focus of Germany's formidable might against Britain. Arguably, he should have turned it first towards Spain.

Göring certainly thought so, believing that of all Hitler's mistakes, 'the gravest and most damaging to German fortunes was [his] failure to seize Spain and North Africa in 1940'. One of Hitler's star generals, the dashing Heinz Guderian, hero of the Ardennes and known to his men as '*Schneller*

Heinz' (Fast Heinz), felt so too, arguing for a postponement of the French armistice in order to give him time to rush through Spain with two Panzer divisions and take Gibraltar. Alfred Jodl, Hitler's chief of operational staff, thinking along the same lines, presented the Führer with a detailed plan urging him to continue the momentum of German forces south-west by invading Spain, taking Gibraltar and cutting Britain off from the Suez Canal, instead of turning north on the hazardous enterprise of a Channel crossing and an invasion of the British Isles.

Many believe that if Hitler had followed this advice, the course of the Second World War might have been very different. German control of the Straits of Gibraltar would have turned the Mediterranean into an Axis lake for the duration of the war. Malta would have been indefensible. British access to its Middle Eastern and Far Eastern colonies would have been much more difficult, and the desert campaign would have been impossible.

External circumstances, too, favoured the Spanish option.

In the aftermath of the fall of France and the humiliation of British forces at Dunkirk, a strong wind of nationalism and pro-German sympathy, encouraged by Franco's government, blew through Spain. There were public demonstrations, with chants of 'Gibraltar Español!' and calls for the immediate recapture of the Rock and of French colonies in North Africa. Franco, catching the mood, wrote to Hitler on 3 June, lauding his victories and calling for an alliance to drive the British and French out of their footholds on the shores of North Africa and the Straits of Gibraltar. He hinted that he would soon join the war on the Axis side. On 12 June, two days before the triumphal entry of German troops into Paris, Spain changed its status from 'neutral' to 'non-belligerent', to which Franco added a few days later the qualification 'with ardent sympathy [for Germany]', to mark the point. Franco had thus far followed a policy of sinuous ambiguity to maintain Spain's strict non-engagement in the struggle between the old European powers and the new Axis dictatorships – always balancing a move which seemed to imply support for one side with another tending in the opposite direction. So this reclassification looked to many like (and was probably intended as) an invitation to Hitler to request free passage for German troops to attack Gibraltar, as Guderian and Jodl had proposed.

But the Führer made no move.

Perhaps he hesitated because he did not wish to interfere in the Mediterranean, which he had previously agreed with Mussolini would be

Carl Goerdeler.

Wilhelm Canaris.

Ludwig Beck.

Henning von
Tresckow.

Hans Oster.

Erwin von Lahousen.

Hans Bernd Gisevius.

Robert Vansittart.

Stewart Menzies with his wife Pamela.

Neville Chamberlain on his return from Munich, September 1938.

Paul Thümmel, Agent A54.

Madeleine Bihet-Richou.

Ursula Hamburger
('Sonja').

Ursula with her children Nina (l) and Micha (r), and Peter Beurton
(second from left).

Leon 'Len' Beurton.

Halina Szymańska.

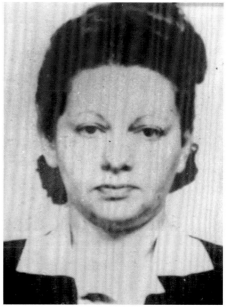

Rachel Duebendorfer.

Alexander Foote.

Rudolf Roessler.

Allen Dulles.

Sándor Radó with his Geopress staff.

Sándor and Helene Radó with their two sons, June 1941.

a strictly Italian preserve. Perhaps, waiting for a British peace proposal which he confidently expected after the fall of France, he did not wish to complicate matters by attacking Gibraltar. Or perhaps he calculated that, in the event that London did not sue for peace, then with Franco now (as he thought) safely on the Axis side of the fence, he could 'park' Spain for the moment while he delivered the *coup de grâce* to a wounded and weakened Britain. If the latter was a factor, then Hitler had calculated without Franco's chameleon ability to change and rechange his policies according to what was, at the particular time, in Spain's interests. For the moment that meant being part of Hitler's victories. But if these were checked – or reversed ...

On 4 June Churchill made it plain that Britain would fight on, with his famous 'We shall fight on the beaches' speech. Hitler was taken aback, bewildered and furious at what he saw as a personal snub. On 2 July he ordered planning to start on Operation Sealion – the invasion of Britain. Though he was careful to keep an attack on Gibraltar in play (on 22 July Canaris was sent to assess Spanish attitudes and conduct a preliminary reconnaissance of the Rock), the vast weight of the German military machine now swung north towards the English Channel.

Probably the first intimation that Hitler was prepared to mount an invasion of the British Isles came in a report sent by Paul Thümmel on 2 May 1940 – that is, even before the Germans launched their attack on the West. This report, which finally reached London (probably via Zürich) on 19 May, read: 'intense preparations for air attacks on England are proceeding but the invasion itself has been postponed, because all available troops are being used in Norway'.

In mid-June, Halina Szymańska reported to London on a conversation with Gisevius indicating that Hitler had already decided that, after he had conquered Britain, he would turn east against Russia. This intelligence was confirmed by a conversation between one of Goerdeler's civilian resistance colleagues, the ex-president of the Reichsbank Hjalmar Schacht, and a diplomat at the US embassy in Bern.

A month later, on 16 July, Hitler confirmed the new policy in Führer Directive No. 16:

> As England, in spite of the hopelessness of her military position, has so
> far shown herself unwilling to come to any compromise, I have decided
> ... to carry out an invasion of England ... and if necessary the island
> will be occupied.

The Führer was, however, far less confident than he sounded about a seaborne invasion: 'I am water shy,' he once remarked. 'On land I am a hero, but on water I am a coward.' His military advisers too were unnerved by their inexperience of seaborne operations, and spent much time wrangling over the details of the assault, and especially how to find an effective way to provide seaborne logistic support for their forces.

Taking advantage of the mood of uncertainty, Canaris began actively exaggerating the strength of Britain's defences. An Abwehr estimate gave thirty-nine British divisions in the invasion area, when in fact there were only sixteen. On 5 September the Tirpitzufer produced a report which would have come as a considerable surprise to the good citizens of Sussex, struggling through their Home Guard drills with wooden rifles: 'The area Tunbridge Wells to Beachy Head (and especially the small town of Rye, where there are large sand dunes) and also St Leonards is distinguished by a special labyrinth of defences.' Before going on to describe Sussex golf courses crowded with armoured vehicles, the report contained a defensive passage designed to get the Abwehr off the hook if there were contrary reports from aerial photography, or German spies on the ground: 'These [St Leonards' labyrinth of defences] are so well camouflaged that a superficial observer on the sand dunes, bathing spots and fields would not discover anything extraordinary.'

In the end Hitler's dreams of an invasion did not founder on his fear of the sea, or on the nervousness of his military planners, or on Canaris's exaggerations. It was the courage of the RAF's magnificent 'few' who, under clear summer skies, defeated Hitler's air armada in what we know as the Battle of Britain which forced him to change tack. Although the Battle of Britain would continue through the Blitz into the early months of 1941, Hitler's attempt to win the air superiority necessary to carry out Sealion was, in reality, defeated by late June.

As early as 10 July, Churchill was able to assure the cabinet (but not yet the country) that the danger of imminent invasion could be ignored, as it 'would [now] be a most hazardous and suicidal operation'. It was not until eleven days later, on 21 July, that Hitler delivered the same message to the generals of German Army High Command, announcing: 'our attention must [now] be turned to tackling the Russian problem and preparing planning' for an attack during the autumn. Churchill's uncanny ability to read Hitler's mind may have been assisted by a series of messages from Paul Thümmel, who was by now sending reports almost daily through a clandestine Czech resistance radio, codenamed 'Spartacus Two', in Prague.

One of these reports in early July gave the first confirmation that Sealion had been 'postponed'. Given Thümmel's close relationship with Canaris, it seems very possible that this message to Churchill originated with his unknown admirer in the Tirpitzufer.

Having previously insisted to his generals that one of his war-fighting principles was never to do battle on two fronts at the same time, Hitler covered his change of mind as a 'postponement', explaining that he had not given up on conquering Britain, but would return to this with renewed energy and force as soon as Russia had been defeated in a lightning strike. But most of his audience would have recognised the truth: the moment for the invasion of Britain had passed. Erwin Lahousen, who had kept Madeleine Bihet-Richou regularly supplied with postcards from different European cities throughout the summer, posted a letter to her in the early autumn confirming that Sealion had been 'postponed'. Paul Thümmel reinforced the fact in a report dated 19 September, putting the delay down 'chiefly to weather conditions and … British air raids' (he probably meant Britain's continuing air superiority over the Channel and the south coast).

While Hitler was telling his generals that Sealion was over for the moment, Wilhelm Canaris was in Spain investigating the possibility of an assault on Gibraltar, codenamed Operation Felix. On the surface he was making a pretty thorough job of it. He set up a new Abwehr station in Algeciras, just across Gibraltar bay, which ran spies onto the Rock. Under the alias 'Señor Juan Guillermo' he paid incognito visits to Algeciras's most famous watering hole, the Hotel Reina Cristina, where he listened to the gossip of British spy-masters and Royal Navy officers. He ordered a report from a leading Brandenburg Regiment expert on the possibility of a surprise special-forces assault on the British bastion. He led a mission to assess operational possibilities, observing the terrain himself from a tower close to the British defences. He commissioned maps to be made, with the help of the Spaniards. He assembled a list of the equipment that would be required for success, and investigated the price that would have to be paid to the Spanish (chiefly in arms, road improvements and financial support) to get them to engage in a joint operation.

All of Canaris's findings pointed to a single conclusion – Operation Felix was at best hazardous, and at worst impossible. The moment had passed for a surprise attack, since the British already knew what was happening. A frontal assault would involve deploying huge resources in aircraft, men and artillery for an uncertain outcome. And neither of these was possible without the active participation of Franco's government, whose ministers, Canaris privately admitted to Erwin Lahousen on 28 July, he had been secretly discouraging from any participation in Felix. The Spanish foreign minister, Serrano Suñer, confused by the different signals he was receiving from Canaris in Spain and Ribbentrop in Berlin, sought clarification from the Italian foreign minister Galeazzo Ciano in Rome. While he was there, Suñer met Canaris's Vatican spy Josef Mueller, who clarified the matter in the bluntest terms: 'The admiral asks you to inform the Caudillo [Franco] that he would like Spain to stay out of the game. It may appear to you that we are in the stronger position – in reality it is hopeless – we have hardly any chance of winning the war. The Caudillo may rest assured that Hitler will not invade Spain.'

Canaris's undercover attempts to undermine Operation Felix did not go unnoticed by his enemies. According to a post-war interrogation of Himmler's representative in the German embassy in Madrid, the Abwehr chief was known to have 'divulged military secrets to Franco and advised him against entering the war on Germany's side in 1940'. At this stage, however, Himmler was content to file this information away for later use.

Having missed one opportunity of attacking Britain, Hitler was not disposed to miss a second. On 24 August he decreed that Felix should go ahead in principle, but the final plan and launch date would be decided at a personal meeting between him and Franco.

Over the next eight weeks Spanish foreign minister Suñer gave a masterclass in the diplomatic game of promise and prevarication, always ensuring that the prospect of Franco joining Hitler was plainly visible on the negotiating table, while always keeping it tantalisingly just out of reach. Ribbentrop tried everything to get the sinuous Spaniard on board, including tantrums, pleading and even a personal interview with Hitler. These discussions turned exclusively on Spain's terms for participating in Felix. The Spanish demands, often based on the secret advice of Canaris, nearly always began with the same plea: 'Spain does not even have the wherewithal to make bread, let alone enough oil to make war.' This was followed by complaints about bad roads, poor railways and even poorer armaments. Canaris advised Franco's government to be especially careful to keep the country's roads in poor repair, as these were regarded by the Germans as a crucial indicator of Spain's readiness for war. When Germany had corrected this imbalance and provided the economic support needed to get Spain into a position to fight a war, Suñer assured Ribbentrop, it would of course be more than happy to do so. On one occasion during Suñer's interview with Hitler, the Spanish foreign minister insisted, at Canaris's secret suggestion, that to attack Gibraltar Spain would need huge 38cm siege guns of the sort that the Germans had installed at Calais on the Channel coast. As Canaris knew very well, Germany had none of these guns to spare. And if any could be found, the local roads were anyway too narrow to transport them and local cranes too puny to lift them.

What the Germans should have realised, but didn't, was that the failure to invade Britain had changed Franco's calculations. With Britain still fighting, Spain's coastline, its North African colonies and its possessions in the Canary Islands would be dangerously vulnerable to the Royal Navy if the Spaniards abandoned their neutrality.

It all finally came down to a face-to-face meeting between the Führer and the Spanish dictator, whom Hitler now privately referred to as 'the Latin charlatan'. This took place on 23 October 1940, at Hendaye, next to the Spanish border on the French Aquitaine coast.

In a minute written three days before Hendaye, and probably intended to be part of Hitler's briefing for the meeting, the German Foreign Office's chief anti-Hitler conspirator, Ernst von Weizsäcker, echoed the views which Canaris was also pressing on Franco: 'My vote is that Spain should be left out of the game ... Gibraltar is not worth that much to us ... Spain is starving and has a fuel shortage ... the entry of Spain [into the war] has no practical value.'

In the days before Hendaye, Canaris carefully briefed Franco through foreign minister Suñer and the Spanish chief of staff, General Martinez Campos. When Campos asked about the status of Sealion and the invasion of Britain, Canaris reassured him, 'Tell Franco no German soldier will ever set foot in England.' Once again he advised that the Spanish dictator should press for financial aid and arms, including, especially, heavy siege artillery.

Hitler's interpreter Paul Schmidt described the Hendaye meeting afterwards as a 'fiasco'. The more the Führer became impatient and angry, the more Franco, with exquisite courtesy, dodged, weaved and ducked to avoid making any commitments whatsoever. On the evening of the talks, Hitler's adjutant wrote in his diary: 'F. [the Führer] very upset, if not actually wild, since Caudillo very reserved and made the Gibraltar operation conditional on fulfilment of comprehensive demands: fuel, coal, weapons. We expected a lot from today's meeting.' During a discussion with Mussolini afterwards, Hitler, who had a pathological horror of dentists, swore he would rather have three teeth pulled out than have another meeting with the eternally mercurial Spanish leader.

On the face of it, Operation Felix did not end with Hendaye. Preparations for the attack, including rehearsals, continued. Hitler even considered attacking Gibraltar without Franco's help. But in reality the moment had, once again, passed. The undertaking was hazardous and expensive enough even with the active participation of Spain. Without it, as everyone knew, it would be folly.

We cannot credit Franco's success in maintaining Spain's neutrality in the face of Hitler's demands to Wilhelm Canaris alone. Franco's over-whelming instinct was not to be drawn in on either side until it was clear who was going to win. There can, for instance, be little doubt that had Sealion succeeded, he would have joined Hitler happily and instantly. But with Britain still in the game he could not, for Spain's sake, side with Germany, even despite the personal debt he owed to Hitler for helping him at a critical moment in the Spanish Civil War.

To these calculations should also be added a well-judged and timely British 'bribe' in the form of a $10 million subvention ($172 million at today's values) which London, through Canaris's old acquaintance Juan March, arranged to be deposited in favour of the Spanish government at the Swiss Bank Corporation in New York. Churchill hoped that this huge sum would, as he delicately put it, 'persuade [the Spanish] of the sweets of neutrality'.

Canaris may not have been the sole reason that Franco kept Spain neutral, but he certainly made it easier by providing the Spanish dictator with the encouragement, support and arguments he needed to push back against the pressure Hitler exerted on him and his country.

Of all the steps Wilhelm Canaris took in pursuit of his self-declared aim of frustrating Hitler's restless expansionism and denying him victory, this was arguably the most important. For now, checked by Britain's stubborn refusal to submit in the north and by Spanish neutrality in the west, Hitler had only one way to go – east.

It seems very probable that MI6 was well aware of Canaris's movements over the period of the Franco–Hitler talks at Hendaye in October 1940, for five months previously, on 19 May, the Bletchley crypto-analysts succeeded in breaking the code used by the Abwehr's administrative wireless network. They were not yet able to decode the main Abwehr traffic, but they could read signals about Abwehr logistics and, specifically, the movements of Canaris and his main subordinates. From now on, with only one break of three months from December 1940, MI6 in London could follow Canaris's movements wherever he went in German-occupied Europe.

It was at this point that Sir Stewart Menzies, the new head of MI6, started to make a close personal study of his opposite number in the Tirpitzufer, giving instructions that he was to be kept intimately informed of everything that Canaris did.

This may account for a highly unusual event that took place at the end of that year.

On 20 December 1940 the newly-recruited British double agent Dusko Popov arrived at Bristol airport on a KLM flight from Lisbon. He was picked up, driven to London and installed in the Savoy Hotel. Ten days later he was taken to the home of Stewart Menzies' brother Ian, 'Little Bridley', a large interwar mansion set in substantial grounds near Woking, where he joined guests including Menzies himself at a New Year's Eve house party. It is, to say the least, most unusual for a newly-arrived, completely untested and untried secret agent to meet the head of MI6 in person, let alone attend a weekend house party with him. At one stage during the festivities Menzies took Popov aside into a small, book-lined study. Even allowing for Popov's tendency to romanticise in the book he wrote after the war, the conversation that took place between the two men seems remarkable. He records Menzies as saying: 'In 1938 Churchill had a conversation with Canaris. Unofficially – he wasn't in office then. Churchill came to the opinion that Canaris is a sort of catalyst for the anti-Hitler elements in Germany. That's why I want to know more about the people he attracts. Eventually I may want to resume the conversation that Churchill initiated. In that event, I must be in a position to evaluate the strength of those around Canaris.'

Whether or not this is an accurate representation of what was said, it is well established that Menzies had a deep understanding of Canaris's personality, traits, habits and opinions, and that he grew to have a high respect for him. 'C [Menzies] understood Admiral Canaris better than he did me,' one of his subordinates complained, commenting on Menzies' uncanny ability to predict the admiral's next move with near total accuracy.

15

The Red Three

At a little before midnight on an evening in the early winter of 1938, a burst of shortwave radio on a frequency of 6.1182 mhz leapt off an antenna camouflaged as a washing line strung between two cherry trees and attached to the upstairs window of an isolated chalet called 'La Taupinière', perched at the end of a north–south-running ridge high above the northern shore of Lake Geneva. Travelling through the cool night air trapped between the troposphere and the surface of the earth, the tiny vibration sped around the world at 186,000 miles a second.

It crossed northern Switzerland, it crossed Germany, it crossed Czechoslovakia, it crossed Poland, until – shortly after it crossed the border of the Soviet Union – an array of aerials hidden in a forest close to the town of Dymovka reached up and plucked it down from the ether.

From here the message shot along telephone lines laid across the Russian steppes until, finally, it emerged into the headphones of a young woman sitting at one of a bank of tables in a corner of the old Moscow Ballroom and Music School, now requisitioned as the wireless room of 'Moscow Centre', the headquarters of Russia's main foreign spy agency, the Glavnoye razvedyvatel'noye upravleniye, or GRU. Scribbling fast, she transcribed the Morse dots and dashes onto a pad. When the transmission ended, she tore off the sheet and put it in a wire basket in front of her.

In due course it was carried to a man in glasses hunched over a table illuminated by a single anglepoise desk lamp. Smoke from his cigarette, balanced on the edge of a full ashtray, ascended in a leisurely spiral to the naked cherubs on the ballroom ceiling, who stared down unconcerned at all this unusual, frenetic activity below.

The man took a pencil and a blank sheet of paper, and began worrying at the message, which consisted of half a dozen 'groups', each comprising five numbers. Frequently referring to a copy of a French novel lying alongside him on the desk, he repeatedly flicked to one of the book's pages, counted the lines down and the words across, and then returned to make a note on his sheet of paper. Gradually the jumble of numbers resolved themselves into a message. It was a short text, the most important part of which was the first three letters – 'SSE', the call-sign of a Soviet secret agent codenamed 'Sonja' who had just moved with her family into the quiet Swiss Alpine village of Caux, above Montreux.

With this tiny pulse of contact in 1938 between a washing line on a Swiss mountainside and Moscow Centre began the assembly of what Russian intelligence would later claim – and with justification – was the greatest spy ring of the entire war. It would be codenamed the 'Dora Ring', and would at its zenith deliver invaluable intelligence to Moscow from Wilhelm Canaris, Hans Oster, Carl Goerdeler and others high in German command which would help defeat Hitler on the Russian Front, and bring about what many regard as the key turning point of the Second World War.

Neither the Dora Ring nor Moscow was ever aware of the true sources of the intelligence it received. Nor did they know that, according to information whose significance has only recently been identified in the British National Archives, Swiss intelligence actively facilitated this crucial passage of intelligence to Moscow – and Britain's MI6 almost certainly knew all about it.

The tenant of 'La Taupinière' was not the first Soviet agent to have established herself in neutral Switzerland.

Two years earlier, in the summer of 1936, with the anti-communist purge reaching its peak in Germany, a short, bald and bespectacled man with a sardonically quizzical smile arrived unremarked in Geneva. Sándor Radó, Fellow of the Royal Geographical Society, Fellow of the American Geographical Society of New York, member of the Geographical Societies of Paris, Geneva, Rome and Washington, and the inventor of aerial mapping, was a much-respected Hungarian geographer of Jewish extraction. The new arrival set up house with his wife Helene (known to her friends as Lene), their two sons, his mother-in-law and the family dog, in the penthouse flat at 113, rue de Lausanne, a substantial granite-faced apartment block looking out over Geneva's Mon Repos park to the lake beyond. Radó's first move was to establish a political cartography business, Geopress, which had its registered address at 2, rue Gustave Moynier, an adjoining sidestreet. Here he got to work making maps illustrating world events – and especially wars. Radó was one of the pioneers of this form of 'political cartography', and his maps were soon in high demand from newspapers, embassies and international enterprises.

Radó's business provided perfect cover for the real reason he had come to Switzerland – to spy for the Soviet Union. Geopress gave him legitimate access to a wide network of foreign diplomats and informants whom he used as his sources. A lifelong communist and already an experienced Soviet agent who had worked in Hungary, Berlin and Paris, Sándor Radó passed the low-grade but useful intelligence he collected through his business on microdots concealed in the text of books which were sent by courier to the Soviet embassy in Paris during 1936 and 1937.

All this changed in the spring of 1938, when crocuses and daffodils carpeted Mon Repos park below the windows of the Radó penthouse. In April of that year a man calling himself 'Kolja' knocked on the door of 113, rue de Lausanne. Kolja was the codename of a Soviet agent called Leonid Abramovitsch Anulow. He had been the 'Rezident' (head) of the GRU in Switzerland, but was suddenly recalled to Russia. On Moscow's instructions 'Kolja' handed over his role in Switzerland to Sándor Radó, who as the new Rezident was to have the rank of major general in the Red Army, and a new codename – 'Albert'. Moscow's orders were for him to lie low and establish his credentials in Geneva. Further instructions would arrive at an appropriate time.

In October 1938, six months after Anulow knocked on Sándor Radó's door in Geneva, Sonja arrived in Caux, above Montreux, and began asking around for somewhere to rent for herself, her husband Rudolf 'Rolf' Hamburger (also a Russian spy), their two children, seven-year-old Mikhail (Micha) and Janina (Nina), aged two, and her old childhood nurse, Olga Muth (known as 'Ollo'). She soon found exactly what she was looking for, a small, isolated chalet called 'La Taupinière', which consisted of three upstairs rooms in which the family lived, and a barn on the ground floor, occupied by a dozen cows.

Reached by a small path across Alpine meadows which blazed with wild scented narcissus in the spring, and with an unparalleled view of Montreux and the full length of Lake Geneva in the distance, 'La Taupinière' was an idyllic spot for a young family – and a perfect place for a spy with a radio. Micha attended the local school, to which he would ski in the winter, and the family soon became an established part of the local community. No one paid any attention to the fact that the new arrivals' washing line was made of wire, and ran almost precisely from north-west to south-east. Or that it was connected by a thin, barely visible filament to the window of a corner room on the chalet's first floor. No one questioned Sonja's purchases of radio parts from a wireless shop run by Edmond and Olga Hamel in a backstreet of Geneva. No one looked into the space under the floorboards of Sonja's built-in linen cupboard, which was just big enough to hide a shortwave wireless transmitter which she and her husband had assembled themselves.

Thirty-one years old, dark-haired, petite, with high Asian cheekbones and smiling eyes, Sonja, alias 'Wiera', alias 'Sonja Schultz', alias 'Ruth Werner', was in reality Ursula Hamburger, the daughter of Robert Kuczynski, an LSE professor of economics and one-time Jewish refugee who lived in Oxford. Born Ursula Ruth Kuczynski on 14 May 1907 in Berlin, she had been brought up, coincidentally, in a lakeside villa on Berlin's Schlachtensee, not far from where Wilhelm Canaris chose to live twenty years later. In the 1930s, after being recruited by the Soviet master-spy Richard Sorge in Shanghai, she operated secret radios for Moscow Centre from Manchuria, Peking and Poland, and for this work had been awarded the Order of the Red Banner and promoted to the rank of colonel in the Red Army.

Sonja, who arrived in Switzerland from Shanghai on 25 September 1938, spent the winter months of that year and the summer of 1939 assembling a spy ring which was tasked to carry out sabotage in Germany. She also gathered political information from Swiss and émigré contacts, which she passed to Moscow Centre in twice-weekly secret transmissions made from her bedroom in 'La Taupinière'. In the early weeks of 1939 her husband left Switzerland, ostensibly 'for business reasons', but in reality on a new spying mission for Moscow Centre.

Nine months afterwards, in mid-October 1939, just six weeks after the war started, two young Englishmen arrived in Territet, on the outskirts of Montreux, and rented rooms in the Pension Elizabeth, a Swiss-style nineteenth-century villa on the shores of Lake Geneva. They drew little attention from the other residents, for the young men were out most days. Like many tourists, their routine was regular. Breakfast in the dining room overlooking the lake. Then, wearing hiking boots and carrying rucksacks, they took a short walk along the waterfront, past municipal flowerbeds and the little rustic harbour of Bon Port, to Territet station, from where a funicular railway took them a kilometre up the mountain to the small town of Glion. Here they caught the open-carriage mountain tram to the station at Caux, from where they walked to Sonja's chalet, 'La Taupinière'.

Thirty-four-year-old Alexander Allan Foote and his friend, Leon Charles Beurton (known as Len), nine years Foote's junior, were not tourists; they too were Soviet agents.

Foote, tall with reddish hair, fair eyebrows, pale skin and blue eyes, was recruited as a Soviet spy by Sonja's sister Bridget Lewis on his return to Britain in 1938 after fighting with the British Brigade in the Spanish Civil War. He in turn recruited his friend and comrade 'Len' Beurton, another veteran of the Civil War. Sometime around the end of 1938 the two men were ordered by Moscow Centre to go to Switzerland and make contact with Sonja, who sent them to Munich, where they spent the year before the outbreak of war in unsuccessful attempts at sabotage. Foote was, by chance, back at 'La Taupinière' in the late summer of 1939, when the Soviet–German Non-Aggression Pact was signed and war broke out. Moscow instructed Sonja to pull all her agents out of Germany, and as soon as Beurton arrived back in Switzerland, ordered her to retrain the two Englishmen as clandestine radio operators.

In December 1939, two months after Foote and Beurton began their training at 'La Taupinière', Sonja was instructed by Moscow Centre to go to Geneva to visit Sándor Radó, who it appears she had never met before. Her instructions were to offer to act as Radó's radio link with Moscow Centre and to 'pool her finances with him'. Radó, recognising that his courier links to Moscow through Italy and Paris could be jeopardised by the outbreak of war, agreed.

From this moment, what would be known as the 'Dora Ring' (the name is an anagram of 'Radó') was established as the Swiss arm of the pan-European Soviet spy network the *Rote Kapelle*.

At first, Sonja, acting alone, was Radó's wireless link with Moscow Centre, sending two transmissions a week with his reports. But by the early months of 1940, with Foote and Beurton now fully trained, Moscow Centre decided that it was time for her to move on – it had more important work for her to do in Britain, where she was to join the growing and extremely fruitful ring of Soviet spies operating in the British scientific community and at the heart of the British establishment. However, while her father, as a Jewish refugee in Britain, did have a UK passport, she did not, having spent the pre-war years spying in China, Manchuria and Poland. Moscow's solution was to instruct her to obtain a British passport by divorcing her absent husband and marrying one of her two English pupils. The first plan was for her to marry Foote, but this fell through for personal reasons, so it was agreed that she should instead marry Beurton, seven years her junior. Beurton, who had lost his father in the First World War and been abandoned by his mother, was not an easy man to live with. Sonja described him as complicated, distrustful, and subject to 'frequent changes in mood [and] depressions I could not fathom'.

The marriage took place in Montreux on 23 February 1940 (Alexander Foote was a witness, and gave false testimony to support Sonja's divorce). The date was chosen by the happy couple because it was the official birthday of the Red Army. Afterwards Beurton moved into 'La Taupinière'.

At first all went well. But soon human nature, which could not be altogether excluded by Moscow Centre's casual attitude to love, marriage and divorce, began to intervene.

Sonja's childhood nurse, Olga Muth, now the devoted carer of her children Nina and Micha, suddenly realised that she had been excluded from Moscow's plans for the family she had grown so attached to. The new Mrs Beurton would get a British passport, but she, Olga, would not – she would be abandoned and separated from the children she adored. Believing that if she unmasked her mistress the children would be left in her care, 'Ollo' visited the British consulate in Montreux and tried to tell an official there that Sonja was a Russian spy – but her English was as bad as the British official's French, and neither could understand a word the other said. Next she revealed Sonja's true role to one of her mistress's closest friends, who also paid no attention. Then she informed the wife of the farmer who owned 'La Taupinière'. Finally she told the local hairdresser.

Now Sonja had to act fast to save her network. She installed both her children in a nearby German-speaking school* and promptly moved with her new husband to a flat on the rue de Lausanne in Geneva, close to Sándor Radó. Ollo was abandoned, to return to Germany.

At about the same time, Alexander Foote moved from Montreux to an apartment block on a small street just behind the Geneva lakefront, midway between the British consulate on the quai Wilson and Radó's apartment in the rue de Lausanne. Here, over the next few months Foote and Sonja trained Olga and Edmond Hamel, the owners of the backstreet wireless shop called 'Radio-Eleman' where Sonja had bought her radio parts, as clandestine radio operators.

---

* The École Internationale 'Les Rayons', in Gland on Lake Geneva. It had been established by the Jewish refugee Kurt Hahn, who also founded Gordonstoun in Scotland, which at this time numbered the present Duke of Edinburgh among its pupils.

As soon as the Hamels were capable of operating their radio, Moscow sent Sonja $3,500 and instructed her to leave immediately for Britain. There she was instructed to join her father in Oxford and await instructions. Len Beurton, at twenty-six, was still of military age, and therefore not able to get a visa to accompany his wife through Spain and France. In mid-December 1940, after introducing Alexander Foote to Radó, handing her microdot camera and enlarger on to her husband Len and depositing her wireless in the Hamels' shop, Ursula Beurton, as she now was, left Geneva with her two children for Lisbon. From there she took a boat to Britain, arriving at her parents' home in the Woodstock Road, Oxford, in February 1941.

With the Hamels' radio – which Moscow Centre knew as 'Station Maude' – now able to take the load after Sonja's departure, Alexander Foote left Geneva for a safer place from which to transmit. Hiding his radio in his dirty laundry, he caught a train to Lausanne, where he moved into a penthouse apartment in a block of flats at the top of a ridge overlooking Lake Geneva. Once settled in, he erected a hidden aerial on the roof, established contact with Moscow on 12 March 1941, and set about constructing a reputation for himself as a rich young Englishman taking refuge from the war in the easy living of the famous Swiss lakeside gambling resort.

By now, trouble was brewing. Ursula Beurton's departure at the end of 1940 seems to have initiated some kind of crisis in the Dora Ring.

In early 1941 a tall, handsome woman with Slavic features and porcelain teeth arrived at the Radós' front door in the rue de Lausanne. She introduced herself as 'Vera', and she was expected. Her real name was Captain Maria Josefovna Poljakova, codename 'Vera', alias 'Gisela', alias 'Mildred', alias 'Meg'. Fluent in English, French and German, she had herself run a Soviet spy ring in Switzerland between 1936 and 1937, and was now acting as the 'case officer' at Moscow Centre responsible for the management of the Dora Ring. She had arrived from Moscow to investigate Radó's organisation and restructure it after the loss of Sonja as a radio operator. She tried to persuade Radó to operate his own wireless, but he refused on the grounds that, with his high-profile position and a family in residence, he would soon be compromised if he operated a radio from his home.

The problem which Vera was sent from Moscow to sort out may well have been more than just organisational, for Sándor Radó, though internationally recognised as a cartographer of the highest calibre, was very far from being the perfect spy-master. After the war MI6 described him as 'not particularly brave or honest, nor had he the strength of character to control his organisation by his own efforts'. He was undisciplined when it came to recruiting his agents, breaching a fundamental principle of espionage that agents who are already members of other espionage rings should be strictly avoided, as they increase the chance of infiltration and contamination. Despite this, at least four of the agents used by key members of the Dora Ring were also agents of other Allied spy-masters operating in Switzerland, including Chojnacki, Sedláček, Swiss intelligence and MI6.

Radó was not held in high regard by those who worked for him either. Alexander Foote described him as an unscrupulous dilettante, and accused him of embezzling Moscow funds provided for his agents (Radó claimed sixty on his payroll) and using them for his own private purposes. In time, Moscow Centre would come to share Foote's view of Radó's dubious accounting practices. Helene Radó, too, was less than discreet, gaining a reputation among the employees of Geopress for her love of jewellery, fur coats and expensive perfumes. In 1942 the couple bought a chalet in the Swiss ski resort of Crans Montana, ostensibly as a refuge if the Germans invaded.

We do not know what conclusions Maria Poljakova took back with her, but there is evidence that at this time Moscow Centre established separate lines to Foote (who was given his own codes which Radó could not read) and to one of the Dora Ring's other principal agents, a forty-year-old pre-war International Labour Organisation (ILO) interpreter called Rachel Duebendorfer, alias 'Sissy', who Poljakova ran independently from Moscow. Sissy seems to have been asked to keep an eye on Helene and Sándor Radó.

For one person, however, the departure of Sonja and the events surrounding Poljakova's visit had a more radical effect.

According to Alexander Foote, it was at this time that Len Beurton sank into a deep depression. Disillusioned with his secret work for the Russians, he withdrew from the Dora Ring and, though maintaining occasional contact with Foote, broke off all contact with the Radós and other Dora agents. Inactive, missing his wife, short of money (he sold the microdot equipment Sonja had left with him for cash), down on his luck and desperate to get back to the UK, Beurton seems to have decided to pay a visit to the British consulate at 41, quai Wilson, half a kilometre from his apartment on the Geneva lakefront. Here, some time around the spring of 1941, he met the consulate passport control officer Victor Farrell, who was also the undercover (but widely identified) head of MI6 in Geneva. As a result of this meeting, Beurton agreed to provide MI6 with what his file in the British National Archives describes as 'useful intelligence information' on his activities in Switzerland in exchange for Farrell's help in getting him back to England. We do not know all the information that Beurton provided to Farrell, but we do know that it included, among other things, the name and details of at least one of Sándor Radó's secret agents, a Chinese journalist who before the war had been accredited to the League of Nations called L.T. Wang, who, Beurton revealed, was a source of secret information.

After a year or so working for Farrell, Beurton was finally able to leave Switzerland, thanks to a false identity provided by the 'passport control officer'. This included papers in the name 'John William Miller' and a complete new background, which wiped clean his espionage activity and described him as a British citizen stranded in Switzerland as a result of tuberculosis and the aftermath of a bad skiing accident. Beurton caught a ship from Lisbon, and landed at Poole on 29 July 1942. On arrival he immediately confessed that he had been travelling under a false identity.

MI5 smelled a rat, and suspected (correctly) that Beurton had been 'in touch with the agents of a foreign power' and was involved in 'espionage on behalf of the USSR against Germany from Switzerland'. This raises the question: why, if MI5 in London had spotted Beurton's true role, had MI6's representative on the ground in Geneva, Victor Farrell – apparently – not?

Unless, of course, Farrell *had* uncovered Beurton's real role in Switzerland, but kept it secret, including from MI5. Correspondence on Beurton's file in the British National Archives reveals that the Independent MP Eleanor Rathbone, who gained a reputation for assisting ex-members of the International Brigade in Spain, as well as no less a person than foreign secretary Anthony Eden, were involved in issuing Beurton with a new identity so that he could return to the UK.

We have no way of knowing exactly what happened between Len Beurton and Victor Farrell. But, given the facts we do know, the most likely course of events is as follows: sometime around the spring of 1941, Beurton, disillusioned and desperate to get back to Britain, revealed to Farrell that he had received secret information from the Chinese journalist L.T. Wang. When Farrell pressed him, as he would have been bound to do, about who was the receiver of Wang's secret reports, Beurton would have had no option but to reveal the existence of the Dora Ring, and was then duly paid off with the false identity he needed to leave Switzerland without delay.

This conclusion is supported by other events that followed Beurton's meetings with MI6's man in Geneva.

In the spring of 1941 (i.e. at about the same time that Beurton first met Farrell) the senior Swiss intelligence officer in Geneva, Captain Bernhard Mayr von Baldegg, suddenly made a totally unannounced approach to one of Sándor Radó's most productive agents, and asked him to help in 'establishing contact with Russian army intelligence in Switzerland'.

It seems most unlikely that von Baldegg's out-of-the-blue request was purely coincidental, given that it happened at exactly the same time that Beurton appears to have revealed the existence of the Dora Ring to Farrell, among whose other functions in Geneva was to act as MI6's contact man with von Baldegg. The most likely explanation for the timing of von Baldegg's approach to one of Radó's key agents is that Farrell, having discovered the existence of the Dora Ring from Beurton, passed this information on to his local Swiss intelligence opposite number, who then picked up the thread.

Sándor Radó must have panicked when he heard the news that the Swiss were aware of his existence. As a foreign spy in Switzerland, he was now at risk of severe penalty. He knew he had no choice but to accept von Baldegg's invitation to make contact. Shortly after this, Swiss intelligence's star agent, Rudolf Roessler, was put in contact with Radó, offering to act as a source of intelligence which would be passed through an intermediary, a Swiss citizen called Christian Schneider, who was Roessler's partner in his Lucerne publishing business, Vita Nova. Significantly, Radó never reported either von Baldegg's approach or his new relationship with Swiss intelligence to Moscow Centre.

Christian Schneider, operating under the codename 'Taylor', now began acting as a go-between, passing Roessler's intelligence reports to a second 'cut-out', Radó's agent Rachel Duebendorfer, whose apartment was 150 metres from the Radó home on the rue de Lausanne.

Once these two 'cut-outs' (Duebendorfer and Schneider) were established in such a way as to obscure the true origins of the intelligence the Swiss wanted to get to Moscow, Swiss intelligence began to feed the Dora network with selected information from Rudolf Roessler's high-level sources in Germany, including Hans Oster and Carl Goerdeler.

On the face of it, the channel between the Swiss and Radó was a complex one. Roessler to Schneider; then Schneider to Duebendorfer; and finally Duebendorfer to Radó. By now, however, the area around Radó's flat on the rue de Lausanne had become a regular nest of Soviet spies, with Len Beurton living at number 129, a hundred metres from Radó, Rachel Duebendorfer just 150 metres further on at number 135, and the ILO, where Duebendorfer and Schneider had met before the war, a hundred metres beyond that. At a kilometre and a half, the distance between Schneider's Geneva home in the place des Alpes and the Duebendorfer flat can be accomplished in a comfortable thirty-minute walk, while that between the Duebendorfer front door and Radós letterbox requires no more than an easy lunchtime stroll through the Mon Repos park. Schneider usually carried Roessler's information, written in manuscript on flimsy notepaper, on his regular journeys to and from Lucerne, either dropping it through Duebendorfer's door or handing it over at clandestine meetings in the Jardin Anglais, adjacent to the Pont de Mont Blanc on the Geneva lakefront.

The fact that Rachel Duebendorfer was one of the key cut-outs in this chain suggests a second probability. We know from her post-war comments, confirmed by the head of MI6 in Switzerland, that as well as working for Radó and Poljakova in Moscow Centre, Duebendorfer was also listed by MI6's industrious spy-master in Geneva, Victor Farrell, as one of his secret sources.

From this distance, peering back into the murk of World War II spying in Switzerland, we cannot be definite. But the conclusion which best fits the facts we do know is that from around mid-1941, not long before the surprise German invasion of Russia, the Swiss intelligence service was, without Moscow's knowledge, feeding the intelligence it received from Rudolf Roessler's high-level sources in Berlin through to the Dora network, which passed it on to Moscow Centre; and the British, at the very least, knew about it and may have actively participated in the exchange. Sándor Radó, writing after the war, confirms that 'important intelligence [from Roessler] was shared with the English by Swiss intelligence'.

Did Hans Oster in the Tirpitzufer know that the information he was supplying to Roessler and the Allies about German plans on the Eastern Front was also being passed on to Moscow through the Dora Ring? It seems very likely that he did, for in a post-war interrogation of Richard Protze, a close personal friend of Canaris and head of the Abwehr's foreign intelligence department, Protze confirmed that one of his agents in

Switzerland, a prominent Swiss communist, had been instrumental in helping Sándor Radó found and fund the Dora Ring. Protze also revealed that 'The Abwehr's penetration of [the Dora] network was upset by a Gestapo investigation.' If this information is accurate, it means that the Dora Ring was penetrated and used as a channel to pass information to Moscow by no fewer than three intelligence organisations: MI6, Swiss intelligence, and possibly even the Abwehr in Berlin – though whether and to what extent they worked together we cannot tell.

We know, of course, why Oster would have wanted to help Russia defeat Hitler. But why were the Swiss and the British also keen to share some of their most precious secrets with Stalin?

The answer is straightforward.

Both had a very strong interest in helping Stalin in any conflict which would develop between Russia and Germany. The Swiss had long been aware of Hitler's plans to invade their country. In 1941 Switzerland was surrounded by an estimated thirty German divisions, which could move at a moment's notice. Britain, only just free of the fear of imminent invasion, was also still under serious threat. If Hitler attacked Russia and got bogged down on the Eastern Front, the immediate effect would be to relieve the pressure on both Britain and Switzerland. MI6 and Swiss intelligence had, as we know, recently picked up clear signals that Hitler did indeed intend to turn east and attack the Soviet Union in the very near future. Helping Stalin was now an urgent priority for both nations.

On 3 April 1941, at about the same time that Len Beurton was approaching Victor Farrell in Geneva, Winston Churchill instructed Sir Stafford Cripps, the British ambassador in Moscow, to pass to Stalin, in disguised form, information he had received from Bletchley's Ultra decrypts that Hitler was transferring armoured divisions from Yugoslavia to southern Poland in preparation for an attack. Stalin declared this a British deception, and refused to believe it.

The Dora Ring in Geneva thus provided an alternative means of supplying Moscow Centre with information Switzerland and London needed to get to Stalin without arousing his paranoid fears of becoming a dupe to British tricks.

The first substantive message sent by Alexander Foote to Moscow Centre, after establishing communications on 12 March 1941, began the process of 'playing' Roessler's extraordinary high-level intelligence on troop preparations for Hitler's coming invasion of Russia through to Joseph Stalin.

12 April: Dora to the Director … In mid March German divisions were positioned as follows: France 50, Belgium and Holland 15, Denmark and Norway 10, east Prussia 17, German-occupied Poland 44 of which 12 are motorised or armoured divisions, Rumania 30, Bulgaria 22, Slovakia, Bohemia and Austria 20, the Munich and Ulm sectors 8, Italy 5, Africa 5 – total 225 divisions, in addition to which a further 25 divisions being formed in Germany.

16

Belgrade and Barbarossa

In the last weeks of 1940, Paul Thümmel accompanied Wilhelm Canaris on a trip to Turkey and the Balkans. A few weeks later, on a cold morning in early February 1941, Thümmel returned to the Balkans on a second and more secret visit, arriving by train with a small overnight case at Belgrade's main station. He walked the short distance from the station to a café called Složna Braća (Brothers in Arms) on Kralja Milana Boulevard. Ordering a coffee, he looked for a bunch of dried maple leaves wedged behind a picture of a past king of Serbia on the café wall. Seeing that it was in place, he finished his coffee and strolled to a modern apartment building in a nearby backstreet, where he climbed the stairs to the second floor. Here he found what he was looking for: a brass nameplate bearing the title 'Kosovska Company'. Knocking on the door, he introduced himself under yet another new alias – 'René' – and was shown into a small lobby where he took off his grey overcoat and announced, 'I am bringing the promised information from Prague.' He was swiftly shown into a small outer room furnished as a typical Belgrade flat. Waiting for him, as arranged, was Major Fritscher of the Czech intelligence service. That evening coded telegram number 12001, carrying a new report from Agent A54, arrived at the Czech government-in-exile's intelligence headquarters at 3–8 Porchester Gate on the Bayswater Road in London, and was swiftly sent by despatch rider to MI6 headquarters at Broadway Buildings above St James's Park tube station. It informed London that Hitler would attack Greece before the end of March: 'Bulgaria has allowed German troops to cross her territory and enter Greece … A similar agreement is expected with the Yugoslavs. The Yugoslav Government has raised no objection …'

A month or so later, on 25 March, despite an earlier declaration of neutrality, the pro-German Yugoslav government signed the Tripartite Pact between Italy, Germany and Japan, and announced that it would soon join the Axis alliance.

The Belgrade government had however reckoned without Julian Amery, the twenty-two-year-old ex-war correspondent in the Spanish Civil War and son of the influential Member of Parliament and one-time First Lord of the Admiralty, Leo Amery. The younger Amery, working as a joint agent of MI6 and SOE, had for some time been encouraging the pro-British Serbs to revolt against their government. The future head of the American Office of Strategic Services (OSS – the forerunner of the CIA), 'Wild Bill' Donovan, was also dashing around the Balkans at this time, trying to persuade the Yugoslavs not to join the Axis powers and calling for a Serb military revolt if this happened. Canaris was aware of Donovan's activities, and had his agents follow him everywhere. They even managed to steal his passport from his unattended coat in a Belgrade restaurant in order to disrupt his travel plans. But the Abwehr completely missed what Amery had been up to.

At 2.15 a.m. on 27 March, following an incendiary BBC broadcast by the elder Amery, a coup d'état was launched in Yugoslavia, replacing the old pro-Axis government with a new pro-British one. Hitler saw the coup as a personal insult and, once again driven by anger rather than logic, issued two directives, the first calling for the invasion of Yugoslavia and its destruction 'militarily and as a nation', and the second ordering a five-week delay to Barbarossa while he brought Yugoslavia to its knees. It was five weeks which the Führer would find he could ill afford to lose at the end of the year, as under thick falling snow and through bitter cold his troops tramped towards the gates of Moscow. A German officer was later to comment: 'The delay cost the Germans the winter battle for Moscow. And it was there that the war was lost.'

The Belgrade coup also came as an unwelcome shock to Canaris, for it brought to an end a delicate set of manoeuvres in which he was involved (probably, on this occasion, with the agreement of Hitler) to pursue a separate peace deal with Britain which bypassed Churchill by using pro-appeasement figures in the British establishment, including, some say, the ex-King Edward VIII (by then the Duke of Windsor). The channels through which these feelers were put out were of truly Balkan complexity. They involved a Luftwaffe captain; a German prince; Sir Samuel Hoare, the pro-appeasement British ambassador to Spain; a Swiss diplomat and historian; and the ex-kaiser's son-in-law Prince Paul of Yugoslavia, an Oxford-educated Knight of the Garter. Prince Paul was also the prime mover behind Yugoslavia's signature of the Tripartite Pact, and thus the person against whom the 'Amery' coup was primarily directed. With his man kicked out of office and his peace plot in ruins, Canaris, who always had another ruse up his sleeve, turned his attention to warning the Allies and the Yugoslavs what was about to happen.

On the day after Hitler ordered his army to prepare for the invasion and destruction of Yugoslavia, Erwin Lahousen took a train to Budapest for a four-day stay with Madeleine Bihet-Richou. 'The coup d'état in Belgrade has thrown Hitler into a pullulating rage,' he warned. 'In his fury he has ordered the destruction of this little irritant country with reprisals which will be catastrophic for Yugoslavia. The country will be destroyed with pitiless rigour – the Luftwaffe has received orders to raze Belgrade to the ground.' Madeleine sent the intelligence back to Colonel Rivet, who following the fall of France had taken up secret residence with the new French 'post-Armistice' government in Vichy. Rivet passed the information on to London and Belgrade.

Senior Yugoslav officers were also warned by Abwehr sources that the German attack would be launched on Palm Sunday, 6 April.

As March 1941 drew to a close, Czech intelligence received one of Paul Thümmel's fat envelopes containing documents which not only confirmed that the attack on Yugoslavia would be launched with a Luftwaffe bombing raid on Belgrade on the night of 5–6 April, but also gave details of the overall invasion plan, the units involved and the precise timetable.

In the first days of April, Madeleine Bihet-Richou watched German forces streaming through Budapest, heading south towards Serbia. There were so many that they crammed the streets of the city for forty-eight hours.

On 2 April, hoping to save the capital, the new Yugoslav government declared Belgrade an 'open city' (i.e. no military resistance would be offered to those wishing to enter). But it was to no avail. On 5 April Stewart Menzies sent an urgent message to the MI6 station head in Belgrade: 'Inform Yugoslav general staff that, from a very reliable agent we learn that German attack will begin early tomorrow morning 6 April.'

The first wave of 230 German bombers struck Belgrade at 6.45 the following morning, killing or maiming, it is estimated, between 10,000 and 17,000 civilians.

Ten days later, Canaris, accompanied by Lahousen and one of his other department heads, Hans Piekenbrock, arrived in Belgrade. As in Poland, the horrors overwhelmed him. 'I shall never forget his complete psychological breakdown under the impression of smoking and devastated Belgrade where the stench of unburied corpses still lingered. At such moments Canaris was not dissimulating,' wrote Hans Bernd Gisevius after the war. That evening, after a day made even worse for the animal-loving Canaris by the sight and smell of decaying corpses of humans mixed with the rotting bodies of animals which had escaped in panic from the city zoo, the old admiral collapsed into a chair and declared, 'I can stand no more of this. We will leave tomorrow for Spain.' It was not the first time, and it would not be the last, that Canaris would seek solace from the horrors around him in the sunlit villages, cobbled streets and bustling communities of peaceful Spain.

There was, however, one legacy of the bombing of Belgrade which Canaris would not be able to escape. Searching the empty rooms of the British embassy in Belgrade, Walter Schellenberg, newly prominent in Heydrich's SD after Venlo, found a copy of a telegram from London which the British military attaché had failed to destroy before he fled. It read: 'The Luftwaffe will commence attack with overwhelming bombardment of the capital, according to our faithful friend "Franz-Josef". Inform the Yugoslav government.' We now know that the origin of this information was Hans Oster, who passed it on through Paul Thümmel, alias 'our faithful friend "Franz-Josef"'.

The ensuing Gestapo investigation soon discovered that the 'Franz-Josef' leak came from secret files held in the safe of the Abwehr offices in Prague. But that was as far as the Gestapo got. Behind the scenes, Canaris manoeuvred to ensure that the Gestapo inquiry once again ran into the sand and was shut down. There the matter seemingly ended.

Except that it didn't. This small event would eventually have profound long-term consequences for both Wilhelm Canaris and MI6's prize agent Paul Thümmel.

On his way back from Spain, Canaris called in to Switzerland for a meeting with Halina Szymańska. Asked if Germany would attack Turkey, he replied, 'No, we won't attack Turkey – Russia perhaps.'

With Belgrade little more than a heap of smoking ruins, all eyes now turned east.

Paul Thümmel began reporting that German intentions were shifting to the east as early as September 1940, when he sent a message warning of an impending invasion of Romania and Bulgaria, a step which many regarded as a necessary prelude for an assault on Russia.

The first proof that this supposition was correct came later that autumn, when Halina Szymańska passed on a warning from Canaris that Hitler had decided to launch an attack on the Soviet Union the following year. To start with the British were sceptical. But then confirmation arrived from the British minister at the Vatican, Sir Francis d'Arcy Osborne, who reported that Canaris's agent Josef Mueller had paid another visit to the Vatican and had warned of Hitler's decision to turn east.

Not long after, on 18 December 1940, Hitler issued Führer Directive No. 21, which ordered that the German armed forces should begin planning for an invasion aimed at crushing Soviet Russia in a lightning campaign even before the conclusion of the war against 'England'.

A week later, on Christmas Day, Thümmel reported through the Czech resistance radio in Prague that the Germans were seeking experts in the Crimea and the Caucasus, and that Operation Barbarossa, the attack on Russia, would be launched in the first half of May 1941.

In March 1941, around the time of Hitler's invasion of Yugoslavia, Hans Bernd Gisevius reported to London through Halina Szymańska that he was 'convinced hostilities between Russia and Germany would start early in May'. At about the same time, rumours about the impending attack reached London through the Swedish businessman and amateur diplomat Johan Dahlerus, a friend of Göring's in Copenhagen.*

Towards the end of March, Thümmel reported in another voluminous letter: 'Attack against the USSR definitely planned. There will be three directions: in the north, against Leningrad; in the centre through White Russia [Belarus], ultimately against Moscow and in the south through the Ukraine against Kiev. About 155 divisions to participate.'

A few days later, on 30 March, perhaps still smarting from having to delay Barbarossa, perhaps in a bid to outflank a repeat of the complaints about the excesses of the Polish campaign, Hitler called 250 senior officers to his Chancellery in Berlin. In a two-and-a-half-hour speech he made it clear that, after the easy victories of what he called the 'flower wars' (the Rhineland, the *Anschluss* and the Sudetenland), this was to be his war – his personal war – the war he had predicted in *Mein Kampf*. It should be, he demanded, a 'struggle of two ideologies ... a struggle of annihilation. The war against Russia will be such that it cannot be conducted in a knightly fashion ... [with] soldierly comradeship ... The fight will be very different from the fight in the west. In the east harshness is kindness towards the future ... leaders must demand of themselves the sacrifices of overcoming

---

* It is possible that Göring, playing a double game, may have deliberately leaked the information.

their scruples.' There was stunned silence when the Führer finished and stalked out of the room – followed by an outburst of protest to commander-in-chief von Brauchitsch, who brushed the objections aside as best he could. Von Brauchitsch and his chief of staff Halder had already had heated discussions as to whether the two of them should resign in protest against Hitler's illegal orders. But, as ever, von Brauchitsch's backbone proved completely incapable of bearing such weighty and decisive action. The German commander-in-chief was, if nothing else, a brilliant exponent of the art of casuistry. 'If because of his upbringing and inner conviction, von Brauchitsch was on the side of the conspirators,' Halder wrote of his chief after the war, 'then he carefully avoided giving any definite undertaking on a matter on which his conscience dictated no plain course and logical reasoning failed to indicate clearly whether the enterprise would succeed or fail.'

What followed Hitler's speech was even worse. A series of guidelines and edicts was issued transferring the governance of captured territory to special Reichskommissars with absolute powers. Himmler's Einsatzgruppen were ordered to carry out 'special tasks', a euphemism which everyone knew meant mass murder on a grand scale. An edict, known as the 'Kommissar order' was issued, requiring all Red Army political commissars to be shot immediately. When Hans Oster read the orders aloud at a secret gathering in Ludwig Beck's mansion in Goethestrasse on 5 April – the day before the invasion of Yugoslavia – 'Everyone's hair stood up on end at these orders for the troops ... [they] would systematically transform military justice for the civilian population into a caricature that mocked every concept of law ... [thus] sacrificing the honour of the German army.'

It was at this stage that, in the face of the crippling ambivalence of the army's senior leadership and with Beck out of action in retirement, a new leader of the military opposition began to come to the fore.

Henning von Tresckow was a most attractive figure. Scion of a noble Prussian family which over three hundred years of unbroken military service had provided twenty-one generals to the armies of Prussia and Germany, he was forty years old, and the senior staff officer at Army Group Centre. Under the Barbarossa plan it was to be Army Group Centre, commanded by von Tresckow's uncle Field Marshal Fedor ('Fedi') von Bock, that was to carry the main burden of the Russian assault leading up to the capture of Moscow.

Top of his class at the war academy, deeply grounded in moral principle, disciplined and cool under pressure, von Tresckow was the natural

Henning von Tresckow

leader of the new generation of young Turks who were increasingly taking over the anti-Hitler resistance in the army. 'He had a personality that simply bowled you over,' commented an admirer. 'He had an incredible gift for connecting with you and winning you over … Have you seen pictures of him? He exercised a very strong immediate influence on his surroundings; he had great personal charm – charm and the ability to convince. You trusted him.' Another said, 'In my life I have met a lot of illustrious people; but none who had the spiritual charisma and force of character of Henning von Tresckow.'

Like many charismatic leaders, von Tresckow possessed great clarity of mind and purpose. Speaking to an Army Group Centre colleague 'on the riverbank in the starlight' one night in the summer of 1941, he said: 'One has to resort to active revolutionary means. To take this path, we have to throw away everything we learned from our forefathers about the honour of the Prussian-German soldier, as well as our property, our family, our personal honour and the honour of our class.'

As preparations for Barbarossa gathered pace, von Tresckow started to assemble around him at his headquarters in Posen (Poznań) a network of middle-ranking officers sympathetic to his views. These included two counts and a scattering of rising young colonels whom he would meet in a private room. In front of a roaring fire they would play chess, consume meals of steak washed down by copious quantities of red wine and conduct long, ardent discussions on politics, military campaigns, the progress of the war and the future of Germany. A subsequent chronicler of the plots against Hitler would describe the von Tresckow group as 'the largest and most tightly knit [army] resistance group of those years.'

When he heard of the 'Kommissar order', von Tresckow immediately flew to see his uncle the field marshal to protest. Walking through a small park leading to the field marshal's villa, he turned to his close friend Rudolf-Christoph von Gersdorff, who was accompanying him, and said: 'If we don't convince the field marshal to fly to Hitler at once and have these orders cancelled, the German people will be burdened with a guilt the world will not forget in a hundred years. The responsibility will fall not only on Hitler, Himmler and Göring and their comrades, but on you and me, your wife and my wife, your children and my children, the old woman who just went into the store over there, the man riding his bicycle over here, and that little boy playing with the ball. Think about it.'

After listening to von Tresckow's explanation of Hitler's new orders, Bock, who had been present at the Führer's two-and-a-half-hour tirade on 30 March, feigned surprise, horror and shock.

'Fedi,' Tresckow insisted, using the diminutive form of Fedor, 'I have had your plane made ready. You must fly immediately to Hitler … You must put a pistol to his chest and demand the immediate revocation of these orders … If you refuse to obey him now, he will have to give in …'

'What if he dismisses us?' von Bock broke in.

'Then you will at least exit the stage of history honourably.'

'Hitler will send Himmler as my replacement,' his uncle responded defensively.

'We'll know how to deal with him!' von Tresckow replied.

The field marshal could be neither persuaded nor browbeaten into confronting the Führer, so Tresckow sent von Gersdorff to army head-quarters in Berlin to express Bock's concern. When the emissary inevitably returned empty-handed, never having got beyond the staff in von Brauchitsch's front office, he found Bock at dinner with Tresckow and other officers. After von Gersdorff had delivered his report, Bock announced to the assembled company, 'Let it be noted, gentlemen, that Field Marshal von Bock protested,' and carried on with his dinner.

In the last days before Barbarossa was launched, Goerdeler, Beck, Oster and others held a series of conferences to discuss whether Hitler's 'Kommissar order' and the other edicts might be sufficient to 'open the eyes of the military leaders to the nature of the regime for which they are fighting ... [but] we came to the conclusion that nothing was to be hoped for now ... They [the generals] were just a bunch of hopeless sergeant majors.'

While Henning von Tresckow, sitting on the Russo–German frontier, was venting his frustration about the spinelessness of his superiors, clear signs of the impending assault on Russia were coming in thick and fast to Allied capitals, including, especially, Moscow.

Stalin resolutely rejected all of them. Apart from Churchill's attempts to pass on Ultra decrypts, he also dismissed as deception similar warnings from the United States, whose codebreakers had been reading Japanese diplomatic despatches since the early days of the war. He even refused to give credence to the information that an attack was imminent which was passed to Moscow Centre by the great Soviet spy in Tokyo, Sonja's old friend and recruiter Richard Sorge.

On 1 May 1941, Max Waibel reported to his Swiss intelligence chiefs that he had received full details of Barbarossa from the Viking Line. This, after the occupation of Holland and Belgium, had become little more than a codename for Hans Oster himself.

On 30 April Hitler changed the Barbarossa launch date from 15 May to 22 June. At the end of May Erwin Lahousen reported this latest decision to Madeleine Bihet-Richou, adding that the reason the invasion would be delayed was the trouble in Yugoslavia.

On 18 May, a Paul Thümmel message detailed:

Wehrmacht railway transport moving east. The Germans have concentrated three bodies of troops along the Soviet frontier. The 'northern' group is in Prussia, the 'central' group around Warsaw and the 'southern' group in Galicia ...

By now the Dora Ring was also passing on Roessler's reports from the Tirpitzufer to Moscow. Alexander Foote in Lausanne sent:

22 April: From Dora. Information from Swiss politician indicates that Governmental sources in Berlin place the date for the attack on Ukraine 15 June. The Germans do not expect strong opposition.

Moscow, faithfully reflecting Stalin's refusal to believe that an attack was being planned, categorically rejected these reports as untrue, and instructed Sándor Radó to send no more reports of this nature in future.

Radó ignored the order, and around the end of May sent two further reports to Moscow through Foote in Lausanne. Both set the projected date for Barbarossa as 22 June. These were followed by a further warning, this time sent through the Hamels' radio, 'Station Maude':

> 6 June: Dora to the Director: All Germany's mobile divisions are in the east. The German troops formerly stationed on the Swiss frontier have been transferred to the south-east ...

On that same day, the British war cabinet in London, after a review of intelligence, still remained uncertain whether Hitler's troop movements near the Russian border were really the preparations for an attack, or were designed to increase pressure on Stalin to provide Germany with more oil, grain and iron ore from the Caucasus. The following day, however, with nine days to go before the launch date of Barbarossa, a US-decrypted telegram from the Japanese ambassador in Berlin to his government finally convinced London that an attack was imminent.

Four days later, with the target date for Barbarossa now only five days away, Foote signalled Moscow Centre:

> 17 June: Dora to the Director: 100 infantry Divisions now stationed on the Soviet German border, one third of which are motorised. There are, in addition ten armoured divisions. A further concentration of German troops are at Galatz in Rumania. The 5th and 10th elite combat divisions, who have a special mission, are positioned in German-occupied Poland.

Stalin, who was himself a master of the art of deception, had by now succeeded in deceiving himself into believing that the more information piled up about an impending German attack, the more it proved that it was all a British plot. When Marshal Semyon Timoshenko, backed by political commissar Nikita Khrushchev, pressed Stalin to give the order for the peasants along the German border to start digging defences, the Russian dictator rejected the suggestion on the grounds that it would 'provoke Hitler'.

On 15 June, just a week before the start date for the invasion, Stalin furiously rejected another Timoshenko request, this time to move his frontier forces to better defensive positions. 'We have a non-aggression pact with Germany,' Stalin insisted. 'Germany is up to her ears with the war in the west and I am certain that Hitler will not risk creating a second front by attacking the Soviet Union. Hitler is not such an idiot and understands that the Soviet Union is not Poland, not France and not even England.' A despairing Khrushchev would later comment that, although Stalin refused to believe in the impending attack, 'sparrows chirped about it at every crossroads'.

And so Russia was unprepared and Stalin taken completely by surprise when, at dawn on 22 June 1941, the greatest invasion in history, Operation Barbarossa, the German attack on Russia, was launched simultaneously along a 2,900-kilometre front.

In Bern, Halina Szymańska was getting ready to take her daughter Marysia to the dentist when she heard the news on the radio and, to the alarm of her children, broke her habitual decorum by leaping to her feet and letting out a most unladylike whoop of delight. Her warnings over the past six months had proved correct – a turning point in the war had been reached.

That night in Lausanne, Alexander Foote, hunched over his radio, tapped out an immediate message to Moscow Centre:

To the Director. In this historic hour we vow solemnly and with unshakeable loyalty, that we will fight with redoubled energy at our forward posts. Dora

17

General Winter

Five days after the launch of Operation Barbarossa, London received a coded signal sent from 'Spartacus', one of the secret radios operated by the underground in Prague. It was from A54 – Paul Thümmel.

At the time Thümmel was being actively pursued by the Gestapo, and had to resort to using 'dead-letter boxes' around Prague old town in order to pass his information to the Czech resistance for onward transmission to London. One of these was a telephone directory in a phone box, between the pages of which Thümmel slipped his reports for later collection; another was in Prague's old military cemetery, where messages were pushed into a large crack in the memorial statue of a nineteenth-century Czech general.

Perhaps more than any other signal Thümmel sent in his remarkable career, this one indicated just how high-level his access was in the German command, for it laid out not just the current disposition of German troops, but also the long-term aims of Barbarossa:

> *60 Divisions are deployed to the north and as far as Brest Litovsk. Another 6 divisions from Brest-Litovsk to Prziemyls.* In the south and as far as the Black Sea, there are 120 divisions. The army in the north is to advance in one column, the centre army in three columns. The two armies should converge towards Smolensk, arriving there about 24 July. Operations will then begin in the south of the Soviet Union, where the Russians have gathered their best trained troops in enormous numbers … At the same time the Finnish army will start moving and, on 10 July, attack in the direction of Leningrad. At the end of July, German troops will be in Moscow. The Germans are preparing a follow-up campaign aimed at gaining control of the Caucasus and the oil wells. The Italians are expected to play the major role in this latter operation …*

---

* Sic. Probably Przemyśl, close to the Polish–Ukrainian border.

Up to this moment, even with Bletchley decrypts, all London would have known was the size and geographical scale of the German assault on Russia. Operation Barbarossa involved four million Axis troops, 600,000 motorised vehicles and more than half a million horses spread out along a front stretching from the Baltic to the Black Sea. These troop concentrations, or some broad indication of them, London might have been able to guess at. But the overall plan of Barbarossa, its intentions and how it would unfold, would still have been a mystery to them.

It was that information which Thümmel's short, and as it would turn out extremely accurate, report gave them.

Churchill famously treated Ultra decrypts with almost religious reverence. But these, like almost all signals and technical intelligence (known as 'sigint'), could only reveal what and who was where, and possibly what they would do next. The Abwehr spies who tried to help the Allies win the war provided human intelligence ('humint') on Hitler's long-term intentions and plans. Unhappily, although Bletchley sigint greatly changed the conduct of the war prosecuted by the Western Allies, the humint for which many in the German resistance risked their lives changed very little, because, after Venlo, it was largely discounted. Maybe it was the West's failure to heed the repeated warnings about the invasions of Norway, the Low Countries and France that caused the Tirpitzufer to begin to divert its efforts through Switzerland, to Moscow.

If so, it was a change of tack which would pay off handsomely.

To start with Barbarossa achieved lightning success, as the entire Russian front, taken completely by surprise, collapsed in panic before the German assault. For the first two weeks Russian command and communication lines from the front dissolved into chaos, leaving Moscow blind, and desperate for information:

> *1 July 1941. To Dora from the Director. Concentrate on the lines of movement of German forces. Follow this carefully and signal regularly, especially all movement of troops toward the east from France and other western countries.*

Once the initial surprise had passed, the pace of the German advance began to slow. After two weeks of continuous manoeuvre battle, the German army high command realised that they had underestimated both their Russian opponents' will to resist and the difficulties they would experience with logistical resupply.

To make matters worse, on 2 July the weather portentously intervened when the *rasputitsa*, a seasonal Ukrainian summer rainstorm, swept in. It lasted six days, filling the marshes and rivers and turning even small streams into impassable barriers and earth roads into ribbons of mud. The German advance stuttered to a stop as its armoured columns tried to regroup.

That same day, Radó replied to Moscow's demands with information indicating a source at very high level – almost certainly provided through Swiss intelligence and the Roessler link with Berlin:

> *2 July. For the Director. The Germans currently have Operational plan No 1 in force. The target is Moscow. Operations that have been started on the flanks are merely diversionary tactics. The emphasis is on the central section of the front. Dora.*

The German pause to let their logistic supply lines catch up and the rainstorms pass gave the Russians the time they needed to regroup and regain their balance. When battle resumed they were able to meet the German advance with repeated counterattacks which, in spite of huge Russian losses in troops and armour, began to wear down the speed of German progress.

On 23 August, Radó warned:

> *For the Director: 28 new divisions are being formed in Germany. They will be ready by September. Dora.*

Hitler was now getting impatient. With the advance towards Moscow slowing he decided, against the advice of his most senior generals, to dilute the main thrust of his assault towards the Russian capital by splitting both his forces and his axis of attack. The centre was to halt and consolidate; one column was to split off and turn south to take the Caucasus oilfields and the industrial centre of Kharkov, and another was to turn north to capture the great city of Leningrad.

In early September, Radó gave Moscow a high-level insight into the long-term aims behind this change of plan:

> *6 September. For the Director: Germany believes that, after the capture of Leningrad, Finland will conclude a separate peace; this would shorten the German front, thereby releasing German troops and easing the transport and supply situation.*

Two weeks later, Radó backed this up with intelligence on an even more strategic scale:

> *20 September. For the Director. The German long-term aim is to occupy Murmansk and cut the line of communication and resupply between the Soviet Union, Britain and the United States. At the same time they intend to use Japanese pressure in the Far East to prevent the Americans resupplying the Russians through Vladivostok. Dora.*

Hitler's diversions to the north and south gave Marshal Timoshenko, who had been tasked with the defence of Moscow, time to stiffen the city's defences.

In the first week of October, Radó sent a report to Moscow Centre which caused Timoshenko to commit troops to the area around Smolensk, in expectation of a German assault on the town of Vy'azma. What Radó did not know, because his information came from Berlin and not from the German front-line headquarters, was that at the last minute the German attack was postponed, leaving Timoshenko's men exposed and in the wrong place. In the German encirclement of Vy'azma which followed, the Russians lost around 700,000 troops wounded, killed or captured. The catastrophe at Vy'azma shook Moscow's trust in Dora. But this did not last long, and was quickly restored in the following months.

Meanwhile, back in Geneva, pressure was building on Dora and its operators. Such was the volume of information coming through to Radó that Alexander Foote now had to collect reports from him twice a week. Helene Radó pitched in to help with some of the Hamels' coding, and the Radó children were recruited as couriers carrying messages to and fro. Foote, who did his own coding and decoding and sent his messages in English, was transmitting to Moscow at the astonishing rate of 30,000 five-figure groups a month. Because shortwave travels better in the cool night air, he usually started working his radio after midnight, often continuing to send and receive until the early hours of the morning. Soon, however, the weight and volume of the reports coming through for Moscow reached proportions which could no longer be managed simply by extending transmission hours. The Dora Ring needed another operator.

In October 1941 Sándor Radó recruited a pretty twenty-one-year-old waitress called Margrit Bolli, alias 'Rosy', whom he found working at the Bear Pit restaurant in Bern. She was swiftly trained up by Foote in Lausanne, and installed with a radio in her parents' house in Basel. But Foote soon discovered that her father constantly interfered with her work, 'causing her to limit her working and sometimes even forbidding her to work at all'. In the summer of 1942 Radó moved Rosy into a guest house looking out on Geneva's famous Jet d'Eau. Later he found her a one-bedroomed flat in a handsome apartment block with iron-balustraded balconies close to a small park in the suburb of Eaux-Vives, on the east bank of the lake.

German listening stations under the control of Himmler's Sicherheitsdienst in Munich, Karlsruhe and Stuttgart had by now picked up on the increased volume of transmissions coming out of Switzerland. They soon identified three radios sending information to Moscow on a regular basis from the area around Lake Geneva. For the moment they could not decode these messages, and did not know who was sending them, or exactly where they were – so they christened them *die Rote Drei* – the Red Three.

The final phase of Barbarossa, the push to Moscow – Operation Typhoon – began on 2 October. Two weeks later, with Panzers within 125 kilometres of the Russian capital, Stalin ordered the evacuation of the city. Only a few essential staff and caretakers were left behind in the echoing rooms and corridors of the Kremlin and other government buildings. Moscow Centre did not think to inform Radó, or his operators, of the move.

All the *Rote Drei* knew was that Moscow Centre had suddenly gone silent. Had the Russian capital fallen, they wondered.

Brushing aside their concerns, Foote and his colleagues continued to send their reports. On 22 October, Foote in Lausanne sent:

> *Radó for Director: As a result of their losses the majority of German divisions on the Eastern Front have lost their cohesion. Apart from some fully trained personnel they consist of men with 4 to 6 months' training and others who have only had one-sixth of the necessary training period.*

Five days later he signalled:

> *27 October, For the Director. Someone who works in Ribbentrop's office (I will refer to him as Codename Agnes in future)* has sent the following confidential information to [the Swiss newspaper] Neue Zürcher Zeitung:*

---

* The journalist Ernst Lemmer.

1. *Armoured propaganda units are stationed in Briansk waiting to enter*
    Moscow. The date of entry is to be between 14 and 22 October.
2. *On 17 October, orders were given to prepare for a long siege of Moscow.*
    Artillery, including those of the calibre of coastal artillery which were
    on the Maginot Line and at Königsberg, have, for several days, been en
    route for Moscow. The German press has been banned from reporting
    anything on the battle of Moscow. Dora

In mid-October, as Army Group Centre, now on the move again, pushed towards Moscow through deteriorating weather, Wilhelm Canaris, on his way back from a tour of the Russian front, took Halina Szymańska out to dinner in Bern. He reported in some detail on the problems the Germans were facing because of unexpectedly stiff Russian opposition and the lack of winter clothing and equipment. Hitler had miscalculated, he explained. The Führer had counted on 'support from dissatisfied elements in Russia [but these] … had completely failed to materialise'.

At the end of October, Foote, again worried that Moscow Centre had been overrun, sent:

29 October. For the Director. We haven't heard from you for several days.
Have you received our messages? Should we continue to send these, or
wait until communications have been re-established? Send instructions.
Dora

A month later, at the end of November, Moscow Centre suddenly came up on the air again, with a long string of new questions. There was no apology, no explanation and no hint that GRU headquarters was no longer in Moscow but was with the rest of the Russian government in Kuybyshev, on a hairpin bend of the Volga river, eight hundred kilometres south-west of the capital.

On the plains before Moscow, the weather was worsening by the day. Temperatures plummeted and cold, penetrating rain fell incessantly, drenching the infantry – who were still mostly wearing summer clothing – and making earth roads impassable to armoured and motorised columns. On 31 October, German commanders ordered another pause for the armies to regroup and the logistics to catch up. The Russians, with shorter supply lines, were once again able to make better use of the lull than their enemy. On 15 November, with the ground hardening as it froze, the Germans continued their push for the Russian capital. 'If we do not make a resolute advance to Moscow now,' von Tresckow at Army Group Centre headquarters, and thus in the thick of it, said to a friend, 'we'll have lost the campaign.'

By now, snow was falling. To start with it came intermittently, sandwiched between periods of freezing rain. Then, on 2 December, with the forward German troops close to the outskirts of Moscow and, they claimed, within sight of the spires of the Kremlin, that old Russian ally, General Winter, blew in with a succession of smothering blizzards. And that, just eighteen kilometres from the centre of Moscow, was where Hitler's great Russian gamble ended.

With the German spring at full extension, and the Soviet one pushed back to its maximum compression, it was time at last for the Russians to strike back.

On 5 December they launched their Winter Offensive, dislodging the German forward columns from the outskirts of Moscow and forcing them into a rapid but orderly withdrawal.

Two days later, on 7 December 1941, the Japanese launched a surprise attack on Pearl Harbor. President Roosevelt, describing the assault as 'a day that will live in infamy', promptly announced that the United States was at war with Japan. Four days after that, on 11 December, Germany and Italy declared war on the United States. It was another example of Hitler's impetuousness. Roosevelt would have had some difficulty in persuading Congress to go to war with Germany as well as Japan, had Hitler not done the job for him. Now, contrary to the hopes and efforts of Canaris, Beck, Goerdeler and their colleagues, the conflict had become truly global, and as they understood too well, could only end in total catastrophe for Germany.

Among the many thousands of casualties of Barbarossa was one of a different kind. On 19 December, in a move designed to shift blame, Hitler dismissed Walther von Brauchitsch as commander-in-chief and took the position for himself. Over the next months four army commanders and dozens of divisional and corps commanders followed von Brauchitsch into retirement, allowing Hitler to consolidate his absolute authority over the Wehrmacht, which was finally deprived of all vestige of its privileged position in the German state and left, as an institution, morally broken.

The following day, the Führer, overriding the protests of his generals on the ground, who were now losing more soldiers to the cold than to the attacking Russians, ordered that the positions around Moscow were to be held at whatever cost.

It was to no avail. When the first phase of the Russian Winter Offensive ended a month later, on 7 January 1942, the entire German front line had been pushed back to a point which, at its closest, was a hundred kilometres from the Russian capital. Hitler had lost the Battle of Moscow. Now there was nothing left for his underequipped and underdressed troops but to dig in and do their best to endure the terrors of the twentieth century's coldest winter. The myth of the Führer's infallibility and his soldiers' invincibility had been broken once and for all. Von Tresckow said to a friend, 'This war … is irrevocably lost, and we serve an arch-criminal. I repeat, an arch-criminal. According to reliable information, SS units are committing massacres beyond anything you can imagine.'

He was right on both counts.

The bald telling of the German army's advance to disaster before Moscow is only half the Barbarossa story. Behind the armoured columns came Himmler's Einsatzgruppen killing squads. Although logistically supplied by the army, these operated autonomously and answered only to Himmler's security apparatus, the RSHA.

Five days before the start of Barbarossa, on 17 June, the Einsatzgruppen commanders were gathered at Pretsch in eastern Poland and briefed by Heydrich. He explained that the central aim of their task was the elimination of the Jews in Soviet territory. It is estimated that over the period of the German operations on the Eastern Front, in excess of 3.3 million Russian prisoners of war were killed or starved to death, 1.4 million Jews were systematically murdered, and probably more than a million from other minorities and the general civilian population were put to death. 'Poland was nothing by comparison,' wrote a German officer in a letter, adding that he felt like 'a tool of a despotic will to destroy without regard for humanity and simple decency'.

A senior officer with Army Group North reported how, three days after the start of Barbarossa, in an atrocity ordered by Heydrich himself, a Lithuanian militia unit under SS command 'herded a large number of Jews together, beat them to death with truncheons and then danced to music on their dead bodies. After the victims were carted away, fresh Jews were brought and the game was repeated.'

In Borisov, seventy kilometres east of Minsk and right in the middle of Army Group Centre's main line of advance, 6,500 Jews were machine-gunned into pits in a single day. This massacre, which took place on 24 October 1941, was observed from an aircraft by a Wehrmacht officer, who reported it to von Tresckow's uncle, the Army Group's commander-in-chief, Field Marshal von Bock. Bock protested in the strongest terms to the Himmler-appointed civilian commissioner for the area, ordering him to report to the field marshal's headquarters in Smolensk without delay. The commissioner replied that it was Bock who should be reporting to him, not the other way round, and refused all requests to provide information on the SS commander who had carried out the slaughter. Later, the Wehrmacht commander on the ground, criticised by his fellow officers for not preventing the massacre, committed suicide.

In Army Group South's area, SS units slaughtered all the Muslim Azerbaijanis and Crimean Tartars they could find amongst their prisoners because, being circumcised, they were presumed to be Jews. Canaris protested that this indiscriminate killing destroyed the Abwehr's ability to get intelligence from local ethnic communities, who had suffered cruelly under Stalin. But his warnings went completely unheeded, and the orgy of mass murder continued unabated across the entire front.

In August, a report from Paul Thümmel gave a graphic description of the problem, viewed from inside the Abwehr:

> The [Abwehr] is up against unbelievable obstacles. Most of its agents took part in the campaigns on the Western Front, where they received support from certain members of the local population. The situation is quite different in the Soviet Union, where the Abwehr has lost a lot of men. Frequently a German intelligence agent fails to return from a rendezvous with people who had been thought willing to cooperate. By 15 August Abwehr units attached to the army in the south had lost half their men.

Defeat and shame now combined to pull new recruits into the anti-Hitler resistance and to harden the attitudes of already-committed conspirators. Carl Goerdeler, whose religious scruples had made him opposed to the assassination of Hitler, now conceded that killing the Führer might be necessary.

Once again, in the absence of anything planned and thought through, wild schemes proliferated.

A paper drawn up by Goerdeler, Beck and others included a new draft constitution based around a British parliamentary-style monarchy. The German commander-in-chief in the west, Erwin von Witzleben (now promoted to field marshal), who had led the September 1938 coup, toyed with the idea of marching his troops on Berlin. With Canaris's agreement, feelers were put out by the German diplomat Ulrich von Hassell to the

United States through the president of the General Motors Overseas Corporation. And, again with Canaris's knowledge, an approach was made to Moscow through a Jewish Abwehr agent in Stockholm and his female bridge partner, who happened to be the Soviet envoy in Sweden. Most of these schemes were quickly dismissed as hopelessly unrealistic.

But some had more practical purpose. Henning von Tresckow's network of plotters in Army Group Centre started to extend its reach as its numbers increased. General Halder, Brauchitsch's chief of staff, with the help of the head of army personnel, began an active policy of planting committed anti-Hitler sympathisers in all the army's key commands.

Among those for whom the atrocities on the Eastern Front were a defining moment was a young staff officer in the German army high command called Claus von Stauffenberg.

In late September 1941, three months after the start of Barbarossa and with its horrors now plainly visible to all, von Tresckow sent Fabian von Schlabrendorff, a lawyer friend whom he had recruited as Army Group Centre's legal adviser, to Berlin with instructions to make contact with Goerdeler, Beck, Oster and von Weizsäcker of the German Foreign Office. He was to tell them that the Army Group Centre conspirators were at their disposal, and 'prepared to do anything'.

MI6 in London soon picked up on the new mood amongst the German generals, reporting on 16 December 1941 that one of its sources in the Vatican (Josef Mueller?) had heard rumours that as a result of the 'collapse of the offensive on Russia' the army had 'prepared a shadow government' to come to power after a coup.

For the first time since the attempted coup of 1938, an instrument was being created capable of delivering an integrated nationwide putsch. It would not happen quickly – and in the meantime those who wished to be rid of Hitler would have to rely on individual assassination attempts. But from this first building block would eventually be created the architecture to deliver the great coup of 20 July 1944.

18

The Great God of Prague

It is rare in the counter-intelligence business for a big thing to happen all at once.

The demise of Paul Thümmel, close associate of Wilhelm Canaris, one of MI6's star agents and arguably among the most daring and reckless spies of World War II, began with an event with which he had no direct connection. On 13 May 1941 a Gestapo search party looking for a Czech underground fugitive stumbled across 'Spartacus', the Czech intelligence radio station in Prague and the channel by which most of Thümmel's information was sent to London. In the firefight that ensued, three Gestapo agents were killed and one Czech resistant was badly wounded and overpowered. The other two Czechs – the radio operator, who was in the act of transmitting to London at the time, and Václav Morávek (not to be confused with the Czech intelligence chief František Morávec in London) – managed to escape by sliding down a cable at the back of the block of flats in which they had been hiding, an escapade which cost Morávek a severed finger.

The Gestapo search of the apartment uncovered a document referring to a certain 'Franta'. This alias was already known to the Gestapo from a 1939 raid on another Czech secret radio. From documents recovered in the earlier raid, it was known that Franta was passing secrets to London which could only have come from the highest level in Berlin. The 1939 Franta information was regarded by Himmler's SD as so serious that a special task force was established to hunt down the traitor, under a gifted counter-intelligence officer called 'Wild' Willi Abendschön.

For two years Abendschön drew a blank on Franta – until the discoveries made in May 1941 at the flat used by Spartacus.

Another Gestapo raid that autumn netted a low-level Czech resistant who, under extreme torture, revealed that one of his comrades had been in touch with an unnamed German officer. Asked for proof, the man identified a Czech resistance member, Colonel Josef Churavý, who was already in Gestapo custody. According to the tortured man, Churavý had handed his Wehrmacht 'spy' a large sum of money. A search of the colonel's home turned up a receipt which precisely matched the details the Gestapo had obtained from their Czech informant – except that it was signed not by Franta, but by 'René'. Later, when debriefing Balkan agents who had been present in Belgrade before the German invasion, Abendschön picked up Paul Thümmel's name as an Abwehr officer who had made frequent visits to the Serb capital. He began to suspect (correctly) that London's 'faithful friend "Franz-Josef"', mentioned in the scrap of paper found in the deserted British embassy after the invasion of Belgrade, along with 'Franta' and 'René', were in fact one and the same person – Paul Thümmel. The net was beginning to close on A54.

But when it came to light that Thümmel was a founder member of the Nazi Party and a close friend of Himmler's, Berlin gave instructions that the file should be immediately closed and declared 'dead'. Abendschön, however, continued to harbour strong suspicions that Thümmel was, nevertheless, his man.

Meanwhile, 'René', as Paul Thümmel was now styling himself, kept on supplying London with regular reports. On 19 September 1941 Czech intelligence in the British capital sent Thümmel a questionnaire: What had Canaris been doing in Turkey? Was Hitler about to invade there too? What news was there from the Eastern Front? Where exactly was Hitler's HQ? Were there plans to invade Bulgaria and Romania? What was Göring up to?

Thümmel answered these rapidly and in detail. London came back on 22 September: 'René's last reports were very good … in future he should always mention his source.'

Then, suddenly, A54 went silent.

On the day before London's congratulatory message to Thümmel, Reinhard Heydrich, lunching with Hitler in the Chancellery in Berlin, mounted a fierce attack on the then Reichsprotektor of Bohemia and Moravia (Czechoslovakia), Konstantin von Neurath. Heydrich told Hitler that the laxness and inefficiency of the Neurath administration in Prague had damaged the respect in which the Führer and the Germans were held in the Czech capital. Chief among the examples he gave to support his case that von Neurath should be replaced was the evidence found in the Abwehr safe in Prague that 'Franz-Josef', the spy who had alerted the British to the attack on Belgrade, was connected to the local Abwehr office. Hitler took the bait. Without even informing Neurath, he appointed the thirty-seven-year-old Heydrich as acting Protektor in Prague, and promoted him to Obergruppenführer, the highest rank in the SS. Significantly, Hitler allowed Heydrich to retain his position as head of the RSHA, whose interests he was now able to pursue even more effectively through the right of personal access to the Führer, which came with his new position as Reichsprotektor.

Heydrich's reign of terror began immediately on his arrival at Prague's Čzernin Palace on 27 September 1941. 'We are going to try to "Germanise" these Czech vermin using the old methods ... there is no other way but to try to incorporate them into the Reich, to re-educate them ... Or if this does not work, as a last resort we shall stand them up against the wall,' he said on 2 October, five days after his arrival.

All this was very bad news, not just for the Czechs, but also for Wilhelm Canaris, for by this time Heydrich, despite his close neighbourly and musical relationship with his old mentor, had become convinced that the Abwehr – and most probably Canaris himself – was deeply immersed in treachery.

Now the hunt for the Abwehr spy – 'Traitor X', as Heydrich called him – gathered pace, with the Reichsprotektor taking personal charge.

It can be argued that Czech intelligence and MI6 should never have allowed so valuable a spy as Thümmel to get so deeply enmeshed with the Czech local resistance, for it meant that his existence was widely known, and he was therefore vulnerable to Gestapo discovery through any weak link. It is, however, unarguable that at this stage, with the Gestapo in hot pursuit and closing in, Thümmel, codename A54, alias 'Franta', alias 'René', alias 'our faithful friend "Franz-Josef"', known to the Germans as 'Traitor X', should have been instructed to break off all contact with the local Czechs and lie low until things calmed down. But he wasn't.

At 3 a.m. on 3 October, the day after Heydrich's speech at the Čzernin Palace, German Gonio wireless-detection vans identified another clandestine radio in an isolated customs and excise post in the Prague suburb of Jinonice. A swift raid was mounted and the radio captured. One of the radio operators committed suicide, but the other was captured. As a result of follow-up arrests the Germans pieced together that Václav Morávek, one of the Prague resistance leaders known locally as the 'the Three Kings', was in touch with 'Traitor X', who was a German and worked at Wehrmacht headquarters in the city.

Even worse, among the documents found lying alongside the captured radio were intelligence reports so highly classified that there were only three people in Prague who had access to them. Two were senior RSHA figures, and so beyond suspicion. The third was the multi-aliased Paul Thümmel, known at the time to Abendschön and the rest of the Prague German security community by his official Abwehr codename, 'Dr Holm'.

In view of Thümmel's high-level status, Heydrich was consulted before 'Dr Holm' was arrested on 13 October 1941.

What followed was a cascade of protest from Berlin, including from Martin Bormann and even Himmler himself, orchestrated, it seems certain, by Canaris. Heydrich in Prague was furious, and let the fact be known in Berlin.

At this time Canaris was in the habit of taking regular morning rides with Heydrich's right-hand man in the German capital, the thirty-one-year-old hero of Venlo, Walter Schellenberg. Schellenberg, clearly briefed by Heydrich, suggested that the best way to deal with the rising tension between the two men was a face-to-face meeting to sort out a new *modus operandi* between the Abwehr and the RSHA.

In November, with his agent Thümmel still in Gestapo hands, Canaris flew to Prague. The first meeting between the two neighbours and old naval colleagues, with Schellenberg also present, was held in the grand surroundings of the Čzernin Palace. According to a witness, it was laden with icy tension from the start.

Heydrich opened the attack: 'I will not hide from you that, after the war the SS will take over all the Abwehr's responsibilities.'

Canaris countered silkily, 'My dear Heydrich, I have never doubted your intentions or your ambitions. Remember I have known you a long time, since … since you were in the navy, I suppose,' he added, without needing to mention Heydrich's junior rank in the navy, or the fact that he had been cashiered from the service. 'And since you know me well too, you will know that nobody will touch the Abwehr as long as I live.'

'Nobody, Herr Admiral? Not even the Führer?'

'Do not imply what I have not said. The Führer is not concerned in this, as you very well know. It is you and I. That is very different, and very clear.'

'Do you imagine, my dear Admiral, that the Führer would not be concerned if he knew that a very important member of your organisation in Prague has been involved in treasonous dealings with the Czech resistance and MI6 in London. Do you really think that the Führer would not react to that? Do you really believe that?'

'I suppose you are referring to Paul Thümmel.'

'Exactly!'

'Allow me to remind you that before Paul Thümmel was a member of the Abwehr, he was a member of the Party – and a founding member at that,' Canaris parried. The fact that Thümmel was a personal friend of Himmler's could be left floating silently in the air for the moment.

'But not a member of the SS,' Heydrich returned. 'He operates exclusively under your authority. If I send his file to the Führer, I should imagine the reaction will be pretty violent.'

'I doubt it, my dear Heydrich – at least not in the way you imagine.' In dangerous waters now, Canaris changed tack. 'That said, who suggested to you that I was not ready to examine, in a constructive way, the problems which have grown up between our two organisations, the Abwehr and the SS?'

'I have never sought to damage you, Admiral. Our friendship, which stretches back a long time, is testimony to that. And as Schellenberg here can witness, I have always defended the Abwehr against criticism.'

'In which case,' said Canaris, seizing the opening, 'release Paul Thümmel. He is an excellent agent who has done magnificent work. Perhaps he has been a bit imprudent with his contacts with the resistance. But he's no traitor.' At this point Canaris played his ace. With an innocent smile he said – the reference to Thümmel's friendship with Himmler unspoken, but unmistakeable: 'I am sure SS Reichsführer Himmler would confirm my opinion. He told me so only last night in Berlin.'

Heydrich visibly stiffened. 'All right, Admiral, we'll release him. But we'll keep him under surveillance. Agree?'

'Agree.'

'But you must know that if we obtain clear proof against him I will report this to the Führer.'

'Of course. Now, in relation to the "frictions" between the Abwehr and the Sicherheitsdienst, can I take it that our friend Schellenberg here will discuss this problem with my senior people and propose a *modus vivendi* to us for approval?'

Heydrich nodded.

It was a big concession, and reflected Canaris's increasingly weak position and Heydrich's rising power. Both men knew that the ensuing talks could only result in increased power for Heydrich's SD at the expense of Canaris's Abwehr.

On 25 November, with Thümmel back in his office, Canaris flew to Madrid, ostensibly for discussions with ministers in the Franco government. The true reason for his visit to Spain was probably as much for solace as for work, for the admiral was again at a very low ebb.

Depressed, probably in part because of what he had seen on the Eastern Front, he was also conscious that he was losing power in Berlin while achieving little towards his goal of stopping, or at least altering the course of, the war. His colleagues in the Tirpitzufer had spotted the change, and were becoming increasingly worried and critical about his management of the Abwehr. He had more or less abandoned all interest in his administrative duties, and his apathy and torpor now extended even to his control of intelligence operations, in which he had previously been very intimately engaged. As the cohesion of the Abwehr started to disintegrate, its department heads began to act more and more autonomously. Hans Oster in particular now pursued his anti-Hitler activities with little reference to his chief.

Despite his depressed mood, Canaris had not lost his irreverent sense of humour. Driving with one of his senior colleagues, Hans Piekenbrock, through winter sunshine from Biarritz to Madrid on 21 November 1941, his open-topped car was held up on a mountain road by a shepherd and a flock of sheep. Canaris, in full admiral's uniform, rose in his seat and solemnly gave the astonished Spanish peasant an exaggerated Nazi salute. Asked why, he replied, 'You can never tell if there isn't a senior officer in there somewhere.'

On this visit to Spain his staff noted that their chief spent even more time than usual finding melancholy comfort in the mixture of gloom, sunlight and splendour of Spanish cathedrals. MI6, watching him closely on the orders of Stewart Menzies, concluded that the Abwehr chief must be 'some kind of Catholic mystic'.

From now on Canaris would seize every opportunity – and even create some of his own – to get back to Spain, where he felt at peace. His favourite place was in Algeciras, on the other side of the bay from Gibraltar. Here, in a house specially set aside for his use,* he cooked Spanish food and ruminated on life with his colleagues from the local Abwehr station. He frequently took incognito trips to the Hotel Reina Cristina, by now well established as a gathering point for the espionage demi-monde from both sides.

He did not go unnoticed.

---

* It is still known in Algeciras as 'La Casa Del Aleman' – The House of the German. (With thanks to Anthony Pitaluga for digging out this information.)

There is a charming account of three British MI6 agents bumping into
him over tea at the Reina Cristina about this time:

We walked through the luxurious, ventilated area of the salon to the
terrace, which at that point was empty – despite the heat of the summer
afternoon. We sat at a table in one corner, from where we could see all
around. We looked across the bay of Gibraltar towards Morocco …
Brian ordered tea and sandwiches … The tea arrived, together with a
variety of sandwiches – tomato, fish pâté – and some pastries. While
Brian was serving the tea, I noticed that the waiter was setting a table for
three, just two tables away from our own. At that point Admiral Canaris
came out on to the terrace, with one man in front of him and another
guarding his back … he made a polite gesture in our direction … Under
the table I kicked Brian, which almost made him spill the milk …
Canaris was a small man with distinguished features. He looked too
kind and friendly, one would think, to be running Germany's secret
services. Donald, totally unaware who the nearby person was, happily
munched his gherkin sandwiches and was enjoying his tea and the view.
He said, with his mouth full, 'Desmond, I can't thank you enough for
talking me into sharing this tea and Sunday with you. It's a holiday! The
sandwiches are a delight and the view from here makes Gibraltar look
like a different world. I'm asking myself why we do what we're doing.' …
I leaned forward and whispered, 'By the way, do you realise who that is
sitting at the table over there?' – 'No,' he said indignantly. 'Why should
I? What matters is how others [the Germans] behave and whether they
are annoying us or not.' I didn't offer a smile in return, because I knew
what I was about to say was going to unsettle him. I leaned forward and
whispered in his ear, 'The person sitting with us is none other than
Admiral Canaris.' Donald was unable to contain himself and spat out
bits of sandwich everywhere. He said, 'Don't talk nonsense Desmond.'
As I didn't want to cause a scene, I said that I was only joking. He
replied with some annoyance, 'Your jokes are in very bad taste. You've
spoilt my enjoyment of the gherkins.' Turning towards the three
gentlemen at the nearby table, he apologised for the incident, saying it
had all been my fault.
      We finished our tea and paid the bill. Brian and I made a polite
gesture towards the Admiral, and walked slowly past his table. He
looked at us and smiled. He knew, no doubt, that we were English, as he
must have heard part of our conversation over his shoulder, but even to

this day I am left with the impression that he knew we were British agents.

Canaris's courtesy on the terrace of the Reina Cristina was deceptive. The truth was, the admiral was growing tired – and tired especially of his constant, futile, dangerous, ambivalent struggle to fight an all-powerful dictator by clandestine means from the heart of his own high command. He asked one of his Balkan experts around this time: 'What do you plan to do after the war?' His friend replied that he hoped to remain in the Balkans. Canaris said, 'We ought to open a little coffee shop in Piraeus harbour. I'll make the coffee, you can wait table. Wouldn't it be great to lead a simple life like that?'

MI6 spotted the change in Canaris: 'It was about this time that we definitely registered that the baddies, that is the SD, were gunning for Canaris,' a senior MI6 man commented after the war. On one level, all this MI6 attention was perfectly normal. Canaris was after all the man who had just succeeded in getting MI6's star agent, A54, out of the hands of the Gestapo. But was there something deeper in Canaris's relationship with London? Canaris himself claimed so, often boasting to trusted friends that he had a direct line to Menzies and Churchill.

If this was so, then MI6 might have been wiser to curb Thümmel's activity, given that his capture had already cost Canaris very dear in terms of political capital and the weakening of his position, not just with Heydrich, but also with Himmler and the rest of the Nazi leadership.

Instead of lying low and getting on with his official job, however, Thümmel tried to persuade his hunter Willi Abendschön that the reason for his relationship with Václav Morávek was that he, Thümmel, was actually an Abwehr double agent, pretending to work for the Czechs in order to unmask their whole network. Abendschön responded by demanding that in that case Thümmel must lead him to Morávek. Thümmel, now dangerously out on a limb, agreed, and an operation was set up. But when the Gestapo raided Morávek's apartment it was empty, save for two wastepaper bins, one marked 'Goebbels' and the other 'Göring'. It was a trademark Morávek joke. On a previous similarly fruitless attempt to catch the phantom Czech resistance leader, Abendschön's men had been confronted by an empty flat adorned with a large notice written, in strict accordance with the Nazi language regulations in Czechoslovakia, first in German and then in Czech. This informed the unwelcome visitors, in the crudest vernacular terms, exactly where they should put themselves.

On this occasion, too, Abendschön found it difficult to see the joke, not least because it was very obvious that he had again been tricked by Thümmel, who had somehow warned off the Czech fugitive.

By now, however, Abendschön had filled in another piece of his jigsaw. In an interrogation of Sigismund Payne Best and Richard Stevens, the two British intelligence officers captured at Venlo, he discovered that a high-level Abwehr officer had visited The Hague in August 1939. There, at a meeting with a Czech intelligence officer called Aloïs Franck, he had warned the West of the impending invasion of Poland. The only person who fitted the bill in terms of position, knowledge and travel schedule was Paul Thümmel. In late January 1942, 'Dr Holm' was arrested for the second time.

Once again, Thümmel made a convincing case to his Gestapo interrogators that he was acting in The Hague as an Abwehr double agent. Once again, in the face of a storm of protest from Berlin, backed up by confirmation of Thümmel's story from Canaris, Abendschön was forced to back down. Once again, Thümmel was released, this time on his 'word of honour' that he would lead the Gestapo to Václav Morávek. Extraordinarily, Thümmel managed to trick Abendschön twice more with arranged meetings that never happened because Morávek had been warned off beforehand. Eventually, on 21 March 1942, Abendschön succeeded in using Thümmel to lure Morávek to a meeting in a small Prague park, where after a shoot-out the Czech chose suicide in preference to being captured by his foes.

Canaris could not save his man a third time. Thümmel was jailed in Prague's Pankrac prison, interrogated and eventually sent to Theresienstadt concentration camp under a final, fifteenth alias, 'Petr Tooman', this time given to him by the Gestapo in order to hide his true identity. Shortly after Thümmel was arrested, Charles and Antoinette Jelinek, the Jewish couple who ran his accommodation address, De Favoriet in The Hague, were taken to Dresden and executed.

While Thümmel and Václav Morávek were playing tricks on Abendschön and the Gestapo all over Prague, negotiations were continuing to sort out the 'new relationship' between the Abwehr and Heydrich's SD. The process was soured by accusations of bad faith on the part of Canaris (who regarded breaking agreements much as he did telling lies – just part of the spy's essential stock in trade). At one stage a petulant Heydrich refused even to meet his opposite number, causing one observer to describe the quarrel between the two men as 'a bit like a lovers' tiff'.

Heydrich, meanwhile, used Thümmel's treachery ruthlessly to exert maximum leverage over his next-door neighbour. He should have reported Thümmel's arrest to Hitler in March, but instead delayed telling the Führer of the Abwehr man's fate until 16 May, the day his negotiations with Canaris were completed, so as to have greater leverage over the Abwehr chief during the negotiations.

The final agreement between the two men consisted of ten points, which would govern future relations between the Abwehr and the SD. Swiftly rechristened 'The Ten Commandments of the Great God of Prague', the document was formally signed off by Heydrich and Canaris at a ceremony in Prague Castle on 18 May. Everyone recognised that the 'Ten Commandments' represented a substantial and irreversible shift of power from the Abwehr and Canaris to Heydrich and the SD.

The ex-naval cadet now had his old patron at his mercy. Heydrich had long suspected that the Abwehr was treacherous, and that Canaris was involved. Now he had the power and the position to find out, and to act.

Heydrich's assassination nine days later, on 27 May 1942, by two émigré Czech British agents at a hairpin bend on his way to work, has become the stuff of legend and film, not just because of the derring-do involved, but also because of the terrible reprisals that followed.

But is there a deeper story behind Operation Anthropoid, which came at the very moment when Wilhelm Canaris, who had done so much to help MI6 and its key agent Paul Thümmel, was under such imminent threat?

Anthropoid was a British SOE (Special Operations Executive) planned and executed operation, not an MI6 one. But as with all SOE operations, it had to be cleared through MI6.

The two-man assassination team who carried out Anthropoid, Josef Gabčik and Jan Kubiš, were parachuted onto a snow-covered meadow east of Prague on the night of 28 December 1941. Making their way to the Czech capital, they met with the local resistance in the city. After a heated exchange of views it was agreed that a signal should be sent to MI6 in London expressing the strong views of the local resistance that Anthropoid would lead to terrible reprisals, and should not be allowed to proceed:

> The assassination would not be of the least value to the Allies and for our nation it would have unforeseeable consequences. It would threaten not only hostages and political prisoners, but also thousands of other lives. The nation would be subject to unheard of reprisals ... Therefore

we beg you to give the order ... for the assassination not to take place.
Danger in delay. Give the order at once.

This signal was shown to, among others, Stewart Menzies, the head of
MI6, whose agreement had to be obtained before Anthropoid could
proceed. Menzies did not respond to Prague's pleas and cancel the operation. Later, the head of Czech intelligence in London would claim: 'I
learned after the war that the British not only did not cancel the operation,
but continued to insist on it being carried out ... I have been told that
Heydrich was on the track of important British agents and that to protect
them it was necessary that Heydrich should die.'

Whether one purpose of Anthropoid was to enable MI6 to save Canaris
we shall never know. But the death of Heydrich was crucial to rescuing the
Abwehr chief from a very deep and possibly fatal hole.

It was not Canaris's only narrow escape from danger about this time.

Sometime in the spring of 1942, on Hitler's instructions Canaris was
ordered to use a Brandenburger special forces team to kidnap or assassinate the French general Henri Giraud.

Operation Gustav, as the plan was known, was the second time Hitler
had demanded that the Abwehr carry out this kind of 'neutralisation'
operation. In November 1940, fearing that the French general Maxime
Weygand might lead a resistance movement against the Vichy government and the German occupation of France, Hitler gave orders for the
general to be killed. Canaris told his senior lieutenants, 'We shall of
course not carry out this order.' Erwin Lahousen had warned French
intelligence through Madeleine Bihet-Richou of the threat to the general's
life, and then, on Canaris's instructions took sufficient steps to convince
them that an operation was under way. The whole matter was quietly
dropped.

In the case of Giraud, however, with the SD now on the alert, it was
much more difficult to sidestep the issue. Giraud, a much bigger target
than Weygand, had been captured at the fall of France and incarcerated
behind the forbidding medieval ramparts of Königstein Castle, near
Dresden. The Allies, not least MI6 (and later President Roosevelt), having
identified him as a potential leader of a liberated France, were keen to get
him out (he had escaped from captivity in World War I). Giraud's escape
from Königstein on 17 April 1942 has attracted much speculation, not
least because it was an almost impossibly romantic affair involving the

general learning German, shaving off his moustache, lowering his sixty-three-year-old, six-foot-four-inch frame on a rope made of twine, wire and bedsheets down the outside of the castle walls, fleeing across Germany in a Tyrolean hat, meeting with British secret agents, miraculously evading search parties sent out to catch him at the Swiss frontier, and finally making it to Vichy France. British intelligence, in the form of at least SOE, was it seems involved in the escape. So, according to the post-war testimony of a senior SD officer in the Paris Gestapo, were the Abwehr and Canaris, though we don't know precisely how.

Following the same course of action as with Weygand, Lahousen warned Madeleine Bihet-Richou of the threat to Giraud's life. Canaris also discussed Hitler's order to kill or kidnap the French general with his key lieutenants. All agreed that this was not a job for the Abwehr: 'It's time … to inform … Herr Hitler that we aren't a murderous organisation like the SD or the SS,' said Hans Piekenbrock. Canaris agreed to arrange for the task to be reassigned to the SS.

On 17 September 1942, Hitler's pliable army glove-puppet, Field Marshal Wilhelm Keitel, called the Tirpitzufer and, in Canaris's absence, demanded to speak to Lahousen. He wanted to know what had happened on the Giraud affair, and reminded Lahousen that Canaris had been instructed to hand the matter over to the SD. Had he done so? And if so, when? Lahousen, who knew very well that Canaris had decided to 'forget' to do this, parried the question by saying the chief was away. Keitel demanded an immediate report on the matter, a copy of which should also be sent to the SD. Coming on top of the Thümmel affair and the Ten Commandments, Canaris was now in real danger. Oster instructed Lahousen to fly immediately to Paris to warn the Abwehr chief.

Canaris, who was at dinner with senior colleagues at the Abwehr's Paris headquarters in the Hôtel Lutetia, was visibly shocked when he heard Lahousen's news. Then, suddenly brightening, he asked to be reminded of the dates of the order to 'deal with' Giraud, the signing of the Ten Commandments, and Heydrich's assassination. When Lahousen recited these, Canaris smiled, raised his glass and said, 'Well, Langer ["Lofty"], is that right? Yes, that is right. Cheers!' What Canaris, full of artifice as ever, had spotted was that Giraud's escape and Hitler's order to kill him had taken place before Canaris's visit to Prague to sign the Ten Commandments. With Heydrich dead and in no position to say otherwise, Canaris told Lahousen to report to Keitel that he had handed the order over to Heydrich when the two had met in Prague, and that he was sure the late and much lamented Reichsprotektor would have swiftly set the wheels in motion before his untimely death.

Reinhard Heydrich was buried with elaborate state honours on 7 June 1942. Wilhelm Canaris openly wept in the front rank of the mourners at the graveside. These were not necessarily crocodile tears, for the admiral was an emotional man, and, like all good spies, perfectly capable of managing two totally contradictory emotions at the same time.

19

Rebound

Defeat in the Battle of Moscow and the United States's entry into the war created just the conditions which the conspirators had long hoped would bring new recruits to their cause. Instead, they faced a new range of obstacles.

The first was the attitude of the Allies.

Even before Pearl Harbor and America's declaration of war, Churchill and Roosevelt had sketched out their vision of the post-war world when their battleships met in the sheltered waters of Placentia Bay, off Newfoundland, in the late summer of 1941. Roosevelt arrived for the meeting on the newly-minted heavy cruiser the USS *Augusta*. Churchill sailed in after a hazardous dash across the Atlantic on the battleship HMS *Prince of Wales*, which, ever the master of theatre, he had insisted should not be repainted, so that she still bore the livid scars of her victory over the *Bismarck* three months previously.

The Atlantic Charter (its official title was 'Joint Declaration by the President and the Prime Minister'), seen by many historians as containing the original seeds of the current NATO alliance, was agreed by the two leaders on 14 August 1941. Along with a commitment to assist each other during the war, it incorporated the first outlines of what would become the architecture of the post-war world, including a carefully drafted clause stipulating that since 'no future peace can be maintained if … armaments continue to be employed by nations which threaten, or may threaten aggression outside of their frontiers, they [the two leaders] believe, pending the establishment of a wider and permanent system of general security, that the disarmament of such nations is essential'. Hitler's propaganda minister Joseph Goebbels seized on this provision, portraying it as meaning that Germany would be forever stripped of her armed forces, a humiliation beyond even the impositions of Versailles.

Ludwig Beck swallowed Goebbels's bait and agonised with two of his resistance colleagues about whether the time for putsches was now over, since it was increasingly likely that, even if Hitler was replaced, a new German government would still not be able to 'obtain an acceptable peace'.

In fact Churchill's position at this stage of the war was much more nuanced. In his briefing to the cabinet on the Atlantic Charter he is recorded as drawing a 'sharp difference' with 1917: 'then we spoke of "the war to end war" ... and of impoverishing them [the Germans] ... Now we look at things differently. We must disarm the Germans ... [but] we now take the view that impoverished nations are bound to be bad neighbours and we wish to see everyone prosperous, including the Germans. In short our aim is to make Germany "fat but impotent"'.

Despite Churchill's good intentions, however, the dynamics of the Alliance now started to work against the possibility of a constructive peace with a post-Hitler Germany.

With the balance of the war shifting in favour of the Allies, Germany's bargaining position weakened. Meanwhile, as victory seemed more and more likely, Allied unity on the conduct of the war began to drift into divisions over how the world would be carved up afterwards. As a consequence, just about the only easy point of agreement at later inter-Allied talks and summits was on how to be more and more beastly to their common enemy.

Other factors also conspired to make it more difficult for Goerdeler, Beck and Canaris to create the space for some kind of peace that did not involve the obliteration and humiliation of their country. The fact that all attempts to re-establish a secret contact between the German resistance and London had, on Churchill's personal instructions, been met with 'absolute silence' only served to reinforce the impression that, come what may, the Allies were determined to punish Germany, even if it got rid of Hitler, rather than making an honourable peace which would shorten the war.

Meanwhile, in the early months of 1942 Hitler returned to the path of victory, with German armies on the Eastern Front scoring some notable early successes. In the Western Desert, too, Rommel's tank columns were sweeping all before them. These triumphs quickly erased the humiliations of the winter defeat before Moscow, causing the weaker-hearted resistants to conclude that this was not the moment; they should once again wait for a more propitious opportunity.

On 5 April, Hitler, seizing the initiative on the Eastern Front, issued Führer Directive No. 41. This called for preparations to start for a new phase of the Russian invasion, Operation Blue, to be launched at the end of June. Hitler's orders swung the axis of the German attack south towards Kharkov, Stalingrad and the Caucasus oilfields. The main burden of operations would now pass from Army Group Centre to Army Group South, whose task was to attack across country perfectly suited to what the German armies did best: manoeuvre battle using armoured columns, backed by close air support to scythe-cut deep into Soviet territory, first outflanking, then surrounding and finally destroying enemy positions one by one.

Very shortly after it was signed off by Hitler in Berlin, Sándor Radó was able to transmit a complete copy of Führer Directive No. 41 to Moscow Centre.

With new German successes on the battlefield and a fresh campaign in prospect, even the more committed in the resistance now began to fall prey to a crippling pessimism about their chances of finding the way to a peace which would enable Germany to survive intact. Phrases such as 'little hope', 'few chances for success' and 'no initial spark' litter their private notes and journals at this time.

Only the irrepressible Carl Goerdeler was immune from this mood of stasis and despondency. He paid a five-day visit to Stockholm on 13 April in an attempt to rebuild a line of contact to London through the Wallenberg brothers and their Enskilda Bank. Goerdeler hoped, in the words of Jacob Wallenberg, 'to get a preliminary peace commitment from the Allies, in case they should succeed in capturing Hitler and overthrowing the Nazi regime'. The Swede was not encouraging: 'I ... tried to make it clear that no preliminary commitments [by the British] could be made ... [and] that [if] he, as a good German patriot, considered that a change of regime was the right thing ... in order to save Germany, [then] he and his friends should try and carry out such a change, regardless of the views that people in London or Washington might take.'

Not long after he returned to Berlin, Goerdeler heard that his eldest and most beloved son, Christian, also a fierce opponent of Hitler, had been killed on the Eastern Front. He declared to a friend that the best memorial to his boy would be to bring to an end the never-ending sacrifice of German youth to the demonic ambitions of Adolf Hitler.

Despite these impediments great and small, some minor victories were scored by the conspirators during this period – and some steps were taken which would prove useful for what was to come.

In a classic Canaris double play, he tipped off the Swedish military attaché in Berlin in February 1942 that 'there were powerful influences at work to persuade Hitler to swallow up Sweden before the summer'. Stockholm immediately announced a rapid mobilisation of troops, enabling Canaris to report to the German general staff that, with Sweden mobilising, an attack on it would be most unwise.

Coup preparations also continued apace during this period.

Over the spring and summer months of 1942, the broad outlines of an ambitious 'grand coup' began to crystallise. This was based around three main 'hubs': the civilian resistance; the army in the field, especially on the Eastern Front; and the Reserve Army in Berlin. The purpose of the grand coup was not just to remove Hitler, but to replace him with a provisional structure capable of governing Germany and negotiating a peace with the Allies. A triumvirate was established between Goerdeler, Beck and von Witzleben, with Goerdeler coordinating the civilian elements of the coup, and Beck and Witzleben, working with Henning von Tresckow, mobilising the German army in the field.

What the conspirators lacked was a senior general in the Reserve Army, whose role in the coup would be to take over the institutions of the Berlin government. Hans Oster solved this problem when in March 1942 he recruited General Friedrich Olbricht, the chief of the General Army Office in the Army High Command, who was also, among other things, the acting commander of the Reserve Army. Bespectacled, punctilious, cautious, religious, cultivated, self-effacing and a holder of the Iron Cross, Olbricht was a brilliant staff officer. He very soon became one of the central figures of the resistance, acting as its chief planning officer and the putative mobiliser of the Reserve Army when the moment came.

With the outline structure for the grand coup now in place, Ludwig Beck was formally nominated as its overall leader, and his villa in Goethestrasse declared as its headquarters.

Over this period Canaris, sunk in one of his periodic moods of depression and pessimism, became increasingly separated from the Abwehr and the main group of plotters. This gave Hans Oster even more space to act autonomously as what one observer called 'the technical centre of the anti-Hitler resistance'. Hans Bernd Gisevius put it more graphically: 'He once described to me in one sentence his own conception of his function within the resistance movement. He was standing at his desk looking down pensively at the four or five telephones whose secret circuits connected him with the most diverse authorities. "This is what I am," he said. "I facilitate communications for everyone, everywhere."'

'Nevertheless,' Gisevius continued, 'he was far more than a human switch-board and his work went beyond those telephone conversations, in which he repeatedly gave brusque warnings to generals and field marshals in their distant headquarters. He was the driving force, not merely the tech-nician of the opposition.'

To assist him in this role Oster could call on the entire communications network of the Abwehr: 'The so-called "A-net" [independent secure tele-phone and teleprinter lines, which were at the disposal of the Abwehr only] ensured that the "conspirators" could transmit news and orders,' one observer noted, adding: 'The Abwehr organisation was the nerve centre from which lines led to the General Staff, to General von Witzleben ... to Schacht, to Goerdeler, to Beck ... to Weizsäcker and through him to a group of diplomats abroad.'

These grand and ambitious plans would take time to mature. For the moment, all attempts to remove Hitler would have to rely on individual endeavour.

At first, Henning von Tresckow wondered whether the simplest way would not be for him just to shoot the Führer with a pistol. Later he went in search of a 'particularly powerful explosive' and a 'totally reliable, completely silent fuse' with which to construct a bomb. Together with two co-conspirators, von Tresckow tried out a dozen or so different explosive charges in the summer water-meadows along the banks of the Dnieper. They finally settled on British plastic explosives and 'time pencil' detona-tors captured from the French resistance.

The British 'time pencil' detonator was silent, and looked, in the words of a British wartime saboteur, 'a bit like a biro pen. It was a glass tube with a spring-loaded striker [above a percussion cap] held in place by a copper wire. At the top was a glass phial containing acid which you squeezed gently to break. The acid would eat through the wire and release the striker. Obviously, the thicker the wire the longer the delay before the striker was triggered. [The pencils] were colour coded according to the [time delay] of the fuse.'

In the month before the German armies launched their attack towards the Caucasus, there was a flurry of peacemaking overtures. George Bell, the bishop of Chichester, met Dietrich Bonhoeffer in Stockholm. The two, who had known each other before the war, discussed a peace plan drawn up by the Kreisau Circle. In Bell's report to foreign secretary Anthony Eden he included one particular point on which the Germans sought clar-ity: would the Allies' hard line on Germany be different if Hitler were got rid of? Eden replied that he was 'satisfied that it is not in the national interest to provide an answer of any kind' to this question.

The English Church nevertheless went on investigating peace possibilities with its German counterparts until, on 17 July 1942, with the new German assault on Russia in full swing, Eden shut the process down on the grounds that if the Church's approaches came to light, they would exacerbate already strained Anglo–Soviet relations. It may be a coincidence that it was at exactly this time that heavy Allied bombing raids started on the residential areas of German cities, in the belief that this was a surer way to get the German people to revolt than peace talks and shadowy plans for putsches which never seemed to materialise. But, as history records, bombing Berlin, like bombing London, stiffened popular resistance rather than undermining it.

Also around this time, a tentative peace approach was made to Washington through an American journalist in Berlin. This too was rejected, on the grounds that it put the US government 'in an awkward position'.

And there this round of peace initiatives, like all the others before it, dribbled away into the sand.

In June 1942 Sándor Radó sent Moscow Centre another ten-page coded message giving further details of the impending German assault south towards the Caucasus. Radó's message confirmed information already obtained by the Russians from documents and maps recovered from a reconnaissance plane* shot down over Kharkov on the morning of 19 June, nine days before the German attack was due to be launched.

Once again, however, Stalin's paranoia about deception won the day. Convinced that the German attack would still come against Moscow, he refused to redeploy his troops south to meet the threat. Once again the Russians were caught wrongfooted. Once again there were glory days for the Wehrmacht and a succession of early and astonishing victories. Once again the Russians fell back in disarray. Once again the German spring extended and the Russian one compressed.

Once again Alexander Foote, bent over his radio in Lausanne, and the Hamels above their shop in Geneva, now joined by Margrit Bolli in a flat

---

* Its passenger was Major Joachim Reichel, chief of operations of the 23rd Panzer Division.

on the eastern bank of Lake Geneva, were busy all night coding and transmitting a flood of messages to Moscow.

In July, relations between London and Moscow began to sour because of a row over the insecurity of Russian codes. As a result, the British significantly reduced the number of Ultra decrypts they shared with the Soviets. A month later, in a series of August raids across Western Europe, the Gestapo smashed the entire *Rote Kapelle* Soviet spy ring, leaving only its small outpost, the Dora Ring in Geneva. With these two crucial intelligence sources shut down, the Dora Ring's reports became by far Moscow's most important foreign window on German plans and intentions on the Eastern Front. Moscow Centre, reflecting Stalin's fear of a deception ploy, began to demand that Radó should press Roessler to reveal his sources. Roessler steadfastly refused.

Perhaps one of the reasons for his reluctance to reveal his sources was that at this time information from deep in Germany was flooding into Switzerland along several channels, and from several apparently different spies. The Polish spy-master Sczcęsny Chojnacki had an exceptional agent with extensive contacts in Germany who was supplying very similar information to that provided by Roessler. Other couriers were bringing intelligence to Gisevius from Berlin. The British too had their sources, as did the Swiss through Max Waibel and his Viking Line (by now just another codename for Hans Oster). Though each of these lines served different customers through different people – and some would have had a few independent sources of their own – tracing them back to their origins, it is remarkable how often the names Goerdeler, Oster and Beck appear as the primary sources of much of the most important information.

We will probably never know exactly how all this worked. But the most likely case is that the anti-Hitler conspirators used several channels – possibly even in a coordinated manner – to get information through to the Allies. And the Allies in Switzerland (or at least the main players) indulged in a degree of intelligence sharing, including, where it was useful to the Allied cause, sending information about what was happening on the Eastern Front through Roessler and the Dora Ring to Moscow.

We know that Swiss intelligence cooperated closely with other Allied intelligence agencies, and that its Captain Max Waibel was key to this process. More worryingly, by late 1941 Himmler's RSHA knew this too. In the autumn of that year the Germans mounted a successful operation on the office of the US military attaché in Bern, Barnwell Legge. Using a disgruntled Swiss employee at the US legation in the Swiss capital, undestroyed sheets of used carbon paper were recovered from Legge's wastepaper basket. These provided a cornucopia of information, including intelligence which could only have come from the very highest sources in Berlin, and which, though Himmler's men did not know it, bore a striking resemblance to the information being provided by Roessler and other agents to the Swiss and the British. After the operation came to an end through the accidental discovery of the leak in March 1942, Germany made a strong diplomatic protest to Switzerland about the involvement of Max Waibel in passing Swiss intelligence to Allied nations. As a result Waibel was removed from his position as head of the Swiss German section and reappointed to be the official liaison officer between the Swiss, the British and the Americans – which can hardly have been the outcome the SD had hoped for. It seems that, from as early as 1941 to the end of the war, a semi-formal intelligence 'clearing house' system was established to pass information between the Allies and their Swiss hosts.

Throughout the summer, coded messages containing German battle plans provided by Roessler streamed out all night from the *Rote Drei*'s hidden rooftop aerials. It is estimated that from 1941 to 1943 the Dora Ring and its three radio operators sent in all around 5,500 clandestine messages to Moscow Centre. But it was in the months from May 1942 to May 1943 that the *Rote Drei* would make the contribution to Soviet victory on the Eastern Front which would be the basis of the Russian claim that the Dora Ring was one of the most successful spy rings in intelligence history. What Radó's team gave Moscow was a regular, unbroken supply of high-level, real-time information on German intentions and battle plans which Moscow used first to slow up and then to destroy the German thrust. The *Rote Drei* operators were often able to get German battle plans to Moscow even before the German generals on the front line received them. Chief of staff Halder complained after the war, 'Almost every offensive operation of ours was betrayed to the enemy, even before it appeared on my desk.'

There has been much puzzlement about how exactly the Dora Ring was able to get its information so quickly – occasionally, according to some claims, within twenty-four hours of a decision being made in Berlin. Rudolf Roessler, speaking after the war, provided the answer. The information was sent by secure Abwehr channels to its station in Milan, and thence by courier to Chiasso, at the southernmost tip of Switzerland near Lake Como. From there it travelled by Swiss railway express post to

Lucerne, where Roessler himself picked it up in the late evening from the post office in the station concourse.

In addition, Hans Bernd Gisevius in Zürich had access, at least twice and sometimes three times a week, to a diplomatic pouch couriered from the Berlin Foreign Office to the German legation in Bern. Hans Oster also introduced a special diplomatic pouch to which only he and Gisevius had access. This was despatched every other day from Wehrmacht headquarters in Bendlerstrasse to the German legation in Bern. For very urgent messages there was always the special Abwehr encrypted telephone lines, which were used to communicate between all the key plotters and must therefore have been secure even from eavesdropping by Himmler's SS.

With the German assault through the southern steppes of Russia gathering pace and the ether around southern Switzerland humming with nightly shortwave radio traffic, the SS listening stations in Karlsruhe, Munich and Stuttgart stepped up their attempts to get a more precise idea of where the signals were coming from. By the late spring of 1942 they had managed to decipher some scraps of the *Rote Drei*'s coded messages, and had identified two wireless transmitters in Geneva and one in Lausanne. Several attempts were made by Berlin to alert the Swiss to the fact that their supposedly neutral country was being used by spies with clandestine radios. When this produced no effect, the SS took matters into its own hands and started sending agents into Switzerland to hunt out the radios and their operators. But these would take time to get into place.

Meanwhile, as with the first phase of Barbarossa, the start of the German sweep south-east down the corridor between the Don and Volga rivers and the Black Sea went well. As with Barbarossa, the forward tank columns soon charged beyond the reach of their logistics and had to stop for the supply lines to catch up. As with Barbarossa, Hitler made difficult logistics worse by splitting his attacking forces into two columns, one heading for the Caucasus and the other for Stalingrad. As with Barbarossa, after battling through constant Russian counterattacks, the Germans finally reached their destination. On 12 September 1942, the Sixth Army entered Stalingrad. That was as far as it got. In the terrible, frozen, meatgrinder of a three-month siege which followed, Hitler's reputation, Germany's pride and its entire Sixth Army would be destroyed.

20

Codes and Contacts

Sometime in mid-September 1942, Claude Arnould, alias 'Colonel Ollivier',* an MI6 agent in Paris, received a most unusual message from London instructing him to go to a certain spot in the Forest of Fontainebleau on the morning of 18 September and make a report on what happened when he got there.

On the appointed day, Arnould, dressed in workman's blue overalls and carrying a labourer's lunchbag containing bread, cheese and the traditional litre of wine, went as instructed to Fontainebleau. The leaves in the forest were already turning, and the dew lay heavy on damp woodland paths. In any other circumstances, this would have been a good day for picking mushrooms. Arnould did not have to wait long before a Citroën came bumping towards him down the forest track. The car drew to a halt alongside him, and a small man with white hair and light-blue eyes stepped out, accompanied by a very large bodyguard.

To Arnould's stupefaction, the man said in perfect French, 'I am Admiral Canaris. What are your instructions?'

'To come here, to listen and to report back.'

The two men spoke for over an hour and a half. We do not have a detailed account of their conversation, but from the information recounted by Arnould after the war, Canaris, who made it clear that he knew the Frenchman was an MI6 agent, went to some lengths to stress that 'he was determined and decided: he wished to work with the "Anglo-Saxon allies" against the Nazi regime who had brought such terrible pain and suffering to his country'. As the two men parted, the admiral said, 'We are working together for the same ideals.'

---

* Arnould, an ex-French army officer, had escaped to London after the fall of France. He was infiltrated back into his homeland charged with helping to raise the resistance in France as head of MI6's Jade-Amicol network.

We have frustratingly little further information about this puzzling meeting, the first details of which were recounted by Arnould during his final illness, thirty-two years after the event.

Some presumptions, however, can reasonably be made. First, it is clear from the chronology that it was Canaris who asked for this meeting. Second, one of his purposes seems to have been to reassure London that he was on its side – though it is perplexing that he had to find yet another channel to assure them of this, given that he already had plenty through which he could have done so (not least Halina Szymańska in Bern). It may be that he was passing his message through French channels as much to General de Gaulle's people in London as to MI6.

There is a further possibility. It was during this three-day trip to attend a meeting in Paris (one of a regular series Canaris held with his Abwehr station heads) that the admiral was warned by Erwin Lahousen that his failure to carry out Hitler's orders for the disposal of General Giraud was about to be uncovered. It may be that one purpose of the strange meeting in the Forest of Fontainebleau was to warn London of Canaris's increasingly precarious position.

A final speculation needs also to be considered. We know that in the early winter of 1942 Canaris started sending messages to his opposite number, Stewart Menzies, that he would like to arrange a personal meeting between the two of them. Was this an early pre-echo of that approach?

Wilhelm Canaris was only too aware that, following the assassination of Reinhard Heydrich and the exposure of Paul Thümmel, events were now moving decisively in favour of Himmler and the Sicherheitsdienst, at the expense of Canaris and the Abwehr. The Abwehr had already lost its monopoly of counter-espionage to the SD, and the SD leadership, dominated by fanatical Nazis, now made it abundantly clear that their intention was to further undermine and then take over the Tirpitzufer's central role as the Wehrmacht's intelligence arm and Germany's main foreign spy service. Canaris knew that his room for autonomous action to undermine Hitler's intentions was about to become increasingly limited. As one close observer put it, Canaris was 'in the process of losing his last battle to the Nazi revolution'. If he was to change the course of the war, it would have to be done soon.

The anti-Hitler conspirators suffered a further blow on 24 September 1942, when after a series of furious rows with Hitler over the conduct of the war in southern Russia, Franz Halder was dismissed from his position as chief of staff of the army. Coming on top of the removal six months previously of Erwin von Witzleben, who had been sacked while in hospital, the loss of Halder was a grievous setback. Both men had been stalwart and reliable conspirators with access to the high command of the army, and Witzleben would continue to play a central role in the plots and planning to come. Their removal meant that, of the early plotters in high positions in Berlin, only Wilhelm Canaris now remained on active duty.

With the 'greybeards' of the conspiracy now being winnowed out of the high command, the young Turks began to make their presence more widely felt.

In October 1942 a young staff officer spoke out at a meeting at army headquarters in the Ukraine about the 'disastrous course of German policy in the east', and the Wehrmacht's 'carpet-layers with the rank of general'. His criticisms did not come as a surprise – he had previously made his views starkly clear. Asked by a senior commander what to do about the atrocities ordered by Hitler in Russia, he had replied laconically, 'Kill him.' Another superior, who suggested that Hitler might change his policies if he knew the truth, was roundly told, 'The point is no longer to tell him the truth, but to get rid of him.' Everyone who came in contact with him knew of the anger of Colonel Claus Schenk von Stauffenberg. In due course he would turn this anger into action. But not yet.

In the late autumn, Henning von Tresckow travelled from his headquarters in Smolensk to Berlin, where he met Olbricht, Oster and Goerdeler to settle details for the grand coup. Olbricht, who had by now taken full charge of the planning process, declared that it would take at least eight weeks to complete the coup arrangements, including recruiting reliable groups who would seize power not just in Berlin, but also simultaneously in Cologne, Munich, Paris and Vienna. Von Tresckow was more impatient, and wanted to bring the operation forward. There was 'not a day to lose ... Action should be taken as quickly as possible. No initial spark can be expected to come from the field marshals. They'll only follow an order,' he declared. But Olbricht stuck to his guns: the earliest date for a properly planned putsch, he insisted, was March 1943. Events would prove von Tresckow's impatience more justified than Olbricht's desire to mount the perfect coup.

In November, Goerdeler paid a reciprocal visit to Smolensk. Travelling under the cover of Bosch business and with supporting travel documents supplied by Oster, he made the hazardous eight-day journey deep into the battle zone to Army Group Centre's headquarters. Here he met von Tresckow and Field Marshal Günther von Kluge, the new commander-in-chief of Army Group Centre. In a two-hour conversation the three men discussed and agreed the role of Army Group Centre when the grand coup was finally launched.

It was about this time that news of a new and even more unimaginable horror began to seep out of Germany. On 17 July 1942 Himmler went to Auschwitz to witness personally the gassing of 449 Jews from Holland. Twelve days later, Eduard Schulte, one of the Polish spy-master Szczęsny Chojnacki's key sources in Germany,* obtained what appears to be the first information of Hitler's 'Final Solution' calling for the total extermination of Europe's Jewish population. The substance of Schulte's report was passed to 'leading Jewish institutions in America [because only] they had sufficient influence to sound the tocsin and to induce the American and the British governments to take some action'. In October, the first intelligence of the Auschwitz extermination programme was passed by Schulte to the World Jewish Congress. And so the wider world found out that the Holocaust had begun.

The effects of Hitler's new policy were not confined to extermination camps. In early October 1942 a highly-decorated twenty-three-year-old Wehrmacht captain called Axel von dem Bussche-Streithorst witnessed the mass execution of Jews at Dubno airfield in the Ukraine. In a report, he wrote: 'The residents of the Jewish quarter, 2,000 to 3,000 people, were made to stand in long lines in front of mass graves, to be killed one by one by shots in the base of the neck. On the following day I was in the ghetto. They began a manhunt after the few who had managed to hide. A woman literally kneeled in front of me and begged for her life, but there was nothing I could do for her.'

Von dem Bussche never recovered from his experience. A previous supporter of Hitler, he commented to friends after the horror that there were only three possible ways for an honourable officer to react: 'to die in battle, to desert or to rebel'. In due course, Claus Stauffenberg would give the young captain the opportunity to make his choice.

Erwin Lahousen too visited the Russian Front that October, and was equally shocked by what he saw, describing the executions in graphic detail to Madeleine Bihet-Richou. But now, alongside these horrors, Lahousen was also witness to another kind of Calvary – the suffering of the German soldiers besieged in Stalingrad.

---

* Schulte, a prominent German industrialist, provided important information to a number of Allied intelligence officers, mostly in Switzerland.

Lahousen's job at the front was to oversee the censorship of soldiers' correspondence to their families and loved ones. Any letters (and there were many) that spoke of misery, poor conditions or the hopelessness of what they were doing were summarily burnt on the spot. But Lahousen, as a soldier, knew well enough that the destroyed letters represented the true state of German morale on the Eastern Front. With Lahousen on the edge of depression, Madeleine worried that 'He seemed to want to finish it all, either by going to the front to be killed, or by doing it himself.'

In November 1942 Hitler suffered three body blows which, in a single month, altered the entire balance of the war. On the 8th, the US-led Operation Torch caught the Germans completely by surprise by seizing the North African ports of Oran, Casablanca and Algiers. Nine days later, on the 17th, for the first time since the war began the church bells of England pealed out to announce General Bernard Montgomery's decisive victory over Rommel's forces at El Alamein. And two days after that, on the 19th, in a ferocious snowstorm, two Soviet army groups launched their offensive on German positions in Stalingrad.

By this time the Dora Ring and its three *Rote Drei* operators were again at full stretch and under huge pressure from Moscow Centre, especially for tactical information on German positions and intentions in Stalingrad.

8 October, Director to Dora for Sissy [Rachel Duebendorfer]: You must learn a code and receive additional instruction ... Your new people ... are not bad workers, but one must always control them and keep them busy.

21 October, Director to Radó: Prepare emergency meeting points for [your key agents] so that if you are temporarily prevented from working these they can remain in contact with us [through others in the Dora Ring]. Explain to Jim [Alexander Foote] what is happening ... take utmost care at meetings and in passing on telegrams. Dear Dora, please bear in mind that the work of your organisation is more important than ever. You must do everything to continue the work.

Early November, Dora to Moscow: South-east of Stalingrad, in a semi-desert and uninhabited area known as 'The Black Fields', the German flank has been left largely unprotected because the German army high command estimates that the Soviet army would not be able to concentrate troops in this area.

On 23 November Russian troops, attacking through 'the Black Fields' between Lakes Barmantsak and Tsatsa, finally closed the ring and surrounded the German Sixth Army.

19 December, Moscow to Radó: In addition to taking measures to safeguard the organisation as a whole, do everything you can to continue working. It is precisely now that it is very important … Organise parallel contacts between Sissy [Duebendorfer] and Maude [Olga Hamel] so that information is forwarded come what may. I want calm, and clear and circumspect decisions. Director

22 December, Moscow to Radó: Make sure that Jim [Foote] and the wireless operators are able to rest despite their daily work. Their nerves have to be protected for the demanding work. Give your wife New Year's presents …

Desperate efforts were made to send in a relieving force to rescue the German Sixth Army besieged in Stalingrad. But all of them failed. The attempt was finally abandoned two days before Christmas. Hitler refused to allow a breakout, ordering his troops to hold on to the last man and the last bullet. They resisted until 2 February 1943, when the remaining German forces capitulated. Among those captured were twenty-two generals and 91,000 troops, most of whom were wounded, starving, emaciated and sick. They were all that was left of the 265,000 men of the German Sixth Army. Of the 90,000 who surrendered, only six thousand returned from captivity.

Thanks to the intelligence from Roessler's high-level sources in the Tirpitzufer, which Swiss intelligence had arranged to be fed through to the Dora Ring, Sándor Radò and his *Rote Drei* operators had made a major, perhaps even decisive, contribution to the Russian victory at Stalingrad.

Moscow Centre was understandably pleased, not least because it knew that Dora's potential to play a major part in the crucial battles still to come was considerable. But it was not alone in understanding this. The SD listening stations around Switzerland were by now locked onto the *Rote Drei's* nightly transmissions, which they were meticulously recording, although their cryptographers could not yet break the codes. Finally, in December 1942, at the height of the battle for Stalingrad, the SD's decoders got a lucky break and succeeded in decrypting two *Rote Drei* messages. Both related to German military dispositions and plans on the Eastern Front, and were alarmingly accurate and detailed.

The problem for the Germans, however, was that the Russians and their *Rote Drei* operators used a 'book cipher'. This kind of code is based on the text in a book, which is used by the coder and decoder as the cipher's source (Alexander Foote's codebook was the 1938 edition of *The Statistical Handbook for Foreign Trade*, published by His Majesty's Stationery Office in London). The coder finds a letter or word in the text corresponding to the one he or she wants to encode, and identifies it by the number of the page, the line of the text and the position of the word or letter. So, for instance, the number 431827 could be deciphered by looking in the source book to find the letter which appears on page 43, line 18, letter 27 counting from the left. Without knowing the source book which the *Rote Drei* operators and Moscow Centre were using, their coded messages could only be broken one at a time, and by an extremely long and laborious process. But if the German codebreakers could find the source book, they could read all the *Rote Drei* messages as quickly and easily as Moscow Centre. Finding the source book, however, could not be accomplished from a distance – it had to be done by an infiltration agent on the ground.

Around the end of 1942, at about the same time that Himmler's SD began sending agents into Switzerland to track down the *Rote Drei*, one of the civilian wireless operators at Geneva airport on the eastern edge of the city, having nothing to do, was idly twiddling the dial on his set, looking for something of interest to listen to (BBC foreign broadcasts also used shortwave). Suddenly he picked up a stream of strong signal-strength Morse transmission coming from somewhere in the city. The Morse 'hand' was fast and competent, but the wireless procedure was clearly that of an amateur radio operator who was transmitting, most unusually, in five-figure groups of code. Since the Swiss had banned all amateur transmissions at the beginning of the war, the airport operator noted the frequency and call-sign of the station and reported it to the authorities. The Swiss army and police investigated and identified, it appears, two unusual amateur radios operating in Geneva, and another similar nightly transmission streaming out from the area of Lausanne. And there the matter rested. Nothing was done. The Dora Ring continued to operate just as before. Perhaps this was no more than uncharacteristic Swiss inefficiency. More likely, the investigators did not discover anything which Swiss intelligence did not already know of and which it was perfectly content – for the time being – to see continue.

For the moment the *Rote Drei* were safe – but for how long?

21

Of Spies and Spy Chiefs

On 7 November 1942, at about the same time that the first SD hunter arrived in Geneva seeking out the *Rote Drei*, a rather crumpled, pipe-smoking traveller arrived at the French–Swiss frontier at Annemasse, just outside the city.

The new arrival had the air of a favourite uncle, and carried a single suitcase containing two travel-worn suits, some shirts, a small collection of bow ties and a $10,000 letter of credit. Flying from Florida to Lisbon at the end of October in a Pan American Airways Boeing 314 flying boat, he had passed low over a vast armada of American troopships heading for the North African coast. From Lisbon the traveller made his way by train across Spain and Vichy France, trying to look as inconspicuous as possible. At the Franco–Swiss frontier he discovered that Marshal Pétain, the Vichy French leader, had just ordered all British and American travellers to be detained. Attempting to slip onto a train for Geneva, he was stopped by a Gestapo official who confiscated his American passport. But, resourceful as ever, he managed to persuade (or bribe?) a sympathetic French frontier official to smuggle him onto the train and over the border while the Gestapo man was having his habitual lunch and glass of red wine at a local café.

The following day, the traveller finally made it to Bern. He had cut it fine. Two days later, following the surprise Allied landings in North Africa, German tanks smashed aside the barriers on France's internal border and invaded Vichy territory. With all France under German occupation, Switzerland was now entirely surrounded by Axis territory.

Allen Welsh Dulles was tall, with a frame which betrayed a podginess not uncommon to forty-nine-year-olds. Fluent in French and German, he had receding dark hair parted in the middle, steel-rimmed glasses, blue-grey eyes, a strangely cheerful face, a moustache more suited to a British colonel, a booming laugh and a trenchcoat which bulged with crumpled newspapers like an overstuffed eiderdown. Dulles's official title was substantial and impressive: 'Assistant to the Envoy Extraordinary and Minister Plenipotentiary of the USA at Bern, Switzerland'. This string of verbiage did not disguise what everyone in Bern knew very well, and Dulles himself took no trouble to hide. The fact that he was in reality a spy would not have been more obvious if he had had the word emblazoned in capital letters and picked out in neon lights on his forehead.

Born in New York State, educated at Princeton and a lawyer by profession, this was not Dulles's first espionage expedition in Switzerland. He had served in the American legation in the Swiss capital during the First World War. During that period he had famously turned down a request for a meeting with a young Russian firebrand called Vladimir Ilyich Ulyanov – better known to history as Lenin – in order to keep a tennis appointment. Afterwards, and right through until he was forced to resign as head of the CIA by President John F. Kennedy after the 1961 Bay of Pigs fiasco, Dulles would insist that anyone who 'walked through his door' offering intelligence should be accorded at least one interview for their pains.

Dulles set up shop in an imposing Swiss mansion with splendid views of the Bernese Oberland and a back door leading out onto a south-facing terrace which looked vertiginously down over sixty metres to the Aare river and its lively weir, from which the sound of tumbling water wafted up on summer nights and still winter evenings. Below the upper terrace of the Dulles mansion were two further terraces containing vines and vegetable plots, accessed by a network of steps and hidden paths which provided perfect cover for after-dark visitors. Herrengasse 23, situated less than half a kilometre from the much more modest British legation, and within touching distance of Bern city centre and the cathedral, was, in short, the ideal spot for a senior spy-master who took himself seriously and expected others to do so too.

Dulles's first act on his return to Bern was to have the lightbulbs removed from the small cobbled square in front of his house so as to make it easier for the surreptitious to come and go. His second was to hire a butler, a chef and a maid. His third was to leak to the local paper that he was back in town and looking for spies. There was not much of the clandestine about Allen Dulles.

All the flotsam and jetsam of the Swiss spying world now washed up at Herrengasse 23, 'bringing to my door', Dulles cheerfully admitted, 'purveyors of information, volunteers and adventurers of every sort, professional and amateur spies, good and bad'. Soon, with United States's largesse at

Dulles's disposal, the price of intelligence titbits began to rise sharply on the Swiss market.

Dulles, who had a reputation for indiscriminate enthusiasm and prolixity, began passing all he received – good, bad and indifferent – in long rambling telegrams to Washington, earning a rebuke from OSS head, General 'Wild Bill' Donovan:

> It has been requested of us to inform you that: All news from Bern these days is being discounted for 100% … Switzerland is an ideal location for plants, tendentious intelligence and peace feelers [where] no details are given.

Along with the dross making its way to Dulles's unlit front door, however, there were also some real nuggets of gold.

These included the ex-minister of economics and president of the Reichsbank, Hjalmar Schacht; a clerk in the German Foreign Office whom the British had turned down as an agent; and, from January 1943, Hans Bernd Gisevius, whom Dulles sardonically nicknamed 'Tiny'. Gisevius had by this time fallen out with the British in Bern, who he found suspicious and arrogant, and much preferred fireside chats in Dulles's dimly-lit study at Herrengasse 23, where the American spy-master alternately pulled on his pipe and pontificated on the world at large.

Allen Dulles may have been an unconventional spy, but he was an effective one, and soon had networks extending deep into Germany and the occupied countries of Europe which rivalled those of the British and Swiss. It was not long before he was welcomed to the Bern intelligence 'club' run by the British (whose codename for the new arrival was 'F.D.W. Brown esq.') and the Swiss. This was not just because he was an American, but also because of the 'product' he brought to the table. Not long after his arrival, Dulles was already exchanging intelligence, including from Rudolf Roessler, at weekly meetings with Swiss intelligence's Hans Hausamann at the home of a Zürich-based publisher.

While Dulles was settling in to Herrengasse 23 and his new role, MI6 in London was also dealing with an unconventional intelligence approach.

This may all have begun with Stalin, who in mid-October 1942 used some words in a speech which seemed to hint at the possibility of a secret peace deal between Germany and Russia. Ribbentrop, probably tempted by the prospect of a peace which would cement German territorial gains in the Ukraine, picked up on Stalin's words. On 2 December 1942, with the

German Sixth Army newly besieged in the bitter cold of Stalingrad, he sent one of his agents to Stockholm to probe Soviet intentions. Although Ribbentrop's instructions were to keep Canaris ignorant of the approach, he almost certainly got to know of it through one of his agents. The British also picked up on the secret discussions through Ultra decrypts.

Soon, other straws in the wind lent substance to the possibility that Ribbentrop's play was serious. Himmler was said to be in favour; the tone of Goebbels's propaganda attacks on Russia had softened noticeably; there were whispers of something afoot between Germany and Russia from Japanese diplomats in Turkey. Furthermore, as Ribbentrop knew very well, relations between Stalin and the Western Allies were going through a particularly bad patch, with the Russian leader accusing Roosevelt and Churchill of doing too little to help Russia defeat the German invaders, but just enough to help hold them at bay, while bleeding to death in the process.

All this fed Churchill's recurring nightmare that Stalin and Hitler would suddenly flip back to the Molotov–Ribbentrop Pact which had so shocked the world when it was announced just a few days before the start of the war. The strategist in Churchill understood very well that Germany's fulcrum position in Europe meant that if Hitler was unable to go it alone, he only had two strategic options to choose from: combine with the West against Russia, or with Russia against the West. If he chose the latter, he could close down the Eastern Front and turn his full might back on Britain before the United Sates had time to get fully engaged in the war. For Churchill and Roosevelt, keeping Stalin in the Alliance was the most important war aim at this point in the conflict.

Canaris, who shared Churchill's fears about what was going on in Stockholm, sensed an opportunity, and started to consider how new feelers could be put out to try to establish contact with Stewart Menzies at MI6.

The Abwehr chief's concerns about a Russo–German rapprochement were, however, different from those of London. They sprang from a deep split among the key anti-Hitler resistants about their vision of Germany after the war.

One group, known as the 'Easterners', who included a number of the army young Turks, saw Germany reverting to its traditional land-based nineteenth-century strategy of alliances with Russia. Among the key Easterners was the ex-German ambassador to Moscow, Friedrich-Werner Graf von der Schulenburg, who at the end of 1942 (coincidentally the same time as the Ribbentrop probe was in progress) even went so far as to volunteer to be smuggled across the Eastern Front into Soviet-held territory in order to make a personal peace appeal to Stalin. The other, stronger group, known as the 'Westerners', included Canaris, Beck, Goerdeler and most of the civilian-dominated Kreisau Circle. For them, the only safe future for a post-war Germany lay in membership of a united community of liberal Western European democratic nations. The best way to ensure a safe post-Hitler peace without national destruction, the Westerners believed, was to seek a pact with the Western Allies in order to protect Germany from the aggressive intentions of Stalin.

That was Canaris's dream. But with his power waning, he needed to act fast.

In November 1942 Carl Goerdeler made another visit to the Wallenbergs in Stockholm, where he again sought reassurance from London that it would respond positively if Hitler was removed in a putsch. Again, Jacob Wallenberg warned him: 'You are a good patriot. You are fighting for the German common weal. You must not ask the enemy what he wants. He cannot give you a fair answer. Everyone knows you want peace, but not at the price of unconditional surrender. Ask yourself what would happen if you were in power. Do you think that a Beck/Goerdeler government has any more chance of avoiding an unconditional surrender than a Hitler one? If your overtures were rejected, your government would be less able than Hitler's to fight on and win an honourable peace.' Goerdeler predictably ignored the advice, believing that he had no option but to continue, even against the odds, in his efforts to remove Hitler as the necessary prelude to a peace with the West.

At around the time Carl Goerdeler was seeking to make contact with London through Stockholm, Canaris's men in Turkey picked up encouraging hints that the United States, 'in order to ensure Germany is not "Bolshevised" … [was] thinking of reaching an agreement with [Germany] against Russia before she is completely routed and [in order to rebuild] her economic position'. This was what Canaris was waiting for. The time had come to act.

Now MI6 too began picking up unmistakeable messages from sundry sources, especially on the Iberian peninsula,* that Canaris was seeking a

---

* MI6's chief sources included Baron Oswald von Hoyningen-Huene, the German ambassador to Portugal (his mother was English); Commander Don Gomez-Beare, the British naval attaché in Madrid; Juan March; Otto John, the Lufthansa lawyer in Madrid; Admiral Godfrey of British naval intelligence; and apparently his assistant, the author Ian Fleming.

personal meeting on neutral ground with Menzies. The young historian
Hugh Trevor-Roper, who worked as an MI6 analyst, commented after the
war on a paper produced in late 1942: 'Admiral Canaris himself at that
time was making repeated journeys to Spain and had indicated a willingness to treat with us; he would even welcome a meeting with his opposite
number, "C" [Menzies]. These conclusions were duly formulated and the
final document was submitted for security clearance to Philby … [but]
Philby absolutely forbade the circulation of the report.'

Kim Philby was at the time the head of the MI6 section dealing with
Spain and Portugal, while also, as a Russian spy, passing on MI6 secrets to
his handler at the Soviet embassy in London. This was not the only time
that Philby tried to frustrate – or worse – the Abwehr chief. In late
November 1943 he proposed a plan to assassinate Canaris on one of his
journeys through Spain. Menzies firmly rejected the plan with a curt
minute written in green ink – the colour reserved for 'C' in Whitehall: 'I
want no action whatsoever taken against the Admiral.'

In both these matters – and probably many others that we do not know
of – it seems very likely that Philby was doing his Russian masters' bidding.
As he himself admitted after his defection to Moscow in 1963, he considered that his most important espionage achievement during World War II
was disrupting Abwehr attempts to broker a separate peace between
Germany and Britain, at the expense of Russia.

Menzies was keen to meet Canaris somewhere in Spain or Portugal,
most possibly in Lisbon. He said to a friend around this time that he
'hoped … that [between the two of them] the conflict could be brought to
an end'. But the Foreign Office had different views. It categorically forbade
any contact 'for fear of offending Russia'. Menzies commented acidly after
the war that a meeting with Canaris 'would certainly not have pleased
Stalin. But why we should fall over backwards to appease those who were
– and are – pledged to destroy our way of life, I shall never understand.'

There has been some speculation by historians after the war as to
whether, despite the Foreign Office's prohibition, Menzies did meet
Canaris over the Christmas–New Year period of 1942. The evidence for
this remains circumstantial. Menzies, who hardly ever left Whitehall, and
almost never left Britain during the war, paid a visit to Algiers in late
December 1942. On Christmas Eve the MI6 chief is recorded as having 'a
splendid lunch on the sun-drenched roof of a little house' in the city with
a senior MI6 colleague. We know from Ultra decrypts and the evidence of
a close colleague that Canaris spent the New Year period on the other side

of the Straits of Gibraltar, at his little house in Algeciras, where he cele-brated the traditional German feast of St Sylvester's Day (31 December) by cooking a roast turkey for his staff wearing his ubiquitous chef's hat. Afterwards he took his Abwehr guests to the Hotel Reina Cristina, where they were seen happily sharing the dance floor with British officers from Gibraltar. For a few hours Canaris 'threw off his preoccupations … and was, once again, the old, jovial, fatherly friend that he used to be to his subordinates', a friend noted.

The Abwehr chief's fifty-sixth birthday fell the following day.

Perhaps Canaris would have been less happy that festive season if he had known that the then governor of Gibraltar, General Mason MacFarlane, who had almost certainly met him when in the post of British military attaché in Berlin before the war, proposed a plan to kidnap the admiral during this visit. This, too, London categorically rejected.

When it came to probing the possibilities for ending the war early, Canaris did not take no for an answer.

Having been turned down by the British, his next approach was to the Americans. In February 1943 General 'Wild Bill' Donovan received a message passed by a circuitous route which included, among others King George II of the Hellenes and an OSS officer visiting Cairo: Canaris would like to make contact.

Donovan was keen, but by then a blanket prohibition had been put in place barring all formal or informal contacts between Allied intelligence officers and Abwehr agents.

There is a tantalising codicil to this story. According to one respected expert on Canaris there was a meeting between the admiral, Donovan and Menzies at Santander on the northern Spanish coast in the early summer of 1943. The evidence for this comes from a quote from an Abwehr officer who claimed to have been there: 'Donovan, his British colleague and Canaris reached agreement on Canaris's proposal [for a peace between Germany and the West?]. It was my most exciting experience as a member of Canaris's staff.'

This is the only flimsy evidence we have for a meeting which, if it did occur, would have been one of the most fascinating of the Second World War.

22

Mistake, Misjudgement, Misfire

It was probably Sándor Radó's affair with his new *Rote Drei* recruit Margrit Bolli, alias 'Rosy', which began the unravelling of the Dora Ring.

We do not know exactly when Radó and Bolli became lovers, but it seems likely that it was around October 1942, when he moved her into the apartment in the Geneva suburb of Eaux-Vives, on the eastern side of the lake.

The affair, which was against all good espionage practice, was made much more dangerous by Radó's insistence on paying daily visits to take messages to and from Margrit. Normally, the task of couriering these would have been shared with his wife and children. But, claiming 'security', Radó packed his family off to Bern, where he rented an apartment for them. Whether his daily visits caused comment among the neighbours we do not know. But they were a gift to Hermann Henseler, an SD agent code-named 'Rhenanus' who had worked before the war in the International Labour Organisation on the Geneva lakefront, 250 metres from Radó's flat. Henseler was ordered by his German bosses to use every means possible to find the *Rote Drei* radio operators.

By the early winter of 1942 the Germans knew that there were two *Rote Drei* radios, codenamed 'Maude' and 'Rosy', working from Geneva, and one, codenamed 'Jim', based in Lausanne. But they needed more precise locations. Lausanne was too far away from German-held territory for their Gonio radio-monitoring cars to be of any use. But Geneva was a different case. The sheer-faced 1,100-metre-high Salève mountain dominates the city from the south. Lying just a kilometre on the French side of the Franco–Swiss frontier, the Salève is today accessed by a cable car and is a favourite viewpoint for visitors, who can look down on Geneva, laid out like a street map below them, with the lake beyond. Following the German invasion of Vichy France on 11 November, SD Gonio cars drove to the summit of the Salève, where they scanned the airwaves for the two *Rote*

Drei transmitters operating somewhere amongst the sprawling jumble of the city below. The distance from the summit of the Salève to the centre of Geneva is around five kilometres; too far for the Gonio vans to pinpoint the precise buildings being used.* But they could – and did – identify with some accuracy the general locations involved: one near the lake in the north-east corner of the city, and one in the working-class and commercial district of Carouge, near the city's southern edge.

The German invasion of Vichy France produced a second windfall for the SD's agents hunting for the *Rote Drei*. On 9 November, two days before the German occupation of southern France, the Gestapo arranged for Vichy French police to arrest one of Sándor Radó's contacts† in Marseille. From his interrogation and from papers found in his flat, Himmler's men were able to obtain Radó's address, full personal details, and code source book, along with the schedules and wavelengths of the *Rote Drei* transmissions. However, since Radó did not have a radio, this only gave the SD interceptors access to the few messages he himself had encoded, not to the far greater number encoded by the *Rote Drei* operators.

Radó's address was passed to Henseler, who set one of his watchers to tail him. It was not long before he was spotted dining with Margrit Bolli at a local restaurant. A tail on Bolli quickly confirmed that she was Rosy, and operated her radio from her flat. The first of the *Rote Drei* had been found.

At this stage the SD's priority would not have been to close down Rosy, but to decipher her messages in the hope that these would lead them to the source of the leak in Berlin. Henseler began to search for someone to get close to her.

Towards the end of 1942, Sándor Radó began to notice a change in Margrit's behaviour. She did not seem so keen to see him, and made excuses to be out when he called. He had her watched, and soon found

---

* Although there is evidence only for the Salève having been used for this purpose, it is likely that there would have been a second point close to Geneva from which the Gonio cars would also have operated. The most accurate means of direction-finding with these vehicles is to have the largest angle, up to a maximum of 90 degrees, between the two detection points. The Salève is not large enough to provide for such a wide angle between two detection points. An ideal place for any second detection point on French territory would have been Mont de Gex, above the French town of Divonne, immediately to the west of Geneva. This, according to local legend, was often used by German Gonio vans (information from the author's social contacts in the pays de Gex).

† Anatoli Gourevitch, alias 'Petit Chef', 'Kent', 'Sukolov' and many others. He was GRU's resident for Belgium and France, and number two in the *Rote Kapelle*.

that she had another lover, a young hairdresser called Hans at one of Geneva's most prestigious hairdressing salons.

Hans Peters, whose German codename was 'Romeo', had fulfilled his eponymous role perfectly. He was now Rosy's lover.

In March 1943 Margrit moved to a one-bedroomed apartment in a crowded residential area a little further back from the lake and just a hundred metres or so from her new lover's flat. It was here, on 16 March, that Hans Peters managed to persuade her to part with a copy of an uncoded message which she had just delivered to Alexander Foote. The Germans now had what every cryptanalyst dreams of: a coded and unencoded version of the same message. By comparing the two they could crack the code. But Peters did even better. He saw a novel lying on Margrit's table – *Es begann im September* ('It Began in September') by Grete von Urbanitzky, a popular romantic novel of the time. The book seemed well thumbed and copiously marked. He reported back to Henseler, who checked the book out with the SD's codebreakers. They swiftly confirmed what Henseler suspected – they had found the source book for Margrit Bolli's book cipher.

From now on the SD could not only read every message sent by Rosy as easily as Moscow, but also begin deciphering all her previous encoded messages, which it had kept a record of over the past months. Now the work could begin in earnest to trace the leak back to its source.

While Himmler's men were busy tracking down the Dora Ring in late 1942 and the early months of 1943, events on the wider scene were creating yet more new challenges for the anti-Hitler resistance in Germany.

On 12 January 1943, in his first political report to Donovan in Washington, Allen Dulles gave an account of a conversation with Hans Bernd Gisevius, who, he said, had stressed 'the importance of receiving encouragement [from the West] that, if the Nazi leaders eliminated Hitler there could be negotiations for a durable peace with the 'United Nations' (a term used by the wartime Allies to describe themselves). The alternative, Gisevius concluded, was 'chaos and revolution, as Hitler, rather than surrender to the Western powers, would turn to Bolshevism'.

A second Dulles telegram followed on 14 January reporting on a meeting with the secretary general of the World Council of Churches, who was clearly speaking on behalf of the German resistance (probably Goerdeler): 'It appears that the fact that their [the resistance's] approaches [to the West] are meeting with no encouragement or understanding is a source of deep disappointment to the opposition … There is … a tendency on the part of the opposition to believe that the Anglo-Saxon countries are merely theorizing and are filled with pharisaic condemnation and bourgeois prejudice. [This is bringing about an] orientation [within the opposition] towards the East [which] is brought about by a belief that fraternization is not possible between the present [Western] Governments, but is possible between the German and Russian peoples.'

At about the same time Dulles also met Adam von Trott zu Solz, a key member of the resistance in both the German Foreign Office and the Kreisau Circle. Von Trott, who appears to have been sent to Bern on a mission to make contact through Dulles with Washington, also complained of the deep disillusion created by the silence from Western governments that had met all attempts by the anti-Hitler opposition to negotiate an early peace. He warned that this was turning many towards a deal with Russia, which would have profound consequences for the future shape of Europe. In an appeal which has echoes of moral internationalism much more akin to our own age than to the 1940s, von Trott insisted that the best way to prevent this was for Europe to unite around liberal principles and a return to 'the spiritual values of Christianity'.

On 13 January, the day after Dulles sent his first report to Donovan, Churchill was with his advisers in the governor's mansion in Gibraltar, preparing for the forthcoming Casablanca Conference with Roosevelt (Stalin had excused himself on the grounds that he was fighting the Battle of Stalingrad). The outcome of the conference dealt a further blow to the German resistance's hopes for removing Hitler as a prelude to an early negotiated peace with the Western Allies. When Roosevelt announced the conclusions of Casablanca at a joint press conference on 24 January, he declared: 'Peace can come to the world only by the total elimination of German and Japanese war power [which] … means unconditional surrender by Germany, Italy and Japan.'

In determining on a crushing victory in preference to a negotiated peace with a Germany that had rid itself of Hitler and Nazism, Roosevelt and Churchill effectively reversed their Atlantic Charter policy of 1941, which preferred a Germany which was, in Churchill's words, 'fat and impotent' to one which had been levelled to the ground.

The policy of 'unconditional surrender', which has attracted more criticism than almost any other Allied wartime strategy, also parted company with three hundred years of established European diplomatic practice. This had replaced the barbarous habits of the Middle Ages, when victory was followed by massacre and destruction, with the more civilised practice of ending wars through negotiations which stopped the killing and left the defeated with the room and dignity to rebuild.

It is a matter of record that at the time of Casablanca the British prime minister privately worried that Europe had more to fear after the war from Stalin's imperialist expansionism than from resurgent militarism in Germany. Despite these reservations, Churchill felt he had to submit to the policy of unconditional surrender, which was sprung on him at the last minute by Roosevelt. One of Churchill's senior advisers said afterwards, 'I think unconditional surrender was originally entirely Roosevelt's idea … Winston felt he must agree because there were so many other issues on which he and Roosevelt were at variance.'

Nevertheless, when, over lunch near the end of the conference, Roosevelt proposed 'unconditional surrender', the British PM responded with apparent enthusiasm: 'Perfect! I can just see how Goebbels and the rest will squeal.' Roosevelt added: 'It's just the thing for the Russians. Uncle Joe [Stalin] might have made it up himself.'

Later, when Roosevelt jokingly proposed at the final press conference that Casablanca should be known as the 'unconditional surrender' summit, Churchill could be heard growling 'Hear! Hear!' in a loud voice from the sidelines.

Many of the two Western leaders' senior advisers, including Sir Robert Vansittart, Stewart Menzies, Foreign Office head Alexander Cadogan and Roosevelt's distinguished secretary of state Cordell Hull, were strongly opposed to the policy. One senior official in London told Cadogan, 'There are two old men out there who have done this without thinking while they were full up with Moroccan red wine.'

It is easy to see why a policy of reducing Germany to rubble and starting again from scratch was popular with the publics of the free world – and, indeed, why even experienced diplomats considered it appropriate to the times. After all, German militarism had held the peace of Europe to ransom and caused the butchery of its young by the millions since Bismarck's armies had marched into Denmark in 1864. Some argued, moreover, that unconditional surrender was necessary in order to leave no space for another 'stab in the back' myth to emerge from any negotiated peace.

These are cogent arguments. But public anger and an instinct in the midst of war for retribution must be weighed against a greater task for statesmen, which is to determine what is needed for a swift victory and a just and lasting peace afterwards.

Whether a flexible policy, more consistent with European diplomatic tradition, would have led to a shorter war, fewer dead, an undivided Germany and a less divided Europe is one of the most intriguing what-might-have-beens of the Second World War. It could, as Churchill feared, have given Stalin the excuse to strike the separate peace with Germany of his nightmares. In due course 'unconditional surrender' would anyway have to be watered down in the case of Italy to 'capitulation with honour'. But despite this and later hints that similar concessions might be extended to Germany if Hitler were removed, the policy of unconditional surrender, underpinned by Churchill's indomitable will and Roosevelt's naïvety towards Stalin, was pursued right through to the point where Berlin was a smoking ruin and two Japanese cities were reduced to nuclear wastelands.

Contrary to Churchill's hope that the Casablanca policy of unconditional surrender would make Goebbels 'squeal', it actually gave the Nazi propaganda chief a powerful new weapon. Now he was able to tell the German people that the Allies' war aim was 'total slavery' – if Hitler failed, the result would be the obliteration of their nation. This was now a fight to the death.

Canaris could hardly believe it when he heard the news: 'Our generals will not swallow that [unconditional surrender]. Now I cannot see any solution … The student of history will not need to trouble their heads after this war, as they did after the last, to determine who was guilty of starting it. The case is, however, different when we consider guilt for prolonging the war. I believe that the other side have now disarmed us of the last weapon with which we could have ended it.'

Despite this, Canaris kept his lines open to the West – especially to Stewart Menzies. He ordered Gisevius to strengthen contacts with Halina Szymańska and Allen Dulles. Gisevius responded by revealing to the American envoy in February that German naval intelligence had cracked one of Washington's codes. This caused panic, and a hurried strengthening of codes in Herrengasse 23 and Washington. It also had the effect of finally winning Dulles's total confidence in Gisevius, whom the British had initially bad-mouthed as untrustworthy.

Meanwhile, other resisters remained active in seeking to persuade the senior generals to act following the humiliation of Stalingrad. Goerdeler and Olbricht worked on Günther von Kluge; von Tresckow on Heinz Guderian; and Beck on Erich von Manstein. But they were met, as before, with obdurate inaction. One field marshal summed up the common view: 'Prussian field marshals do not mutiny in the field.'

Some young students at the University of Munich, mostly in their twenties, were, however, prepared to go where no Prussian field marshal dared tread. The White Rose, a non-violent intellectual resistance group based around some students, including Hans and Sophie Scholl,* and Professor Kurt Huber, began distributing leaflets calling on Germans to resist in the summer of 1942. They were caught in February 1943, after the fall of Stalingrad. Following a show trial, the leaders were led to the guillotine.

During a bitterly cold spell in mid-February 1943, at about the same time that the Gestapo began arresting the White Rose protesters, Allen Dulles was entertaining a certain 'Herr Pauls' at three meetings held in the cosy fireside seclusion of his study at Herrengasse 23. From records that have survived, it seems that the purpose of Herr Pauls's late-night calls was to probe Western views on the ingredients of a possible peace deal. We do not know whom he was working for on this occasion, for Herr Pauls was an indiscriminate spy who separately served both Canaris and Himmler – sometimes individually, sometimes together. Either way, the German emissary's masters must have been pleased with his conversations in Bern. Expressing personal views which would have horrified his superiors in Washington, Dulles made it clear that he did not favour unconditional surrender or a vindictive peace, nor did he support the dismemberment of Germany. On the contrary, he preferred a federal structure for a united country. He did not even wish to see Austria returning to independence, regarding *Anschluss* as a necessary bulwark against Soviet post-war expansionism. He rejected Britain's view that Europe after the war should return to the age of spheres of influence, preferring instead a united Europe made up of sovereign states which could act as a counterbalance to Russia. In short, Dulles's views were, on the surface at least, almost identical to those of the German resistance, and especially those of Goerdeler and the Kreisau Circle.

Herr Pauls's true identity, as Dulles knew very well, having met him previously, was Prince Maximilian Egon Maria Erwin Paul zu Hohenlohe-Langenburg,† described by MI6 in a report to prime minister Churchill as

---

* Other ringleaders included Alexander Schmorell, Willi Graf and Christoph Probst.

† Prince Maximilian was assigned OSS code number 515, and was also referred to as 'Ben'. His other OSS aliases were 'Horseman' and 'Caballero'. He is not to be confused with 'Princess' Stephanie Julianne von Hohenlohe, divorced wife of Friedrich Franz von Hohenlohe-Waldenburg-Schillingsfürst, who started life as plain Stephanie Richter, a ballet dancer in Vienna. She was a notorious 1930s *grande horizontale* in various Western capitals – including London, where she was, it is said, the mistress of Lord Rothermere, the owner of the *Daily Mail* – and, it was rumoured, an active German spy.

'a very special and trusted agent who worked directly to [Canaris] … on matters [involving] high diplomatic or social circles abroad'.

We should not necessarily take this report of the Dulles–Hohenlohe meeting at face value, because the record was mischievously released (and perhaps subtly altered) by the Soviet Union after the war, for propaganda purposes. Dulles himself later claimed that he had been on a 'fishing expedition', hoping to extract information from 'Herr Pauls' by appearing to agree with his views.

Did Dulles's words nevertheless result in yet another tragic misunderstanding about what was possible? Did his comments encourage the German resisters to hope, when there was in fact none? Did the anti-Hitler resistance realise that Dulles was only fishing, and did not mean his words to be taken at face value? Himmler certainly took them seriously enough. He was informed in a report from an SD officer in Berlin on 19 February that Canaris had once again been in touch with the 'English' to discuss terms for ending the war. Once again, Himmler was content to add this new damning information to the already fast-growing file he was assembling on Canaris's treachery.

All of these initiatives to find a way round the bleak conclusions of Casablanca perished against the impenetrable granite wall of silence which Roosevelt and Churchill had erected to exclude all proposals for a separate peace coming from the anti-Hitler conspirators in Germany. It was against this wall that senior figures in the German resistance would cast themselves uselessly, again and again, over the coming years, right up to the point of their own destruction.

Once again, Goerdeler refused to submit to the despair and dejection that gripped the rest of the main players in the resistance after Casablanca. In the days before Roosevelt's announcement of 'unconditional surrender' there was a meeting between the Kreisau Circle and key leaders of the resistance movement, including Goerdeler and Beck.* Despite a tetchy atmosphere, an agreement was reached that, after Hitler was removed, Goerdeler should be the putative chancellor in the transitional government that would follow.

While Goerdeler and Beck were making plans for a still-distant future, Canaris, as so often, smothered his pessimism in intrigue. He had up to

---

* The meeting was held on 8 January at Yorck von Wartenburg's house. Others present included Ulrich von Hassell, Fritz-Dietlof von Schulenburg, Johannes Popitz, Jens Jessen, Adam von Trott and Helmuth von Moltke.

now kept his distance from detailed involvement in coups, plots and assassination attempts. But in early 1943 he seems to have decided that desperate times needed even more desperate measures. In February he received a cryptic message from von Tresckow: 'It's time to act.'

A few days later, Erwin Lahousen was summoned to Hans Oster's office.

'Have your people got sufficient time-clock fuses?' Oster asked.

'I assume so.'

'Then you should know that … von Tresckow is very much interested in such things … In the near future Hitler is expected to visit [Smolensk] … We hope that Himmler is going too. Fatso [Göring] will likewise [be there] and will likely burst of his own accord, like a balloon … To set your mind at ease I shall see to it … that this very morning a consignment of the best precision fuses is shipped by plane to Smolensk.'

On 20 February Canaris flew with Lahousen and Hans von Dohnányi to Army Group Centre headquarters in Smolensk to attend an intelligence officers' conference. In his briefcase Dohnányi carried a slab of British plastic explosive and a 'time pencil' detonator. The three men met von Tresckow on 22 February, and the explosive was handed over. Canaris was brutally clear about what was at stake: 'It would be good if you succeed and I will protect you. But after all these immense crimes, it will not be possible to deceive history. There must be *expiation* [he used the French word].' In a later conversation he said, 'You will be judged by only one thing – your success.'

A little less than three weeks later, on 13 March, Hitler and a delegation which included his personal cook and his doctor, Theodor Morell, flew to Army Group Centre HQ in Smolensk in a convoy comprising two specially adapted transport planes and a fighter escort. This was the opportunity for von Tresckow to do what he had long planned to do – kill the Führer. Not taking any chances, he set up three simultaneous assassination attempts in the hope that one of them would be successful. The first involved slipping a bomb beneath Hitler's car; but the SS cordon was too tight to enable the device to be planted. The second involved soldiers brought in as extra bodyguards, who were to shoot Hitler if the opportunity presented itself – but it never did. The third involved a bomb constructed from the plastic explosive and time pencil which Dohnányi had brought to Smolensk in his briefcase. The bomb was packed into a wooden Cointreau box designed to hold two bottles of the famous French liqueur. During a midday break for lunch in the officers' mess, as Hitler bent low over his plate, was shovelling vegetables into his mouth with his left hand, von Tresckow, sitting nearby, turned to one of Hitler's staff officers, Lieutenant Colonel Heinz Brandt, and asked him if he would mind taking a box containing a pair of Cointreau bottles back on the Führer's aircraft to a friend as 'payment for a wager'. Brandt readily agreed.

With the plot now in play, one of von Tresckow's co-conspirators, Fabian von Schlabrendorff, rang his designated contact in Berlin, giving the codeword – 'Flash' – to indicate that the long-hoped-for coup was under way. Then he raced after the Führer's column, which had already left for the airfield.

'I waited until Hitler … was about to board his plane,' he wrote later. 'Looking at Tresckow, I read in his eyes the order to go ahead. With the help of a key I pressed down hard on the fuse, thus triggering the bomb, and handed the parcel to Colonel Brandt, who boarded the plane shortly after Hitler. A few minutes later … Hitler's plane … escorted by a number of fighters, took off for East Prussia. Fate now had to take its course. Von Tresckow and I returned to our quarters … Operation Flash … was underway.'

The 'Cointreau' bomb was set to go off thirty minutes later, as Hitler's plane crossed over Minsk. Von Tresckow and his co-conspirators huddled around a radio tuned to the frequency used by the Luftwaffe, waiting to hear the report of the explosion from Hitler's fighter escort. An hour passed – and then two. Finally they received a routine signal saying that the Führer had arrived back safely at his 'Wolfsschanze' (Wolf's Lair) forward headquarters near Rastenburg in eastern Prussia.

Now von Tresckow had a problem. He had to rescue the box containing the 'Cointreau bottles' before it was opened. He coolly telephoned Brandt at Wolfsschanze to find out if he had delivered the package. Relieved to discover that it remained undelivered and unopened, Tresckow explained that he had sent the wrong bottles, and asked for the parcel to be held until the following day, when Schlabrendorff would come on the regular morning plane and exchange them for the right ones.

The next day the Cointreau bomb was recovered and carried gingerly to a train to Berlin, which was waiting at the special station which served the Wolfsschanze complex. In the safety of the train's lavatory the device was delicately examined. Von Schlabrendorff recalled later:

After gently removing the wrapping, I could see that the condition of the explosive was unchanged. Carefully dismantling the bomb, I took out the fuse and examined it. The reason for the failure immediately became clear. Everything but one small part had worked as expected. The capsule with the corrosive fluid had broken, the chemical had eaten through the wire, the firing pin had been released and had struck forward – but the detonator had not ignited! One of the few duds that had slipped past a British inspection was responsible for the fact that Hitler did not die on 13 March 1943.

Von Tresckow and his team of assassins were disappointed, but not downhearted. Almost immediately they heard that a second opportunity to assassinate Hitler was about to present itself. On 21 March, eight days after the failure of the 'Cointreau plot', Hitler was to attend an exhibition of captured enemy weapons in Berlin. This time the bomb could not be planted – it would have to be carried by a suicide bomber able to get close enough to kill Hitler in the explosion. On a long walk through the Smolensk countryside, von Tresckow persuaded his close colleague Rudolf-Christoph von Gersdorff, who had been chosen to accompany the Führer around the exhibition, that it was his duty to act as the bomber. 'Is it not extraordinary,' Tresckow said, 'that two officers of the German General Staff are discussing the best method to assassinate their commander-in-chief? But this has to be done. It is the sole means of saving Germany from total destruction. The world must be rid of the greatest criminal history has ever seen. He must be put down like a rabid dog who threatens the whole of humanity.'

Tresckow's plan required his friend to conceal two British 'Clam' magnetic mines, normally used for rail sabotage, one in each sleeve of his greatcoat. These would be initiated on a ten-minute time-pencil fuse just before Hitler's tour began.

In the event von Gersdorff was only able to arm the bomb in his left sleeve, because he had to raise his right arm to give the Nazi salute as Hitler approached. 'I stuck like glue to Hitler's left side,' he wrote later, 'and tried to slow him down by attempting to describe some of the exhibits. But he paid me not the slightest attention, even when I showed him one of Napoleon's eagles which our engineers had found in the Bérézina river while constructing a bridge. Hitler listened to nothing and said nothing but marched – or rather nearly ran – through the exhibition by the shortest possible route to the exit door. He had come and gone in less than the ten minutes necessary for the fuse to detonate, leaving me to dash into the nearest lavatory and remove the fuse as quickly as I could.'

To most of von Tresckow's frustrated assassins, it must have seemed that Hitler did not need the SS for protection: he had fate – or some other malignant supernatural force – already doing the job for him.

On 23 March, two days after the failed attack, Carl Goerdeler sublimated his disappointment by returning to work on what has come to be known as his 'great memorandum'.

Entitled 'The Aim', the 'great memorandum', which Goerdeler started in 1941 and continued to work on right up to the eve of his death, began with a statement of mighty defiance cataloguing German guilt under Hitler, who had 'thrown on the scrap heap the tradition of honour and integrity we have inherited', and committed actions which 'will for ever be a stain on our history'. Next it railed against Britain's inability to see that the real threat for the future was Soviet Russia, and that this danger could only be met by a 'détente ... [between Germany and] the Western Powers ... to concentrate our whole strength in the east'. The main body of Goerdeler's work, however contained a detailed picture of Germany and Europe after the war. He foresaw a quasi-federal European Union comprising all anti-Bolshevik countries, in which national states would be free to organise themselves according to their own traditions. Russia could be included, but only after it had abandoned communism. In such a union, Goerdeler argued, Germany would have a natural position of leadership: 'Their central position, their numbers and their great efficiency ensure for the German people the leadership of the European bloc, provided they do not let themselves be corrupted by immoderate ambition and mad lust for power. It is stupid of them to speak of a master race; it is folly to claim for themselves the preservation of national honour and independence and yet refuse that to others. The leadership of Europe will go to the states which respect the smaller nations ... [what is needed is] the British method [of] unobtrusive and well nigh invisible leadership ... leaving to each member, room for its own organic development ...' Goerdeler's 'great memorandum' ends by asking the question which many Germans still ask themselves today: '[But] Can the German people do [this]?'

It is difficult to read these words without marvelling that they were written at a time of great general pessimism amongst all those who thought as Goerdeler did; and without being impressed by how close his words come to Europe's view of itself after the war, and modern Germany's view of its opportunities and challenges even today.

23

The Worm Turns

Walter Schellenberg, the mastermind of Venlo and Canaris's occasional companion on early-morning rides in Berlin, was not a man much given to outright happiness. But on the morning of 5 March 1943 he felt contented as he sat in a wicker chair in the spring sunshine on the terrace of Wolfsburg Castle in Switzerland, looking down on the Untersee, the lower section of Lake Constance. On the far bank he could see the fields and woods of Germany stretching into the distance. The lake was calm and intensely blue, and the fields were already turning a more verdant green with the retreat of winter.

Schellenberg's good mood was not just the product of a fine day and a beautiful view. His visit to Switzerland had, so far, proceeded most satisfactorily.

His black Mercedes with its German plates and Nazi flag had caused something of a stir when, three days previously, it had turned up at the Swiss frontier post at Kreuzlingen on the shores of Lake Constance. Frontier formalities were waved aside by a small delegation from Swiss intelligence, who shepherded his car the few kilometres to Wolfsburg Castle, where they changed his German numberplates for Swiss ones. The following evening he had been taken to an old Alpine inn at the Bernese village of Biglen, where at a table specially decorated with a Swiss flag he dined with General André Guisan, the head of the Swiss army, Roger Masson, the head of Swiss intelligence, and members of their staffs. It had been a most convivial occasion, enlivened by the general's spicy anecdotes of his time as a farmer in his native canton of Vaud. Schellenberg, though apparently relaxed and informal, was clever enough to know that the general's farming tales and the Swiss flag on the table were no accident. They were intended as none-too-subtle assertions of Swiss pride and confidence in their Alpine redoubt and their citizens' army.

After dinner, Schellenberg, Guisan and Masson withdrew into a smaller room with sliding glass-panelled doors, where they could speak privately. Schellenberg explained at length his attempts to 'ward off any danger of Hitler attacking Switzerland', but stressed the Führer's unpredictability on these matters. It would be easier to placate him, the German suggested, if Switzerland could show itself to be genuinely neutral and fully prepared to defend its status against any attacker, including the Allies. Would Guisan perhaps provide a signed document to this effect? The following day the Swiss general gave Schellenberg the document he sought, which included an even-handed warning, as much to the Allies as to Germany: 'The balance [of power] in Europe requires Switzerland to be neutral towards all sides and in every respect ... Whoever invades our country is our enemy. He will face a highly powerful, united army and a people imbued with one and the same determination ...' Schellenberg had got what he came for – an explicit signed statement of Swiss neutrality that could be used in the future, either to bring the Swiss to heel or as a pretext for invasion.

The main business of his visit over, Schellenberg could now get down to detailed discussions of spying in and between the two countries. It was for this reason that he had returned to Wolfsburg Castle for a weekend of private talks with the Swiss intelligence chief, Roger Masson.

This was not the first time the two men had met. In September 1942 Masson had asked Schellenberg to meet him to discuss some secret documents captured by the Germans at the fall of France* which had the potential to threaten Switzerland's neutrality. Schellenberg, who after Heydrich's death had taken over direct responsibility for dealing with foreign spies operating from Switzerland, agreed to meet Masson, but only on German territory. As dusk approached on 8 September 1942, Masson and a colleague, all too conscious of what had happened at Venlo, walked nervously, unarmed and without identity papers, over the old cobbled stone bridge which, watched over by a crumbling medieval tower, crosses the Rhine and the Swiss–German border at the little hilltop town of Laufenburg. When they reached the German side, the Swiss were told that Schellenberg's car had been delayed because of a traffic accident. Masson and Schellenberg finally met in the station buffet at Waldshut, a little way back from the border.

---

* The documents, which were captured at Charité-sur-Loire by a German armoured column on 19 June 1940, showed that France and Switzerland had agreed to cooperate in the event that either was attacked by Germany.

Masson was at a distinct disadvantage in the discussion that followed, as he had demands to make. Apart from the embarrassing documents, he also needed Schellenberg's help with the release of a Swiss spy captured in Stuttgart, and with a request from the Swiss government for the Germans to curtail the activities of a press agency in Vienna which was hostile to Bern. To Masson's surprise, Schellenberg agreed to both without asking anything in return. But the German did show Masson a deciphered telegram from the US attaché in Bern. The implication was clear: be careful of the games you play with the Americans, because we can read their codes. This business done, the meeting abruptly ended. The embarrassing documents which the Swiss wanted to discuss were never brought up.

The weekend of talks between Masson and Schellenberg at Wolfsburg Castle went at first as congenially as had the dinner at Biglen two days previously. Schellenberg was again expansive, charming and obliging. Over two days he discussed the war, his youth, his rise in the SS and his family, all in such an informal manner that Masson wondered if he was not probing about the possibility of his acting as a mediator for a peace deal. When Masson raised the delicate question of the documents, Schellenberg responded airily that he would deal with the issue, assuring him that they would never again see the light of day. But then, on the last day, the tone subtly changed. Schellenberg explained that he was deeply concerned for the Führer's safety because of a circle of traitors at the highest level in the army who were passing information through Switzerland to the Allies. He wanted to warn them off before the Gestapo got to them. Could the Swiss help, he asked artlessly. By the time the meeting ended, Roger Masson was in no doubt that all this cooperation from the German side was in the clear expectation that the Swiss would help roll up the Dora Ring. Naturally, the Swiss spy chief denied all knowledge of any such ring of foreign spies on Swiss territory – and there, for the moment, the matter rested.

On Sunday, 7 March, Masson delivered Schellenberg back to the Kreuzlingen crossing and, no doubt with a sigh of relief, waved him goodbye.

If Masson thought he could now relax, he was very soon proved to be mistaken.

Eleven days after Schellenberg's departure from Switzerland, on 18 March, Hans Oster reported through the Viking Line that 'A German Operation is imminent against Switzerland and is very likely to be carried out before April 6, 1943.' Masson panicked, and having been fooled by

Schellenberg into believing that he was genuinely on Switzerland's side, sent an urgent message to Berlin asking for a meeting. He had walked straight into Schellenberg's trap. It was all a play. Schellenberg had planted the invasion scare to flush out Masson's sources.

A little over two weeks later, on 5 April, a senior judge, accompanied by an SS officer, arrived in the Tirpitzufer and asked to see Canaris. Ushered into his office, they presented the Abwehr chief with papers authorising the arrest of Hans von Dohnányi for corruption, treason and currency violations involving the transfer of money to the foreign banks of Jews. The old Wilhelm Canaris would have peremptorily kicked the SS arrest party out, as their search order violated the agreed procedures which should have been followed when Himmler's men wanted to question an Abwehr officer. Instead he mildly led the intruders to Dohnányi's office, which was next door to that of Oster.

Canaris had been warned that very morning that something unpleasant was stirring, and that all the evidence pointed to the probability that Oster was the target. He had even gone to Oster's office and ordered him to get rid of all incriminating documents. But Oster, tempting fate as ever, omitted to do so.

Incriminating documents were found in both offices, some describing relations with the Allies and attempts to find a way to an early negotiated peace. Oster, accused of using $100,000 of Abwehr funds to secure the safety of fourteen Jews who he had sent to Switzerland as 'Abwehr agents',* was placed under house arrest and then sacked from the Abwehr. Dohnányi, who was also involved in the rescue operation, was arrested along with his wife Christine, Pastor Dietrich Bonhoeffer and Canaris's Vatican 'spy' Dr Josef Mueller, who was picked up in Munich just after returning from another journey to the Holy See. They were put in separate prisons awaiting trial, though Christine von Dohnányi was released soon afterwards.

The arrests left behind what Hans Bernd Gisevius referred to as a 'conspiratorial vacuum'. Oster would still be able to be cautiously active in the conspiracy, but not from his key position in the Tirpitzufer. The conspirators had lost the man whom one of them called their 'general manager'. They were also rocked by the psychological shock of the arrests,

---

* The large amount of money was required by Swiss authorities to guarantee the financial independence of the refugees, who included Annemarie Conzen and her two daughters Gabriele and Irmgard, a school friend of Canaris's daughter Brigitte.

and perhaps especially by the fact that Canaris had allowed the inner sanctum of the Tirpitzufer, up to now seen as a safe space for plotting, to be violated.

Arguably, the shock should not have been as great as it was, for the signs of impending trouble had been clear enough for some time.

Secret warnings had been given to key plotters, including Dohnányi and Ulrich von Hassell, that they were being shadowed; a medium-level plotter had been arrested for conspiracy in March; and von Tresckow's friend Fabian von Schlabrendorff had only narrowly escaped sanction, or worse, when it came to light that he was canvassing for new recruits to the resisters' cause. On 20 April, von Hassell wrote in his diary: 'I have been warned 4 times that my phone is tapped and that I am probably being watched in other ways.'

Despite this, Goerdeler, undaunted as ever, wrote a letter in March for circulation to army officers: 'How is it possible that so basically decent a people as the Germans can put up for so long with such an intolerable system? Only because all offences against law and decency are carried out under the protection of secrecy and under the pressures of terror.' In April, on a visit to Budapest, Erwin Lahousen too seemed unconcerned, informing Madeleine Bihet-Richou that, despite everything, resistance among the generals continued to grow.

But these small acts of defiance and this irrational optimism could not alter the facts. The resisters' freedom of manoeuvre, and their ability to conspire safely, had been curtailed, and the threat against them personally was rising.

It took all Canaris's skills at deception and obfuscation to extract himself and his people from the investigation which followed the Tirpitzufer raid and, in the process, get the indictments against Dohnányi and Bonhoeffer reduced to some minor non-political offences, for which Oster was also charged with being complicit. But the damage to the Abwehr as an organisation could not be so easily mended. Canaris was forced to agree that he and his staff would vacate the Tirpitzufer and relocate to army headquarters at Zossen, thirty kilometres south of Berlin. Though this was explained away as necessary because of increasingly intense RAF bombing, everyone knew that in the Nazi regime, where access was the true measure of power, it was in reality a political move intended to reduce the Abwehr's influence in the capital. What was worse, Canaris also had to submit to the replacement of nearly all of his department heads.

Cut off from the heart of the action, emasculated and under constant surveillance, the Abwehr now began to fade into the background, both as a centre for resistance and as a political force. To add to the battalion of setbacks, Ludwig Beck, who despite being in retirement was still a prime mover in army circles, fell ill with suspected stomach cancer in the spring, and was out of action for over a month. His loss was immediately felt: 'Only now his importance becomes clear … no one can replace him … may God watch over Beck,' prayed one conspirator.

With resignation and pessimism once again filling the air, new high-level recruits to the conspiracy were more difficult to convince, and some who were already engaged began once again to melt away into the shadows. Field Marshal Erich von Manstein complained to his friends that however much he wanted to, it was impossible to resist Hitler. In a conversation with von Tresckow, one general complained that there was no way to escape Germany's fate. Canaris too, sunk in one of his regular pits of depression and fatalism, described Hitler as the 'scourge of God', which could not be fought against, but had simply to be endured to the very end.

Only Carl Goerdeler, bobbing along in his own private bubble of optimism, refused to submit to what everyone else began to see as a conspiracy of fate. At a dinner with friends he had to be persuaded away from a scheme to recalibrate the entire anti-Hitler plot into an attempt on the life of some more accessible Nazi figure, if the Führer proved impossible.

On 17 May he wrote a 'cheer-up-and-get-on-with-it' letter to Friedrich Olbricht at Reserve Army headquarters:

My dear General,
*… We must not wait for the 'psychologically right' moment to come, **we must bring it about** [emphasis in the original] …*

Stalingrad and Tunis are defeats unparalleled in German history since Jena and Auerstädt. In both cases the German people were told that for decisive reasons armies had to be sacrificed. We know how false this is … The truth is that our leadership is incapable and unscrupulous …

The number of civilians, men, women and children of all nations and of Russian prisoners of war ordered to be put to death before and during this war exceeds one million. The manner of their deaths is monstrous and is far removed … even from the most primitive ideas of decency among savage tribes. But the German people are falsely led to believe that it is Russian Bolshevists who are constantly committing monstrous crimes against innocent victims …

'De Favoriet', the Jelineks' shop in The Hague, *c.* 1939.

Bernhard Mayr von Baldegg, Alfred Rosenberg and Max Waibel.

The Wolfsschanze map room after Stauffenberg's failed assassination attempt, 20 July 1944.

(Left to right) Claus von Stauffenberg, Karl-Jesko von Puttkamer, Karl-Heinrich Bodenschatz, Adolf Hitler, Wilhelm Keitel, 15 July 1944.

Carl Goerdeler on trial.

The Tirpitzufer, c.1939.

'La Taupinière', c.1937.

Alexander Foote's flat in Lausanne (top floor, note the aerials).

Halina Szymańska's fake French passport.

Foote's radio.

Station Maude, Olga and Edmond Hamel's radio.

The Radó family's apartment building at 113, rue de Lausanne in Geneva (top floor).

The Hamels' radio shop in the Geneva suburb of Carouge, *c.* 1939.

*If we can find no other way I am ready to do everything to talk
personally to Hitler. I would tell him what he must be told, namely that in
the vital interests of the people, his resignation is essential ... The risk must
be taken ... It is not unreasonable on my part to demand that action must
be taken immediately ...*

With my best wishes.
Yours sincerely,
Carl Goerdeler

Three days later Goerdeler was back in Stockholm, depositing a voluminous paper with Jacob Wallenberg, which he asked to be transmitted to
Churchill as the basis for a negotiated peace. It proposed a detailed new
constitution for Germany, a new world order based around a world
confederation of states, and a Europe governed by a European economic
community, complete with a president, a council of ministers and a
parliament.

What Goerdeler could not have known, as he laboured over his visions
for the future, was that opinion in London had if anything hardened
against any kind of deal. On 30 May 1943 the head of the Northern
Department of the FCO, commenting on peace feelers from 'one of
Canaris's officers' in Stockholm, wrote to the chief of naval intelligence:
'There have recently, as you know, been an increasing number of attempts
on the part of the enemy to establish contacts with British Representatives
in neutral countries ... such approaches should receive no encouragement
or response.'

The wilful ignorance at high levels in London about the true nature and
record of the German resistance upon which this opinion was based can
be seen in a comment made by foreign secretary Anthony Eden at about
this time. When the bishop of Chichester, George Bell, who had met
Dietrich Bonhoeffer in Sweden in 1942, protested to Eden that other
nations had been promised liberation in return for particular actions, but
Germany had been offered nothing but unconditional surrender, Eden
responded that unlike others, the Germans had never shown a thoroughgoing determination to oppose the Hitler regime. This hard line was very
much in tune with the public mood. Noël Coward's satirical song of the
time 'Don't Let's be Beastly to the Germans' contained the lines:

Don't let's be beastly to the Germans
When we've definitely got them on the run –
Let us treat them very kindly as we would a valued friend
We might send them out some Bishops as a form of lease and lend.

Churchill, hearing Coward's song for the first time, loved it and called for repeated encores.

By a strange quirk of fate, two days after the loss of Hans Oster as 'managing director' of the resistance, a chance event in the North African desert changed the fate of the man who would take over from him as the dominant energising force of the last phase of the resistance.

On 7 April, patrolling Curtiss P40-E Kittyhawk fighter bombers of the Allied Desert Air Force chanced upon a German unit conducting a tactical withdrawal near the Kesserine pass in Tunisia. In the attack that followed, the young German colonel directing the withdrawal, Claus von Stauffenberg, was badly wounded, losing his left eye, most of his right hand, two fingers on his left hand and some of the movement in his back and legs, which were peppered with shrapnel. Stauffenberg, who was not expected to survive, was sent to Munich for treatment. In September, on the way to recovery, he was introduced to Henning von Tresckow, who recruited him into the plot and arranged for him to be sent to the Reserve Army in Berlin as a staff officer reporting to the conspiracy's chief planner, Friedrich Olbricht.

By now the main focus of the war in the European theatre was not the North African desert, but once again the Russian steppes, and especially the city of Kursk, which lies astride a key road and rail confluence 725 kilometres south-west of Moscow.

Although Hans Oster's removal from the Tirpitzufer severely curtailed his usefulness to the resistance, the sources which he had created remained in operation, and began again to supply Moscow Centre with a steady stream of crucial information about the developing situation around Kursk, courtesy of Rudolf Roessler, Swiss intelligence and the Dora Ring. By now, however, nearly all the Dora messages were being read by Schellenberg.

As early as mid-March, Sándor Radó warned Moscow Centre that Hitler was probably intending an attack on the Kursk salient. Moscow checked this information with its British spy John Cairncross, whose smuggled raw decrypts out of Bletchley Park confirmed a German build-up around Kursk.

The origins of the great battle to which Kursk would give its name lay in a brilliant series of counterattacks around Kharkov, masterminded by the great German strategist Field Marshal Erich von Manstein in February 1943. These drove the Russian line back by nearly two hundred kilometres and regained the initiative for the Germans on the Eastern Front after their defeat at Stalingrad. When Manstein's offensive stuttered to a halt because of the spring rains and exhaustion on both sides, it left a bulge of Russian-held territory two hundred kilometres wide and 140 deep, sticking westwards out from the Russian front line into German territory. The textbook strategy would have been to wait patiently for the inevitable Russian counter-offensive. Manstein even saw his successes as the prelude to a peace: 'I was convinced that, after our successful counter-offensive across the Dnieper at Kharkov, we still had the possibility, under a skilful leadership, to fight for, at the very least, an armistice.' In April, Swedish sources too were predicting an imminent German–Russian ceasefire – no doubt giving rise to more Churchillian nightmares.

But, on 15 April, Hitler, as much a stranger to peace as to patience, issued Operational Order No. 6, which called for an all-out assault to cut off the offending Kursk bulge. The broad target date for the attack, to be known as Operation Citadel, was 3 May, just a little over two weeks away.

Five days later, on 20 April, in a message passed on from Goerdeler, Radó informed Moscow Centre of Hitler's intentions and of an apparent change in the launch date for Citadel:

Dora to Director: Mayor Goerdeler from … Bendlerstrasse [German army headquarters in Berlin]

a) *The first fixed day for the German attack on the East Front is 14 June. Only operations of modest proportions are planned.*
b) *The General Staff expects the event by the end of April at the earliest; it could snowball. The … generals who already wanted to take action against Hitler in January, have now decided to liquidate Hitler and also his supporters. An earlier attempt failed because Hitler was warned by Manstein.*

In fact, Radó's prediction that Citadel would be launched on 14 June, and would be of 'modest proportions', was a deliberate deception, approved by Hitler and probably initiated by Schellenberg, who seems to have decided that since he could not yet shut down the Dora Ring, he would use it as a channel to pass on false information.

On 30 April, London sent Moscow information from Bletchley Park decrypts which confirmed the messages Moscow Centre was receiving from Geneva, that an attack on the Kursk salient was imminent.

By now, however, logistical problems were beginning to have an effect on both the Citadel timetable and on the German order of battle. Again, Radó picked these up almost immediately, sending on 6 May:

> To the Director ... The re-formation [redeployment?] of the mobile and armoured divisions is subject to delays. The deadlines for the re-formation and readiness to move of the 60th mobile and 16th armoured division have been postponed by four weeks because these units are insufficiently equipped with vehicles and tanks as a result of delayed deliveries.

On 13 June, the day before the rumoured start of Citadel, Churchill wrote to Stalin: 'Our information about German intentions is conflicting. On balance I think Hitler will attack you again, probably in the Kursk salient.'

Dora, meanwhile, was providing a series of reports to Moscow Centre detailing German problems with lack of equipment and the unreadiness of certain units. These culminated in a signal sent by Radó on 23 June which closely reflected the case being put to Hitler by his key commanders – that the strengthening of Russian positions at the two points at which the Germans intended to break into the Kursk salient made the forthcoming operation extremely hazardous.

> From Radó: Army Command does not wish to provoke a large-scale Russian offensive in the central sector under any circumstances. [They consider] the German ... attack planned for May/early June in the southern sector no longer serves a purpose ... Soviet build-up in the Kursk area since early June is now so great that German superiority there no longer exists.

At about the same time, Field Marshal Manstein's chief of intelligence, Colonel Reinhard Gehlen,* made an uncannily similar assessment of the

---

* Gehlen had been approached by von Tresckow and Stauffenberg to support the anti-Hitler plot, and gave tacit protection to the plotters on the Eastern Front. After the war he became the head of the West German intelligence service.

prospects of success: 'The Russians have anticipated our attacks in the key sectors for weeks … they have done everything to block our threat quickly. It is … most unlikely that the German attack will achieve a breakthrough.'

Once again, Hitler preferred his own instincts to his generals' judgements, and, investing almost his last strategic reserves in the operation, insisted that Citadel must go ahead, setting first 3 and then 5 July as the launch date for the assault on the Russian salient.

For the Germans, Citadel, planned around two simultaneous armoured thrusts intended to cut through the 'neck' of the Kursk pocket from the north and the south, was a disaster almost from the start. The Russians were fully informed, and well prepared. By 17 July, with the German attacks blunted or thrown back on all fronts, Hitler was forced to call off the operation. The Germans lost some 54,000 dead, wounded and missing on the Kursk salient, along with 323 tanks and self-propelled guns and 159 aircraft. Russian losses were even higher, at around 180,000 casualties, 1,800 tanks and assault guns, and 450 aircraft.

One expert has calculated that at Kursk 'the Red Army lost five armoured vehicles for every German Panzer destroyed'. The difference was that whereas the Red Army could absorb these losses, the Wehrmacht at this stage of the war could not. The worm had turned. With the nation's reserves exhausted, the era of German victories was at an end. Now it was Stalin's armies that were on the march, with a series of counterattacks which over the next two years would carry his forces across occupied Russia, over the nations of Eastern Europe, right to the gates of Berlin.

Shortly after the battle ended, Sándor Radó's Geopress business at 113, rue de Lausanne in Geneva published one of his much-sought-after maps. It depicted the Russian counterattack at Kursk, which the secret reports he had prepared in a next-door room had done so much to determine.

It would be wrong to ascribe the German defeat at Kursk wholly, or even mainly, to intelligence on German plans from the Dora Ring. The information about German positions and intentions provided by local Russian field intelligence was probably greater than that coded and sent over many long nights of painstaking clandestine transmissions from the *Rote Drei*. Nevertheless, the stream of high-level, real-time and accurate information provided to Moscow Centre by Sándor Radó and his Dora team must have been of enormous assistance to the Russian victors of Kursk, the greatest tank battle in history and one of the key turning points of the Second World War.

Geopress map of the Russian counterattack at Kursk

It was on this achievement, more than any other, that the Dora Ring's claim to have been one of the great spy rings of the Second World War, and amongst the most remarkable in the history of intelligence, was based. Moscow never knew at the time, nor has it acknowledged since, that its victory at Kursk actually came courtesy of Hans Oster and his colleagues in the Tirpitzufer, with the assistance of Swiss intelligence, and almost certainly with at least the knowledge of Britain's MI6.

24

The End of Dora

Walter Schellenberg would have had a bird's-eye view of the build-up to the Battle of Kursk as a result of the decrypted signals he was reading daily from the *Rote Drei* to Moscow Centre. It must have been frustrating that he was still able neither to close down the *Rote Drei* radios, nor to stem the leaks, which were now posing a mortal threat to German operations and to the lives of thousands of German soldiers.

But he was experienced enough to know that counter-intelligence operations cannot be rushed.

In the mid-summer of 1943, the SD formed a special squad to hunt down the Dora Ring radio operators, under a seasoned German counter-intelligence officer from Paris, Heinz Pannwitz. At this stage Schellenberg's men already had their infiltration agent Hans Peters in regular contact with Margrit Bolli. The next move was to send in an agent to make contact with Radó, Foote and the Hamels. The Gestapo's agents had no difficulty making contact with Radó and Foote, but they failed to find the Hamels, who following a security scare in May had moved their radio from above their shop in the Geneva suburb of Carouge to a large urban villa which Radó had rented for them. This was set in a substantial garden in the midst of a copse of trees at 192, route de Florissant in Chêne-Bougeries, on the outskirts of the city.

The first SD agent sent in was a Franco-German Jewish journalist who approached Radó masquerading as 'Yves Rameau', a survivor from the collapse of the *Rote Kapelle* network. Radó smelt a rat, and, suspecting that he was dealing with an agent provocateur, replied that he knew nothing of the *Rote Kapelle*. Moscow later confirmed that the man was a fraud.

With Radó alerted, Schellenberg's men next tried Alexander Foote. In late 1942 a married couple calling themselves 'Laura' and 'Lorenz' made contact with Foote and, with Moscow Centre's approval, began to help him with his work. They were in fact double agents who had been turned by the Germans while working for Moscow Centre in Japan, and had recently installed themselves in a suspiciously sumptuous villa above Lausanne. Foote, by now an experienced spy with a sixth sense for trouble, very quickly became suspicious. He told Moscow Centre of his concerns, only to have them peremptorily dismissed – Laura and Lorenz, Moscow insisted, had worked for the GRU for a long time and were completely trustworthy. Soon however the evidence that the couple were playing a double game became so strong that Foote broke off all contact. It was only after the war that he discovered the couple were indeed working for the Germans.

The second attempt to get alongside Foote was better prepared. Schellenberg knew from decrypted *Rote Drei* messages that in April 1943 Moscow Centre had instructed Foote to meet a courier from the French Communist Party, to whom he was to hand over 15,000 francs. Pannwitz managed to get a false message through to Moscow that the French courier had been arrested, and then sent one of his agents, who claimed to be a replacement. A meeting was arranged in the botanical gardens in Geneva, but once again Foote's hackles rose. The man was too garrulous, and far too inquisitive – and, worst of all, tried to follow him home. He reported his suspicions to Moscow Centre, which confirmed that the contact was an imposter, and that this was indeed another attempt at a plant.

At about the same time an unannounced visitor called at Rachel Duebendorfer's apartment claiming to be an old friend from Foote's RAF days. A quick phone call to Foote revealed the lie.

By now Moscow Centre had recognised the signs. The *Rote Drei* had been blown. The Germans were on to them. It would have to act fast to save its network.

On 4 July, the day before Hitler launched Operation Citadel, Moscow Centre sent an urgent message to Radó:

Director to Dora:
We have been able to determine, just in the past few days, that the courier from France, who was supposed to pick up the money from Jim [Foote], was arrested; and in his place a Gestapo agent came to Jim and, it appears, followed him to his apartment and in this way was able to learn his name. At the same time but independently of this event, [they have made contact with Rachel Duebendorfer]. For the time being, you must break off your connection with Sissy [Duebendorfer] completely … She should keep her apartment absolutely clean and, above all else, [be careful

what she says]. You must also cut off all contact with Jim immediately. We
will allow you one ... meeting with him outside the city [provided you
take] all due care and attention, particularly after the meeting. Give Jim
another 2,000 dollars so that he has enough money for 3 or 4 months. And
has some in hand.

Advise him on how to hide his radio and where. In our opinion it
would be best for him to go off for a couple of months to Ticino or another
distant resort, so that he can shed the ties in Lausanne. It would also be
good for him to change where he lives ... Discuss all of this with him in
detail. We are relying on you to arrange everything properly and
recommend rest and steadiness to Jim. Agree with him an entirely neutral
way of finding out how he is every now and again ... Director

In response to Moscow's telegram, Radó asked the local Communist Party
to prepare safe refuges for the Dora Ring members, in case they needed
them.

On 8 July, Maria Poljakova at Moscow Centre sent a message in Rachel
Duebendorfer's code instructing her to leave immediately for an extended
stay in Ticino. Four days later Poljakova warned Radó that the Germans
now had his address too.

Alexander Foote followed Moscow's instructions and left Lausanne for
a two-week 'holiday', not at Ticino, but on Lake Lugano. Rachel
Duebendorfer however refused to leave Geneva, telling Moscow Centre
that it was all a storm in a teacup. Moscow replied in no uncertain terms
on 16 August:

Dear Sissy,
We, the Centre, which has its people everywhere and can determine what
is happening in other countries and around you, have told you clearly and
explicitly that we have hard evidence that the Gestapo knows that you
work for us and will try to uncover your connections into Germany. You,
however, deny this possibility ... You must understand ... that you know
nothing of the danger which threatens you and Taylor's [Christian
Schneider's] people, especially those in Germany. Your behaviour is
frivolous and irresponsible. We demand that you recognise the seriousness
of the situation and place full confidence in our statements. We repeat: the
Gestapo knows that you have or had a connection with us and will
attempt all possible provocations ...

The *Rote Drei* and the Dora network were now in very grave danger.

But the real threat came in the end not from Schellenberg and the SD in Stuttgart, but from Hans Bernd Gisevius on the orders of Hans Oster in Berlin.

In early September 1943, Gisevius met the head of Swiss intelligence, Roger Masson, in the ornate surroundings of the Schweizer Hof, Bern's most prestigious hotel. Gisevius's orders from Oster were to inform the Swiss that the SD had identified all three *Rote Drei* transmitters and had assembled a 'Swiss Dossier' listing how Switzerland was being used as a centre for spying against Germany. Berlin would now be able to claim that this undermined Swiss undertakings to remain neutral. Gisevius warned Masson that Himmler's man, Walter Schellenberg, planned to blackmail the Swiss government with this information in order to obtain concessions, including giving German troops the right of passage through Swiss territory to Italy. Gisevius's warning may not have been as altruistic as it appeared. It seems much more likely that the real reason for getting the Swiss to close down the *Rote Drei* was to protect the German resistance from an unravelling of the Dora Ring which would lead Schellenberg back to Roessler and the high-level German sources he shared with Swiss intelligence – including, of course, Oster himself.

And so, a full year after a bored Geneva airport wireless operator stumbled across illegal coded transmissions being sent from Geneva to Moscow, Swiss intelligence finally decided that the Dora Ring's useful role in passing intelligence to Russia was at an end, and its members should be rolled up. But to protect themselves they now had to be seen to be going through the official motions to close the ring down.

On 10 September, Lieutenant Maurice Treyer of the Swiss radio-monitoring service set up his headquarters on the first floor of an apartment block in the centre of Geneva and set about tracking down the precise locations of the two *Rote Drei* operators in the city. At 0203 on the following night Treyer's monitoring vans picked up 'a very strong radio signal' coming from the general direction of the suburb of Chêne-Bougeries. The next phase would have to be on foot. On 20 September Treyer set out with a colleague discreetly looking at the houses in the suspect area. At first they found nothing. But then, peering through the undergrowth surrounding a handsome villa, Treyer saw an aerial some sixty metres long, running up from a loft window into a nearby tree. The address was 192, route de Florissant, the villa Radó had rented for the Hamels following their scare a few months earlier.

Margrit Bolli's flat, in the more densely populated suburb of Eaux-Vives, was more difficult to locate. Eventually Treyer was forced to replace technology with guile. Over a period of six nights he waited for Bolli to start transmission and then, one by one, turned off the electricity supply to each of the individual distribution networks in the area. When Bolli's signal cut out, he knew he had the right spot. The rest would have to be done by footwork.

But this time Treyer was spotted. Bolli reported to Radó that she had noticed strange men claiming to be from the electricity board on the stairs of her building. She thought they had been examining the aerial she had installed on her roof. On 10 October, Radó reported to Moscow Centre that he thought Rosy was being watched, and that Foote too would probably be in danger.

Four nights later, in the very early hours of 14 October, Swiss police with dogs surrounded 192, route de Florissant and silently made their way to the first floor. There they found Olga Hamel in her dressing gown, bent over her transmitter. Along with the radio they found 129 messages and a complete set of Sándor Radó's records and accounts, which he had left with the Hamels earlier in the month because he thought he was being followed.

Simultaneously, a second police detachment raided Margrit Bolli's apartment. But it was empty. They rushed to Hans Peters's apartment 150 metres away in rue Muller-Brun, where they found Bolli and her lover in bed together.

What the Swiss police should have done when they raided the Hamels' apartment in route de Florissant was also to keep an eye on their radio shop in the Geneva suburb of Carouge. If they had, they would have netted Radó too, for early the following morning he took some messages there for later collection and transmission to Moscow. As he approached the shop he saw that the hands of a large clock in its downstairs window were not set in the way they should have been to signal that the coast was clear. He left in a hurry. Later that morning, spotting banner headlines in the local paper, *La Tribune de Genève*, announcing that foreign agents had been captured in the city, Radó phoned Foote: 'Edouard [Hamel's codename] has been taken ill suddenly and is in hospital.' Then he caught the next train to Lausanne, where he found Foote decoding messages from Moscow Centre urgently demanding to know why Bolli's and the Hamels' radios had suddenly fallen silent. That evening Foote hid his radio and left for Bern. Helene and Sándor Radó took refuge in a safe house at Geneva University.

If all these dramatic, well-publicised events were, at least in part, the Swiss acting out an elaborate charade for German consumption, then they were timed to perfection. The day following Lieutenant Treyer's 'successes', Walter Schellenberg arrived in Zürich for another discussion with Roger Masson on how Germany's enemies spying from neutral Switzerland could be stopped. This time Masson had a good story to tell of how he had followed up the Germans' warnings and had nearly all the culprits in the bag. Whether Schellenberg went away satisfied, history does not relate.

Over the next month, events tumbled over each other as Moscow Centre tried desperately to reconstruct its network. Foote, now back in Lausanne, tried to avoid saying anything over the phone, which he was sure was bugged, and took long circuitous routes back to his flat to shake off a plainclothes tail who, he suspected, was now following him everywhere.

Meanwhile, Radó, desperate to find a safer refuge, did something extraordinary and revealing. He reached out to a 'Mr Cartwright' at the British legation in Bern asking if, in view of their common desire to help Russia against Hitler, the British would provide him with a place from which to continue his transmissions to Moscow. Mr Cartwright was all too happy to oblige.

Moscow Centre was horrified when it heard of Radó's plan, instructing him:

> You must do everything without delay to somehow reverse and hush up this extremely unwise act.

Two days later, after further thought, it added:

> After a thorough study of all your telegrams and an in-depth analysis of your affair, we are inclined to think that the whole business was organised … [by] British intelligence in Switzerland who appear not to understand the great importance of this historical moment for the common cause of the Allies.

Later, in answer to another appeal from Radó, this time an approach to the Swiss for help, Moscow sent a message which reveals that by this time it knew that Rudolf Roessler was working for the Swiss:

You can and must immediately arrange for the most important
information to be sent from Lucy [Roessler] via Jim [Foote] … Your
interpretation of our proposal – that Lucy, as the representative of a
friendly power, should endeavour to intervene with the Swiss – is [just
another] way to turn to the English. This is unacceptable.

Moscow would have been even more horrified if it had known that, in a
search for radios to replace the ones lost in the Swiss arrests, one of Radó's
other key agents, a man called Otto Puenter (who had his own contacts
with MI6) had offered Radó an ex-Swiss army wireless. This offer also
came, almost certainly, courtesy of MI6. London was bending over backwards to keep the Dora Ring running and providing intelligence to Moscow.

The revelation of Radó's contact with British intelligence seems to have
terminally damaged Moscow Centre's confidence in its chief agent in
Switzerland. On 8 November it told Radó that, rather than team up with
the 'English', he should continue to attempt to operate as before. If he felt
unable to do this, then he should go into hiding for two or three months.
It instructed Foote, however, to go on transmitting reports from Roessler,
which he would in future receive directly from Rachel Duebendorfer.

In mid-November, Foote spotted a monitoring car roaming the streets
of central Lausanne. For four days he maintained radio silence, hoping
that they would move on. But then, on 19 November, with important
messages for transmission piling up, he powered up his wireless and began
tapping out his call-sign. A little after midnight, as he was in the middle of
transmitting a long message, there was a mighty series of blows on his
door, which eventually burst into splinters, giving way to a torrent of Swiss
police, accompanied by two radio technicians. The technicians seized
Foote's wireless and attempted to continue his transmission to Moscow.
But they weren't quick enough – in the seconds before his door was beaten
down, Foote had burnt his messages over a candle and smashed his wireless set with a heavy hammer. Later the Swiss would try to 'play back'
Foote's radio to Moscow Centre. But they failed, because they did not have
his codes and addresses, which he had transcribed onto tissue paper and
hidden in his torch a few days previously.

Moscow Centre kept trying to raise Foote until 14 April 1944, when it
finally gave up and accepted that he must have been arrested, and that the
Dora Ring was dead.

Sándor and Helene Radó, who had left their two sons in the care of
Helene's mother, spent the next few weeks being transferred from safe

house to safe house by friends and members of the local Communist Party. They ended up in a single-roomed attic, furnished only with an ancient collapsible bed. Here they were required, despite the bed's springs protesting loudly whenever it was sat on, to remain silent all day for fear of discovery. In December 1943, MI6 in Bern somehow managed to make contact with the Radós through intermediaries and again offered them sanctuary. Radó refused.

In the late spring of 1944, Rachel Duebendorfer and her live-in boyfriend Paul Boettcher, along with Rudolf Roessler and Christian Schneider, were arrested.

After nine months on the run, dodging from house to house, Sándor and Helene Radó finally got out of Switzerland. On 16 September 1944 they were smuggled by local communist activists onto an early-morning milk train which took them through the railway tunnel which connects Geneva station with France. From there they made their way to a small chalet near Abondance in the Haute Savoie which they had used for family holidays. Here they spent the final months of the war acting as interpreters for a local French resistance group. Not long after he arrived in France, Sándor Radó heard that following the break-up of the Dora Ring, all his relatives in Hungary, including his seventy-three-year-old mother, his brother, his sister, her husband and their children, had been rounded up by the Gestapo and killed at Auschwitz.

The arrested Dora Ring conspirators were subsequently tried under Swiss law. When the prosecution attempted during his trial to read out the list of Alexander Foote's contacts, the judge prevented him on grounds of national security. Given the heavy penalties for spying in Switzerland, the accused received only the lightest of symbolic sentences. Olga Hamel was released on 7 June 1944, after eight months in prison; Margrit Bolli was freed five days later; Christian Schneider was given bail; Rudolf Roessler left prison on 6 September 1944; Foote and Rachel Duebendorfer were released two days later; and Paul Boettcher at the end of that month. For some reason we do not know, Edmond Hamel was not released until a year later.

The remarkable history of the Dora Ring, which made such an important contribution to the Second World War on the Eastern Front, was over. But its tangle of riddles, rumours, eddies, mirrors, mysteries and enigmas remains a matter of speculation and puzzlement even today. It probably always will.

25

Enter Stauffenberg

As with the winter retreat from the gates of Moscow in 1941, German sorrows following their defeat at Kursk came, like those of Hamlet, not as single spies but in battalions.

On 9 July 1943, with the battle for the Kursk salient swinging decisively in favour of the Russians, the Allies landed in Sicily. Two weeks later, Hitler's most important partner, Benito Mussolini, fell.

Sometime in the fortnight between the Allied invasion of Sicily and the fall of Mussolini, Erwin Lahousen was called to a secret meeting at Hitler's mountain retreat at Berchtesgaden. Only six people were present. In Hitler's absence, the participants were told, on the Führer's express order, that the meeting was to be kept an absolute secret: 'You gentlemen know what the slightest infringement of this will mean.' The purpose of the gathering was to draw up plans for the invasion of the Italian peninsula. The Führer, it was explained, had 'no confidence in Italy, even in Mussolini'. As the conclave ended, Lahousen was drawn to one side and told – again on the personal orders of Hitler – that Wilhelm Canaris was on no account to be informed of the plans.

Lahousen was now in a most difficult position: 'It was clear that both Hitler and those closest to him already deeply distrusted Canaris … I … knew Canaris's unpredictably impulsive and … emotional way of reacting to things which concerned him personally … [especially now, when] he already showed the marks of his desperate struggle against a system stronger than he.' Lahousen decided that his duty to his friend and chief compelled him to disobey the Führer's order, and warn Canaris of the danger he was in.

Canaris seemed less concerned about his own peril than about the threat to his friends in Italy. On 28 July, just three days after Mussolini's fall, Bletchley decrypts show that he sent a signal to the head of the Abwehr station in Rome asking him to deliver an urgent message to the chief of

Italian military intelligence, General Cesare Amè: 'Personal conversation with General Amè urgently desired. Request immediate answer when meeting in Venice is possible.' The Rome Abwehr head replied the following day: 'General Amè is ready to go to Venice immediately on call in order to meet. Your suggestion requested.' The previous meeting between the two men had been in the vast echoing space below the dome of St Peter's in Rome, where, away from inquisitive ears, they had shared pessimistic views about the progress of the war.

Canaris, accompanied by Lahousen, arrived at Venice airport from Munich at 8 a.m. on 30 July 1943. It was a brilliant Italian summer day, with a light northerly breeze. The early-morning sun was already drawing a thin mist off the waters of the Venice lagoon. Canaris was met at the airport by the head of the Rome Abwehr station and taken in a fast launch across the bay to the city. As they sped across the lagoon the dome of Santa Maria Salute and the tall finger of the campanile of San Marco rose out of the murk ahead of them. It was a sight to lighten even Wilhelm Canaris's mood of blackness and despair.

The Abwehr chief and his delegation were deposited at the steps of the private entrance of the Hotel Danieli. Here Canaris and Amè enjoyed a sumptuous lunch on the terrace overlooking the Grand Canal. Cesare Amè, a Piedmontese, an anglophile and politically close to the Italian king, was, like Canaris, a secret anti-fascist. But it was not just their views and their professional relationship which drew the two men together. They were also close personal friends. 'Canaris presented him to me as enjoying his absolute confidence,' Lahousen wrote later.

Over lunch, with Lahousen taking notes, Canaris told Amè that the SS were plotting to release Mussolini, and to kidnap the Italian king and possibly even the pope: 'Be careful, be very careful,' he warned the Italian. Amè listened attentively and then, smiling, raised his glass in the sunshine and proposed a toast to Canaris and the German visitors. It was probably at this point that Amè unveiled the research he had commissioned on Canaris's forebears, proving that they did not come from Greece, as the family believed, but were originally the Canarisi from Lake Como. 'He looked at the papers I gave him,' Amè said later. 'His hands trembled and, with his eyes brimming with tears, he said simply, "Thank you Amè, thank you."'

Afterwards the party was taken in a launch to the Lido, the long sandbar scattered with hotels and villas which protects the Venice lagoon from the ravages of the Adriatic. Instructing Lahousen to distract the attention of Amè's entourage, Canaris took his friend's arm and led him on an hour-long walk along the beach. They talked first about the removal of Mussolini five days earlier, on 25 July. 'Heartiest congratulations. We hope our 25 July will come quickly,' Canaris commented dryly. Then he turned to German plans to invade Italy: 'Take my advice. Let as few German troops into Italy as you can. Otherwise you will regret it,' he cautioned. As their walk ended, Canaris raised the main purpose of his visit, urging his friend to encourage Marshal Pietro Badoglio, shortly to become Mussolini's replacement as the leader of Italy, to reach a deal with the Allies which would withdraw Italy from the war. 'He loved Germany deeply,' Amè commented afterwards. 'After the events of 1943 he believed that every setback for the Nazis was beneficial because it hastened the collapse of the regime, and that might avoid total catastrophe for his country.'

After their return to the city from the Lido there were farewell speeches, including a long one from Amè which dwelt on their 'brotherhood of arms' and 'sacred duty' to work together. Canaris reportedly listened to this with 'great seriousness'. On the way back to his aircraft he instructed Lahousen to write a report for Berlin emphasising the absolute determination of Italy to remain loyal to its alliance with Germany.

In June, Sir Francis D'Arcy Osborne, the British minister to the Vatican, returned from a visit to London with instructions to begin testing the ground for a separate peace between Italy and the Allies. It is very likely that Canaris knew of this, and welcomed it as a move which would weaken Hitler and increase his isolation. But there may have been a second reason for Canaris's enthusiasm for an Italian armistice. On 28 June, a month before Canaris's meeting with Amè, Osborne, who was strongly opposed to the Casablanca policy of a punitive peace, circulated a document designed to distance Italy from the strictures of unconditional surrender. Osborne proposed that any Italian peace with the Allies should 'not portend any ill-treatment of the Italian people after surrender or any ill-will towards a future non-Fascist Government and state'. Canaris would undoubtedly have been aware of this important statement offering 'peace with honour' to the Italians, and would have seen it as an encouraging sign of Allied flexibility on the Casablanca conditions which might still open the way to a similar opportunity for Germany.

For a brief moment it looked as though the British prime minister too was softening his line on unconditional surrender. On 14 August, two weeks after Canaris's return from Venice, Churchill wrote a minute to the Foreign Office instructing: 'there is no need for us to discourage this process [of peace feelers from Germany] by continually uttering the slogan "Unconditional Surrender" … we certainly do not want, if we can help it, to get them all fused together in a solid block for whom there is no hope'. Sadly, just a month later Churchill's brief second thoughts reversed themselves, leaving Canaris's hopes once again stillborn: 'I am sure we should not depart from our policy of absolute silence', he wrote to foreign secretary Eden, who had suggested a minor softening of the policy. 'Nothing would be more disturbing to our friends in the United States or more dangerous to our new ally Russia. I am absolutely opposed to the slightest contact.'

Canaris's meeting with Amè had not gone unnoticed. Even before he left Italy, the Abwehr station in Berlin reported that the Hitler loyalist (and subsequent rescuer of Mussolini from his mountain prison) Otto Skorzeny had noted and reported the Abwehr chief's visit to Venice. Worse still, Walter Schellenberg, who had a spy in Amè's household, soon got to hear of the meeting, and reported it to Himmler. But to Schellenberg's surprise the SS chief told him to drop his enquiries and to leave 'the old man in peace'. Schellenberg concluded that Canaris must have some leverage over Himmler. But it seems more likely that Himmler, who at this stage of the war was already beginning to take out his own insurance against an Allied victory, was content for the moment to leave Canaris putting out peace feelers which might prove useful to him later.

On 6 September 1943, five weeks after his visit to Venice, Canaris made a secret journey to Bern, travelling on a false passport. The head of the local Abwehr station was instructed to meet him at the Swiss frontier and 'take care that [his] entry permit is to be found in all circumstances at the appropriate frontier station'. We do not know the purpose of his visit, though given that the Wehrmacht occupied Italy in force three days later, it is probable that at least one reason would have been to alert the West to the impending invasion, perhaps through Gisevius or Halina Szymańska.

While Canaris was in Venice warning Cesare Amè, Henning von Tresckow was suddenly posted to command an operational battalion on the Eastern Front. This was another serious blow to the plotters. Von Tresckow's position at Army Group Centre headquarters in Smolensk had enabled him to play a pivotal role in organising front-line support for the coup, when it came. This would be lost once he was isolated in a fighting unit – which indeed may have been the reason for the posting. Fortunately, before his departure to the front, von Tresckow managed finally to bring Field

Marshal Günther von Kluge,* who had taken over from von Tresckow's uncle Fedor von Bock as Army Group Centre's commander, to the brink of committing himself to the plotters. Getting Kluge on board was essential, as without him the plot would not have a senior general able to lead the revolt on the Eastern Front.

Carl Goerdeler threw his weight behind von Tresckow's persuasions, writing to Kluge in late July:

> My dear Field Marshal,
> I take the liberty of making a last appeal to you … The hour has now come at which we must take the final decision on our personal fate …
> We must put an end to the state of affairs in which we allow fools to force their delusions and lies on the German people. We must make the war of conquest, started from a spirit of domination, into a war of necessary defence … German interests must once again be represented with force and reason by decent Germans.
> I will not trespass any further on your time, my dear Field Marshal … One thing I ask you; not to refuse to answer because you are afraid. I have learned not to be silent and I shall not forget the lesson.
>
> With best wishes.
> Yours sincerely.
> Goerdeler

A few days later, Goerdeler asked Jacob Wallenberg to pass the word to London that the putsch was ready and would be mounted in September, followed by peace talks, which would be led by Fabian von Schlabrendorff, who would be sent to Stockholm.

In the course of a visit to London in May and June, Wallenberg's brother Marcus had managed to pass on Goerdeler's plans for a peace deal to Desmond Morton, the principal No. 10 assistant to Winston Churchill. Morton told the Swede that this was 'interesting information', and hoped he would be kept informed about any further developments, emphasising that he could make no pledges.

Jacob Wallenberg now needed to bring Morton up to date on the latest news from Goerdeler that the coup was imminent. His secret channel for

---

* His nickname was 'Kluger Hans', a play on the fact that kluger means 'clever one' in German.

passing written information to London was a British banking contact, Charles Hambro, whose second wife Dorothy had previously been married to Jacob Wallenberg's brother, Marcus. A former officer in the Coldstream Guards, at the time chairman of the board of Great Western Railways and a senior partner at Hambros Bank, which had been founded by his Danish immigrant forebears in the early nineteenth century, Charles Jocelyn Hambro MC was also a wartime officer in the Special Operations Executive. His connections in London extended, as befitted a senior banker and an Old Etonian, into every nook and cranny of Whitehall, including, naturally, Desmond Morton in the prime minister's private office.

It was through this conduit that, following Goerdeler's tip-off of the impending coup, a highly secret exchange of unsigned handwritten letters was initiated around 6 September 1943 between Marcus Wallenberg and Desmond Morton:

> *Enskilda Bank*
> *Stockholm*
> *Dear Desmond,*
> *… I shall give you some indication of how the wind …*
>   *The interested parties have come very far in their preparations …*
> *Outlines over procedure and the names of those in the organization have been furnished, showing the great width and scope of [their] plans.*
>   *Once the plan is carried through it is their desire to establish some unofficial contact with you … to give you information of their intentions and … with a hope of receiving some indications … of measures for reaching an end to this war.*
>   *Such a personal contact could be arranged on neutral territory and their representative would be a personal acquaintance of W.C. [Wilhelm Canaris]*

Three weeks later a letter arrived at the Enskilda Bank, with stern instructions that it was not to be seen by anyone else and especially not the British legation in Stockholm.

Great Western Railway
Board Room
Paddington Sta.
29.9.43.
My dear Marc,
... you spoke to someone in high circles about ... plans of some of the professional warriors in a neighbouring country unfriendly to mine. Following this ... you wrote a letter.

You should ... reply ... to the effect that they should certainly go on with their plans and take the action they contemplate.

Action will be construed as an act of good faith and proof that they are serious people with standing and influence in their country.

No undertaking of any kind can be given or expected ...

If the event contemplated really happens it may be possible for someone (perhaps myself) to come and see you.

Please forget that you have communicated to anyone but me about this matter.

Good luck to you.
(Probably wise to destroy these pages)

It seems certain that Charles Hambro would have checked the broad lines of this letter, if not its precise text, with 10 Downing Street. We do not know if it was ever seen by Goerdeler – probably not, given Hambro's injunctions on confidentiality. But if its substance was passed on by Wallenberg, it would have come as a huge encouragement and relief to the plotters, as it hinted strongly that if Hitler were removed, the punitive aspects of 'unconditional surrender' would be, if not abandoned, then considerably softened.

In fact, the information Goerdeler passed to Downing Street by way of Jacob and Marcus Wallenberg and Charles Hambro was inaccurate – but only by a fortnight.

Von Kluge finally threw his weight behind the plotters at a meeting in Berlin in September attended by Goerdeler, Beck (recently released from hospital after his illness), von Tresckow (on pre-posting leave) and Olbricht. But once again there was a wobble. The field marshal had no sooner crossed the Rubicon in one direction, than Carl Goerdeler crossed it in the opposite one. Seized by one of his fits of utopianism, he announced to his startled co-conspirators that no coup would be necessary because he, the ex-mayor of Leipzig, would 'speak frankly with the Führer', and that would do the trick. 'Anyone could be won over to a good cause,' he declared, to disbelief all round. Unsurprisingly, Goerdeler's suggestion died without trace.

With von Kluge finally on board, Friedrich Olbricht decided that all was now in place and the coup could be launched, setting mid-October as the date. But then, as so often, fate played her hand against the conspirators. On 12 October von Kluge was seriously injured in a car crash and put out of action for several months. Worse still, he was replaced as commander of Army Group Centre by Ernst Busch, a dyed-in-the-wool Hitler loyalist. The coup had to be postponed once again.

Two days after Hambro's letter from the director's office at Paddington station to Marcus Wallenberg in Stockholm, Claus von Stauffenberg arrived at the Bendlerblock to assume his new post as the chief of staff to Friedrich Olbricht. It was not an accidental appointment. Von Stauffenberg had spent five months recuperating from his North African wounds, first in Munich and then at his family castle, Schloss Lautlingen in southern Germany. In the second week of August he met Henning von Tresckow at Olbricht's house, and was fully recruited to the cause. It had not been difficult to secure a post assisting Olbricht, who as head of the Reserve Army was tasked with employing wounded men incapable of service at the front (like Stauffenberg). The Reserve Army's other duties were to recruit and train replacements for front-line units, administer those home on leave, test new military equipment, and act as a reserve force in an emergency for the protection of the government in Berlin.

It is notable how many anti-Hitler conspirators were scions of the heroes whose military, civil and artistic prowess helped create the flowering of modern Germany in the nineteenth century. Among these were a Bismarck, a von Moltke, a Dohnányi, and three direct descendants of Field Marshal August Neidhardt von Gneisenau – Claus von Stauffenberg and his twin elder brothers Berthold and Alexander.

Count Claus Philipp Maria Justinian Schenk von Stauffenberg was, at first sight, a classic product of his upbringing: aristocratic, Catholic, born to command, formidably gifted, definite in his views, dedicated to public service in the tradition of his ancestors, and driven by pride of family and the Fatherland. A school friend described him somewhat breathlessly: 'His glowing eyes clearly expressed his cheerfulness ... and generosity. Their colour was dark blue ... His hair was shining black ... always cut short. His development from youth to adulthood ... was rapid. He was tall and flexible with a slender, powerful body.'

Claus von Stauffenberg

Like so many of his social class, Claus von Stauffenberg was at first seduced by Hitler's rise to power, seeing it as a necessary antidote to the humiliations of Versailles and the failures of the Weimar Republic. This led to a brief enthusiasm for the Hitler Youth and, later, some glorification of his early military successes.

With that exception, Stauffenberg was in many ways a man who stood apart from his military colleagues. He had thought about becoming an architect in preference to a life in the military. He was a good enough musician to have seriously considered a musical career. A man of powerful passions and strong views, he was greatly influenced by one of the foremost poets of his time, the mystic nationalist Stefan George, and wrote some poetry himself. His views, founded on a strong moral code based on his Catholic beliefs, were nevertheless heterodox and somewhat contradictory. A strong nationalist, he was dedicated to the cause of German political and moral revival. A believer in order, he was yet more romantic revolutionary socialist than middle-class liberal. A practical and highly professional soldier, he also had a deep fascination, almost an obsession, with the spiritual and the mystical. Stauffenberg was a man of extremes. Whatever he believed, and whatever he did, he believed and did with absolute certainty, absolute commitment and absolute energy. Timidity and self-doubt had no part in his make-up.

Von Stauffenberg was also a natural leader who radiated charisma through a potent combination of an attractive physical presence, powerful eloquence, intellectual drive and spiritual force which some (like Gisevius) found sinister and others irresistibly captivating. The power of his will and the strength of his influence over others made him, in some strange way, the precise Zoroastrian counterbalance to Hitler, whose similar talents were committed to a diametrically opposite purpose.

Younger than Ludwig Beck by twenty-seven years, and almost seven years Henning von Tresckow's junior, von Stauffenberg brought to the resistance an almost electric charge of vigour, leadership and energy. This was exactly what it needed most in October 1943 in order to fill the vacuum of leadership left by the removal of Oster, the sickness of Beck, von Kluge's accident and von Tresckow's posting to a front-line command.

For many of the conspirators, even those who knew that they had to be shaken out of their torpor and emotional exhaustion, the von Stauffenberg of October 1943 was, however, not an easy bedfellow.

His nobility and charisma were somehow enhanced by his mutilated form, with his right arm dangling limp and the black eyepatch which he regularly lifted to dab a watery empty eyesocket with a piece of lint. The disfigurement of his personality was almost as striking as that of his body. His near-death experience in the North African desert had changed him – not fundamentally, but in scale. He was still the same character, only more so. All his natural characteristics seemed to have been magnified by his suffering and the humiliations of a broken body.

Always determined, he was now driven – his anger had turned into obsession, his directness into disdain, as though his disfigurements and the great task he had set himself of killing Hitler excused him from the need for politeness and the social graces. His strong will had transmuted into obduracy; his persuasive self-confidence into didactic impatience, peppered with asperity; his conversation, which previously had had an attractive directness, now meandered in wide arcs of circumlocution uttered in a hoarse, soft voice which some compared to Bismarck's, until, like a circling hawk, he would suddenly swoop on a conclusion which brooked no contradiction. Treason, from which he had recoiled before Stalingrad, had now become 'a duty'. His habit of leading a generally purposeful life was now subsumed into a single Messianic enterprise, complete with the probability of martyrdom. It was as though his damaged body had turned into a metaphor for the mutilation of all he valued in his country, his army and his honour. For this, a single person – Adolf Hitler – bore the entire blame. Stauffenberg had no time for those who would not, or could not, share his dedication to tyrannicide.

'It's time for me to save the German Reich,' he said to his wife Nina. He told a friend, 'The struggle against National Socialism … could be done only one way; by eliminating Hitler and the men around him.' The army alone could achieve this, he believed, so the army alone concerned him – a civil role in the putsch held no interest, nor did attempts to negotiate an early peace with the West: 'It is too late for the West,' he declared; Stalin would be standing in Berlin in weeks anyway. The October 1943 version of Claus von Stauffenberg had exchanged the romantic soldier for the implacable crusader waging total war by any means, and at any cost, on behalf of good, against the absolute evil of Adolf Hitler; 'The High Priest of Vermin extends his domain', he would say, quoting Stefan George, whose poem 'The Anti-Christ' he carried with him at all times.

All the complexities of Claus von Stauffenberg, the man of action, art and refinement, had now been distilled down to a single deadly purpose – that of creating, or if necessary becoming, the assassin's bullet.

26

Valkyrie and Tehran

Claus von Stauffenberg's takeover of the military elements of the anti-Hitler conspiracy was swift, and very soon complete.

Supported by Hans Olbricht and a growing staff at the Reserve Army office, he got to work on von Tresckow's as-yet incomplete plan, finalising the host of details which had still to be settled – the mobilisation table, the schedule for occupying the offices of the Reich, the secret orders to be issued to various Reserve Army units, and the notices to be promulgated to the population and the public services on Hitler's death. To help him with the mountain of paperwork he recruited three female volunteers: von Tresckow's wife Erika; Stauffenberg's close personal friend Margarete von Oven; and Ehrengard von der Schulenburg. Much of the typing – which Stauffenberg insisted should be carried out in gloves to avoid leaving fingerprints – was done in the newly-acquired Stauffenberg house, a steep-roofed, half-timbered property straight out of Grimms' fairy tales, set among fir trees on a leafy road in the quiet Berlin suburb of Wannsee.*

At the core of the Stauffenberg/Olbricht coup was an already existing Reserve Army operation codenamed Operation Valkyrie.

Earlier in the year, Friedrich Olbricht, as part of his duties in the Reserve Army, had reviewed and updated Valkyrie, a contingency plan which used units of the Reserve Army to protect Berlin in the case of 'internal disturbances'. Hitler himself had signed off on Olbricht's revised plan on 31 July 1943.

Operation Valkyrie was divided into two phases. Valkyrie I consisted of a running training programme to ensure the combat-readiness of all units of the Reserve Army, which included provisions for regular rehearsals in Berlin; one dress rehearsal during a British air raid in the spring of 1944

---

* The property remains almost completely unchanged today from the morning Stauffenberg walked out of it on his way to attempt to kill Hitler.

involved tanks from the armoured and infantry training schools storming in to occupy the government quarter, causing Goebbels to complain furiously about the disruption.

Valkyrie II, the operational element of the plan, was made up of a series of detailed orders, copies of which were deposited in sealed envelopes in the safes of all Berlin unit commanders. These included the codewords to initiate Valkyrie I and II ('Swallow' and 'Seagull' respectively), battle orders, communications details, assembly points, routes, and a complete scheme for troop deployment at key locations in and around the German capital. Every Friday evening, commanders in the Reserve Army were required to render a Valkyrie report, giving their units' strengths and states of readiness, to Stauffenberg in his role as chief of staff to Olbricht. Under the Valkyrie II provisions, troops were required to be ready for deployment within six hours of the codeword being given. At this point all units, including those formed from the students at the armoured and infantry schools, were to be organised into combat commands and given their tasks. These included securing telephone and telegraph exchanges, radio transmitters, power plants, bridges and government buildings. Some units were also specially trained in the arrest of personnel, the detention of prisoners, the occupation of government buildings and the overwhelming of rebel strongpoints.

Communications played a central role in the Valkyrie plan, especially the management of telephone exchanges and wireless traffic. The Stauffenberg/Olbricht version of Valkyrie called for the establishment of a discrete, secure parallel communications network which would only come into operation as soon as the Valkyrie codeword was given. This was to be managed by General Erich Fellgiebel,* the chief of the army's Signal Establishment and therfore responsible for all the links with Hitler's Supreme Command Headquarters (OKW), including with his forward headquarters at Wolfsschanze. Fellgiebel's most important task in the plot was to sever all communications between Hitler and the outside world from the moment the coup was launched. His second task was, in the words of a fellow conspirator, 'to keep open, on the day of the coup, all means of communication between the centre of the resistance movement, the office of General Olbricht, and all other key offices'. Fellgiebel's success would in due course cause the plot to be nicknamed by the Gestapo the 'Switchboard Putsch'.

---

* Fellgiebel was one of Rudolf Roessler's key sources for information passed to the Allies and the Dora Ring.

We do not know precisely when the conspirators realised that Operation Valkyrie, designed to protect Hitler, could also be used to remove him. This possibility was greatly enhanced by a provision in the Valkyrie orders that stipulated: 'Under no circumstances may agencies and individuals outside the Wehrmacht be informed of the intentions [of Valkyrie] or of any preparatory work' – meaning that the Gestapo and the SD could justifiably be excluded from all Valkyrie-related activities. Training, preparation, mobilisation and deployment of the Reserve Army could all thus take place perfectly legitimately and secretly under the cover of Valkyrie I's provisions. The true, subverted purpose of Valkyrie II would only need to be revealed at the very last moment, when commanders gave their final orders. If Hitler was already dead or out of contact by that time, then the Reserve Army commander's orders to take over and protect the instruments of government in Berlin, including military headquarters, communications routes, broadcast transmitters and channels, police stations and administrative departments, would all be entirely legal and appropriate. Valkyrie was, in short, a perfect instrument both to deliver power to the conspirators and to protect their ability to hold onto it in the case of external attack.

Except for one factor – General Friedrich Fromm. As the overall commander of the Reserve Army, Fromm's signature was necessary on a Valkyrie II mobilisation order to give it authority with unit commanders. The fifty-five-year-old Fromm, a big figure with a weak and vacillating personality, was appointed by Hitler to command the Reserve Army after the defeat at Moscow. He was a lazy, self-regarding, vain man, and as someone who in his own words 'always came down on the right side', an expert at bending to the prevailing wind. Approached to support the October 1938 coup plot, Fromm had taken twenty-four hours to politely decline, while expressing the hope that it would succeed. To cover his back, he recorded the approach and his refusal to take part – but not, obviously, his hope that it would succeed – in his official diary.

Before being posted to the Reserve Army staff, Stauffenberg had several conversations with Fromm, during which the younger man made clear his view that the war was lost, and that the blame lay exclusively with Hitler. When Fromm made no objections to what was, at the time, officially regarded as defeatism punishable by death, Stauffenberg concluded that his commander would, at the very least, not stand in the way of the coup when it was launched – especially if by that time Hitler was dead. But the matter would need to be clarified nearer the moment.

By mid-November, Stauffenberg had laid down the final military details of the 'grand coup'. The conspirators were now ready for what they referred to as 'the initial spark' which would set the process in train – the assassination of Hitler. The problem was: who would do the deed? They needed someone with regular access to the Führer.

The final weeks of 1943 were peppered with plan after plan to assassinate the dictator, all of which failed, for reasons either of human weakness or bad luck. The first would-be assassin, who as head of the organisation of the OKW briefed Hitler almost daily, stalled on the grounds that he didn't believe a bomb could be brought into the briefing room without being noticed. The second, also of the OKW, agreed to think about doing the job, but then got cold feet. Finally von Stauffenberg was put in touch with 'a reliable young officer', Captain Axel von dem Bussche-Streithorst, the man who had turned from a Hitler enthusiast to an implacable enemy ready to 'die in battle, to desert or to rebel' after witnessing a mass execution of Jews in the Ukraine in October 1942.

The plan was for Bussche-Streithorst to attend a presentation at the end of November 1943, at which he would brief the Führer on some new uniforms. In the course of their discussion he was to secretly initiate an explosive hidden in his clothing, and then leap onto Hitler and hold him down for three or four seconds until the bomb exploded, killing them both. Bussche-Streithorst agreed to this somewhat bizarre suicide attack without hesitation. He travelled with his bomb to the Führer's Wolfsschanze headquarters, and waited: 'The sunny late-autumn days amid the forests and lakes are imbued with the heightened intensity a soldier feels before an attack,' he wrote in his diary. The presentation was first postponed, then postponed again – and again – until finally it came to light that the railway wagon carrying the new uniforms had been destroyed in an Allied bombing raid on Berlin. Replacements would not be available until January 1944. Once again it seemed to the plotters that some kind of evil providence was protecting the tyrant in order to ensure that Germany could not escape its full appointed measure of agony before he could be got rid of.

Von dem Bussche-Streithorst, however, suffered more than disappointment. Ordered to return to the front in a hurry before he could get rid of the bomb, he was badly wounded in early 1944, losing a leg. Accompanied by his suitcase, complete with the bomb, he was transferred down the line from hospital to hospital, and was unable to rid himself of the embarrassing leftover until, a full nine months later, he persuaded a friend to throw it into a lake.

At about the same time, a second bomb, which had been hidden at Wolfsschanze after a previous failed attempt, also had to be disposed of. In this case the conspirators decided to bury it under one of the watchtowers in the woods close to the Mauerwald barracks, which served Wolfsschanze. The two men assigned to the task of disposing of the package were spotted by a patrol and only just managed to escape, leaving the bomb behind. It was recovered, made safe and put away in an Abwehr store near Berlin. It would not be long before this particular slab of British explosive would be flown back to Wolfsschanze for a second chance to do the deadly work originally intended for it.

Luckily, the investigation that followed the bomb's discovery was led by a friend of Hans Oster's, who managed to sidetrack the inquiry into a cul de sac from which it never emerged.

Not long afterwards, Erwin Lahousen visited Oster at his home and found his colleague in deep depression over the repeated failures to kill Hitler, and especially over Canaris's disengagement from the plot process and his haphazard and careless management of the Abwehr. Though Canaris remained a figure in the background who could be called on to assist, the admiral's mind and spirit seemed to his old friends to have retreated into their own private domain.

Others, however, though no doubt set back by Hitler's repeated miraculous escapes, continued to busy themselves with filling in unfinished elements of the grand coup.

It was probably during this process that, sometime in the early autumn of 1943, Claus von Stauffenberg and Carl Goerdeler met for the first time. It was never likely to be an easy encounter, for the two men were larger-than-life representatives of two totally opposite Germanies. Goerdeler, stiff, serious, intellectual, traditional, morally superior and committed to change through political process rather than violence, was unlikely to find an easy conversationalist in the passionate, impulsive, impatient Stauffenberg, who did not shrink from violence in the service of the greater good, and was instinctively distrustful of politicians, especially when there was soldiers' work to be done.

The two men swiftly decided that they heartily disliked each other. 'A cranky and obstinate fellow who wanted to play politics,' Goerdeler later wrote of Stauffenberg. 'I had many a row with him but greatly esteemed him. He wanted to steer a dubious course with the left socialists and the communists and gave me a bad time with his ego.' Stauffenberg, meanwhile, dismissed his elder as 'the leader of the revolution of greybeards' whose reactionary ideas were out of touch with the realities of the modern world. The grating mismatch between the two went deeper than personalities. Goerdeler had always believed that the end of Hitler would be brought about by a senior general. It may have irked him to find his precious dream now in the hands of this upstart youngster. There was wide political disagreement between the two as well. Goerdeler looked to engagement with the West for Germany's future. Stauffenberg was a confirmed 'Easterner' who followed the more traditional German view that his country's best linkages lay with Russia.

In late November, Ludwig Beck, still seen as the presiding father figure of the conspiracy from his mansion amongst the trees at Goethestrasse 9, asked Goerdeler to begin the process of assembling an alternative government that would come into being after Hitler had been killed. Goerdeler, who like von Stauffenberg did not know how to approach a task except at full bore, spent the last weeks of 1943 assembling a comprehensive list of 'ministers' for a shadow government. Some worthy candidates were excluded because they would create a political, cultural or even religious imbalance. Once the list was assembled and agreed, Goerdeler set about getting approval (not always easily) from his fellow conspirators, and then approaching the chosen individuals to secure their acceptance to serve. Beck was to be the new head of state, Goerdeler himself chancellor, and so on right down to ministers of foreign affairs, agriculture, culture and the arts, the interior, trade, etc.

But Goerdeler did not stop there. Assisted, despite their personal differences, by Stauffenberg, he undertook the extremely dangerous task of travelling around the country recruiting teams of people who would take over the regional civilian and military authorities on receipt of the codeword sent from Berlin. On his travels he made contact with civilian resistance organisations, most notably with the leaders of what was left of the pre-war German labour, Catholic and socialist movements.* These were also recruited to the cause – though Goerdeler had to work hard to overcome deep suspicion from the left about trusting the army with the main action. In time, as successive attempts to kill Hitler raised hopes only for them to be dashed, it became increasingly difficult to maintain the unity of Goerdeler's broad coalition. By the end of 1943, however, a small army of willing conspirators had been painfully assembled, stretching into

---

* These included Josef Wirmer, Julius Leber, Graf Helldorf, Jacob Kaiser and Max Haberman.

almost every corner of Germany and German life. Sadly, Goerdeler, in his neat, organised way, made careful lists of all the names, which would later become death sentences in the hands of Himmler's hunters.

Although they appear to have known nothing for certain at this stage, by the late months of 1943 the Gestapo began to sense that something was stirring. In early December the whole plot very nearly became exposed when one of the conspirators' stores of explosive blew up. A nationwide hunt was instituted in an attempt to find out what was going on, and Hitler's personal protection was strengthened. As Beck and Goerdeler came under more and more Gestapo pressure, they were increasingly forced to rely on von Stauffenberg, protected by his army position, to act as the coup's chief driver, organiser and motivator. All realised that with the Gestapo closing in, they were now in a race between killing Hitler and discovery.

While Claus von Stauffenberg and Carl Goerdeler were busy, the first trying to kill Hitler, the second assembling a shadow government to replace him, Churchill, Stalin and Roosevelt were meeting in the comprehensively pre-bugged Soviet embassy in Tehran to settle the strategy for the final phase of the war.

Tehran was more than just a war-planning conference. It also marked the pivotal moment when the Allied chiefs began to turn their full attention to what would happen when the war was over. In that sense it should be seen alongside the Yalta and Potsdam Conferences as one of the 'great three' summits which decided the shape of the post-war world.

For those among the anti-Hitler resistance who hoped against hope that it might still be possible to reach an early peace after getting rid of Hitler, the public portents from Tehran were encouraging. The final declaration from the conference on 1 December 1943 included a statement that the Allies would welcome 'into the world family of democratic nations' all those ready to join the fight against tyrants. Stalin went so far as to condemn the policy of unconditional surrender as unnecessary and unwise (a view which did much to add weight to those among the resisters who believed they should look east rather than west for salvation). He suggested instead that the Allies should make a concrete statement of peace conditions. The British lobbied Washington in favour of this, as did, behind the scenes, Roosevelt's secretary of state Cordell Hull. But Roosevelt was unmovable, insisting that the policy of unconditional German surrender must be fulfilled to the letter (even though this policy had by now been relaxed for other Axis states such as Italy, Finland, Hungary and Bulgaria). What this meant was that there would be – could be – no room for dealing with Germany even after Hitler had been removed.

The victories at Stalingrad and Kursk had turned the Soviet Union into a major world power. Basking in this glory, and with his leverage enhanced by Roosevelt's insistence on having no other partner than him, Stalin dominated the discussions at Tehran. He told his advisers before the conference: 'Now the fate of Europe is settled, we shall do as we like, with the Allies' consent.' Which was more or less exactly what he did.

After clarifying the strategy for the conclusion of the war (including the opening of a second front with an invasion of northern France) the trium-virs turned their attention to Eastern Europe – and specifically Poland. At this stage Roosevelt, whose health was failing, excused himself from the discussion in order, he said, not to damage his ability to secure Polish-American votes in the coming US election. Stalin and Churchill were left alone to make the decision on what would turn out to be the crucial centrepiece that determined the shape of post-war Europe – the extent and position of Poland. In order to give Stalin a defensible buffer along his western frontier, the two leaders unilaterally moved Poland, lock, stock and barrel, a hundred kilometres to the west. This meant handing the east-ern Polish marshlands over to the Soviet Union so as to give Stalin strength in depth on his western border. Poland, in compensation, was given terri-tory in east Prussia, Pomerania and the industrial heartland of Silesia right up to the line of the Oder and Neisse rivers. The matter of Poland concluded, the three leaders reconvened and turned their attention to laying the groundwork for the post-war partition of their enemy into Allied zones of occupation. Churchill was prepared to go much further, writing after Tehran: 'Germany is to be decisively broken up into a number of separate states. East Prussia and Germany east of the Oder are to be alienated forever and the population shifted. Prussia itself is to be divided and curtailed. The Ruhr and the other great centres of coal and steel must be put outside the power of Prussia.' Far from being left 'fat but impotent' as Churchill had proposed in 1941, Germany, according to Churchill at Tehran, should be first diminished and then dismembered.

Churchill did not have a comfortable conference at Tehran. Now the junior partner between two superpowers, he was repeatedly humiliated by Roosevelt in front of Stalin, with whom the US president sided on almost every contentious issue. Roosevelt mistakenly believed that he could handle the Russian dictator by being nice to him. Churchill, in contrast, had no illusions about Stalin. He knew that, though the Soviet leader was a necessary wartime ally, he was unlikely to be a congenial peacetime friend. But since the United States, the only power capable of counterbalancing Stalin's imperial intentions, was not prepared to do this – at least not in 1944 – the only practical alternative was to accommodate Stalin in order to win the war, while hoping to reach a more just settled peace afterwards.

Of all this the plotters knew nothing. They ploughed on, with increasing and ultimately tragic desperation, trying to find a way to a peace which, from Tehran onwards, was never going to be available.

The two Western Allied leaders were now bound together by the Faustian bargain they had made to keep Stalin on board at any cost. For the time being the price for this was to be paid by Germany. At the Moscow Conference a year later, however, the cost of keeping Stalin satisfied became the whole of Eastern Europe.

At this summit, held in October 1944, Churchill and Stalin returned to the business of privately redesigning the post-war Continent. The crucial moment in the poker game came when Churchill pushed a piece of paper, which he later referred to as his 'naughty document', across the table to Stalin. This proposed that Eastern Europe should be divided into 'spheres of influence'. Stalin looked briefly at Churchill's scrap of paper, ticked it and pushed it back. By the time the last card was played in the ensuing negotiations, the two men had parcelled out Hitler's eastern conquests between them. Britain would have 90 per cent of what was referred to euphemistically as a 'predominance of influence' in Greece, the two countries would divide Yugoslavia 50/50, and Russia would have 90 per cent 'predominant influence' in Romania and 80 per cent in Hungary and Bulgaria. The basis for the post-war Soviet occupation – some might say enslavement – of Eastern Europe, which was the almost inevitable consequence of the lack of room for manoeuvre which the rigid application of 'unconditional surrender' imposed upon Roosevelt and Churchill, had been established.

27

Disappointment, Disruption, Desperation

Not long before Christmas 1943, a gangly, two-metre-tall figure with a sallow complexion, thinning hair and sharp, questioning eyes arrived at the Abwehr offices in Istanbul.

Though he was a great-grandnephew of the victorious hero of the Prussian wars of the nineteenth century, Count Helmuth James von Moltke was not a soldier, but a lawyer. Leader of the Kreisau Circle* which met at his estate, member of the English Bar and the child of an English mother, he had been recruited by Wilhelm Canaris into the Abwehr and had spent much of the war so far plotting with his friends at Kreisau, advising Canaris on legal matters and trying to mitigate the worst effects of the brutal racial laws and practices of the Hitler regime.

The thirty-six-year-old von Moltke was a quiet man whose personality stood in sharp contrast to his Prussian roots and heritage. The very opposite of the classic Junker reactionary, he was a liberal and a European who would have found himself thoroughly at home in the Germany of today. General 'Wild Bill' Donovan, the head of the American OSS, considered him 'very well read and educated ... quiet and reserved [with a] strong sense of decency, justice and fairness ... Everyone who knows him agrees about his integrity, his intelligence ... [he] would risk more than the average [to be in contact with us].'

Von Moltke's December trip to Istanbul had been preceded by a visit sanctioned by Canaris in July, during which he probed the possibilities of getting Kreisau Circle proposals for an early peace to Washington through an old Berlin friend, Alexander Kirk, at the time the US ambassador in Cairo. This second visit, again conducted on the instructions of Canaris, who also provided him with a cover story (the pretext was a dispute over

* Moltke's OSS codename was 'Hermann'; the Kreisau Circle was also referred to as 'the Hermann Group'.

the fate of a fleet of French river steamers interned in the neutral waters of the Sea of Marmora), was made in expectation of a meeting with Kirk, who was apparently flying from Cairo to meet him. In the event, however, Kirk never turned up, forcing von Moltke to return to Berlin commenting, 'Now all is lost.'

But it wasn't – quite. During his July visit to Istanbul, von Moltke had been persuaded by German friends* who were in touch with US intelligence that there was no possibility of Washington watering down the policy of unconditional surrender, and that any peace proposal to the West would explicitly have to accept this if it were to have any chance of success. Following his departure, and based on comments he had made during his visit, von Moltke's Istanbul colleagues made one last attempt to persuade the Americans of the merits of an early peace after Hitler had been removed. Their paper, 'Conditions for Collaboration with the Allies', was passed through an OSS agent in Istanbul to the US embassy in the Turkish capital Ankara, and thence to General Donovan, who was at the time setting up an OSS office in Cairo. It comprised the most detailed and substantive peace proposals ever made by the German opposition to the Western Allies.

In a radical departure from all previous peace proposals, 'Conditions for Collaboration with the Allies' accepted, in terms, President Roosevelt's insistence on unconditional surrender. It specifically acknowledged that the 'unequivocal military defeat and occupation of Germany' was a 'moral and political necessity', and that this fact rendered 'untimely' any 'discussion of peace terms before this surrender has been accomplished'. Having accepted the Allies' ground rules, the document, in a remarkably prescient passage hinting at the Cold War to come, laid out a long-term vision of a Europe in which Germany, firmly anchored among the democratic nations, would act as a bulwark against communism: 'the natural convergence of interests between post-Nazi Germany and the other democratic nations ... [and] the possibility of the Bolshevisation of Germany through the rise of a national communism [which is] the deadliest imminent danger to ... the European family ... [requires] radical decisions in the West as the only means of forestalling the overpowering threat from the East'.

With the groundwork of their argument laid, the conspirators moved on to propose what amounted to outright treason when the Allies carried

---

* Paul Leverkuhn, the head of the Abwehr office in Istanbul, Professor Hans Willbrandt, and Dr Alexander Rüstow.

out their planned invasion of northern France: 'If it is decided [by the Allies] to create the second front in the West ... and follow it up ... to the goal of total occupation of Germany ... the Group is ready to support the Allied effort with all its strength and all the important resources at its disposal ... This victory over Hitler ... would set free the real voice of Germany which would acclaim the action of the Group as a bold act of true patriotism.' More importantly, the document suggested that this strategy would release German and Allied resources to hold 'an unbroken ... front' in the east of Poland, along a line from Tilsit to Lemberg (i.e. almost exactly along the line which Churchill and Stalin would settle on as Poland's eastern frontier at the Moscow Conference ten months later).

Parts of the 'Conditions for Collaboration' document are so submerged under thickets of verbiage as to be almost unreadable. If these are stripped away, however, a number of extraordinarily bold propositions are revealed. When the Allies landed on D-Day, the conspirators would remove Hitler, surrender unconditionally to the Western Allies, open the entire Western Front to Allied troops, permit the peaceful occupation of Germany by Allied forces, and shift all German military resources to the east to protect Germany and Eastern Europe from Soviet occupation. If these proposals were acceptable to the West, then peace would come sooner, thousands of lives would be saved, huge destruction would be avoided, and most of Eastern Europe would remain free.

Whether or not this was a proposition that should have been accepted by the West is open to serious debate. But it should certainly have been considered, even if only as a means to bring about the early demise of Hitler (as Donovan himself suggested at the time). Sadly, the entire document, in which so many of the conspirators had placed their last hopes, was dismissed wholesale by von Moltke's friend Alexander Kirk, who wrote that it was rejected 'on my own responsibility without consulting anyone, solely on my conviction that the war must end by the military defeat of the German armed forces and not by dickering about with factions within Germany'. Ambassador Kirk may have been correct. But hindsight suggests that had Western leaders known in advance the numbers who would be killed as the Allies fought their way through to Berlin, had they understood the consequences of the more than four decades of Soviet occupation of Eastern Europe that would ensue, they might have given a little more thought to this extraordinary proposal from responsible and powerful figures in an as yet undefeated country.

The last, best, most practical and most thought-out attempt to strike a separate peace with the Western Allies had met with rejection. All future plots to remove Hitler would now take place against the backdrop of resignation and desperation, rather than hope.

On 19 January 1944, Helmuth von Moltke was arrested by the Gestapo. He had apparently been discovered trying to warn the members of a small resistance group called the Solf Circle, mostly Berlin intellectuals and civil servants who hid Jews, that they were under surveillance. In fact Himmler had been aware of the Solf Circle for some time, and had allowed them to continue in operation so as to seek out their connections with others. The arrest of Solf members as they were having tea on 12 January 1944 was the start of a major SS crackdown aimed at exposing the treachery of the Abwehr, as a prelude to subsuming Canaris's organisation into the SS.

Himmler's cunning in staying his hand until he was in a position to exploit the connections between resistance groups was handsomely rewarded. Among those arrested for links with the Solf Circle was Otto Kiep, an important senior Foreign Office official whose contact list in turn led the SD to a twenty-five-year-old junior Abwehr officer serving in Istanbul called Erich Vermehren. Vermehren, whose determination not to join the Hitler Youth before the war had led to him being refused permission to take up a Rhodes Scholarship to Oxford, was now summoned to Berlin for questioning.

As it happened, Vermehren, who had already been identified as a possible defector by Nicholas Elliott, the head of the MI6 station in Istanbul, had recently returned to the Turkish capital from home leave in Berlin. While on leave, he and his wife Elisabeth had secretly discussed defecting to the British. With this in mind, Vermehren applied to Canaris to take his wife back to Istanbul with him in September 1943, a request which Canaris summarily refused. Elisabeth Vermehren, a self-possessed and strong-willed woman, was not prepared to take no for an answer, and arranged with friends in the German Foreign office to be given a job at the German embassy in Turkey. The couple left Berlin by train together, but crossing the Bulgarian–Turkish border at Svilengrad they were stopped by a German official. Although Vermehren was permitted to continue his journey, Elisabeth was taken to the embassy in Sofia to await further orders. Once again refusing to accept her fate, she appealed to the local ambassador, a family friend, for help. With the assistance of the local Abwehr office, the ambassador arranged for his house guest to be smuggled onto a diplomatic courier aircraft and flown to Istanbul, where on 24 December she rejoined her husband.

Vermehren's summons to Berlin for questioning by the SS now forced the couple's hand. They got a message to Nicholas Elliott offering to defect. In early February 1944, after a 'kidnapping' staged by Elliott to protect their families from reprisals, the Vermehrens were smuggled to London by way of Izmir, Aleppo, Cairo and Gibraltar. On arrival they were taken to the South Kensington flat owned by the mother of Kim Philby, where they stayed until MI6 could arrange suitable alternative accommodation.

In a move which seemed sharply to contradict MI6's earlier attempts to cover up the Vermehrens' defection as a 'kidnap', a major propaganda campaign was now launched to exploit it. This included entirely false reports that the couple had brought valuable German codes with them to London.

It is sometimes claimed that the Vermehren defection was the sole cause of Wilhelm Canaris's dismissal by Hitler. This is not true. Other factors were also involved, such as the Abwehr's failure to predict Allied landings in North Africa, Sicily and Anzio. Thanks to Canaris's lax control of the Abwehr, a series of clumsy sabotage attacks mounted on British and Italian interests in Spain and Argentina had also caused serious damage to German interests in both neutral countries.

Nevertheless, the Vermehren affair, skilfully exploited by Himmler, who exaggerated the couple's role in order to increase the damage to Canaris, was the final straw which caused Hitler to act.

On 11 February 1944, returning from a visit to Spain, where colleagues had remarked on his depressed spirits and haggard appearance, Canaris found a summons from the Führer waiting for him. According to one record, during the stormy meeting that followed there was a physical confrontation between the two men: Hitler, out of control with anger, leapt at Canaris, grabbed him by the coat and accused him of defeatism. Canaris was relieved of his duties and given three hours to vacate his office and make his preparations to leave. Having already sent his wife and children out of Berlin to avoid the bombing, he had only to return to his house on the Schlachtensee, collect his dachshunds Seppl and Sabine, and leave in his official Mercedes. He was driven to Lauenstein Castle, a brooding medieval fortress south of Hanover, whose setting on a hilltop among mountains and dark winter woods must have been an affliction to Canaris's spirit, with its love of sunlight and the southern way of life.

A week later, on 18 February, Hitler issued a decree ordering that all German intelligence services, including the Abwehr, would henceforth be combined under the command of Himmler and the SD.

Each step along Wilhelm Canaris's journey into exile can be fully explained in its own context and without reference to external factors. For most of them he was himself fully responsible. Nevertheless, there is a thread of coincidence here, which has to be explored – and behind it lies, once again, the dark shadow of Kim Philby. If, as seems most likely, MI6 in Istanbul was shown the 'Conditions for Collaboration with the Allies' sent to 'Wild Bill' Donovan, it would definitely have come to the attention of Philby, for it was to him that Nicholas Elliott, the head of MI6 in Istanbul, reported. We know that Philby regarded his work to frustrate a separate peace between Germany and the Western Allies as his greatest service to Moscow in the Second World War. Given that the 'Conditions' document, the delivery of which to the West had been facilitated by Canaris, proposed a 'Western' peace which would prevent a Soviet expansion into Eastern Europe, it seems certain that Philby would have passed that information to Moscow. In these circumstances, the betrayal and arrest of von Moltke very soon after his return from Istanbul would have been entirely in Moscow's interest.

We also know for certain that Philby was actively involved in the defection of the Vermehrens, since the fugitives spent their first night in England in his mother's South Kensington flat. In fact, instead of assisting Elliott to arrange the Vermehrens' defection, Philby should have forbidden it. Allied intelligence policy of the time specifically discouraged Abwehr defections, on the grounds that anything that weakened Canaris's position in favour of that of Himmler was unhelpful to the Allied cause. Here the line of supposition ends, except to note that, as Wilhelm Canaris was the chief architect of numerous attempts to persuade the Western Allies to a separate peace which would preserve Germany and Eastern Europe from Soviet occupation, his removal after the Vermehren affair would have been a most welcome development from Moscow's point of view.

Canaris's banishment from Berlin was by far the most grievous of the blows which fell on the conspirators in the early months of 1944. But it was not the only one. In January, Erwin Lahousen was sent to command a regiment on the Eastern Front. The Solf Circle arrests were followed by a determined SD drive against resistance circles all over Germany. Everyone felt that the net was tightening and the opportunities were slipping away.

In February 1944, Carl Goerdeler, whose habit of responding to failure by turning to even more ambitious dreams never ceased to amaze his friends, startled his colleagues again by repeating his insistence that any coup to remove Hitler must be bloodless. In order to achieve this, he suggested that a public meeting between him and the Führer should be held, and preferably broadcast over the radio. During this Goerdeler promised to 'eliminate' Hitler by exposing him in debate and causing him to resign.

Stauffenberg treated Goerdeler's proposal with predictable contempt, and pushed on relentlessly with plan after plan to kill the Führer and strike the 'initial spark'. Many of the ensuing attempts, which all depended on opportunity and a single-minded, lone, soldier assassin, have vanished in the fog of history, often because their would-be perpetrators were either killed at the front or executed after the 20 July plot.

Some, however, we know about.

Early in 1944 an announcement was made that the much-delayed pre-Christmas presentation to Hitler of new uniforms had been rescheduled for mid-January. With Axel von dem Bussch-Streithorst, the would-be suicide assassin on that occasion, wounded, Stauffenberg asked von der Schulenburg to approach Ewald-Heinrich von Kleist-Schmenzin, the son of the emissary who had sought to obtain Churchill's support for the coup in 1938. Years later, the younger Kleist-Schmenzin described his meeting with Stauffenberg: 'He got straight to the point by telling me, "Look, we're ready. Everything is in place. But we need a volunteer to assassinate Hitler. Are you willing to do it?" He explained to me that it would have to be a suicide attempt in which I would blow myself up with Hitler ... I said, "All right, give me twenty-four hours to think it over." I went home to brief my father about it.' The following day, father and son met on the Kleist-Schmenzin family estate. The young man explained that killing Hitler would cost him his life, and asked for advice. His father stood up, walked to the window and, staring out over the fields of his estate, replied: 'You have to do it. Anyone who falters at such a moment will never again be at one with himself in this life.'

Once again, the presentation was postponed, and the moment passed.

Once again, Stauffenberg cast around for a new assassin.

The next candidate suicide bomber, Stauffenberg's ADC Werner von Haeften, also agreed, but was then dissuaded on religious grounds by his brother. Nerves and tempers were now becoming frayed by this emotional rollercoaster of plans, agreements, delays, disappointments, fresh plans,

more excuses, more heightened security around the Führer, more disappointments and more raids by the SD as the net closed around the
conspirators. At one meeting a key plotter suddenly burst out in frustration that Hitler was still alive: 'That swine DOES after all have a mouth
that somebody could just shoot into!'

This too, or something very like it, was also tried. On 11 March 1944
Field Marshal Ernst Busch, who commanded Army Group Centre, was
called to a conference with the Führer at his Berghof retreat at Obersalzberg.
Early on the morning of the conference the field marshal's adjutant, a
friend of von Tresckow's, was approached 'on spec' and asked if he would
shoot Hitler during the meeting. He agreed without hesitation. But, filing
behind the senior officers through the great doors to the Führer's inner
sanctum, the would-be assassin, a loaded and cocked Browning automatic
pistol in his inside pocket, was barred from entry by two SS guards who
told him that adjutants were excluded from the meeting. Asked if he
would try it again, he said, 'You only do something like that once.'

With the reservoir of would-be assassins becoming exhausted, morale
amongst the plotters dropping, and a mood of pessimism and stasis
spreading, Claus von Stauffenberg began to wonder – if no one else could
be found with the steel to do the deed, then he himself would have to.

28

The Tip of the Spear

As the spring of 1944 brightened into summer, the 'Westerners' amongst the plotters made their last desperate attempts to get some kind of answer in place of silence from the Western Allies to their proposition that if they killed Hitler and overthrew the Nazis, Germany would get a better and sooner peace.

Early in April, Adam von Trott zu Solz, the senior Foreign Office official and key member of the Kreisau Circle who had visited Allen Dulles in early 1943, made a second trip to Bern. He warned Dulles that, in contrast to the Western Allied leaders, who only talked of the destruction of Germany, Moscow was conducting a subtle campaign of whispers promising a 'liberation programme' which would provide massive help for reconstruction. The effect, Trott claimed, was a visible rise in extreme left-wing support for the Soviet Union amongst the German working classes. If the West did nothing, there was a real risk of Germany passing into the hands of the communists after the war.

On 6 April Dulles sent telegrams to Washington giving an update. The first reported that a courier had just arrived from Germany with messages from Goerdeler and Beck:

> They are anxious to know whether we have any interest in following up this matter [removing Hitler] indicating that time is fast running out when such a group could effectively take action ... Would appreciate any guidance you can give me ...

Later that day he followed up with a second telegram:

> Group prepared to proceed only if they can get some assurances from Western powers that upon removal of Nazis they can enter into direct negotiations with Anglo-Saxons ... Group also says that if surrender is

to be negotiated primarily with Moscow [then] a different set of men [i.e. not from the Beck/Goerdeler group] would do the negotiating … After overthrow of Nazis, German generals now in command on Western front … would be prepared to give up resistance and to facilitate landing of Allied troops … Principal motive for their action is ardent desire to prevent Central Europe from becoming ideologically or factually under the control of Russia. Likewise arrangements could be made for receiving Allied parachute troops in key points of Germany.

Five weeks later, on 12 May, Dulles reported that 'some Nazi generals … want to … [collaborate] on the construction of a firm Anglo-American bulwark against a Russian-controlled Europe'. These reports were circulated at the highest levels of the US government. But, despite their prescient predictions of Eastern Europe falling under Russian control, the policy remained unchanged. Dulles was firmly instructed to give no responses and make no promises.

Throughout April, May and June, Goerdeler was again in frequent contact with Jacob Wallenberg in Stockholm, assuring him that 'the assassination was certain to take place' and asking him to pass the word to London and report back on its response.*

To all these pleas and requests there came, from both London and Washington, a thunderous silence. Eventually, in late April, Beck and Goerdeler concluded that it was useless to keep pressing for answers. They would have to go ahead, and hope for the best.

Tucked away in the medieval gloom of Lauenstein Castle, Wilhelm Canaris knew little if anything of this, though he picked up a few bits and pieces from official bulletins and from occasional visitors. Some ex-Abwehr colleagues managed to get to see him, and his wife Erika was permitted one visit in the late spring. He questioned these visitors closely, especially about the progressive dismantling of the Abwehr, which by the early summer of 1944 had been more or less completely absorbed into Himmler's SD.

Canaris was not alone in Lauenstein. The great castle's echoing rooms and baronial halls were filled with the buzzing activity of workshops and

---

* Wallenberg was running a very high risk in helping Goerdeler at this time, since his famous brother Raoul was already deeply involved in saving Jews in Germany. After the war, Raoul, who was regarded by the Russians as an American spy, was 'disappeared' by the KGB.

laboratories producing clandestine equipment for spies and the German security departments: secret inks, microphotography, forged papers, concealed microphones and all the other indispensable paraphernalia of the espionage trade. Amongst this hustle and bustle, Canaris cut a strange, almost ghost-like figure, pursued by his beloved dachshunds as he patrolled the battlements, echoing corridors and walled gardens of his gigantic prison, always under the watchful eye of his jailer, a staunch Nazi who had specific orders from Berlin that the admiral was to be given no privileges and allowed only carefully vetted visitors.

On 10 March Canaris was informed that he was to be removed from the active service list at the end of June. Two weeks later, a letter from the navy personnel office stated: 'Admiral Canaris will be placed at the navy's disposal. No re-employment is contemplated.' Officially he had ceased to exist.

And then, out of the blue, a little after D-Day (6 June 1944), Hitler rescinded the order removing Canaris from the active list and appointed him as the head of the Sonderstab für Handelskrieg und Wirtschaftliche Kampfmassnahmen (HKW – the Special Staff for Mercantile Warfare and Economic Combat Measures), a small and unimportant department based in Potsdam which dealt with maritime and economic warfare. It seems likely that the Allied landings in northern France and Canaris's rehabilitation were linked. Now that the Western armies had managed to carve out a secure bridgehead in France, Germany would find itself caught in the jaws of an inexorably tightening vice closing in from east and west. As one of Canaris's Swedish friends told the Gestapo later, 'the admiral's removal would destroy every possibility of some kind of accommodation between Germany and the Western Allies'. In these uncertain times, the admiral would be more use to Hitler close by, than hidden away in Gothic isolation.

Canaris did not delay leaving Lauenstein. Sweeping up his dachshunds, he called his Mercedes and driver and was very soon back in his house near the Schlachtensee, where he found his Moroccan manservant and Polish cook waiting to welcome them all home.

The admiral's new job in Potsdam required very little work, and allowed him considerable freedom of manoeuvre and even travel. Sometime in mid-1944 he managed to get a message through to an MI6 agent he had previously used to communicate with Stewart Menzies in London. There is no reliable record of the substance of the communication, but given that his colleagues Beck and Goerdeler were trying desperately to get answers to their proposals for peace, it seems safe to presume that Canaris was using his line to Menzies for the same purpose.

Around the end of June, Canaris, on a visit to Paris, received a secret message from Claude Arnould, alias 'Colonel Ollivier', the MI6 agent he had met in the Forest of Fontainebleau in September 1942. Could Canaris meet him at 11.15 the following day in the garden on the walled terrace which surrounds the base of the windmill overlooking the Longchamp racecourse? The meeting was short and hurried, because Canaris thought he was under surveillance. Arnould said he had been instructed to deliver a letter from London, but it was too dangerous to carry in public. Could the admiral meet him again that evening at Le Couvent des Soeurs de la Sainte Agonie, a Lazarite convent at 41, rue de la Santé? Arnould did not explain that the convent was also the headquarters of a Paris MI6 spy ring called Jade-Amicol.

At 9.30 sharp that evening Wilhelm Canaris entered the convent gates in the rue de la Santé and walked across the cobbled courtyard to the front portico. With his diminutive stature and shock of white hair, and wearing a dark suit in place of his habitual admiral's uniform, he must have seemed a vulnerable figure under the magnificent pillared front porch of La Maison des Dames, emblazoned with the words 'À LA GLOIRE DE JÉSUS PAR LE SAINT COEUR DE MARIE'.

He knocked on the heavy oak doors, which were opened without delay by the deputy to the mother superior, Sister Marie Vianney. 'Canaris seemed non-plussed,' the mother superior of La Maison des Dames recounted later. 'He said that he had come to pray.' Sister Marie, who had taken the precaution of confining her twelve fellow nuns to their cells for the evening, shut the door, drew the bolts and led the admiral across the chapel, past the sacristy, and down a long stone corridor which echoed to their footfalls, to her cell. Here a table was set for a 'simple but wholesome meal' for two. Arnould was already there, and stepped forward to shake the admiral's hand. Sister Vianney withdrew, leaving the two men alone. While they were eating, Arnould handed Canaris an unaddressed sealed white envelope. The admiral opened it, pulled out two typewritten sheets with a signature at the bottom, and began to read. A long period of silence followed, and then a sharp intake of breath and a little gasp. 'Finis Germaniae' – thus ends Germany – he said, looking across at Arnould and reiterating the words he had growled at Gisevius in the Tirpitzufer on the day war had been declared, five long years previously.

He pushed the letter into an inside pocket and asked to leave. Arnould, who had no knowledge of the contents of the letter, walked him back in silence to the front doors and let him out into the summer evening.

Back in Berlin, Canaris kept his distance from the plot and from von Stauffenberg, whom he regarded with energetic suspicion. The young colonel was too brash, too passionate, too left-wing, too idealistic, too impulsive, he thought, to run a successful coup. The feeling was mutual. Stauffenberg regarded the greyhaired old has-been, tucked away in a non-job granted at Hitler's pleasure, as too conservative and too cautious to be of any use in these more revolutionary times. He went to some lengths to keep Canaris in ignorance of his plans.

The admiral did, however, receive an outline briefing on what was planned from two old Abwehr colleagues. He was specifically aware of one crucial aspect of the plot. Stauffenberg had requested – and been given – the package of British plastic explosive which had been handed to the Abwehr for safekeeping after its discovery under the watchtower close to Wolfsschanze, following the failed bomb attempts of autumn 1943.

D-Day on 6 June 1944 caused a further decline in morale amongst the plotters. Given the Allied sacrifices made on the beaches of Normandy, most believed that there was now little chance of Western capitals accepting anything less than Germany's painful humiliation. Goerdeler contacted Jacob Wallenberg again, asking for advice on whether it was worth continuing. He received a pessimistic reply on 20 June.

For a period even Goerdeler, his irrepressible optimism briefly broken, wondered to his brother Fritz if the plot should be abandoned, since there was now almost no chance of it succeeding. Von Stauffenberg too, though maintaining a public face of undiminished determination, questioned in private whether the whole scheme had any future. He sent a message through a mutual friend to Henning von Tresckow on the Eastern Front suggesting that since the assassination of Hitler could no longer have any appreciable effect on saving Germany from 'unconditional destruction', it was perhaps time to end the project. Von Tresckow's instantaneous reply perfectly typifies the mood of fatalism that enveloped the plotters in the summer of 1944, as they approached the final act: 'The attempt must succeed *coûte que coûte* [at whatever price]. If it fails, we must act in Berlin. It is now no longer a question of practical results, but of showing to the world and to history that the [German] resistance movements risked the last throw. Nothing else matters now.'

Von Stauffenberg's brother Berthold, speaking to a friend around this time, put the same sentiment in different words: 'The most terrible thing is knowing that we cannot succeed and yet that we have to do it, for our country and our children ...' Colonel Albrecht Mertz von Quirnheim wrote what would turn out to be a last letter to his wife a week before the plot was launched, agonising: 'It is quite clear to me that we shall bring about the end of the German military forces, for, whatever sort of peace we achieve, it will remove the military class once and for all; yet we must act for the sake of Germany and the West.'

The killing of Adolf Hitler was now no longer just a patriotic act to save post-war Germany; it had taken on the character of a crusade driven by personal conscience and the imperative need, as the plotters saw it, to lighten the burden of guilt that would be carried by future generations of Germans.

On 1 July 1944 von Stauffenberg was promoted to full colonel, and simultaneously appointed chief of staff to General Friedrich Fromm, the commander of the Reserve Army. Although Fromm knew perfectly well what von Stauffenberg was up to, it was he who personally appointed him as his chief of staff – possibly in order to ingratiate himself with Hitler, who had commented approvingly on von Stauffenberg: 'Finally a general staff officer with imagination and intelligence!' Or possibly Fromm, the man who by his own boast 'always came down on the right side', was re-insuring himself in case the coup succeeded. Or possibly both, which would have been very Fromm.

Von Stauffenberg now had the right of attendance whenever Fromm saw Hitler. He had already met the Führer once, on 7 June, the day after D-Day, and found him incoherent and 'in a daze', pushing maps back and forth and glancing around the room like a hunted animal. Now he would, God willing, be one of the last people to see him alive.

Early on the morning of 6 July, von Stauffenberg and Fromm flew to the Berghof to present the latest version of the Operation Valkyrie plan for the Führer's approval. According to some claims, alongside the Valkyrie papers in von Stauffenberg's briefcase was a bomb constructed from the package of British plastic explosive previously provided by the Abwehr. But this seems unlikely, since the success of the 'grand coup' depended on Valkyrie, and that could not be assured until the plan had the full authority of the Führer – which was not given until the meeting was almost over.

It is more likely that von Stauffenberg had the bomb with him in order to hand it over to yet another newly-recruited assassin, who, Stauffenberg

hoped, could be persuaded to kill Hitler at the repeatedly delayed presentation of new uniforms – which was, at last, to be held the following day.
But no sooner had Stauffenberg handed over what he called 'all the stuff'
to do the deed to the prospective assassin, than he got a sudden attack of
cold feet and pulled out.

It was at this point that Claus von Stauffenberg finally decided that if
the job was to be done, and done properly, it would have to be done by
him. Initially he had some difficulty persuading his senior conspirator
colleagues that he must be the assassin. Ludwig Beck in particular was
adamant that the coup could not be run without Stauffenberg in Berlin.
He only finally agreed to Stauffenberg undertaking the role of assassin on
the condition that, having armed and placed the bomb, he returned to
Berlin before it went off in order to take charge of the remaining elements
of the coup.

It is important at this moment, with the focus on Stauffenberg and his
bomb, to remember that he and his package were just the tip of a very long
spear. Behind them lay a vast organisation reaching into almost every
corner, class, underground political organisation and many departments
of government in Germany. What Olbricht, Stauffenberg and their
colleagues had by this time created was a truly remarkable organisational
superstructure for the coup – perhaps even a miraculous one, given that it
was all built under the constant, suspicious, ever-watchful eyes of Hitler's
all-pervasive security networks.

Alongside the official Valkyrie operational orders, Stauffenberg and
Olbricht drew up a number of other supporting documents, including
draft proclamations to the public, replacement orders for the institutions
of the state, instructions for the treatment of prisoners arrested during the
coup, and even a new oath of loyalty, composed largely by Stauffenberg
himself, which was to be taken by all servants of the state.

The main announcement, to be broadcast on all radio outlets and
printed in all newspapers, was entitled 'An Appeal to the German People'.
This too is believed to have been drafted largely by Stauffenberg.

It read:

Germans!
The tyranny of Hitler is broken!
In the last years terrible things have taken place in front of our very eyes.
Hitler, never entrusted with power by the German people, usurped the
chancellorship using the worst kind of manipulations … To keep power in

his own hands, Hitler established a reign of terror. In the past our
compatriots were able to take pride in their honesty and integrity, but
Hitler despised the word of God, undermined the law, destroyed integrity
and devastated the happiness of millions. He ignored honour and
magnanimity, the liberty and lives of others. Countless Germans, as well
as people from foreign nations, have been languishing for years in
concentration camps, where they suffer agony and are subjected to
horrifying tortures. Many of them have died. With bloodstained hands,
Hitler continues to walk the path of madness, leaving behind him a trail of
tears, grief and agony … his phony military ingenuity has brought disaster
on our brave soldiers … The … sacrifices of the nation have all been
squandered in vain. Ignoring expert advice, Hitler has sacrificed entire
armies to satisfy his craving for glory and his megalomania.

Meanwhile, with the assistance of Goerdeler and Beck, a slate of nineteen names had been assembled to form a government-in-waiting capable of taking over after Hitler's death. Resistance elements, which would rise on a codeword from Berlin, had been established in many of the big cities and regional centres of Germany. Alongside these, workers' leaders had constructed an elaborate underground network of workplace cells whose members were ready to rise to give support to the new government once it was announced. Similar units of resisters ready to 'come out' when called on had been set up in many German departments of state, especially in the Foreign Office. A parallel simultaneous coup to take over the army command structures was to be launched in Paris by Stauffenberg's cousin, the chief of staff to the military commander of German forces in France, Carl-Heinrich von Stülpnagel. Similar 'mini-coups' were to be launched in Vienna and the capitals of some other occupied countries.

By the beginning of July 1944, perhaps as many as six thousand people, including three field marshals, nineteen generals, twenty-six colonels, two ambassadors, seven diplomats, one minister, three secretaries of state and the head of the Berlin police were, in one way or another, implicated in the coup d'état which would be launched at the instant Stauffenberg's bomb killed Hitler.

This extensive resistance network was both the coup's strength and its weakness. So many people and organisations were now involved that the structure was highly vulnerable to infiltration by Himmler's SD. In June, to the shock of all, death sentences were pronounced on the leaders of the Solf Circle. At about the same time, an army colonel close to

Goerdeler was arrested. In early July the two key leaders of the clandestine German workers' movement were taken into custody and interrogated. Nerves became very frayed; an Abwehr officer who knew of the plot threatened to reveal everything and 'blow the whole nest on Bendlerstrasse sky high'.

Time was running out – and not just because everyone sensed that the Gestapo net was closing in. Soviet forces were less than a hundred kilometres east of Wolfsschanze at Rastenburg. Many believed, Henning von Tresckow among them, that the entire Eastern Front was in imminent danger of collapse, precipitating a Soviet rush to Berlin. Not for the first time it was von Stauffenberg who, in mid-July, gave voice to the general mood of urgency among the plotters: 'It's time now for something to be done. He who has the courage to act will probably go down in German history as a traitor. But if he fails to act, he will be a traitor before his own conscience.'

On 11 July, Hans Bernd Gisevius (who was on Goerdeler's shadow government list as state secretary for information) left Basel on the night train to Berlin. He did not say a personal goodbye to Dulles, fearing that the American would try to dissuade him from leaving the safety of Switzerland. Instead he deposited a long farewell minute at Herrengasse 23 informing Dulles of what was about to happen: 'Hitler's overthrow is not the result of a counter-revolution. He has ended as a political and military failure … Total exhaustion is coupled with total dejection. The danger is that disappointed people will shift from one revolutionary mentality to the next … Ten years of revolution and war have brutalised morals and deadened feelings. What takes over from the Hitler revolution … will come to terms with Bolshevik methods if … they are not offered a new way ahead and hope for the future.'

Dulles sent a report warning Washington that the coup was imminent. In London, sources also told MI6 that it was to be expected any day.

On the same day that Gisevius left Switzerland, Claus von Stauffenberg once again flew to Berchtesgaden to attend a morning briefing with Hitler at the Berghof. This time he came equipped not just with the bomb, but also with the resolve to use it. But before reaching Berchtesgaden he discovered that neither Göring nor Himmler was to be at the meeting. When someone suggested that, since the coup plan called for both of them to be killed along with the Führer, they had better postpone, Stauffenberg muttered, 'Good God, oughtn't one to go ahead regardless?' But he didn't, and carried his bomb back to Berlin that evening.

On the morning of 14 July, Stauffenberg and Fromm were instructed to fly the following day to attend another briefing from Hitler, who had now moved to Wolfsschanze. They left Berlin at seven o'clock the following morning, arriving at Rastenburg at around ten. At 11 a.m. Freidrich Olbricht, believing the 'initial spark' to be imminent, issued the preliminary Valkyrie codeword calling all troops in and around Berlin to move to the centre of the city in order to suppress 'internal disturbances'. It was not until mid-morning that von Stauffenberg learned that, once again, neither Himmler nor Göring was going to be present. Twice during the ensuing briefing with Hitler he left the room to telephone the plotters' headquarters in the Bendlerblock and seek their agreement to go ahead with the assassination. On the second call, the coup managers in Berlin finally agreed that the attempt should proceed. Stauffenberg returned to the briefing room to initiate the fuse on his bomb – only to find that Hitler had left.

Olbricht had great difficulty persuading the Valkyrie troops and commanders whom he had ordered to Berlin the previous day that the mobilisation had been only a practice.

Two days later, arriving back in Berlin from a visit to Leipzig, where he had been taking leave of his family, Goerdeler was told by one of the plotters that the Gestapo had just issued a warrant for his arrest.* Stauffenberg instructed him to 'disappear as quickly as possible and not endanger the entire conspiracy by running around Berlin making telephone calls'. Goerdeler left hurriedly in a car provided by the Berlin chief of police and took refuge at a friend's country estate at Rahnisdorf, a hundred kilometres south of the capital.

On that same day, 18 July, a naval officer told von Stauffenberg that he had heard a rumour from a Hungarian nobleman that Hitler's headquarters was to be blown to smithereens in two days' time. The leak was swiftly traced to Stauffenberg's loose-mouthed ADC Werner von Haeften. 'The Rubicon has been crossed,' was Stauffenberg's grim response. The entire plot now perched at the edge of catastrophe. If the next attempt to kill Hitler failed, it would be too late.

Next day, Stauffenberg received a summons to Wolfsschanze to make a report to Hitler on the following morning – 20 July.

---

* The information came from Arthur Nebe, the head of the Berlin criminal police, and was passed to Goederler at Gisevius's request by Jacob Kaiser.

29

Thursday, 20 July 1944

In the early evening of 19 July 1944, as Claus von Stauffenberg's driver Karl Schweizer was collecting a briefcase containing two heavy packets wrapped in brown paper tied with string from the home of an officer in Potsdam, von Stauffenberg himself was shooting hares with a friend near army headquarters at Zossen, thirty kilometres south of Berlin.

He had spent the day checking that all was as ready as it could be for the putsch that would kill Hitler on the following day. His last meeting that evening would be with Adam von Trott zu Solz, the Foreign Office diplomat and prime mover of the Kreisau Circle who had been a key contact with the Western Allies.

On his way back from Zossen, Stauffenberg asked for his car to stop at the church of St Matthew the Evangelist in the Berlin suburb of Steglitz. Despite the fact that he was Catholic and the church was Protestant, he spent half an hour alone in the vast nave below its magnificent vaulted neo-Romanesque ceiling. Arriving back at his house near Berlin's Wannsee just after dark, he showed his brother Berthold the two brown-paper-wrapped packages of British explosives, each weighing two pounds, which, together with their primers* and 'time pencil' detonators, were hidden under a shirt and a pile of documents in his briefcase. If he was asked about the shirt, he explained, he would say that it was hot and that he wanted to look his best for the Führer. Before going to bed that evening he tried to telephone his wife, who had left Berlin the day before 'to avoid the bombing'. But he couldn't get through, probably because the lines were down following the day's British air raids.

20 July broke hot and sultry. There would be oppressive heat and thunderstorms before evening. Claus and his brother Berthold rose at

---

* A primer is a small, usually conical-shaped explosive charge pierced by a hole into which a detonator can be placed. It is used as pre-explosive to set off the main charge.

five. They were collected in Stauffenberg's black Mercedes an hour later and driven the thirty kilometres to Rangsdorf airfield, south of Berlin. Even at this early hour the streets of the city were busy, mostly with military traffic. Shortly before seven the big Mercedes swung through the gates at Rangsdorf, receiving a salute from the sentries as it swept past. Von Stauffenberg's ADC, Werner von Haeften, was waiting at the airstrip for the two brothers with a second briefcase. A mist which had crept up overnight from the nearby lake, the Rangsdorfer See, was billowing over the airfield. They would have to wait for the sun to do its work.

While they stood around smoking and passing the time, Stauffenberg shepherded Haeften to a discreet corner, where he transferred one of the brown-paper packages to his ADC's briefcase. Finally, at around 7.30 a.m. the von Stauffenberg brothers said their goodbyes, and Claus, with Haeften and a staff officer, climbed on board the waiting Heinkel HE 111. The plane taxied briefly and took off without further delay, heading east-north-east for Rastenburg, 350 kilometres away.

By now the sun was well into the sky. Little pools of mist, which had gathered during the night in hollows and river valleys, were being drawn into wisps which curled up towards the plane as it flew across Germany's eastern plains. By and by, a black line began to grow on the horizon ahead of them – the forests of east Prussia. They touched down at Rastenburg airstrip, eight kilometres south-west of Wolfsschanze, at a little after ten. The day was already hot, humid and sweaty.

Leaving Haeften (who was now carrying both explosive briefcases) to go about other duties, von Stauffenberg was driven to Hitler's headquarters, described by one of his most senior commanders, General Alfred Jodl, as a cross between a monastery and a concentration camp. Paul Schmidt, the Führer's personal interpreter, writing after the war, captures the oppressive atmosphere of Wolfsschanze in the 'gloomy East Prussian forest [where] … the electric light in Hitler's rooms often had to be left on all day, even in full sunshine … [the concrete bunkers] grey and green and windowless … squatted in the wood like primeval monsters … the rooms were very small … the dampness from the mass of concrete, the artificial light and the perpetual buzzing of the ventilating machinery increased one's sense of unreality … [with Hitler] growing daily paler and more puffy … the general effect was of the lair of a legendary evil spirit … It was like a film studio … One witty colleague … announced [imitating an American film producer] "The woodland used in the Hansel and

Gretel film ... will be taken down tomorrow and the day after we are going to start shooting *Antony and Cleopatra*; the pyramids are already in place.'"

The Wolfsschanze complex was contained within an area of mosquito-infested marsh and woodland, a kilometre and a half deep and two kilometres long. Encircled by a stout exterior wooden perimeter fence, it was served by its own railway station, a small airstrip and a comprehensive layout of internal roads. These connected three 'citadels', each protected by its own electrified wire-netting fence and checkpoints. The innermost 'command' citadel comprised a number of wooden huts and concrete bunkers set amidst a crowd of alder and silver birch trees festooned with camouflage nets. Among these were the Führer's accommodation and briefing bunker, guest bunkers for dignitaries, a bunker reserved for Reichsmarschall Göring, and another containing a state-of-the-art communications centre, managed by Stauffenberg's fellow conspirator General Erich Fellgiebel. Facilities in the outer 'administrative' enclosures of the complex included a cinema (where British and American films, banned in Germany, were shown), a sauna, mess halls, a heating plant, a teahouse, a garage, office buildings and accommodation for secretaries. The whole area was protected by an interlocking network of machine-gun nests and anti-aircraft-gun positions, and a twenty-kilometre-wide outer defensive zone which included fourteen 88mm anti-aircraft batteries.

Once through the checkpoints guarding the outer perimeters of the complex, von Stauffenberg was driven to one of the mess halls, where he breakfasted with the camp commandant and officers on his staff. At around eleven o'clock he went to a briefing room for a rehearsal of his presentation to the Führer with two senior officers, whom he then accompanied to a final pre-meeting rehearsal with a jittery Field Marshal Wilhelm Keitel, the chief of the Armed Forces High Command. By this time Haeften had arrived with his two briefcases, but having no role in the meeting, he was left standing outside nursing his deadly charges. At a little before noon, Keitel received a phone call saying the meeting with Hitler had been moved forward from 13.00 to 12.30 because of the impending arrival of Mussolini – recently rescued from captivity – at the Wolfsschanze railway station later in the afternoon.

Von Stauffenberg asked if he might be allowed a room in which to exchange his sweat-soaked shirt for the clean one he had brought in his briefcase. Because of his injured arm, he asked Haeften to assist him. The two men went into a cramped cubicle where, after Stauffenberg had changed his shirt, they began the process of arming the explosive charges. Using a pair of pliers specially adapted for the remaining two fingers and thumb of his left hand, Stauffenberg crushed the glass phial filled with sulphuric acid to start the timer. He then inserted the detonator into a primer, and wrapped the whole contraption into the body of the plastic explosive. The procedure required delicacy and precision at the best of times, let alone handicapped with a mutilated hand and cramped in a confined space with a dirty shirt, two briefcases and another heavily perspiring human being. No sooner had the two men completed arming one of the bombs than the door behind them was roughly pushed against von Stauffenberg's back by a messenger who had been sent to tell him to hurry, as the Führer was now approaching. In the confusion that followed, Stauffenberg, deciding that it was better to have one successfully armed charge than to risk being discovered arming a second, pushed the redundant package back at Haeften and left with his briefcase containing the bomb, now set to go off in thirty minutes' time.*

On the way to the map room in which the briefing was to be held, Keitel's adjutant, Ernst von Freyend, reached out to carry the maimed man's briefcase. Stauffenberg snatched it back. Then, worried that his rudeness might attract attention, he relented and handed it over, asking his benefactor to find him a place close to Hitler, because his hearing had been impaired when he was wounded in North Africa.

In normal times, Hitler's briefings took place in the cramped and enclosed space of the briefing room in his concrete bunker. But in this hot weather it was cooler in the wooden map room under the shade of the trees. Walking the four hundred metres through dappled sunshine towards his rendezvous with fate, von Stauffenberg noted that all the windows were open to allow a breeze to blow through the room. In comparison with the tightly enclosed space of a concrete bunker, the open windows and light wooden construction of the briefing room would mean that the explosive effect of his bomb would be much more dispersed. But, with his fuse running, there was no turning back.

By the time Stauffenberg arrived, the Führer's briefing was already in progress. There were twenty-five men in the crowded room, all gathered around a large, heavy ten-by-four-metre oak map table, on which lay

---

* It is a matter of puzzlement why Stauffenberg did not simply place the unarmed charge alongside the armed one, as it would have been detonated 'sympathetically' when the armed charge went off.

sheaves of papers, maps and diagrams. Hitler, dressed in baggy black trousers, knee-length boots and a grey tunic, was bending over a map listening to one of his generals explaining the fast-deteriorating situation on the front, seventy kilometres away.

Though Hitler did not at first look up at the new arrival, one of his generals did, and later described von Stauffenberg's entry: '[He was] the classic image of the warrior through all of history. I barely knew him, but as he stood there, one eye covered by a black patch, a maimed arm in an empty uniform sleeve, standing tall and straight, looking directly at Hitler who had now also turned round, he was ... a proud figure, the very image of the ... German General Staff officer of that time.'

Keitel introduced the new arrival: 'Colonel Count Stauffenberg, mein Führer. The man who is working on the new units to be sent to the front.' Hitler swivelled briefly to shake the new arrival's hand and then returned to his position, bent over the maps on the table. Von Freyend showed Stauffenberg to a position two places to Hitler's right, and placed his briefcase on the floor to the left of his chair. Sitting down, von Stauffenberg tried discreetly to move the case as close to Hitler as possible, but found himself blocked by one of the table's massive supports.

At this stage Keitel intervened to suggest to Hitler that Stauffenberg should give his briefing immediately. But the Führer insisted that the report he was receiving on the Eastern Front should be completed first. This was the window von Stauffenberg needed. He rose, leant over Keitel's right shoulder and whispered that he had to take an urgent call from Berlin with information which the Führer would need to hear in his briefing. Keitel frowned and, with a look of annoyance, nodded. Outside, von Stauffenberg asked to be connected on the internal phone system to Erich Fellgiebel, the head of the Wolfsschanze communication centre.

A communications officer was called out from the conference room to make the connection. When the officer returned to the briefing, Stauffenberg, instead of continuing the call, put the receiver down and, leaving his cap and belt behind, left for a nearby building where, as previously arranged, he met Fellgiebel, Haeften and the car that would take him back to the airfield as soon as the bomb exploded.

Meanwhile, one of Hitler's briefers, asked a question by the Führer, moved into the empty space left by Stauffenberg. Leaning over the table to point at a map, he pushed Stauffenberg's briefcase over. His point made, he reached under the table and stood the briefcase upright again, in the process pushing it further under the table. By now it was nearly von

Stauffenberg's turn to brief the Führer. Concerned that the young colonel hadn't returned, Keitel hurried out of the room to find him. Outside, the field marshal was informed that von Stauffenberg had left in a hurry and without explanation. Keitel, perplexed, returned to the briefing.

The man Keitel was looking for was by this time standing outside one of the huts about two hundred metres away, smoking a cigarette and trying to look as normal as possible as he chatted to Fellgiebel and Haeften. His staff car, which had been turned round to face the exit gate, waited nearby, its engine purring, ready for a swift getaway.

At 12.42 Hitler's briefing hut erupted with a flash and a deafening roar, which Stauffenberg later described as like a direct hit from a 155mm shell. Wooden beams, planks, plasterboard and a hail of splinters flew in all directions. A cloud of smoke and dust billowed up, engulfing the whole scene. General Alfred Jodl, who had been blown clean through an open window, got up unhurt but dazed, dusted himself down and hurried off to get help. General Walter Warlimont, who was in the hut, said later: 'In a flash the map room became a scene of stampede and destruction. At one moment … a set of men … a focal point of world events; at the next there was nothing but wounded men groaning, the acrid smell of burning; and charred fragments and papers fluttering in the wind. I staggered up and jumped through an open window.'

As the dust settled, there was one question in the minds of the three spectators standing by Stauffenberg's staff car. Was Hitler dead? They waited and watched for a few minutes. Then they saw a body on a stretcher being carried out, covered by the Führer's cloak. Stauffenberg turned on his heel, threw his cigarette onto the grass, jumped into the waiting car and ordered full speed for the airfield.

The staff car was quickly waved through the first checkpoint. But the sentries at the final barrier guarding the outer perimeter fence refused them passage. The man in charge insisted, 'The colonel is not permitted to pass any longer.' Stauffenberg replied, 'I have an urgent order from the Führer to fly to Berlin immediately.' The sergeant was resolute – his orders were clear. Von Stauffenberg walked calmly into the guard post, called one of the Führer's adjutants, spoke a few sentences to him, and handed the receiver to the sergeant: 'Of course the colonel is allowed to pass,' the adjutant ordered.

Once through the checkpoint, Stauffenberg's car lurched at speed along the narrow winding road to the airfield. On the way Haeften threw the unused package of explosive, still in its brown-paper wrapping, into a wood. Arriving back at the airfield at a little after 1 p.m. they found a

THURSDAY, 20 JULY 1944

Heinkel which another conspirator had arranged waiting for them, its engines running. They took off for Berlin at 1.15.

By now the heat of the day had piled up tall pillars of cumulonimbus clouds, some of them black with rain and beginning to rumble and flash with thunder. It must have been a turbulent and bumpy two-and-a-half-hour flight back to Rangsdorf field. Landing at 3.45, Stauffenberg, surprised to see neither his personal staff car nor the armoured personnel carrier he expected, was forced to scrounge a car from the local Luftwaffe. Before they left the airfield, Haeften rang Bendlerstrasse to report that Hitler was dead.

It wasn't true.

The blast had killed or mortally wounded four of those who were in the map room* and injured many others, some seriously. It was one of the dead that Stauffenberg had seen carried out from the briefing hut, covered in Hitler's coat. The Führer himself, protected by the heavy oak table, had somehow miraculously survived. About fifteen minutes after the explosion he staggered out of the door of the wrecked hut, supported by Keitel and one other. He was partially paralysed by shock, his right arm dislocated and hanging useless like some grisly imitation of Stauffenberg's, his hair singed, his right leg badly burned, one eardrum perforated, his trousers shredded by the blast, and his buttocks, in his own words, bruised 'as blue as a baboon's behind'.

One of the earliest arrivals on the scene was Hitler's private secretary, Gertraud 'Traudl' Junge: 'I almost laughed at the sight of Hitler. He was standing in the little anteroom, surrounded by several of his adjutants and servants. His hair was never particularly well cut, but now it was standing on end so that he looked like a hedgehog. His black trousers were hanging in strips from his belt, almost like a raffia skirt ...'

The first news of the Führer's survival reached Bendlerstrasse at 1.30 p.m., not long after Stauffenberg had taken off from Rastenburg. It was Fellgiebel who telephoned the bad news, delivering what was obviously a carefully constructed message designed to deceive eavesdroppers: 'Something terrible has happened ...' – then a long, long pause – '... The Führer is alive.' The Wolfsschanze communications chief could say no more, because all communications from Rastenburg were now cut off – not by him, as planned, but by Hitler himself, in order to flush out the

---

* Generals Günther Korten and Rudolf Schmundt, Colonel Heinz Brandt, and a stenographer, Heinrich Berger.

conspirators. The only communications left open were personal telephone lines, and these, as Fellgiebel well knew, were closely monitored by the SS.

After a moment of panic and dithering on hearing the news, Olbricht and two of his colleagues, who were at this stage controlling the plot from Bendlerstrasse, decided to say nothing, proceed as though Hitler was dead, and await more news from Rastenburg. At 1.50 the codeword ('Swallow') for the first stage of Valkyrie was given. Unfortunately, since this was sent on the secret telex net, it had to be encoded, causing considerable delay. At 2 p.m. an announcement was made that, the Führer having been assassinated, the army would now take control of the country under a triumvirate of Field Marshal Witzleben as commander-in-chief, Ludwig Beck as head of state, and Carl Goerdeler as chancellor. The codeword to initiate the coup was also issued to Paris, Prague and Vienna. Over the next hours a steady stream of plotters gathered in the Bendlerblock, which was by now buzzing with a potent mixture of tension, apprehension and excitement. 'What I will never forget about 20 July was the sensation that we all felt, of being part of a moment in which history was balancing on the edge of a knife,' said one.

By the time von Stauffenberg landed at Rangsdorf, Himmler had already carried out enough investigation to know that he was the would-be assassin, and was in hot pursuit.

When von Stauffenberg reached Bendlerstrasse at 4.30, a confrontation was under way with Fromm, who, having heard that Hitler was still alive, refused to sign Valkyrie. He was curtly informed by Mertz von Quirnheim that his signature was not needed, since the codeword for Valkyrie II had already been issued. Fromm responded by telling von Quirnheim that he was under arrest. A quarter of an hour later, the newly-arrived von Stauffenberg led a delegation into Fromm's office to tell the general that, on the contrary, it was *he* who was now under arrest, and would therefore be locked in his own adjutant's office, under armed guard, until further notice.

Back at Rastenburg, Hitler, nursing his wounded arm, his singed hair concealed beneath a battered hat and still unaware of the extent of the coup, made the short journey to the nearby station to greet Mussolini's special train and accompany him back to the Wolfsschanze's nerve centre. There, as the tussle in Fromm's office was under way in Berlin, Hitler and Mussolini had tea and got down to discussions. At 5.30, Goebbels – the most senior Nazi in Berlin – interrupted the talks between the two leaders to tell Hitler by telephone that the coup was much wider than had been presumed: a military putsch was under way; orders to initiate Valkyrie had been issued. Action must be taken swiftly to nip the attempt in the bud before it got out of control. Hitler ordered Goebbels to make an immediate broadcast reporting what had happened and announcing that the Führer himself would speak to the German people later that evening.

Up to this moment, resolute action, including the execution of Fromm and Goebbels, might have saved the day. But the conspirators seemed paralysed by indecision – even von Stauffenberg immersed himself in making telephone calls rather than giving orders.

According to one version of events, von Stauffenberg phoned Canaris at 3 p.m. to tell him that the Führer was dead, to which the admiral, feigning ignorance for the benefit of eavesdroppers, replied, 'Dead? Good God, who did it? The Russians?' Since von Stauffenberg was still in the air at 3 p.m., this story – which came from a Canaris loyalist – has to be doubted. It seems more likely that Canaris first heard of the bomb, and of Hitler's survival, at about five o'clock that afternoon. He immediately concluded that if Hitler was alive, the plot was dead. That evening he despatched an obsequiously worded telegram to Hitler, congratulating the Führer on his miraculous escape and sending him best wishes.

At 6.45 p.m. Goebbels took to the airwaves: 'Today an attempt was made on the Führer's life with explosives. The Führer himself suffered no injuries beyond light burns and bruises. He has resumed work immediately and – as scheduled – received Il Duce for a lengthy discussion ...' It was all that needed to be said. Normal service had been resumed.

It was over. The stream of conspirators who had flowed into Bendlerstrasse during the afternoon now flowed back out again. Later that evening the coup in Paris collapsed, as did the parallel coups in Prague and Vienna.

The final act came at 10.50 p.m., when Olbricht's secretary heard a commotion and shouts of 'For the Führer!' in the corridor. A moment later, a crowd of army officers burst in. Confronting Olbricht, they demanded to know the truth, and to speak to Fromm. Alerted to what was happening, von Stauffenberg rushed into Olbricht's room. In the melee that ensued shots were fired, one of them wounding von Stauffenberg in the shoulder. He staggered into an adjacent office, a red stain spreading over his white summer-uniform jacket. While Stauffenberg put in a call to Paris, hoping in desperation that the coup there had fared better, Haeften tried to burn incriminating papers in a corner of the room. Suddenly the door burst open and the bulky silhouette of Fromm appeared through the smoke. Grinning with self-satisfaction, he said, 'And now, gentlemen, I am going to do to you what you wanted to do to me. You are all under arrest.'

Ludwig Beck asked for a pistol 'for personal use'. Fromm agreed. 'But make it quick!' he barked.

The old general, his hands shaking, cocked the weapon, pointing it inadvertently for a moment at Fromm, who sharply ordered him to take care. Standing to attention, Beck said, 'At a time like this I remember the old days ...' Fromm cut him short, and told him to get on with it. Beck drew himself up and, his hands still shaking, put the gun to his temple and fired. But the bullet only grazed his forehead. Collapsing in a chair, he asked, dazed, 'Did the gun fail to function?' Fromm ordered two officers to 'help the old man', but before they could relieve him of his pistol Beck fired again. This time the bullet entered his head, but it still did not kill him. He collapsed to the floor, unconscious.

Fromm, leaving Beck lying where he had fallen, turned to the others. 'Now, you gentlemen, if you have any letters to write you have a few minutes in which to do so.' As the condemned men sat writing their final letters, with the still-living body of their co-conspirator lying in a widening pool of blood at their feet, Fromm left to organise a firing squad* and choose a site for the executions. Having selected a pile of builders' sand, used to douse incendiary devices, in a corner of the Bendlerblock courtyard, he called in some army trucks to illuminate the scene with their headlights.

Then he returned to his office. He had no interest in delaying matters, or in due process. These men knew just how much he himself was implicated by acquiescence in the plot. Alive, they were a threat to him. Dead, they could not speak.

'In the name of the Führer,' he intoned, 'a court martial convened by me has pronounced sentence: Colonel Mertz von Quirnheim, General Olbricht, the colonel whose name I will not mention [here he pointed an accusing finger at von Staffenberg] and Lieutenant von Haeften are condemned to death.'

Stauffenberg, faint from loss of blood, stood to attention and said that he took full responsibility – the others had only been obeying orders. Fromm made no reply, but stood wordlessly to one side and motioned the four men out of the room with a sweep of his hand. On their way out, Beck stirred. Fromm turned to one of his officers and told him to finish the old

---

* Under the command of Lieutenant Werner Schady, it consisted of ten NCOs.

man off. Unwilling to do the deed himself, the officer turned to an NCO and ordered him to administer the coup de grâce. As the little cortège filed down the stairs and out into the cobbled courtyard, a shot rang out behind them.

It was half an hour past midnight. The night was still warm and sultry, and distant flashes from a thunderstorm far away lit the sky. Small knots of onlookers stood around in the pools of darkness. The trucks' headlight beams were trained on the firing party and the four men lined up in front of the pile of sand, their long shadows stretching up the walls of the building behind them. And then they were shot, one at a time: Olbricht first, then von Stauffenberg, then Haeften, then Mertz von Quirnheim. As von Stauffenberg stood waiting for the volley, he drew on his last reserves of energy and shouted, '*Es lebe das heilige Deutschland*' – Long live blessed Germany. One version relates that, just as the execution squad fired, Haeften, shouting 'Long live freedom,' threw himself in front of von Stauffenberg to take the bullets.

Somewhere in a washroom or a game pantry south of Berlin, the hares von Stauffenberg had killed the previous evening hung on hooks, waiting for the butcher.

30

Calvary

In the very early hours of 21 July 1944, possibly even before the executions in the Bendlerblock courtyard, Henning von Tresckow heard what had happened, and knew what it meant.

A friend related: 'In a totally calm and collected way he said, "Now they will all fall upon us and cover us with abuse. But I am convinced, now as much as ever, that we have done the right thing. I believe Hitler to be the arch-enemy, not only of Germany, but indeed of the entire world. In a few hours' time, I shall stand before God and answer both for what I have done and what I have left undone. I think I can with a clear conscience stand by all I have done in the battle against Hitler. Just as God once promised Abraham that he would spare Sodom if only ten just men could be found in the city, I also have reason to hope that, for our sake, He will not destroy Germany. No one amongst us can complain about his death … A man's moral worth is established only at the point where he is prepared to give his life for his convictions."'

Not long after dawn, Henning von Tresckow, for three long, dangerous, disappointment-strewn years one of the indispensable pillars of the anti-Hitler resistance, drove into the no-man's land between the German and Russian front lines and blew himself up with a grenade.

A few hours before, shortly after midnight, at about the same time as the executions were taking place in the Bendlerblock courtyard, Carl-Heinrich von Stülpnagel, the German military commander in France and deeply implicated in the coup in Paris, went to the Hôtel Raphaël in avenue Kléber, next to his headquarters. There, in the unofficial officers' mess for Germans in Paris, he found a riotous party in full swing. The Paris coup had gone like clockwork. More than 1,200 SD, SS and Gestapo officers had been arrested and were now in prison. The champagne was flowing, and there was much clinking of glasses to the new dawn that was about to break. Suddenly, penetrating the din, the unmistakable voice of Adolf Hitler came over the radio. Silence fell like a smothering blanket on the room. Stülpnagel took several involuntary steps towards the radio, and then stood stock still, like a man turned to stone.

'My fellow countrymen! I do not know how many times an assassination attempt on me was planned and carried out.' The raucous voice from the radio struck like an icy blast into the room. 'If I speak to you today it is, first, in order that you should hear my voice and that you should know that I myself am unhurt and well; second, in order that you should know about a crime unparalleled in German history. The claim made by the usurpers that I am no longer alive is being contradicted at this very moment as I am speaking to you. A very small clique of ambitious, irresponsible, and at the same time senseless and criminally stupid officers have formed a plot to eliminate me, and with me the German Wehrmacht command … I myself am completely unhurt … The circle of these conspirators is very small and has no connection with the German Wehrmacht, and above all none with the German people. It is a miniature group of criminal elements who will now be ruthlessly exterminated.'

Stülpnagel waited to the end without a sign of emotion, save for his hands, which, clasped behind his back, slowly twisted and untwisted his leather gloves. Then he turned on his heels and left. A little later, he received orders to return to Berlin. Declaring simply, 'Providence has decided against us,' he took leave of his officers and set off to meet his fate. As his car approached Verdun, where he had fought in the First World War, Stülpnagel asked his driver to stop, let him out, and drive a little way ahead to wait for him. Not long after, a shot rang out in the night. His companions rushed back to find their general lying half in and half out of the Meuse Canal, blood gushing from a wound in his head. They dragged him out and found him, though blind, still alive. Slowly and meticulously he was nursed back to health under guard in Berlin. On 30 August he was sentenced to death and led, sightless, straight to the gallows.

Even before Stülpnagel's failed attempt at suicide, the Gestapo hunting parties were already out rounding up suspects and perpetrators.

Carl Goerdeler was only narrowly able to slip away from his friend's estate south of Berlin before his pursuers arrived. He took refuge for three days on the estate of an old World War I comrade twenty kilometres away. The next few days he spent back in Berlin, changing his sleeping place every night and meeting with fellow conspirators during the day. He had intended, if arrested, to claim that he knew nothing of the plot. But by this time the Gestapo had found the full list of the post-Hitler shadow government, all neatly typed out and filed away in Olbricht's safe. Denial was now useless.

Finally, with the help of friends, Goerdeler was found a bed in a block of flats in the suburb of Friedrichshagen, on the south-eastern edge of Berlin, at the home of a junior clerk who had no idea who Goerdeler was, and had agreed to give him shelter out of simple humanity.

Goerdeler stayed in Friedrichshagen only two nights before travelling on again, this time to the home of a friend in north-east Berlin. He moved again the following day, to spend the night of 29–30 July with his cousin Willy Ullbrich at Nikolassee, south-west of the capital. By now, with the arrests in full swing and Goerdeler's photograph in circulation everywhere, Ullbrich strongly advised him to disguise himself and try to escape to the Russians. But Goerdeler, a 'Westerner' to the end, preferred to throw himself on the mercy of the Swedes, whom he hoped to reach through an acquaintance, the pastor of the Swedish German Confessional Church. He went to the church on Sunday, 30 July, to find that the Swedish pastor was away. A German pastor who was standing in to cover the Swede's absence promised to contact the Swedish embassy, but nothing came of it.

Goerdeler moved on once more, this time to an old university friend in Potsdam, Dr Brodfuehrer, who held a small ceremony to mark his guest's sixtieth birthday on 31 July. By now, with a reward of a million marks on his head, Goerdeler decided that central Berlin was too dangerous. He moved back to the home of the clerk in Friedrichshagen, where he spent almost a week, passing his days writing and improving his 'great memorandum' on the future of Germany and Europe.

Finally, Goerdeler decided that he must accept his fate and could no longer risk the lives of those who gave him refuge. On 8 August he packed his rucksack and, taking his hiking stock, set out to pay a last visit to the graves of his parents at Marienwerder in western Prussia. Travelling by little rural railway lines and side roads, and with many detours, he reached Marienwerder station on the evening of 10 August. Conscious that he was very well known in the town, he did not risk booking into a hotel, but spent the night in the station waiting room. The following morning he walked by back roads to the cemetery. As he approached its gates he was recognised by a local woman. Deciding that it would be too dangerous to be seen at his parents' graves, he turned away and tried to shake off his pursuer by taking a winding route to nowhere along small lanes and minor roads. He eventually arrived at Stuhnsdorf branch-line station late that afternoon, checked his rucksack into the left-luggage office and spent the night in the open air on the shores of nearby Stuhmer Lake. Next morning, exhausted and hungry, he made his way to a local inn and ordered breakfast. There he bumped into Helene Schwaerzel, a woman from a nearby Luftwaffe base who had known him and his family at Rauschen-Düne, the Goerdeler summer-holiday resort on the Baltic coast. She recognised him immediately. Leaving his breakfast unfinished, he tried to find refuge in a nearby wood. He was swiftly found, arrested and taken to the Gestapo prison at Prinz-Albrecht-Strasse in central Berlin.

Wilhelm Canaris's turn came on 23 July.

He was having coffee with two friends in his house near the Schlachtensee when his Moroccan manservant announced the arrival of two men. Shortly afterwards, Walter Schellenberg and one of Canaris's ex-colleagues in the Abwehr walked in. Looking his one-time riding companion straight in the eye, Canaris said, 'Somehow I thought it would be you.'

The admiral was not taken immediately to a Gestapo prison, but to a police college where the officers' mess had been turned into a temporary holding centre for senior officers under suspicion of being implicated in the plot. Initially it was difficult to prove Canaris's involvement, but by the end of August enough information had been extracted from others to enable the Gestapo to have him transferred to its cells at Prinz Albrecht Strasse. From then on, Canaris would never be out of the hands of the secret police. In a cell two and a half metres by one and a half, shackled at night, kept in solitary confinement and on near starvation rations, the lover of sun, fresh air and the company of his dogs did not cope well with his new conditions.

By now the great purge was in full swing. According to best estimates almost five thousand people of all ranks, backgrounds, professions and positions were executed in the months after 20 July 1944. Many of them were strangled, on Hitler's specific orders, with piano wire. Some, like Erwin Rommel (who was only marginally implicated), were offered the chance to commit suicide and took it. Others killed themselves before capture. Many, innocent of any involvement, were picked up by the Gestapo, which took the opportunity of the wave of killings to settle old scores. Under Himmler's so-called *Sippenhaft* (blood guilt/kin liability) laws, the relatives of key figures were arrested and imprisoned – some were killed. The large majority of these horrors took place in darkness, away from the public gaze.

A special kind of very public humiliation was, however, reserved for the main figures. Starting as early as 7 August, little more than two weeks after the Wolfsschanze bomb, a series of public show trials began in the Volksgerichtshof (People's Court) under Judge-President Roland Freisler, Nazi ideologist, enthusiastic enforcer of Germany's racial laws, and an early architect of the Final Solution. Modelling his style on that of Andrei Vyshinsky, the chief prosecutor at Stalin's purge trials of 1938, Freisler denied his victims any due process and publicly humiliated them in front of a hand-picked audience made up chiefly of fanatical Nazi supporters. One by one the key figures in the 20 July plot were paraded before the 'court', wearing ill-fitting civilian clothes which hung off their gaunt skeletons. They were denied ties or belts, and were forced to stand within spitting distance of Freisler's tirades, with their heads bowed, one hand on the back of a chair and the other holding up their trousers. Cut short when they tried to speak, and without any defence lawyers to help or advise them, they were first raged at, then shouted down, and finally summarily condemned to death.

In most cases the passing of sentence was followed by immediate execution, often by hanging, which was expertly carried out to ensure the process took as long as possible. Thus died, on the second day of the court's sitting, Field Marshal Erwin von Witzleben, the leader of the 1938 coup attempt, together with seven of his colleagues.* On being sentenced to death, Witzleben told Freisler, 'You can have us hanged, but within three months' time the people will drag you alive through the filth of the gutter.'

On 10 August, Claus von Stauffenberg's brother Berthold was amongst five who were sent to their deaths. One of them was General Erich Fellgiebel, the head of Hitler's communications system, who also warned Freisler, 'You had better hang us in a hurry, otherwise you'll hang before we do.'

Five days after that, four more were 'tried' and sentenced to death. Among them was Adam von Trott zu Solz, the Oxford-educated messenger to Allen Dulles who had so often tried to get the Allies to listen to his proposals for an early peace.†

---

* Colonel General Erich Hoepner, Major General Helmuth Stieff, Lieutenant Albrecht von Hagen, Lieutenant General Paul von Hase, Lieutenant Colonel Robert Bernardis, Captain Friedrich Klausing and Peter Yorck von Wartenburg.

† The other three were Lieutenant Colonel Bernhard Klamroth, Berlin police chief Wolf-Heinrich von Helldorf and Lieutenant Hans-Bernd von Haeften (the brother of von Stauffenberg's ADC).

Freisler's 'show trials', however, did not live up to Nazi expectations. Most of the accused behaved with such great dignity and composure that they won the sympathy even of spectators hand-picked for their loyalty to Hitler and the Nazi cause. Letters to the court from their wives were especially impressive and moving.

The Berlin socialite and journalist Ursula von Kardorff wrote in her diary of some friends returning from a day in Freisler's court:

> They looked like ghosts [when they came in]. They were in such a state that they blurted everything out, although they were under an oath of silence. Freisler in his scarlet robes shouted at the top of his voice from nine until noon. [Ex-ambassador to Rome and leading plotter Ulrich von] Hassell abandoned his reserve when he realised there was nothing more to be saved. They said he was very impressive. The SS people in the court were so impressed by Goerdeler that they were very nearly guilty of high treason themselves ... [the accused] made much more impression on their enemies than did Freisler, for all his ranting and roaring. [Dr Josef Wirmer], a very big man, shouted back at Freisler so loudly that it took Freisler's breath away for a moment ... [After a long argument on Lutheran opposition to Nazism] Freisler said, with a cynical smile, 'All right, when I am in Hell and you are in Purgatory, we can talk about it over the telephone.'

Helmuth von Moltke, the leader of the Kreisau Circle and emissary of the January 1944 peace proposal to Donovan, was hanged in Plötzensee prison on 11 January 1945. His last words, written in a letter to his son, were: 'Since National Socialism came to power, I have striven to make its consequences milder for its victims and to prepare the way for a change. In that, my conscience drove me – and in the end, that is a man's duty.'

And so it continued, and continued and continued, until providence, in the form of a bomb delivered by the US Eighth Air Force, fell on Freisler's court on 13 February 1945, killing him and many of his officials outright, and destroying their records. This mercy, though late, came as a miraculous deliverance to many still awaiting trial, who were thus saved from the hangman's terrible noose.

Eight members of Carl Goerdeler's family were sent to concentration camps under the *Sippenhaft* laws, while his brother Fritz was sentenced to death and executed on 1 March 1945. Goerdeler himself was sentenced to death on 9 September 1944. But, unlike most of his colleagues, he was too valuable to be sent to the hangman immediately.

Under interrogation, Wilhelm Canaris used all his experience and skill at sidetracking investigations, dodging questions and scattering false leads and half-truths to try to slip the noose. With his interrogators getting nowhere, he sought to bypass them by writing a personal statement to their superiors, which he signed on 21 September 1944, two weeks after Goerdeler had been condemned to death. Uneasy and awkward, it is a masterpiece of the spy's art of distorting mirrors and sinuous adaptations of the truth:

> I still hold today that the final phase of the war will make further
> demands of us and can only be surmounted if we genuinely fight to the
> last … I drew attention to the difficulties that might be expected to arise
> if the enemy neared our frontiers … we have to attune ourselves to the
> idea that everyone must continue to make sacrifices and place himself
> entirely at the service of the Fatherland … I have briefly restated these
> ideas because I believe that many officers regarded these [honest]
> appraisals … as pessimistic … But my principal realisation … was that a
> war of such vast dimensions had been ordained by fate … [and] that the
> great sacrifices which our nation made at the front line and at home
> under firm and united leadership could never have been in vain … even
> if the war did not end as optimists thought.

It was a good try. And it might have worked. But, as is often the case in the game of spies, it was the knock-on consequences of an event which took place almost two months previously, with which the Abwehr chief had no connection, that finally did for Wilhelm Canaris.

On 28 July, a week after the execution of von Stauffenberg and his colleagues in the Bendlerblock courtyard, Werner Schrader, the Abwehr officer who had provided the British explosives and fuses to Stauffenberg, shot himself in preference to falling into the hands of the Gestapo. His driver was closely interrogated after the suicide, but was then freed as it was decided that he had no information to give. On 21 September, the day of Canaris's personal statement, the released driver turned up at Gestapo headquarters claiming that he had suddenly remembered a fact that might prove of interest. He led a search party to a safe lying amongst 130 others in an army bunker in the OKW headquarters at Zossen. A locksmith was called, and after several tries, the safe was opened, revealing the entire archives of the anti-Hitler resistance, along with excerpts from Canaris's diaries detailing many of his activities and private thoughts over these years. These diaries have disappeared. Some say that all, or some of them, were burnt on Hitler's orders because he did not want the extent of Canaris's betrayal ever to be known. Others claim that they are in MI6's secret archives. Others still, that they were captured by the Russians and are in Moscow Centre. Their whereabouts remain, even today, one of the most intriguing unsolved mysteries of the Second World War.

For Wilhelm Canaris, however, they were a death warrant. He was too big a figure to be publicly tried, but his fate was sealed.

In the remaining months of 1944 and the opening weeks of 1945, Carl Goerdeler gave far more than he should have done to the Gestapo. Naïve and seduced to the end by his sense of personal mission, he allowed himself to be manipulated into believing that by cooperating he was at last influencing Hitler towards peace, and that in giving up the names of colleagues he was ensuring their pardons. On 2 February 1945, his usefulness over, he was hanged from one of the meathooks arranged on a bar in the execution shed at Plötzensee prison. His last days were spent writing a series of memoranda culminating in a 168-page political testament under the title 'Our Ideal'. His last letter pleaded: 'I ask the world to accept our martyrdom as penance for the German people.'

A little over a month later, Friedrich Fromm, the man who 'always came down on the right side', found himself on the wrong side of a firing squad in the courtyard of Brandenburg-Görden prison. In the final instance, his careful manoeuvrings convinced no one. Unable to prove he was directly connected with the conspirators, the 'People's Court' found him guilty of not doing enough to expose the 20 July plot, and sentenced him to death for cowardice in the face of the enemy – which, to many of the plotters, would have been an infinitely more shameful verdict than treason.

Five days after Goerdeler was hanged, Wilhelm Canaris and Hans Oster were taken to the German death camp at Flossenbürg. From there Oster, *preux chevalier* to the end, wrote a final letter to his son: 'To our last breath we all remain upstanding men, as we were taught to be from our childhood and in our soldierly discipline. Come what may, we fear only the wrath of God that will fall upon us if we are not clean and do not do our duty.' The new arrivals at Flossenbürg were kept alive a little longer, perhaps because Himmler believed they might be useful as bargaining chips, in case he wanted to strike a separate peace with the Allies. But eventually it was too late even for that.

Dietrich Bonhoeffer

On the night before their execution, which was the Sunday after Easter, Dietrich Bonhoeffer led a service of worship for the prisoners, all of whom had now been subjected to hasty 'courts martial' condemning them to death. He preached on the scripture for the day, 'Through His stripes we are healed' (Isaiah 53:5), and 'Blessed be the God and Father of our Lord Jesus Christ, which according to His abundant mercy hath begotten us again unto a lively hope by the resurrection of Jesus Christ from the dead' (1 Peter 1:3).

The final act could have been a scene from Wilhelm Canaris's favourite opera, *Fidelio*, except with tragedy in place of triumph.

At 6 a.m. on 9 April 1945, Canaris was ordered to get undressed and was led, naked, through the chilly April morning with Hans Oster, Dietrich Bonhoeffer, Karl Sack and Ludwig Gehre to the execution shed. Canaris went first. He did not die quickly. An SS witness said: 'The little admiral took a very long time – he was jerked up and down once or twice.'

The camp doctor witnessed Dietrich Bonhoeffer's last minutes: 'On the morning of that day between five and six o clock, the prisoners were taken from their cells and the verdicts of the court martial read out to them. Through the half-open door in one room of the huts I saw Pastor

Bonhoeffer, before taking off his prison garb, kneeling on the floor praying fervently to his God. I was most deeply moved by the way this lovable man prayed, so devout and so certain that God heard his prayer. At the place of execution, he again said a short prayer and then climbed the steps of the gallows, brave and composed. His death ensued in a few seconds. In the almost fifty years that I worked as a doctor, I have hardly seen a man die so entirely submissive to the will of God.'

As the executioners burnt the corpses later that day, the sound of the guns of the approaching American army could clearly be heard.

According to legend, on his way to the gallows Canaris said, 'I die for my country and with a clear conscience ... I was only doing my duty to my country when I endeavoured to oppose Hitler and to hinder the senseless crimes by which he dragged Germany to ruin. I know that all I did was in vain, for Germany will be completely defeated. I knew that she would be as far back as 1942.'

The quote is probably apocryphal. But in its mixture of prescience, principle and pessimism, it remains, quintessentially, Wilhelm Canaris.

31

Epilogue

There are no flawless heroes in this story.

Almost all the major anti-Hitler resisters had helped him to power in the first place, and bear a degree of complicity for this. Few of them could be said to have been natural democrats. Many were monarchists and aristocrats, and nearly all were nationalists who sought to preserve the old Germany, rather than build a new one. Some remain tainted, even today, with accusations of anti-Semitic attitudes. Others, mainly army officers, did not object when they should have done, and were thus passively complicit in the early mass killings of the SS.

Some, perhaps especially in the senior ranks of the army, were weak men. Once they saw the true nature of Hitler and the Nazis, they wanted to remove him with a putsch, but faltered when it came to initiating one. Nor were they good revolutionaries. In their various attempts to rid themselves of Hitler, there was stupidity in abundance, along with misjudgement, unreality, vanity, utopianism and, when it came to carrying out their plots, a host of almost infantile faults of execution and tradecraft.

But – and it is a very big but – though flawless heroes are absent here, heroism and heroic acts are not.

In war, blacks and whites are difficult to come by. It is easy from the safety of distance to find fault with the decisions people have to make, and the things they have to do, in terrible times.

One fact, however, stands out clearly. When much of the world, in Germany and beyond, was either seduced by Hitler or cowered before him, those who, even if a little late, felt compelled to oppose what he stood for, saw him clearly when others did not, and had the courage to resist when others, for whatever reason, failed to do so.

It is worth noting that many of the leaders of the resistance put their lives at risk in their attempt to rid Germany of Hitler long before it was obvious that he would lose the war. Some did so years before the war started, and continued their dangerous work even at the height of Hitler's success and power. Carl Goerdeler, for instance, was writing to army officers warning them of national catastrophe and encouraging them to resistance even in the immediate aftermath of Hitler's extraordinary triumphs in France and the Low Countries in mid-1940. The claim put about after the war that those who opposed Hitler were no more than 'fair-weather' resisters trying to ingratiate themselves with the soon-to-be-victorious Allies is a demonstrable and shameful lie.

These long years of resistance in a surveillance state took their toll of the leaders in very different ways.

Wilhelm Canaris, the swashbuckling adventurer and master of all he surveyed from his balcony at the Tirpitzufer, was transformed into a depressive recluse by pessimism, disappointment and the constant duplicities of serving Hitler while opposing him. As others risked all, he just sat and waited for fate, in the form of Walter Schellenberg, to collect him from his house on Berlin's Schlachtensee.

It is almost too painful to try to reconcile the Ludwig Beck who with such prescience and self-confidence resigned over Czechoslovakia in 1938 with the old man whose pistol shook so violently that he twice failed to kill himself on the night of 20 July 1944.

Carl Goerdeler, sustained by unshakeable optimism, went the other way. The man who resigned as mayor of Leipzig in 1936 in protest against the Nazi regime was a classic Prussian administrator – traditionalist, hierarchical, mildly monarchist, nationalist, nervous about too much democracy, and dedicated to form and order. But by the time he reached his death cell in 1944 Goerdeler had turned into a visionary who had already mapped a new constitution for his country and a detailed blueprint for the united, democratic Europe which he rightly saw as the only sure basis for a peaceful European future. His designs bear a striking resemblance to what exists today. By the end of the war Goerdeler's attitude towards the Jews had changed too. He had abandoned his ambivalence over the Jewish question, asserting that all forms of racism were contrary to basic humanity and a threat to civilised values.

Whatever their failures, whatever their flaws, whatever paths they followed, whether circuitous or not, these men, and those who joined them, arrived at the right moral judgements when so many others did not. The younger resisters, especially in the army and the Kreisau Circle, were intellectually, morally and in their world-view a gifted generation such as only comes along once in a while in the history of a nation. They were the flower of the Germany of their day, who sustained the courage and moral purpose to carry their chosen course right through to the hangman's noose. For this at least they deserve history's admiration.

A.E. Housman's great World War I epitaph to the fallen applies to them, too:

> Here dead we lie because we did not choose
> To live and shame the land from which we sprung.
> Life, to be sure, is nothing much to lose;
> But young men think it is, and we were young.

Those who share the deep Christian faith which inspired most of the anti-Hitler resisters – and those, like me, who do not, but who recognise the power of catharsis – may find something almost biblical in the fact that Germany, having allowed itself to be submerged under the tide of Hitler's evil, could not find its way back to true expiation until it had suffered its full measure of misery, including the sacrifice of its brightest and its best, who would have made such a huge contribution to the post-war reconstruction of the German state.

Two questions remain to be answered.

First, could the Second World War have been avoided if, in 1938, Britain and France had been prepared to stand up to Hitler?

Second, if war was unavoidable, could it at least have been shortened by a peace that did not involve the occupation of Eastern Europe by the Soviet Union?

The case made for Neville Chamberlain at Munich is that he had no option but to let Hitler have his head. He could not risk a war that Britain was in no position to fight. By allowing Hitler to have the Sudetenland, some historians claim, Munich delayed war for a year, giving Britain time to prepare itself for conflict. The military case for this view is strong – especially when it comes to airpower, where Britain was hopelessly under-equipped to defend itself. It should also be acknowledged that Chamberlain's policy of appeasement was overwhelmingly supported by all his advisers and most of the British public at the time.

But that policy was founded on two crucial misjudgements.

The first was the belief that, provided Hitler was sufficiently appeased, he could be rendered, as Chamberlain put it to his sister in the months before Munich, 'sated, indolent and quiescent'. In May 1939, eight months after his promise of 'peace for our time', Chamberlain wrote another letter to his sister in which, now relying for salvation on the coup plotters he had so summarily dismissed the previous September, he insisted that Munich had succeeded: 'I myself still believe that Hitler missed the bus last September and that his generals won't let him risk a major war now.' But this was never going to be the case. Hitler was bent on war whatever the circumstances, and would not be diverted from it. Winston Churchill and the German resistance understood this. Neville Chamberlain and the appeasers did not.

Chamberlain's second miscalculation was that Hitler was a conventional politician with whom he could negotiate conventionally: 'I saw in his face ... that here was a man who could be relied upon when he had given his word,' he wrote after his first meeting with the Führer at Berchtesgaden in September 1938.

Chamberlain and his advisers (as with French prime minister Édouard Daladier and his) thought they were dealing with just another German militarist in the direct line of German militarists who had caused wars in Europe for the best part of a century. Neither realised that Hitler's pathology set him apart from all normal modern European leaders. He was, rather, so abnormal that his like has been seen only rarely in history, and never in the democratic age.

If he had understood this, as Churchill and the anti-Hitler resistance in Germany did, and if he had understood the seriousness and potential of the 1938 coup, as he should have done, would Chamberlain have behaved differently?

The answer appears to be yes. For he said so – and in terms – in his famous radio address made on 27 September 1938, the evening before Hitler's agreement at Munich. The key passage has become rather lost behind Chamberlain's famous reference to 'a quarrel in a far-away country between people of whom we know nothing'. In the sentence which precedes and sets the context for that much-criticised statement, Chamberlain declared: 'I am myself a man of peace to the depths of my soul. Armed conflict between nations is a nightmare to me; **but if I were convinced that any nation had made up its mind to dominate the world by fear of its force, I should feel that it must be resisted** [emphasis added].' It was only, the British prime minister concluded, because he believed Hitler was *not* such a threat that he considered it wrong to go to war. History now knows that this judgement was catastrophically wrong; Hitler at the time of Munich had indeed determined, come what may, 'to dominate the world by fear of … force', and as such, according to Chamberlain's own words, 'must be resisted' – but wasn't.

To be sure, if Chamberlain had decided to stand up to Hitler rather than appease him at Munich, he would have been taking a risk with Britain's unpreparedness for war. But would this have been a reasonable risk to take if he had better understood – as, again, Churchill did – what would otherwise come next: a near-six-year global war involving unprecedented destruction and loss of life, along with every horror imaginable, and many beyond imagination?

We cannot of course be sure that the 1938 coup would have succeeded, any more than Chamberlain could. But given the relative forces backing it (including the commanders of the army and the police in Berlin) and those protecting Hitler (fifteen SS guards), it seems very reasonable to conclude that it might have. No other attempted putsch against Hitler would be better prepared, more strongly backed, or more likely to succeed than that of 1938. After Munich, removing Hitler grew more and more difficult as his power and standing rose, and his personal protection became stronger and stronger.

This is not to say that the 1938 coup would have produced a German government congenial to Britain and the democracies of Western Europe. A post-Hitler administration in 1938 would have been nationalist, subliminally anti-Semitic, uncertain in its commitment to democracy, overinfluenced by militarism and dedicated to righting what it believed were the injustices of Versailles. But – and this is the key point – it would *not* have been a government led by a man intent on total war and unconstrained by any moral code or the norms of civilised behaviour.

The second question – could there have been an earlier peace with a better outcome? – is more difficult to answer.

It is argued that the policy of initially dismissing the German resistance and then imposing the demand for 'unconditional surrender' was tough but right – not least to prevent the emergence of another 'stab in the back' legend leading Germany back to militarism.

But this policy was also based on two miscalculations.

The first was in relation to the seriousness, power, organisation and potential of the anti-Hitler resistance. An example of prevailing Whitehall thinking is given in a Foreign Office paper of April 1941 which concluded, in terms which mix disdain with wilful ignorance: 'The other principal element alleged to be in favour of peace was a section of the German army. These gentlemen were said to fear the outcome of a pact with the Soviet

Union and to favour a peace compromise accompanied by the removal of Hitler ... They never suggested, however, any detailed basis for discussion, and they never afforded any evidence of their ability to carry out such terms as might be agreed ... It seems clear ... that their influence has been greatly overstated by the emissaries ... all the proposals amounted to suggesting that we should purchase peace at the sacrifice of the cause for which we had taken up arms.' Two years later, in May 1943, foreign secretary Anthony Eden repeated this established Foreign Office view when he declared to George Bell, the bishop of Chichester, that the resistance could not be relied on to create a space for peace because 'they had never shown a thoroughgoing determination to oppose the Hitler regime'. There are many things of which Carl Goerdeler, Ludwig Beck, Wilhelm Canaris and their colleagues can be accused – lack of coordination, prevarication, failure of will, naïvety, inability to organise. But dilettantes they were manifestly not.

Even after the war, most of the Allied intelligence community (with the notable exception of Stewart Menzies at MI6) continued this habit of comfortable ignorance, supplemented by insult.

A post-war CIA assessment delivered a judgement of Canaris and the Abwehr which is typical of the prevailing sense of superiority, buttressed by near total ignorance of what had actually gone on in the Tirpitzufer. Canaris, it said, had 'an incapacity for organisation and an inability to choose good men. The Abwehr was filled in its higher ranks with personal friends and dependents of Canaris and they were (in general) idle and corrupt ... The Abwehr was thus a loose and irresponsible collection of worthless characters whom Canaris refused to dismiss.'

Perhaps this failure properly to understand the enigma of the double face of the Abwehr is best expressed in the divided post-war assessments of its chief. 'Inefficient, intriguing, traitorous, lisping queer' was the uncompromising verdict on Canaris of Colonel Sam Lohan, a high-level member of the UK defence and intelligence establishment. Hitler loyalist Otto Skorzeny, on the other hand, condemned Canaris as having 'betrayed his country's secret services directly and wittingly from the beginning of his career to the end'. The post-war historian John Wheeler Bennett stressed his cunning, calling him the 'grey fox with a lair in the Tirpitzufer'. Perhaps those who knew him best were his opponents in the Allied secret services. Louis Rivet of the French Deuxième Bureau described Canaris as a 'trapeze artist ... [and] even the best trapeze artists sometimes fall'; Allen Dulles lauded him as 'one of the bravest men of modern history – gentleman, patriot, visionary of a United States of Europe led by England, France and Germany'. Reinhard Gehlen, a senior intelligence officer at the Battle of Kursk and the future head of the post-war West German foreign intelligence service the BND, credited his old chief with being 'endowed with intellectual traits not seen in officers since the first half of the nineteenth century'. Perhaps the best epitaph was the simplest one, from the man who of all foreign intelligence chiefs probably knew Wilhelm Canaris best, the head of MI6 Sir Stewart Menzies, who declared him 'damned brave and damned unlucky'.

This ignorance of the true nature of the German resistance was compounded by naïvety – in particular on the part of President Roosevelt – about the true nature of Stalin. From as early as the Casablanca Conference in January 1943, Churchill understood that the future threat to the post-war world from Soviet imperialism was far greater than that from a resurgence of German militarism. But he was not prepared to attempt to dissuade Roosevelt from his insistence on unconditional surrender: 'Personally, I am not going to address the President on the subject. For good or ill, the Americans took the lead, and it is for them to make the first move. It is primarily a United States affair.'

Meanwhile, in a strange mirror-image of Chamberlain's view of Hitler at the beginning of the war, Roosevelt believed towards the end of it that Stalin was someone with whom he could do business for a better world.

'Unconditional surrender' and the post-war destruction of Germany as a unitary state was a policy designed to keep Stalin in the Alliance during the war – and Soviet occupation of Eastern Europe was the price that had to be paid for it.

The argument can, once more, be made that this was a brutal policy but a necessary one. The Allies had a simple strategy, and they were winning; why take the risk of changing tack? The publics of the Allied nations strongly supported the aim of unconditional surrender – a more nuanced end to the war would have been confusing and difficult to explain after so much suffering. And, most important of all, there was the great unknown – the German resistance could dream, but could it deliver the German people?

The strategy of unconditional surrender may, in short, have been an effective one to win the war. But whether it was the right strategy to gain a sustainable and just peace afterwards is much more open to question.

The Allied policy of refusing to consider any proposal, of whatever nature, for an earlier negotiated peace led in the end to the unilateral rejection by Alexander Kirk, the American ambassador in Cairo, of the final and most comprehensive peace proposal, 'Conditions for Collaboration with the Allies', in early 1944. Given that this accepted, in terms, the unconditional surrender of all German forces in the west after D-Day and offered the possibility of the bloodless liberation of Western Europe, the unopposed advance of Western forces to Berlin and a framework for post-war peace which would not have involved the enslavement of Eastern Europe, it seems a mistake that this proposal did not receive more serious consideration.

There are also, as Dietrich Bonhoeffer and Bishop Bell argued, moral questions to be addressed here.

For Hitler's sins, the Allies insisted, all Germans, good and bad, had to pay. Today we call this collective punishment, and declare it illegal under international law. Even two hundred years ago this kind of peace was accepted as an unwise – and perhaps even an immoral – way to proceed against an enemy. In March 1775 Edmund Burke, calling for a peace with honour for the American Revolutionaries, famously said: 'I do not know the method of drawing up an indictment against a whole people … for wise men, this is not judicious; for sober men, not decent; for minds tinctured with humanity, not mild and merciful.' There is tragic irony in the fact that, more than 250 years later, it was an American president who insisted on imposing on Germany a capitulation of the kind Burke so wisely argued against for the colonists of America.

It is of course always easy to have perfect vision in hindsight. Even allowing for this, however, it might still be said that, in their single-minded pursuit of an unconditional surrender which admitted no end other than the apocalyptic destruction of Germany, the Western Allied leaders, too, allowed militarism to triumph over statesmanship.

And so perished the old Europe.

And so began a new Europe.

Almost all the plotters who thought about the future, most notably Goerdeler, Canaris and the Kreisau Circle, saw a unified Europe as a necessary bulwark against Soviet expansion, and the only safe context for a peace capable of containing the old European contagion of destructive nationalism. In this they would have found themselves completely at home in the European Union of today. And they would probably have been justifiably proud that the Germany that has emerged to such a powerful position today is, in very large measure, the kind of post-war Germany they hoped for, and for which they gave their lives.

And so, though there may not be any unblemished heroes here, there are many examples of human triumph.

For us, living in similarly troubled and turbulent times, it must surely be inspiring that there was such a rebellion of conscience and moral anger from human spirits who refused to submit, even in the face of such terrible power and even at the seemingly futile cost of their own lives.

32

After Lives

A few of the anti-Hitler conspirators escaped the great purge.

Erwin von Lahousen, commanding a unit on the Russian–Latvian border, was wounded by an artillery shell on the day before Stauffenberg's bomb exploded. The wound was serious, but it saved his life.

Taken first to a field dressing station, he was subsequently transferred into the German hospital system along with thousands of others. Here his existence was soon swallowed up in the army of the wounded. Göring angrily grumbled about Lahousen after the war, 'That's one we forgot about after 20 July.'

It was an oversight for which the Reichsmarschall would pay dearly, for Lahousen, aided in the background by Madeleine Bihet-Richou, was called as the first witness for the prosecution at Göring's trial for war crimes at Nuremberg. In the witness box he gave damning evidence about the treatment of Soviet prisoners and the mass murder of Jews. The Reichsmarschall was found guilty on all counts, but cheated the hangman's noose by committing suicide, with the unwitting help of one of his American jailers.

It was not until May 1947 that Lahousen was finally released from Allied captivity and allowed to return to live with his wife Margarete in the Austrian Tyrol. After 'Marga' died of a brain tumour in November 1950 he took up studying French again, meeting an Austrian widow with three children who taught French in Innsbruck. The couple were married in 1953. Two years later, in February 1955, Erwin Lahousen died of a massive heart attack at the age of fifty-seven. He was buried with full military honours in the cemetery in Innsbruck, and later reburied in the Vienna Central Cemetery. Though he maintained contact with Madeleine Bihet-Richou after the war, there is no record that they ever met again.

Madeleine returned to France, and continued to work for French intelligence. In 1946 she was made a Chevalier de la Légion d'Honneur. Beyond that, apart from the fact of her death thirty-two years after that of Erwin Lahousen, in 1987 in Montpellier, nothing more is known of her. Like the best spies, having played out her part, she vanished into obscurity.

Hans Bernd Gisevius's public role in the 20 July plot was to make a broadcast announcing the death of Hitler and the formation of the new government, as its incoming state secretary for information. He was in the Bendlerblock when Erich Fellgiebel phoned from Wolfsschanze to report that Hitler had survived. Using one of the Abwehr secure telephone lines, he immediately contacted Allen Dulles in Bern to give him the news. Shortly afterwards he received orders calling him urgently to a meeting with another of the key plotters, the Berlin police chief Wolf-Heinrich Helldorf. By the time this meeting was finished, access to the Bendlerblock was barred by soldiers. Gisevius went to ground in the cellar of the agents Theodor and Elizabeth Strünck, who had couriered secret Abwehr information to him in Zürich. That night, together with his hosts, he listened to Hitler's broadcast and knew that he must flee for his life.

Due to a case of mistaken identity, it took three days for the Gestapo to get onto Gisevius's trail. His bulk and size made him an easy man to identify and follow. Nevertheless, thanks to a head start, numerous acts of courage by friends and an extraordinary succession of lucky breaks and narrow escapes, Gisevius survived, moving from refuge to refuge over the next six months with the Gestapo always just a pace behind him. Eventually, in mid-January 1945, Allen Dulles managed to smuggle him a Gestapo badge and identity card, specially forged for him by MI6 in London in the name of 'Dr Hoffman'. With his new identity and an 'official letter' authorising him to undertake a special mission in Zürich, Gisevius finally managed to talk his way over the border into Switzerland through the frontier crossing at Kreuzlingen, on the shores of Lake Constance, early in the morning of 23 January 1945.

By October 1944 – with the exception of Edmond Hamel, who would remain incarcerated until July 1945 – all those from the *Rote Drei* who had been arrested and tried by the Swiss were free. In early November of that year Alexander Foote slipped over the Swiss frontier into France with the help of the local communist resistance. Arriving in Paris on 9 November, his first stop was the Soviet embassy, where he made himself known to Colonel Novikov, the head of the Paris GRU station. Novikov arranged for Foote to rent a flat, and paid him a regular stipend to live off. On a visit to the Russian embassy in mid-December, Foote, quite by accident, bumped into Sándor Rádo, who had arrived in the French capital with Helene a fortnight previously. The Radós, who were joined shortly afterwards by their children, were also supported by Novikov, in their case with regular payments of 25,000 francs a month (£2,000 at today's values).

Sometime around Christmas 1944, Novikov appears to have told Radó that he had to report back to Moscow. No doubt fearing the consequences of his proposal to link up with MI6 in the last days of Dora, Radó declined the invitation. Novikov replied that in that case, 'means would be found to compel him', and promptly cut off his allowance.

On 6 January 1945, the first Soviet plane to leave France since the country had fallen to Germany took off from Paris airport, carrying nine passengers. In order to avoid overflying areas still occupied by the Germans, the flight plan to Moscow took it via Marseille, Tripoli, Cairo and Tehran. Every person on the plane was travelling on false documents, for the passengers were Moscow Centre's top surviving spies in Europe. Sándor Rádo, travelling as 'Mr Ignati Iakovlevitch Koulicher', was one of them, and Alexander Foote, carrying a passport in the name of 'Mr Alfred Fedorovitch Lapidus', was another.

Foote and Radó did not get a chance to talk until they reached Cairo on 10 January, when they shared a room in the Luna Park Hotel. Out of earshot of their Soviet handlers for the first time, they were able to exchange experiences. When Foote told Radó that he had continued to pass important information to Moscow Centre in the days between Radó's flight into refuge and his own arrest in Lausanne, Radó visibly panicked. Foote concluded that the Hungarian had suddenly realised that Foote's last reports to Moscow had exposed Radó's lie that he could not remain at his post because all his sources had been liquidated.

Early on the morning of 11 January, without a word and leaving behind his hat, scarf and suitcase, Radó left the hotel and defected to the British.

Even allowing for the fact that the British embassy staff in Cairo would have been unused to dealing with defectors from an Allied nation, their handling of one of the Soviet Union's top spies, with much information of interest to MI6, was puzzling in the extreme. The following morning, 12 January, after examination by a doctor, Radó – referred to in the local British correspondence as 'Mr Lane' – instead of being welcomed as he expected, was locked up in a cell. Over the next few days he tried twice to commit suicide – but not very seriously, according to a fellow patient at the local hospital, who described his wrists as not so much cut as 'only scratched'. Not long after Radó arrived at the British embassy seeking asylum, the Russians, who somehow already knew the whereabouts of their missing spy, also turned up on its doorstep, asking for 'Mr Koulicher'.

A week later, Radó, who was 'still displaying suicidal tendencies', begged the British to tell the Russians he was dead, in order to avoid reprisals against his family in Paris.

Not until 17 January, a full six days after Radó's defection, did the Cairo embassy finally report his arrival to London, suggesting that it should respond to Russian questions that 'the man who appears to be the one they have enquired about has presented himself at the Embassy, claiming not to be a Russian and not wishing to continue his journey to Russia'.

On 19 January, MI6 in Cairo reported to MI6 in London that Radó claimed to have had 'something to do' with British intelligence in Switzerland.

On 23 January the Foreign Office telegrammed the British ambassador in Cairo saying 'we do not wish to be interested in' Radó (who had again tried to commit suicide three days previously). It instructed that the defector should be handed over to the Egyptian authorities, who should be left to negotiate his future directly with the Russians.

An internal minute of two days later confirmed that MI6 knew about Radó's defection and had no objection to his 'disposal' to the Egyptian authorities. Taken at face value, this appears to be an extraordinary decision by MI6, given Radó's long-term service as a Soviet agent and his importance as one of its most valuable spies in World War II. On the basis of this MI6 advice, the Foreign Office sent a telegram to the Cairo embassy confirming that it should go ahead and hand its embarrassing guest over to the Egyptians.

On 2 February the British ambassador wrote to London confirming that a letter had been written to the Russians informing them that the man they were looking for was going to be handed over to the Egyptian Ministry of the Interior on 5 February.

On 16 February, more than five weeks after his defection, and with Radó now firmly in Egyptian hands, MI6 suddenly changed its mind and declared that he was after all 'of considerable interest'.

On 22 February, in a letter to MI5, Kim Philby, who it now transpired had been handling the matter for MI6, confirmed that he had Radó's file, which included a report on his interrogation.

Three weeks later, on 13 March, MI5 in London wrote complaining that it had still not received the report on Radó's interrogation, which seemed mysteriously to have gone missing, and asked for a copy to be sent urgently.

On 26 March MI5 again complained bitterly that it had not been given the full details of this 'interesting and important case'.

Three weeks later, on 16 April, the much-delayed interrogation report was finally sent to MI5 – by Kim Philby.

On 14 June MI5 wrote again, saying that since he was still in Egyptian hands and on British-controlled territory, 'a good deal more might yet be got out of Radó by questioning him'.

Despite these clear expressions of interest from MI5 – and from some in MI6 – no further action was taken to see, question, or recover Sándor Radó from the local authorities of a foreign country in which Britain was the occupying power. Radó remained, despite MI5's request, firmly in Egyptian hands, finalising his will and writing pleading letters to Helene, friends with influential contacts and anyone else he could reach, saying that if he returned to Moscow his life would be at risk.

Finally, at 0200 on 30 July 1945, more than six months after Radó's defection, Soviet Major Dimitri Potohatkov, accompanied by an unidentified Russian colonel, a junior attaché of the Russian legation and two Egyptian policemen, arrived at the emigration desk at Cairo airport with 'prisoner Ignati Koulicher Radó', whom they said they were taking to a Soviet transport plane. The British emigration control officer noted in his report: 'subject was definitely unwilling to depart and did not wish to sign the clearance sheet. A Russian officer printed subject's name on the sheet and attempted to sign for him, but was prevented from doing so … After private discussion with his guard, however, subject signed the sheet.' Radó was escorted onto the Soviet plane and flown, via Tehran, to Moscow.

Eight weeks later, on 26 September, another potential Russian defector to the British was also hustled onto a Soviet plane and flown to Moscow against his will. Russian intelligence officer Konstantin Volkov was kidnapped by Soviet agents in Istanbul and flown to his death because Kim Philby, who was tasked with flying out to the Turkish capital in order to help Volkov defect, had instead betrayed him to his Soviet handler in London, and then delayed his journey to Turkey so as to give his Russian masters time to kidnap and subsequently execute him. Given the bizarre handling, delays and lost documents in the Radó case, the question must be asked: had Philby done exactly the same thing to Sándor Radó in Cairo two months earlier?

When Radó arrived in Moscow he expected to be shot. Instead he was sentenced without trial to ten years in a Siberian labour camp. A year after the death of Stalin in March 1953 he was released, and in due course appointed as chief of the Hungarian cartographic service. It was only after he returned to Hungary that he discovered that his sister had in fact survived Auschwitz. In 1958, two years after Helene died, Sándor Rádo married again. He died in Budapest, aged eighty-one, in 1981.

The plane that had brought the Russian spies from Paris did not wait for Radó after his disappearance in Cairo. It left the next day, and flew Alexander Foote and his colleagues to their new life in Moscow. Foote quickly became disillusioned with the Soviet Union: 'My first six weeks in Moscow convinced me that Nazi Germany as I had known it was a paradise of freedom as compared with Soviet Russia. I was determined to get out of it as soon as possible and return to a world where freedom was more than a propaganda phrase.' Giving his Soviet handlers the slip, Foote re-defected back to Britain in 1947. He died on 1 August 1956, at the age of fifty-one.

Rachel Duebendorfer, who through Victor Farrell also had contact with MI6, followed Sándor Radó to Moscow in February 1946 and was immediately imprisoned in the KGB's Lubjanka jail. After nine months of terrible interrogation she was sentenced to a term in a labour camp for psychiatric patients in eastern Russia. Released in 1956, she returned to East Germany, where after a further year's psychiatric care to repair the damage done by the terrors of the Lubjanka she was able to resume a normal life. In 1969 her rehabilitation was completed with the award of the Order of the Red Banner for her espionage services to the Soviet Union during the war. She died, at the age of seventy-two, on 3 March 1973.

Halina Szymańska was reunited with her husband after the war. But the marriage broke up, and she married again. MI6 honoured its promise to educate her three daughters in British schools at public expense.

Halina's Polish intelligence handler Szczęsny Chojnacki, who had burned with concealed love for Halina all the years of the war, returned to England, where, unable to speak English, he found it difficult to get a job and began drinking heavily. Early on the morning 7 December 1960 Chojnacki, the great spy-master who the Germans thought outshone the British in Switzerland as the sun outshines the moon, committed suicide with a revolver in front of the Albert Memorial in Kensington Gardens.

Paul Thümmel, MI6's 'Agent A54', the spy with many aliases who played such a crucial part in warning the Allies of Hitler's assault on the West in 1940, was also kept alive until just before the end of the war. Finally, on 20 April 1945, Hitler's fifty-sixth birthday, he was taken out of his cell at Terezin concentration camp and shot.

Ursula Kuczynski, codename 'Sonja', who trained Alexander Foote and married Len Beurton to get a British passport, returned to her work as a Soviet spy. Not long after her arrival in Britain she became the secret courier for the Soviet atomic spy Claus Fuchs. She managed to avoid being caught when Fuchs was exposed, escaping to East Germany on 27 February 1950. Later she worked in East Berlin as an 'information officer', a journalist and a freelance author. Showered with honours, she was awarded the Soviet Order of the Red Banner in 1969, the National Prize of the German Democratic Republic and the Order of Karl Marx in 1978, the Fatherland Order of Merit in 1982, and the medal of the fortieth anniversary of victory in the Great Patriotic War 1941–45 in 1986. She died in Berlin in 2000, aged ninety-three, and was posthumously awarded the Russian Order of Friendship.

Hans Bernd Gisevius wrote his autobiography, *To the Bitter End*, the year after the war. Sándor Radó (*Sous le Pseudonyme Dora*, 1973) and Ursula Kuczynski (*Sonya's Report*, 1977) wrote theirs too, but under the control of the KGB. Alexander Foote also wrote his tale, *Handbook for Spies* (1949), which was more than probably heavily influenced by MI6. In these Cold War years, spy biographies were often more instruments of propaganda than records of history.

Although those who died in the cause of opposing Hitler during the war are today memorialised as martyrs in the places where they lived and died, they were, in most cases, regarded by Germans immediately after the war as traitors responsible for the defeat of their country and the death of thousands of its young men. Many of the widows and families of those executed after 20 July 1944 were the subject of sharp public opprobrium, and some suffered severe hardship and even hunger as a result of the denazification process, a pre-existing Prussian law denying pensions to those convicted of high treason, and an inability to obtain welfare because of delays in getting death certificates for their executed husbands. During this period – and later – they relied on food parcels and aid from a charitable organisation in the United States in which Allen Dulles was closely involved.

After her release from incarceration with her four children, under terrible conditions, in a concentration camp in northern Italy, Anneliese Goerdeler was granted a small pension by the West German government. This was supplemented by the support and kindness of pre-war friends in Britain.

Erika Canaris too lived in straitened circumstances until Allen Dulles arranged for her a modest pension from US funds in recognition of her husband's work. She also received a small Spanish pension from General Franco, no doubt given for the same reason. She spent much of her post-war years strenuously protecting the reputation of her husband Wilhelm, dying on 8 November 1972 in Bad Oldesloe, Schleswig-Holstein, aged seventy-nine.

In July 1945, just three months after Dietrich Bonhoeffer's execution, a service of remembrance in celebration of his life was held at the Holy Trinity church, just off the Brompton Road in London. To many who had suffered the trials and sacrifices of the war, holding a service in the British capital to remember a dead German was incomprehensible, distasteful and disturbing. The public prints were especially critical of the event. Nevertheless, the memorial service for Bonhoeffer's life was full to over-flowing. Speaking of his murdered friend, Bishop George Bell, who had tried so hard to make the voice of the German resistance heard by those who led the Western Allies, said: 'Dietrich has gone … Our debt to [him] and to all others similarly murdered is immense. His death is a death for Germany – indeed for Europe too … He was inspired by his faith in the living God and his devotion to truth and honour. As one of a noble company of martyrs of different traditions, he represents the resistance of the living God to the assaults of evil, but also the moral and political revolt of the human conscience against injustice and cruelty.'

In 1998, empty niches above the Great West Door of Westminster Abbey were filled with the statues of ten 'modern martyrs'. One of them is Dietrich Bonhoeffer.

Afterword

Cock-up or Conspiracy?

The question that has plagued me while writing this book is this: given that Germany was a police state, why were the plotters and the plots not discovered earlier? On the face of it, those charged with protecting Hitler appear not to have really got wind of the high-level plots until the latter months of 1943 or the early months of 1944. Yet these conspiracies had been serious and widespread at the top of Hitler's hierarchy from at least 1937.

How can this be explained?

Some reasons can be advanced for why it may have been so.

Hitler's Germany was not just a bureaucratic state, it was a hierarchical one too. Those at the top could never be held in suspicion, and were, at least until 20 July 1944, never seriously questioned. For example, despite the extremely strict security surrounding Wolfsschanze, the most senior Nazi functionaries were not required to carry identity documents, and objected most violently if they were not recognised immediately at checkpoints and permitted to sweep through without being stopped.

Moreover, questioning or suspecting one of the mandarins of Nazi Germany, even by another mandarin, was a political act, not a legal- or security-driven one. Heinrich Himmler had his suspicions of Wilhelm Canaris from as early as 1941, when he started assembling a secret file on the Abwehr chief (Canaris had started a secret file on Himmler even before the war started). But although Himmler had a fair idea of what his rival was up to – not least through Reinhard Heydrich – he did not feel strong enough to make his move until Canaris was sufficiently weakened for it to be safe to do so. Even when Willi Abendschön in Prague had more than good reason to believe that Paul Thümmel, a relatively low-level Abwehr officer, was a traitor, he was twice forced by pressure from Berlin to abandon his investigations because Thümmel was one of Himmler's early friends, a founder member of his local Nazi Party, and benefited from the protection of Canaris.

The second barrier to the effective uncovering of potential traitors in the army was the culture of *Üb Immer Treu und Redlichkeit* amongst senior Wehrmacht officers. The unwritten code that an officer never betrayed a brother officer provided a screen behind which plotters could plot and test a fellow officer's loyalty to Hitler, even in an explicit way, without too much risk of betrayal.

The coup managers also successfully used legitimate processes and structures to hide their preparations. Operation Valkyrie, behind whose façade the entire military element of the 'grand coup' of 20 July 1944 was constructed, is a good example of this. But as far back as 1941, Helmuth von Moltke was describing to a friend 'an interdepartmental group of officials and officers [which] has been formed with the full approval of the OKW [army command] ostensibly to formulate the wishes of the armed forces in the event of final victory: in reality one is trying to discuss, under a cloak of legality, what should be done when the National-Socialist regime ends'.

The final boon for the conspirators was the fact that, thanks to Hans Oster, they had the Abwehr's secure communications at their disposal. The role of Oster in keeping the coups' secrets should not be underestimated. His extensive network of spies within the structures of the Nazi state meant that, together with the head of the Berlin police, Wolf-Heinrich Helldorf – another committed conspirator – Oster was nearly always the first to hear if a conspirator was under surveillance or about to be arrested. As Hans Bernd Gisevius wrote after the war, 'Oster managed to encircle the German opposition with a cordon of silence.'

But the use of this communications network would probably have been confined to military and espionage matters only. Even by 1941 the anti-Hitler conspiracy had spread far beyond those circles. Carl Goerdeler, for instance, was heavily involved both inside and outside Germany in communicating secrets to the Allies and encouragements to plotters and would-be plotters, mostly by perfectly normal, conventional means. One thinks of his open letter to army officers encouraging revolt straight after Hitler's 1940 triumphs in the west. This was a clear call to treason, and was presumably widely distributed. But its existence never came to light at the time. Goerdeler, naïve, inexperienced and unstoppably loquacious, was a counter-intelligence officer's dream. And yet his deep involvement in all the major putsch attempts seems to have come as a complete surprise to Himmler's men after 20 July.

Or perhaps it didn't?

What counter-intelligence operators fear most is what former US defence secretary Donald Rumsfeld called 'known unknowns' – that is, the conspiracy they *don't* know about, and the would-be spy who has passed below their radar. For this reason, if a plot is uncovered, those who practise counter-intelligence often prefer to let it run, so as to flush out other conspirators and conspiracies. They call this 'drawing moths to the flame'.

We know that Himmler used this technique, for instance when he rolled up the Solf Circle in January 1944, having let the network run for months, if not years.

So, the question has to be asked: could it be that the reason Himmler apparently took so long to discover these plots was because he was in fact secretly controlling them?

Having examined this possibility, I have concluded that it was not so.

The primary reason for this is that, if Himmler and his men were secretly controlling the conspirators in order to 'draw moths to the flame', they would have been running risks with their core task – protecting Hitler and the Nazi state – that they would never have taken.

Take a simple case – the March 1943 plot to blow up Hitler using a suicide bomber while he was inspecting captured weapons. If Himmler was aware of this attempt on Hitler's life, would he really have allowed a suicide bomber armed with a bomb to walk beside Hitler through the presentation, relying only on the hope that the Führer could move fast enough to get out of the door before the device detonated? I very much doubt it. That would have been taking a risk with the Führer's life which I think no counter-intelligence operator would ever take.

Of course, the would-be bomber himself, Henning von Tresckow's friend Rudolf-Christoph von Gersdorff, may have been under Himmler's control. But von Gersdorff, who survived the aftermath of 20 July, wrote his memoirs after the war, and recounted the incident in full detail. It hardly seems likely that he would have acted as he did – or have got away with it without exposure – if all the time he had in fact been Himmler's agent.

In the same way, all the main personalities involved in the 'Cointreau bomb' plot of March 1943 either killed themselves or were tried and executed after 20 July. How could this be so, if they had a ready defence to the charges they faced, by revealing that they were actually working for Himmler at the time? At the very least, they would surely have mentioned this during their trials – but no such claim was ever made, by any of them.

The case for Heinrich Himmler controlling Hans Oster and the various spies and spy networks passing vital German secrets to the West and Russia is easier to counter. Counter-intelligence spies often allow low-level intelligence to be passed to the enemy in order to convince them that their 'play' is genuine. This kind of information is known in the trade as 'chickenfeed' – i.e. unimportant secrets which can be sacrificed for a higher goal.

But the information passed, mostly from Hans Oster, to Paul Thümmel and, especially, the Dora Ring was anything but chickenfeed. It was, in the main, genuine war-changing information, which cost thousands of German lives and diminished the chance of German victory in a number of key strategic battles, such as at Kursk.

It is simply inconceivable that Himmler would have allowed this to happen if he had known about it.

For all these reasons, I conclude that the simplest answer to the conundrum 'How did they get away with it?' is most likely to be the right one: that the failure of the Sicherheitsdienst to uncover the grand coup earlier was not conspiracy, but cock-up.

The most likely answer to the question of whether Himmler knew of the plots earlier is that he did not. Though the usually highly efficient SD was gifted plenty of opportunities by the mistakes, stupidities, bad trade-craft and naïvety of the conspirators, it probably did not begin seriously penetrating the high-level conspiracy against Hitler until near the end of 1943; it did not 'run' the plots in any meaningful way, and the scale of the threat posed by the resistance conspiracy came as a very unpleasant surprise to it after 20 July.

Reader's Note

Very few of the facts in this book are new. They were mostly known, and in many cases published, after the war. But to the Allies it was inconvenient at that time to acknowledge that there had ever been 'good Germans'. And in Germany itself it was regarded as shameful that there were some in high positions who contributed to the nation's defeat, and the deaths of so many of its young.

In the decades after the war numerous books were written which describe one or other aspect of the high-level resistance against Hitler. Many of these books (and one major film) deal with attempts to kill the Führer, most notably the plot of 20 July 1944. Other works describe the resistance's struggle to strike an early peace with the Allies. A few books, all of them minor and published in the years immediately following the war, chose as their subject the individual spies used by Canaris and his conspirators to pass German secrets to the Allies. This book aims to draw all these separate threads together, in order to provide the first comprehensive picture of the high-level anti-Hitler resistance during World War II. Inevitably, extensive use has been made of previously published works, for which I am much indebted to the authors. My colleague Sylvie Young and I have found other information in recently opened archives. Some of this has led us to conclusions which do not concur with those of previous authors (as for instance with the Dora spy network in Geneva). Where this is the case, reference is made in the endnotes.

This book does not cover the whole of the German resistance movement, which involved many tens of thousands of ordinary people who risked their lives, and in many cases lost them, in the process of opposing Hitler. Their story too needs to be told. But I fear it would severely tax the patience of the reader (not to say the endurance of the writer) to include them here. So this work concentrates on those who opposed Hitler from high in his command structure.

I have also not included those stories which seem to depend too much on conjecture. This means that some individuals who could – maybe should – appear in these pages do not: Alexis von Roenne, for example, who was among those executed for treason after the 20 July plot. There is very strong circumstantial evidence that von Roenne, who provided intelligence assessments to Hitler which he greatly trusted, played a key role in Canaris's project to assist an Allied victory by overstating Allied threats and certifying as truthful Allied deception plans which he knew to be false – such as Operation Mincemeat and the Double Cross deceptions before D-Day. I am personally convinced that he did play this double role, but I can find no evidence beyond conjecture to support this, and have therefore not included von Roenne in this story.

There is some overlap in German spelling between the umlaut and the diphthong, especially in proper names. For instance, the Soviet spy in Switzerland, Rachel Duebendorfer, can also be written as Dübendorfer. I have adopted the practice of employing the spelling most commonly used by the individuals themselves, or failing that, the most common spelling employed in the sources I have used. In many cases the Swiss use the diphthong, whereas Germans use the umlaut. Thus, since the Swiss Rachel Duebendorfer spelled her name using 'ue', and the spy Rudolf Roessler 'oe', these are the spellings I have used in this book. Similarly, since Hermann Göring used the umlaut, I have too.

Adolf Hitler was a master of the practice of divide and rule. This applied particularly to Nazi security structures, which were complex, overlapping and numerous. The Abwehr under Admiral Wilhelm Canaris, which is the main organisation covered by this book, is always referred to by its proper name. All other German security structures during World War II fell under the command of Heinrich Himmler. For simplicity's sake I have referred to these interchangeably as the SS (Schutzstaffel), the SD (Sicherheitsdienst), the RSHA (Reichssicherheitshauptamt – Himmler's umbrella security command structure) and the Gestapo (Geheime Staatspolizei).

Finally there is the problem of names. Many aristocratic Germans use 'von' before their surname, rather as many in France use 'de'. In France, however, if a 'de' is appropriate, it is always used (hence 'de Gaulle'). Modern Germans are more relaxed, sometimes including the 'von' and sometimes not. I have followed this practice and omitted the 'von' before a name when I judged it interrupted the flow of the text.

Acknowledgements

This is the third book on which Sylvie Young and I have collaborated. The previous two works would have been greatly diminished without her help. This one would have been impossible.

The scale of this enterprise turned out to be far, far bigger than either of us realised when we first began it. Our research has involved almost 150 published works, and about the same number of files from a wide variety of archives. The greater burden of this work, especially when it came to the books, fell on Sylvie's shoulders.

As did the very difficult task of restraining me.

I am sure it must be my Irish blood which causes me to get irritable when the facts treacherously refuse to support the story I want to tell. Sylvie has used every means, not excluding being disagreeable when she needed to, in order to keep me firmly tethered to the facts. It was, I fear, tough going for her, as I can be quite difficult to work with when I want to get my way. But by the time the dust had settled, she nearly always won. Thanks to that, this is a history book and not a romance. I am very proud of that. For her fierce spirit, her patience, her friendship and her extraordinary capacity for work, I owe Sylvie a great debt as my collaborator-in-chief on this book. My thanks are also extended to her husband Gordon for his forbearance in what will be, by the time it is published, a near-three-year obsession with writing this story.

Once again I must thank my wife Jane, who is the first reader for all of my books when they are written, and the last before they go to press. Other readers have generously commented on the chapters as I wrote them, and given me vital judgements and corrections. These include Steph Bailey, Bob Beecroft, Janet Berridge, Rosemary Billinge, Bill Caswell, Neil Cobbett, Ellen Dahrendorf, Sam Evans, Marysia Fabian-Akehurst, David Harrison, Steven Kippax, Ian Patrick, Steve Radley, Boris Ruge, Linda Siegle, Alistair Sommerlad, Bob Staples and Martin

Thursfield. I know that comparisons are odious (or is it invidious?), but nevertheless I need to pick out three of my wonderful readers for special mention. Peter Hennessy is very widely admired as a historian and commentator on history and current affairs. I owe him a huge debt for his generosity in agreeing to read my book in full and commenting on it in detail. Similarly, I am much indebted to my friend Anthony Lester for doing the same thing. The third is my old colleague in writing these books, Janet Smith, who as previously has spent long hours acting as my nitpicker-in-chief, spotting and correcting infelicities, and errors of spelling and grammar.

I am grateful also to Peter Kamber and Bernd-Rainer Barth, both experts and writers on the Swiss spy rings of World War II, for their help with archives and comments; to Heiko Suhr, who is writing a PhD on Wilhelm Canaris and who has also been generous with his advice; and to Richard Bassett for allowing me to plunder his book on Canaris and his knowledge of this era.

Special thanks are due to Philip Cole, who very kindly came to my rescue by providing not just comments, corrections and suggestions but also excellent German translations of difficult pieces that I could not cope with, and to Archie and Emina Tuta for advice on a Serbo-Croat translation. Another European linguist friend, Gareth Williams, helped with translations from Spanish, for which I also record my thanks. I am, in addition, very much in debt to Bruce Dennis, whose ability to find hidden treasures in the National Archives at Kew makes him, in my opinion, the Indiana Jones of the research world.

Others who should be thanked are all those at the library of the House of Lords for their patience in dealing with my questions and book requests; Father Roger Highcrest of Market Drayton for his information on Canaris; Ed and Lorraine Davis for their hospitality at the governor's house in Gibraltar; Jennifer Ballantine for her kindness during my stay on the Rock; Anthony Pitaluga, Yasmin Cosqueri and Alfonso Escuadras for their help with the history of Gibraltar and Algeciras during World War II; and Carola Kapitza of the Lufthansa Archives in Cologne. Thanks also to Alice, the Weather Office desk adviser at the Met Office in Exeter, and the wonderful Mark Beswick, Archive Information Officer of the Met Office National Meteorological Archive, who has neither complained nor seemed surprised over the last ten years when, in the process of writing books, I have asked him for impossibly detailed weather information on specific days at specific places during World War II. The lyrics from Noël

Coward's 'Don't Let's be Beastly to the Germans', © NC Aventales AG, 1943, are reproduced by permission of Alan Brodie Representation Ltd, www.alanbrodie.com.

Among those who should not be forgotten when it comes to thanks for being so generous with help and hospitality at crucial times are Christine Longworth, who did heroic work securing me a wi-fi connection during the Lib Dem Conference in Bournemouth in 2017; Bü Low, undoubtedly one of the most helpful taxi drivers in the world, for uncomplainingly taking us round all the addresses we needed to see in Berlin; Alicia Gonzalez and Andrew Stallybrass for their help in seeking traces of the Russian spy Ursula Kuczynski in the Swiss village of Caux-sur-Montreux; Julie Janet and her charming daughter Céleste for a splendid and most welcome lunch in Lausanne; the Polish ambassador to Switzerland, Jakub Kumoch, and his wife Joanna Kułakowska-Kumoch for their hospitality at dinner at the Polish residence in Bern and their help in uncovering the activities of Polish spies in Switzerland during the Second World War, and Mike van der Heijden for his assistance in finding the Jelineks' shop, De Favoriet, in The Hague.

Inevitably, research for this book has meant a lot of time in archives. I am, as always, very grateful to the superb staff at the National Archives in Kew for their unstinting helpfulness and patience. My thanks are also due to Natalie Adams, Sarah Lewery of the Churchill Archives in Cambridge, John Andrews and Kira Charatan of the Cadogan Archives, Martin Sanders, Carole Jones, Helen Ford and Thom Frew at the University of Warwick.

As with my previous books I need to express my appreciation and gratitude to the wonderful staff at my agents Peters, Fraser and Dunlop, especially Michael Sissons, who has been generous with suggestions and encouragement, and to Arabella Pike at William Collins for her patience and advice on where my text could be improved. This complex story is much more readable and ordered because of her. Meanwhile, the fact that my text is presented to the reader adequately punctuated, decently spelled, free of clumsy repetition and careless mistakes of syllogism and of fact is in very large measure due, along with much else, to my copy editor Robert Lacey, whom it has been a joy to work with.

There is an old riddle which goes – Question: How do you eat an elephant? Answer: A bite at a time. This is an elephant of a book which has at times almost overwhelmed me. In the end, taking it a mouthful at a time, I am surprised to find that it is done. Without the help of all this army of friends and generous strangers I suspect it could not have been completed – at least not in this form.

As always, if there are mistakes here – and there are bound to be many – they are down, exclusively, to me.

Bibliography

Karl Heinz Abshagen, *Canaris*, London, Hutchinson, 1956

Pierre Accoce & Pierre Quet, *La guerre a été gagnée en Suisse*, Paris, Presses Pocket, 1966

Jefferson Adams, *Historical Dictionary of German Intelligence*, Scarecrow Press, 2009

Anthony Allfrey, *Man of Arms: The Life and Legend of Sir Basil Zaharoff*, Thistle Publishing, 2013

C. Amort & I.M. Jedicka, *The Canaris File*, Paris, Robert Laffont, 1970

— *On l'appellait A.54*, Paris, Robert Laffont, 1965

Christopher Andrew, *The Defence of the Realm: The Authorized History of MI5*, London, Penguin, 2010

— *Her Majesty's Secret Service: The Making of the British Intelligence Community*, New York, Penguin Books, 1987

Drago Arsenovic, *Genève appelle Moscou*, Paris, Éditions Lattès, 1981

Michael Balfour, *Withstanding Hitler*, London & New York, Routledge, 1988

— & Julian Frisby, *Helmuth von Moltke: A Leader Against Hitler*, London, Macmillan, 1972

Mary Bancroft, *Autobiography of a Spy*, New York, William Morrow & Co., 1983

Richard Bassett, *Hitler's Spy Chief*, London, Phoenix, 2011

Antony Beevor, *The Second World War*, London, Weidenfeld & Nicolson, 2012

Gill Bennett, *Churchill's Man of Mystery: Desmond Morton and the World of Intelligence*, London, Routledge, 2007

Michael Beschloss, *The Conquerors*, New York, Simon & Schuster, 2007

Christabel Bielenberg, *The Past is Myself*, London, Corgi, 1988

Laurent Binet, *Hhhh*, London, Harvill Secker, 2012

Pierre Blet, *Pie XII et la Seconde Guerre Mondiale d'après les archives du Vatican*, Paris, Perrin, 1997

Yves Bonnet, *Les Espions d'Hitler*, Rennes, Éditions Ouest-France, 2012

Guillaume Bourgeois, *La véritable histoire de l'Orchestre Rouge*, Paris, Chronos, 2015

Rodric Braithwaite, *Moscow 1941: A City and its People at War*, London, Profile Books, 2007

Pierre Th. Braunschweig, *Secret Channel to Berlin*, Philadelphia, Casemates, 2004

André Brissaud, *Canaris: chef de l'espionnage du IIIème Reich*, Paris, Perrin, Librairie Académique, 1970

John Bryden, *Fighting to Lose*, Toronto, Dundurn, 2014

Sir Alexander Cadogan, *The Diaries of Sir Alexander Cadogan: 1938–45*, London, Cassell, 1971

Anthony Cave Brown, *Bodyguard of Lies*, Guildford Connecticut, The Lyons Press, 2002

— *The Last Hero: Wild Bill Donovan*, New York, Times Books, 1982

— *The Secret Servant*, London, Sphere Books Ltd, 1989

Galeazzo Ciano, *Ciano's Diplomatic Papers*, London, Odhams Press, 1948

— *Diary 1937–1938*, London, Phoenix Press, 2002

Angelo M. Codevilla, *Between the Alps and a Hard Place*, Washington, Regnery Publishing Inc., 2000

Ian Colvin, *The Unknown Courier: The True Story of Operation Mincemeat*, London, Biteback Publishing Ltd, 2016
— *Admiral Canaris: Chief of Intelligence*, London, George Mann Ltd, 1973
— *Vansittart in Office*, London, Victor Gollancz Ltd, 1965
John Cornwell, *Hitler's Scientist*, London, Penguin Books, 2003
— *Hitler's Pope*, London, Penguin Books, 2000
Rabbi David G. Dalin, *The Myth of Hitler's Pope*, Washington, Regnery Publishing, 2005
Hugh Dalton, *The Second World War Diary of Hugh Dalton, 1940–45*, ed. Ben Pimlott, London, Jonathan Cape, 1986
Peter Day, *The Bedbug*, London, Biteback Publishing, 2015
— *Franco's Friends*, London, Biteback Publishing, 2011
Richard Deacon, *A History of the British Secret Service*, London, Frederick Muller Ltd, 1978
Sefton Delmer, *The Counterfeit Spy*, London, Coronet Books, 1976
Harold C. Deutsch, *Hitler and His Generals*, Minneapolis, University of Minnesota Press, 1974
— *The Conspiracy Against Hitler*, Minneapolis, University of Minnesota Press, 1970
Allen Welsh Dulles, *Germany's Underground*, Boston, Da Capo Press, 2000
— *Secret Surrender*, Guildford Connecticut, The Lyons Press, 2006
Anthony Eden, *The Eden Memoirs: Facing the Dictators*, London, Cassell, 1962
Bob Edwards & Kenneth Dunne, *A Study of a Master Spy*, London, Housmans, 1961
Louis R. Eltscher, *Traitors or Patriots?*, Bloomington Indiana, iUniverse LLC, 2013
Major Gerhard Engel, *At the Heart of the Reich*, Barnsley, Frontline Books, 2017
David Faber, *Munich 1938: Appeasement and World War II*, London, Pocket Books, 2009
Ladislas Farago, *The Game of the Foxes*, London, Hodder & Stoughton, 1971
— *Burn After Reading*, Los Angeles, Pinnacle Books, 1978
Joachim Fest, *Hitler*, London, Penguin Books, 2002
— *Plotting Hitler's Death: The German Resistance to Hitler 1939–1945*, London, Weidenfeld & Nicolson, 1996
Alexander Foote, *Handbook for Spies*, Greenville Ohio, Coachwhip Publications, 2011
André François-Poncet, *Souvenirs d'une Ambassade à Berlin 1931–1938*, Paris, Perrin, 2016
Herman Friedhoff, *Requiem for the Resistance: The Civilian Struggle Against Nazism in Holland and Germany*, London, Bloomsbury, 1988
Saul Friedlander, *Pie XII et le IIIe Reich*, Paris, Éditions du Seuil, 1964
James Gannon, *Stealing Secrets, Telling Lies*, New York, Brassey Inc, 2001
Josef Garlinski, *The Swiss Corridor*, London, J.M. Dent & Sons, 1981
Marie Gatard, *La Source MAD*, Paris, Michalon, 2017
Reinhard Gehlen, *The Service: The Memoirs of General Reinhard Gehlen*, New York, Popular Library, 1972
Rudolf-Christoph von Gersdorff, *Tuer Hitler*, Paris, Éditions Tallandier, 2012
G.M. Gilbert, *Nuremberg Diary*, New York, Farrar, Straus & Co., 1947
Anton Gill, *An Honourable Defeat*, New York, Henry Holt & Co., 1994
Hans Bernd Gisevius, *To the Bitter End*, New York, Da Capo Press, 1998
— *Valkyrie: An Insider's Account of the Plot to Kill Hitler*, New York, Da Capo Press, 2009
John Green, *A Political Family: The Kuczynskis, Fascism, Espionage and the Cold War*, London, Routledge, 2017
Agostino von Hassell & Sigrid MacRae, *Alliance of Enemies*, New York, Thomas Dunne Books, 2006
Ulrich von Hassell, *The Ulrich von Hassell Diaries: The Story of the Forces Against Hitler Inside Germany*, Barnsley, Pen & Sword, 2011
Max Hastings, *The Secret War: Spies, Codes and Guerrillas, 1939–45*, London, William Collins, 2015
Nevile Henderson, *Failure of a Mission: Berlin 1937–39*, New York, G.P. Putnam's Sons, 1940
Wilhelm Hoettl, *Secret Front: Nazi Political Espionage 1938–1945*, New York, Enigma Books, 2003

Peter Hoffmann, *Stauffenberg: A Family History*, Montreal, McGill-Queen's University Press, 2008
— *The History of the German Resistance: 1933–1945*, Cambridge Massachusetts, MIT Press, 1977
— (ed.), *Behind Valkyrie: German Resistance to Hitler*, Montreal, McGill-Queen's University Press, 2011
Heinz Höhne, *Canaris*, London, Secker & Warburg, 1979
— *Codeword Direktor*, New York, Coward, McCann & Geoghegan, 1971
Thaddeus Holt, *The Deceivers: Allied Military Deception in the Second World War*, London, Phoenix, 2004
Colonel F. Hossbach, *Entre la Wehrmacht et Hitler*, Paris, Éditions Payot, 1951
Keith Jeffery, *MI6: The History of the Secret Intelligence Service, 1909–1949*, London, Bloomsbury, 2010
David Alan Johnson, *Righteous Deception: German Officers Against Hitler*, Westport, Praeger, 2001
Nigel Jones, *Countdown to Valkyrie: The July Plot to Kill Hitler*, Barnsley, Frontline Books, 2008
Traudl Junge, *Until the Final Hour: Hitler's Last Secretary*, New York, Arcade Publishing, 2003
David Kahn, *Hitler's Spies: German Military Intelligence in World War II*, New York, Da Capo Press, 2000
Peter Kamber, *Kamber Geheime Agentin*, Berlin, Basis Druck, 2010
Ursula von Kardorff, *Diary of a Nightmare: Berlin 1942–1945*, London, Rupert Hart-Davis, 1965
Eric Kerjean, *Canaris*, Paris, Perrin, 2012
Ian Kershaw, *Making Friends with Hitler*, London, Penguin Books, 2005
— *Hitler 1936–45: Nemesis*, London, Penguin Books, 2001
Louis Kilzer, *Hitler's Traitor: Martin Bormann and the Defeat of the Reich*, Novato, Presidio Press, 2000
Sir Ivone Kirkpatrick, *The Inner Circle: The Memoirs of Ivone Kirkpatrick*, New York, Macmillan & Co., 1959
— *Mussolini: Study of a Demagogue*, London, Odhams Books, 1964
Klemens von Klemperer, *German Resistance Against Hitler: The Search for Allies Abroad 1938–1945*, Oxford, Clarendon Press, 1994
Philip Knightley, *Philby: KGB Masterspy*, London, André Deutsch, 2003
Richard Lamb, *The Ghosts of Peace: 1935–1945*, Wilton, Michael Russell, 1987
Walter Laqueur & Richard Breitman, *Breaking the Silence*, New York, Simon & Schuster, 1986
Guy Liddell, *The Guy Liddell Diaries Vols 1 and 2*, ed. Nigel West, London & New York, Routledge, 2005
Basil Liddell Hart, *The Other Side of the Hill*, London, Pan Grand Strategy, 1948
Vejas Gabriel Liulevicius, *The German Myth of the East: 1800 to the Present*, New York, Oxford University Press, 2009
Callum Macdonald, *The Assassination of Reinhard Heydrich*, Edinburgh, Birlinn Ltd, 2016
Giles MacDonogh, *A Good German*, London, Quartet Books, 1989
— *1938: Hitler's Gamble*, London, Constable, 2010
Ben Macintyre, *A Spy Among Friends: Philby and the Great Betrayal*, London, Bloomsbury, 2014
— *Double Cross*, London, Bloomsbury, 2012
— *Operation Mincemeat*, London, Bloomsbury, 2010
Roger Manvell & Heinrich Fraenkel, *The Men Who Tried to Kill Hitler*, Barnsley, Frontline Books, 2008
Ernst May, *Strange Victory*, New York, Hill & Wang, 2000
Jean Médrala, *Les Réseaux de renseignements Franco-Polonais 1940–1944*, Paris, L'Harmattan, 2005

Patricia Meehan, *The Unnecessary War*, London, Sinclair-Stevenson, 1995

Mungo Melvin, *Manstein: Hitler's Greatest General*, London, Weidenfeld & Nicolson, 2010

Helmuth James von Moltke, *Letters to Freya, 1939–1945*, New York, Vintage Books, 1995

Hans Mommsen, *Alternatives to Hitler*, Princeton & Oxford, Princeton University Press, 2003

Roger Moorhouse, *Killing Hitler: The Third Reich and the Plots to Kill Hitler*, London, Vintage, 2007

František Morávec, *Master of Spies: The Memoirs of General František Morávec*, New York, Doubleday & Co., 1975

Gavin Mortimer, *The SBS in World War II*, London, Osprey, 2013

Michael Mueller, *Canaris*, London, Greenhill Books, 2017

Henri Navarre, *Le Service de renseignements 1871–1944*, Paris, Plon, 1978

Danny Orbach, *The Plots Against Hitler*, New York, Houghton Mifflin Harcourt Publishing Company, 2016

Pierre Ordioni, *La Fracture: De Londres 1941 à Sétif 1945*, Paris, Nouvelles Éditions Latines, 1995

Peter Padfield, *Hess, Hitler and Churchill*, London, Icon Books, 2013

Léon Papeleux, *L'Amiral Canaris: Entre Franco et Hitler*, Paris, Casterman, 1977

Terry Parssinen, *The Oster Conspiracy of 1938*, New York, HarperCollins, 2003

Stanley G. Payne, *Franco and Hitler: Spain, Germany, and World War II*, New Haven & London, Yale University Press, 2008

Gilles Perrault, *L'Orchestre Rouge*, Paris, Fayard, 1989

Neal H. Petersen, *From Hitler's Doorstep*, University Park, Pennsylvania State University Press, 1996

Janusz Piekalkiewicz, *Secret Agents, Spies and Saboteurs*, London, Garden City Press Ltd, 1974

Dusko Popov, *Spy Counterspy*, London, Weidenfeld & Nicolson, 1974

Otto Puenter, *Guerre Secrète en pays neutre*, Lausanne, Payot, 1967

Sándor Radó, *Sous le Pseudonyme Dora*, Paris, Julliard, 1972

Ian Rankin, *Ian Fleming's Commandos*, London, Faber & Faber, 2011

Anthony Read & David Fisher, *Colonel Z: The Secret Life of a Master of Spies*, London, Hodder & Stoughton, 1984

— *Operation Lucy: Most Secret Spy Ring of the Second World War*, Newton Abbot, Readers Union, 1981

Nicholas Reynolds, *Treason Was No Crime*, London, William Kimber, 1976

Vincent Ricci, *Target Hitler: The Plots to Kill Adolf Hitler*, Westport & London, Praeger, 1992

Mark Riebling, *Church of Spies*, New York, Basic Books, 2015

Werner Rings, *La Suisse et la Guerre 1933–1945*, Lausanne, Ex Libris, 1975

Gerhard Ritter, *The German Resistance*, London, George Allen & Unwin Ltd, 1958

Général Louis Rivet, *Carnets du Chef des Services Secrets: 1936–1944*, Paris, Nouveau Monde, 2010

Christian Rossé, *Guerre Secrète en Suisse*, Paris, Éditions Nouveau Monde, 2015

Hans Rothfels, *The German Opposition to Hitler*, London, Oswald Wolff Ltd, 1961

Raymond Ruffin, *Les Espionnes du XXème siècle*, Chaintreaux, France-Empire, 2013

Harry Carl Schaub, *Call Your First Witness*, self-published, 2016

Walter Schellenberg, *Hitler's Secret Service*, New York, Pyramid Books, 1958

— *The Labyrinth: Memoirs*, New York, Harper, 1956

Fabian von Schlabrendorff, *The Secret War Against Hitler*, London, Hodder & Stoughton, 1965

Paul Schmidt, *Hitler's Interpreter*, Port Stroud, The History Press, 2016

William L. Shirer, *Berlin Diary: The Journal of a Foreign Correspondent 1934–1941*, London, Hamish Hamilton, 1942

— *The Rise and Fall of the Third Reich*, New York, Touchstone, 1990

James Srodes, *Allen Dulles: Master of Spies*, Washington, Regnery Publishing, 1999

V.E. Tarrant, *The Red Orchestra*, London, Cassell, l998

Leopold Trepper, *The Great Game: The Story of the Red Orchestra*, London, McGraw Hill, 1977

Hugh Trevor-Roper, *The Last Days of Hitler*, London, Pan Books, 2012
— *The Secret World*, London, I.B. Tauris, 2014
Karina Urbach, *Go-Betweens for Hitler*, Oxford, Oxford University Press, 2015
Marie 'Missie' Vassiltchikov, *The Berlin Diaries 1940–1945*, London, Pimlico, 1999
Hal Vaughan, *Sleeping With the Enemy: Coco Chanel's Secret War*, London, Vintage Books, 2012
Ernest Volman, *Spies: The Secret Agents Who Changed the Course of History*, New York, John Wiley & Sons, 1994
Douglas Waller, *Disciples*, New York, Simon & Schuster Paperbacks, 2015
John Waller, *The Unseen War in Europe: Espionage and Conspiracy in the Second World War*, London, I.B. Tauris Publishers, 1996
Gerhard L. Weinberg, *Germany, Hitler and World War II*, Cambridge, Cambridge University Press, 1996
Ruth Werner, *Sonya's Report: Fascinating Autobiography of One of Russia's Most Remarkable Secret Agents*, London, Chatto & Windus, 1991
Nigel West, *MI6*, London, Panther, 1985
John Wheeler-Bennett, *The Nemesis of Power: The German Army in Politics, 1918–1945*, London, Macmillan, 1967
Paul Winter, *Defeating Hitler*, London & New York, Continuum, 2012
F.W. Winterbotham, *Secret and Personal*, London, William Kimber, 1969
— *The Ultra Secret*, London, Futura Publications Ltd, 1975
Neville Wylie, *Britain, Switzerland and the Second World War*, Oxford, Oxford University Press, 2003
A.P. Young, *The 'X' Documents*, London, André Deutsch, 1974

Notes

Prologue

xxix 'If we aim at' John Maynard Keynes, *The Economic Consequences of the Peace*, Transaction Publishers, 2009, p.xv

xxx 'a life's savings' https://www.historyonthenet.com/authentichistory/1930–1939/4-roadtowar/1-germany/index.html

xxx 'In [these] times' Fest, *Hitler*, p.373

xxx 'Within two months' Eltscher, *Traitors or Patriots?*, p.16

xxxi 'I confront everything' Fest, *Hitler*, p.376

xxxii 'a feeling as if' Ibid., p.384

xxxii 'Harsh rulers don't' Ritter, *The German Resistance*, p.42

1: Carl Goerdeler

1 'Schneidemuehl' Now Pila in Poland

2 'Goerdeler was a' Fest, *Plotting Hitler's Death*, p.146

2 'Königsberg' Now Kaliningrad

3 'Goerdeler accepted' Young, *The 'X' Documents*, p.27

4 'Night of the Long Knives' Its official title was 'Unternehmen Kolibri' (Operation Hummingbird). In fact the German phrase *'Nacht der langen Messer'* long predates this event as a description of acts of unrestrained mass violence

4 'the army general' General Kurt von Schleicher

4 'personal secretary of another Chancellor' Herbert von Bose, head of the press division of the Vice Chancellery under Vice-Chancellor Franz von Papen

5 'local Leipzig Nazi leader' Hans Rudolf Haake

5 'There is one of' quoted in Deutsch, *The Conspiracy Against Hitler*, p.11

5 'All of us' Orbach, *The Plots Against Hitler*, p.24

5 'his position' See Mommsen, *Germans Against Hitler*, p.259

5 'a local Gauleiter' Gauleiters were the Nazi district governors. In this case Martin Mutschmann, the Gauleiter of Saxony

6 'as a patriot' Ritter, *The German Resistance*, p.82

6 'call black, black' quoted in Young, *The 'X' Documents*, p.24

6 'He has decided' Sir William Deedes, quoted in ibid.

6 'ex-World War I fighter pilot' Leslie Satchell

6 'industrialist' Hugh Quigley

6 'civil servant' Sir Wyndham Deedes

7 'His Master's Voice' quoted in Colvin, *Vansittart in Office*, p.148

7 'an alarmist' Ibid., p.147

7 'an impressive, wise' TNA FO 371/20733

7 'Suppressed by Eden' Vansittart Papers: Vnst 1/20 Churchill College, and Colvin, *Vansittart in Office*, p.154

2: Ludwig Beck

8 'a degree of anti-Semitism' Mommsen, *Germans Against Hitler*, p.257

8 'I have wished' Ludwig Beck letter to Fraulein Gossler, 17 March 1933, in May, *Strange Victory*, pp.33–4

9 'facial skin' Ibid., pp.31–2

9 'tense, sensitive' Deutsch, *Hitler and His Generals*, p.43

9 'Everyone who knew him' Count Rüdiger von der Goltz in Hoffmann, *The History of the German Resistance*, p.70

11 'humiliating retreat' quoted in May, *Strange Victory*, p.35

11 'a policy with moral' F. Hossbach, *Zwischen Wehrmacht und Hitler*, Hanover, 1949, p.152 (translation from Ritter, *The German Resistance*, p.76)

12 'I swear by God' Shirer, *The Rise and Fall of the Third Reich*, p.227

12 'blackest day of my life' From Gisevius's testimony at Nuremberg, 25 April 1946. (http://avalon.law.yale.edu/imt/04–25–46.asp) and in Ritter, *The German Resistance*, p.73

12 'could never rid himself' From Gisevius's testimony at Nuremberg, 25 April 1946

13 'It is not what' Note to Karl-Heinrich von Stülpnagel, then a colonel, in Peter Hoffmann, 'Ludwig Beck: Loyalty and Resistance', *Central European History*, Vol. 14, no. 4, December 1981, p.337

13 'All hope is placed' Ritter, *The German Resistance*, p.76

13 'The first German objective' Shirer, *The Rise and Fall of the Third Reich*, p.357, and Hossbach, *Entre la Wehrmacht et Hitler*, p.209 (and in Annexe II)

14 'forced to resign' Cave Brown, *The Last Hero*, p.287. The site of the alleged offence was Privaat Strasse, by Berlin's Wannsee station

14 'I exercise henceforth' Colvin, *Vansittart in Office*, p.179

14 'Mutiny and revolution' Ritter, *The German Resistance*, p.78

14 'It is my unalterable decision' Faber, *Munich 1938*, p.186

14 'The Führer's remarks' Hoffmann, 'Loyalty and Resistance', op. cit., p.345

3: Wilhelm Canaris

15 'shop soiled and old' Bassett, *Hitler's Spy Chief*, p.103, quoting Gerhard Henke, 'Bericht und Erinnerungen eines Ic', *Die Nachhut*, 13 Nov 1967

15 'He gave the impression' Bassett, *Hitler's Spy Chief*, p.103

16 'one of the most' Klemperer, *German Resistance Against Hitler*, p.23, quoted from Ernst von Weizsäcker in his *Erinnerungen* (Munich, 1950), p.175

16 'the Canarisi family' See Erika Canaris's letter to Allen Dulles of 24 Aug 1947; Allen Dulles Papers; Public Policy Papers, Department of Rare Books and Special Collections, Princeton University Library, Box 11, Folder 6. Findingaids.princeton.edu/collections/MC019/c00163

16 'believed in the supernatural' Ibid.

16 'Canaris had a profound' Manvell and Fraenkel, *The Men Who Tried to Kill Hitler*, p.193. The words are those of Dr Wolf Werner Schrader

16 'What had gone' Colonel Louis Rivet, 'L'énigme du Service de renseignements allemand sous le régime hitlérien', *Revue de Défense nationale*, décembre 1947, pp.778–807

16 'a friend noted' Erwin Lahousen, quoted in Gisevius, *To the Bitter End*, pp.439–42

17 'a kind person' Kessel speaking to Erika Canaris. See Erika Canaris's letter to Allen Dulles of 24 Aug 1947; Allen Dulles Papers; Public Policy Papers, Department of Rare Books and Special Collections, Princeton University Library, Box 11, Folder 6

17 'tender emotions' Erika Canaris's letter to Donovan of 15 November 1945, http://lawcollections.library.cornell.edu/nuremberg/catalog/nur:01696

17 'light cruiser *Dresden*, on which Canaris was a junior officer' Some subsequent accounts report that Canaris was the *Dresden*'s intelligence officer and closely involved in sowing misinformation which confused the British. But this is untrue. He in fact held a junior position as the Captain's secretary. Heiko Suhr, email to the author

18 'bay on an isolated island' Cumberland Bay, Robinson Crusoe Island, near the Chilean island of Más a Tierra

18 'back in Germany on 30 September 1915' File note Admiralty Staff, 5 October 1915, BA-MA, RM 5/2228, folio 247, quoted in Mueller, *Canaris*, p.265 fn 11

18 'If a Spaniard' Canaris to Piekenbrock, who told the author of Brissaud, *Canaris: chef de l'espionnage*, p.408

19 'put together the spy networks' Canaris contributed to the set-up of the Ettapendienst organisation which provided secret economic support to the German Navy in foreign waters and maritime Intelligence, TNA KV 3/384, and Robert H. Whealey, *Hitler and Spain: The Nazi Role in the Spanish Civil War 1936–1939*, University Press of Kentucky, 1989, pp.121 et seq.

19 'According to rumour' Bassett, *Hitler's Spy Chief*, pp.54–5

19 'the Croatian port of Cattaro' Modern-day Kotor in Montenegro

20 'Miss Hill terminated' See Heiko Suhr, email to the author

21 'he accompanied Erika' Heydrich also played first violin in Erika Canaris's string quartet

21 'twice choose to live' Both families lived on the Dollestrasse in the Dahlem district in Berlin up to January 1936 (Brissaud, *Canaris*, p.86), when they moved to adjacent houses connected by a garden gate in the Schlachtensee (Canaris's address was Waldsängerpfad, Bet-Teil 17, Schlachtensee: Bassett, *Hitler's Spy Chief*, p.99) – the street in which Canaris lived has had a number of names. It was called Dianastrasse until 1940, and then Betazeile during the war years. Heiko Suhr, email to the author, 10 November 2017

21 'Mrs Canaris played' Lina Heydrich, 7 Mar 1951: http://www.fpp.co.uk/Heydrich/Lina_Heydrich_070351.html and Kerjean, *Canaris*, pp.47–8

21 'kill all disabled children' Heiko Suhr, email to the author

22 'Canaris considered them' Manvell and Fraenkel, *The Men Who Tried to Kill Hitler*, p.193. The words are those of Dr Wolf Werner Schrader

22 'One of his superiors' Captain Arno Spindler. Ibid., p.84

22 'tipped off the British' Bassett, *Hitler's Spy Chief*, pp.122–4

22 'film-making enterprise' Ibid., p.89

23 'his immediate superior' Rear Admiral Bastian

23 'Swinemünde' Swinoujście in modern Poland

23 'adopted son' Colonel Louis Rivet, 'L'énigme du Service de renseignements allemand sous le régime hitlérien', *Revue de Défense nationale*, décembre 1947, pp.778–807

23 'avid reader of British spy novels' See Hugh Trevor-Roper article in TNA HW 5/23

23 'What I want' Cave Brown, *The Last Hero*, p.129, quoting Peter Fleming, *Operation Sea Lion*, New York, Simon & Schuster, 1957, p.211

24 'Hitler called in' There are some claims that Canaris himself was present, but it seems likely that he has been confused with another unnamed admiral. See especially Höhne, *Canaris*, p.231

25 'If you are looking' Richard Protze in 'The Double Life of Admiral Canaris', *International Journal of Intelligence and Counterintelligence*, 1996, Vol. 9, part 3, and Waller, *The Unseen War in Europe*, p.278

25 'one reported after the war' Special Interrogation Report of Franz, Maria Leidig, CSIR/6, 4 Oct 1945, Hoover Library T's Germany USA 7 F 697

4: Madeleine and Paul

26 'Above all' Lahousen's evidence, The International Military Tribunal, Nuremberg, Vol. II, 30 November 1945, morning session, p.444

27 'A high-pressure zone' Information from Mark Beswick, Archive Information Officer, Met Office National Meteorological Archive, 23 May 2017

27 'The oldest eastern' Liulevicius, *The German Myth of the East*, p.184

29 'He knew nothing' TV film *MAD, une héroïne de l'ombre*, by Label Image, broadcast Sunday, 25 February 2018, on France 5, 12:43

29 'the full report' TNA KV 2/173

29 'begun on 8 February 1936' Lieutenant-Colonel František Morávec, then head of the research group, puts it in March 1937. Morávec, *Master of Spies*, p.58. However, the photo of one of Thümmel's letters shows that it is dated 1936: in Amort & Jedicka, *The Canaris File*, p.80

29 'medium height' Amort & Jedicka, *The Canaris File*, p.124

30 'The author of this' Piekalkiewicz, *Secret Agents, Spies and Saboteurs*, p.133

31 'I shall await' Amort & Jedicka, *The Canaris File*, pp.12–13

31 'one of Bartik's officers' Lieutenant Kyrinovic

31 'so badly tortured' Amort & Jedicka, *The Canaris File*, p.19

32 'Saturday 4 April' Piekalkiewicz, *Secret Agents, Spies and Saboteurs*, pp.135–6

32 'Grüss Gott' Ibid.

33 'the code number by which' Evidence of Alois Frank, ibid., p.136

33 'warn the Czech government' Morávec, *Master of Spies*, p.107

33 'Both SIS in Prague' Andrew, *Her Majesty's Secret Service*, pp.393–4

34 'His Majesty's Government' Henderson, *Failure of a Mission*, p.139

34 'Thümmel was needy' See Igor Lukes, *Czechoslovakia Between Stalin and Hitler*, Oxford University Press, 1996, citing Jaroslav & Stanislav Kokoška, *Spor o agenta A-54*, Naše Vojsko, Prague, 1994, for an unflattering description of Thümmel's character, and also a different view on his activities in relation to the May 1939 invasion scare

5: Germany in the Shadow of War

35 '*Mittwochgesellschaft*' PAGH p.26. Schlabrendorff, *The Secret War Against Hitler*, pp.165–6. According to Schlabrendorff, the 'Wednesday Society' consisted of 16 scientists. Beck was admitted to the club as a military scientist, and Ulrich von Hassell as a political scientist. They met every other Wednesday. http://deacademic.com/dic.nsf/dewiki/966410

36 'Weizsäcker chose' Klemperer, *German Resistance Against Hitler*, p.26

36 'senior position in Ribbentrop's Berlin office' Head of the Ministerial Office

38 'race of carnivorous sheep' Sir Hugh Dalton in Fest, *Plotting Hitler's Death*, p.78. Dalton seems to have borrowed this colourful description from Churchill, who used the same phrase when talking to his military advisers (Earl Mountbatten, *Churchill the Warrior*, Fourth Winston Churchill Memorial Lecture (1970), 8.). For other examples of Dalton borrowing from Churchill see Ben Pimlott, *Hugh Dalton: A Life*, p.672. I am indebted to Prof. Piers Brendon for drawing my attention to this

38 'Canaris Familie GmBH' CIA-RDP78-03362A002500070002-3 GIS, SCF 52/20, 1 December 1945, https://www.cia.gov/library/readingroom/document/cia-rdp78-03362a002500070002-3

38 'eternal plotter' Fest, *Plotting Hitler's Death*, p.100

39 'the Swine' Shirer, *The Rise and Fall of the Third Reich*, p.716

39 'an elegant cavalry' Colvin, *Admiral Canaris*, p.46

39 'Being anti-Nazi' Colonel Louis Rivet, 'L'énigme du Service de renseignements allemand sous le régime hitlérien', *Revue de Défense nationale*, décembre 1947, pp.778–807

39 '*grande éminence grise*' Gersdorff, *Tuer Hitler*, p.120

40 'I have penetrated' Deacon, *A History of the British Secret Service*, p.274

40 'a Moroccan' Colonel Louis Rivet, 'L'énigme du Service de renseignements allemand sous le régime hitlérien', *Revue de Défense nationale*, décembre 1947, pp.778–807

41 'It had six' Erika Canaris, letter to General Donovan of 15 November 1945. http://lawcollections.library.cornell.edu/nuremberg/catalog/nur:01696

41 'Passive leadership' Gisevius, *To the Bitter End*, p.443

41 'known affectionately as' Abshagen, *Canaris*, p.71

41 'the little sailor' From Balfour & Frisby, *Helmuth von Moltke*, p.226

41 'Canaris was the most' Gisevius, *To the Bitter End*, pp.439 et seq.

41 'Admiral Canaris was' Special Interrogation Report of Franz, Maria Leidig, CSIR/6, 4 Oct 1945, Hoover Library T's Germany USA 7 F 697
42 'An intelligence officer worthy' Said by Canaris in Brussels during a tour of the Abwehr's offices in 1940 in Brissaud, *Canaris: – chef de l'espionnage*, p.249
42 'any officer who slept' Ibid., p.52, quoting Col. Franz Seubert, head of the Abwehr in Bulgaria
42 'By 1943 it had surged' Bassett, *Hitler's Spy Chief*, p.114; Colvin, *Admiral Canaris*, p.76
43 'sated, indolent and quiescent' Fest, *Plotting Hitler's Death*, p.77
43 'You know' Young, *The 'X' Documents*, p.43
44 'Canaris issued instructions' TNA KV 2/173
44 'the campaign against' Ritter, *The German Resistance*, p.88
44 'From his new' Email exchange dated 16 June 2017 with Peter C. Hoffman on a telephone conversation he had on 16 October 1979 with Harold C. Deutsch
44 'England must lend' Colvin, *Admiral Canaris*, p.55

6: The Emissaries
45 'Suddenly they came' The details in the following paragraphs are taken from Young, *The 'X' Documents*, pp.45 et seq.
45 'Rauschen-Düne' Now Svetlogorsk, 39 km north-west of Kaliningrad
46 'A revolution is no place' Young, *The 'X' Documents*, p.57
46 'Hansa Airlines 0800 flight' Lufthansa Berlin to London 1938 timetables, courtesy of Carola Kapitza of Lufthansa archives, Berlin
47 'Bring me certain' Fest, *Plotting Hitler's Death*, p.73, and Colvin, *Admiral Canaris*, p.62
48 'It would be unwise' TNA DBFP 3,ii, p.683
48 'For the first time' Colvin, *Admiral Canaris*, pp.53–4
48 'I must warn you' Ibid., p.54
48 'The Admiral [Canaris]' Ibid., p.60
49 'A friend of mine' TNA DBFP 3, ii, pp.683–9
49 'a conservative, a Prussian' Colvin, *Vansittart in Office*, p.226
49 'He spoke with' TNA DBFP 3, ii, p.685
49 'Of all the Germans' Colvin, *Admiral Canaris*, p.65
49 'Hitler has made' As reported by Vansittart to Halifax in a note dated 18 August 1938, in Colvin, *Vansittart in Office*, p.224
50 'Kleist started by' The Sir Winston Churchill Archives Trust, Cambridge, CHAR 2/331
50 'There can be no' W.S. Churchill, *The Gathering Storm*, Boston, Houghton Mifflin, 1948, p.280
50 'Nevertheless I confess' TNA DBFP 3, ii, pp.688–9
51 'My Dear Sir' The Sir Winston Churchill Archives Trust, Cambridge, CHAR 2/331
51 'Kordt's brother' Klemperer, *German Resistance Against Hitler*, p.102; Parssinen, *The Oster Conspiracy of 1938*, p.100
51 'conspiracy against Hitler' Colvin, *Vansittart in Office*, p.235
52 'We could not be' Fest, *Plotting Hitler's Death*, p.74

7: 'All Our Lovely Plans'
53 'The silence of' Ibid., p.57, and Parssinen, *The Oster Conspiracy of 1938*, p.161
54 'Tonight Hitler will be' Major Groscurth to his brother, Deutsch, *The Conspiracy Against Hitler*, p.37
55 'from the end of August' Colvin, *Vansittart in Office*, p.232
56 'I thought I saw' Cadogan, *Diaries*, p.100
56 'Hitler has given' Faber, *Munich 1938*, p.349
56 'with a view to' TNA DBFP 3/11 No 1118, p.552
57 'Finally we have' Fest, *Plotting Hitler's Death*, p.94

57 'Don't give away' Meehan, *The Unnecessary War*, pp.177, 181
58 'It won't be long' Fest, *Plotting Hitler's Death*, p.95
58 'in the last useful' Ciano, *Diary 1937–1938*, p.133
58 'Go to the Führer' Kirkpatrick, *Mussolini*, p.360
58 'suggesting Mussolini supports' Ibid., p.134
59 '*Il Duce* informs you' Faber, *Munich 1938*, p.387
59 'I had already' *Trials of War Criminals before the Nuremberg Military Tribunals*, Green series, Vol. 12, 'The Ministries Case', p.1083
59 'What can troops' Fest, *Plotting Hitler's Death*, p.97
60 'Silent, mournful' Speech by Churchill on the Munich Agreement, House of Commons, 5 October 1938
61 'Peace for our time?' Gisevius, *To the Bitter End*, p.326
61 'The Munich agreement' Ibid., pp.427–8
61 'Never since 1933' Orbach, *The Plots Against Hitler*, p.60, quoting from Erich Kordt, *Wahn und Wirklichkeit*, Stuttgart, Union Deutsche Verlagsgesellschaft, 1947, p.12
61 'all our lovely plans' Gisevius, *To the Bitter End*, p.326
61 'One general' Franz Halder

8: March Madness

62 'strove unremittingly' Cave Brown, *The Secret Servant*, p.193
62 'By keeping the peace' Mueller, *Canaris*, p.139
62 'the British chargé d'affaires' George Forbes
62 'authoritative circles' Ritter, *The German Resistance*, p.118
63 'Of our top military' Cadogan was speaking in 1951; see Cadogan, *Diaries*, p.93
65 'In the middle of October' 14 October, in Young, *The 'X' Documents*, p.110
65 'Goerdeler's finest' Gisevius, *To the Bitter End*, p.327
65 'had a message' Cadogan, *Diaries*, p.128
66 'a job had been arranged' Schaub, *Call Your First Witness*, p.30
66 'it will be war' Gatard, *La Source MAD*, p.70 (The basis of this book is a memoir by Madeleine Bihet-Richou, written after the war. It is kept at the French Centre historique des archives, Service Historique de la Défense, Vincennes. Unfortunately, we were informed on 5 June 2017, having requested it, that the file – GR 1 KT 271 – was missing)
66 'a German diplomat in Paris' Ernst vom Rath. His assassin was Herschel Grynszpan
66 'The government has secretly' Ibid., p.59
67 'violent nationwide attacks' Orbach, *The Plots Against Hitler*, p.76, quoting from Leni Yahil, *The Holocaust: The Fate of European Jewry*, New York, Oxford University Press, 1990, p.111
67 'The shame and bitterness' Ritter, *The German Resistance*, p.115
67 'Canaris was later thanked' TNA KV 2/173
67 'In the afternoon of 9th November 1938' Evidence of Mrs C.K. Rosenstiel, Association of Jewish Refugees, Vol. 2, February 2014, front page – by kind permission of Mr Colin Rosenstiel. Mrs Rosenstiel did not accept Oster's offer, as she felt it would be too compromising for him if she did. The block of flats, at Bayriche Strasse 9, remains today exactly as it would have been at the time. It is now adorned with a plaque marking the fact that Oster lived there
67 'The son of Canaris's pastor' Dr Stefan Heyden
67 'Thirteen Jewish men' Bassett, *Hitler's Spy Chief*, p.15, quoting a letter to the author from Dr Stefan Heyden
68 'a secret organisation' TNA KV 2/173
68 'On 20 February' Papeleux, *L'Amiral Canaris*, p.76
68 'an agreement with France' The Bérard–Jordana agreements between France and Franco secured the neutrality of Spain in exchange for French recognition of Franco as the legitimate leader of Spain

69 'Meanwhile … Paris and Berlin' After the signing in Paris on 6 December 1938 of a treaty by which Germany and France guaranteed the inviolability of one another's borders and agreed to engage in mutual consultation to resolve all disputes peacefully, France and Germany engaged in serious discussions about commercial collaboration. It ended when Germany invaded Czechoslovakia

69 'a huge loan' Bassett, *Hitler's Spy Chief*, p.168

69 'the complete German plan' Navarre, *Le Service de renseignements*, p.59

69 'The March madness' Gisevius, *To the Bitter End*, p.336

69 'on 11 March' Some accounts give the date as 3 March – see Fryc in Piekalkiewicz, *Secret Agents, Spies and Saboteurs*, p.137

69 'his Czech handler' Captain Fryč

69 'On 15 March' Piekalkiewicz, *Secret Agents, Spies and Saboteurs*, p.137

69 'interrogation with great severity' Morávec, *Master of Spies*, p.138

69 'Two of these were' *Het Koninkrijk der Nederlanden in de Tweede Wereldoorlog* – Deel 2 – Neutraal pp.89–90. With thanks to Mike van der Heijden

70 'Good luck Colonel' Morávec, *Master of Spies*, p.139

70 'If such events' Amort & Jedicka, *The Canaris File*, p.41

70 'in the immediate future' Colvin, *Vansittart in Office*, pp.288–9

70 'a year or two' TNA BDFP 3/IV, ibid., p.289

70 'The following day' Ibid., pp.289–90. The speech was based on a briefing given by Chamberlain to lobby journalists the previous evening

70 'numerous boxes' Other files were sent back by Gibson through the British Diplomatic bag: Jeffery, *MI6*, p.308

70 'At 5.15 p.m.' Amort & Jedicka, *The Canaris File*, p.44; Piekalkiewicz, *Secret Agents, Spies and Saboteurs*, p.138

9: The March to War

71 'As an experienced' Orbach, *The Plots Against Hitler*, p.92

71 'elsewhere in army circles' Witzleben and his chief of general staff Georg von Sodenstern, Goerdeler, Gisevius and General Georg Thomas from the Army High Command were all active on this front – see Fest, *Plotting Hitler's Death*, p.108

71 'The other, hidden purpose' Schaub, *Call Your First Witness*, p.193

72 'it is natural' Young, *The 'X' Documents*, p.170, and Colvin, *Vansittart in Office*, p.294

72 'We wanted to establish' Gisevius, *To the Bitter End*, p.344

72 'person of considerable influence' Dr Reinhold Schairer. Ibid.

72 'in the event' Statement by the Prime Minister in the House of Commons on 31 March 1939

73 'Now I will mix' From Gisevius, in Ritter, *The German Resistance*, p.132

73 'one of these bearers of bad news' Erich Kordt

73 'Keep calm' Ritter, *The German Resistance*, p.134

73 'What have we' Colvin, *Admiral Canaris*, p.78

73 'one of the German general staff' Hans Böhm-Tettelbach

74 'a false British passport' TNA KV 2/1657

74 'Karel Sedláček' Thomas Selzinger, working for Narodni Listy, in Morávec, *Master of Spies*, p.38

74 'The Jelineks ran' Amort & Jedicka, *The Canaris File*, p.47. There are two rather different accounts of the meetings in The Hague with Thümmel: *The Canaris File*, which is based on sourced documents, and Morávec's autobiography, *Master of Spies*. They differ markedly in some areas (such as dates). In writing this account I have had to make judgements as to which account to use, according to what seems most logical and fits the other known facts

74 'the first return card' Ibid.

74 'These were sent through' *Het Koninkrijk der Nederlanden in de Tweede Wereldoorlog* – Deel 2 – Neutraal, pp.89, 90. With thanks to Mike van der Heijden

74 'a German refugee' Karl Hespers
74 'Dear Uncle' Morávec, *Master of Spies*, p.166
75 'I will be in' Ibid.
75 'a twenty-five-year-old junior diplomat' Gordon Etherington-Smith
75 'My dear fellow' Bassett, *Hitler's Spy Chief*, p.169
75 'Nazi leaders think' Amort & Jedicka, *The Canaris File*, p.48
77 'Throughout June' *Ulrich von Hassell Diaries*, entry 15 June 1941, p.130
77 'Poland is now' Fest, *Plotting Hitler's Death*, p.109
77 'two Swedish bankers' Gert Nylander, *The German Resistance Movement and England: Carl Goerdeler and the Wallenberg Brothers*, Banking & Enterprise, No. 2 Stockholm 1999, electronic issue, p.20
78 'under the condition' TNA FO 371/57648
78 'one of his adjutants' Colonel Rudolf Schmundt
78 'I must unfortunately' TNA FO 371/57648
78 'promptly rescinded' Ibid.
79 'The first inkling' Laqueur & Breitman, *Breaking the Silence*, p.67 (the information originated from Eduard Schulte, a German businessman who often travelled to Switzerland)
79 'A few minutes after' There are slightly different versions of the story in Mueller, *Canaris*, pp.149–50 and 305 fn 66
79 'a small group of German' Operation Himmler, also referred to as 'Operation Konserve', or Operation Canned Goods
80 '*Finis Germaniae*' In Latin in the original version of Hans Bernd Gisevius: *Bis zum bitteren Ende: vom Reichstagsbrand bis zum 20. Juli 1944. Vom Verfasser auf den neuesten Stand gebrachte Sonderausgabe*, Rütten & Loening, 1960, p.336

10: Switzerland

82 'The Swiss themselves' In 1939, with war around the corner, Swiss intelligence head Roger Masson began expanding his service, increasing its budget sixfold in that year alone. The Swiss service was divided into a security section, with responsibility for counter-intelligence, and an intelligence section, under Captain Max Waibel, who had very good links to German military circles, having attended the German Military College in Berlin during the pre-war years. Waibel's intelligence section was headquartered in Lucerne and had eight operational subsections based in St Gallen, Basle, Zürich, Schaffhausen, Samedan, Brig, Bern and Lugano. It also had a curious, half-privately run 'intelligence-gathering cell' called Büro Ha, established with private money under Captain Hans Hausamann, in the Villa Stutz, on the shores of Lake Lucerne
82 'Schloss am Mythenquai' Also known as Das Mythenschloss
83 'his team of five officers' Andrew King, Sheila Deane, Joanna Shuckburgh, Richard Arnold-Baker and Norman Wells
83 'the official history of MI6' Keith Jeffery, *MI6: The History of the Secret Intelligence Service 1909–1949*
83 '150,000 of its citizens' TNA KV 3/245, paper on German Intelligence in Switzerland of 21 June 1943
83 'centred on their legation' The German intelligence team included Prince Alois Auersperg, Lothar Philipp, Hans von Pescatore, Heinrich Piert and Dr Fritz Albert: TNA KV 2/281
84 'the sun outshone' Laqueur & Breitman, *Breaking the Silence*, p.199; and C.G. Mckay, *Major Chojnacki's Ace: the Solution to an Old Puzzle of Wartime Intelligence* (https://intelligencepast.com/2015/11/02/major-choynackis-ace-the-solution-to-an-old-puzzle-of-wartime-intelligence) quoting Wilhelm Flicke
85 'triumphant welcome' Jeffery, *MI6*, p.294
85 'ran a network' TNA KV 2/1329/2

85 'probably the biggest' Laqueur & Breitman, *Breaking the Silence*, p.198
85 'in direct clandestine' *Gisevius/Masson – EN Archiv für Zeitgeschichte, Hans Bernd Gisevius/4.6.3 Personal account of some of my experiences in connection with Brigadier Masson (written by Hans Bernd Gisevius, 5.2.1945), MS 15 pp.Date: 1945.* With thanks to Peter Kamber, and for translation to Philip Cole
86 'Three years before' For a full discussion of this including a traffic analysis of the Rote Drei wireless signals to Moscow, see Mark Tittenhofer's CIA paper 'The Rote Drei: Getting behind the "Lucy" Myth' https://www.cia.gov/library/center-for-the-study-of-intelligence/kent-csi/vol13no3/html/v13i3a05p_0001.htm
86 'his spies in Berlin' Post-war comment based on *Rote Drei* messages presumes that Roessler had four sources, codenamed 'Werther', 'Teddy', 'Olga' and 'Anna' (see for example the CIA study into the Dora Ring at https://www.cia.gov/library/center-for-the-study-of-intelligence/kent-csi/vol13no3/html/v13i3a05p_0001.htm). Based on this presumption, it has always been thought that the most likely identification for 'Werther' is Hans Oster. However, we now know (email from Peter Kamber to the author of 30 July 2017) that the four codenames were invented by Rachel Duebendorfer, who under pressure from Moscow to identify Roessler's sources assembled the information according to type and allotted one of the codenames to each type – e.g. 'Werther' was primarily military information. While this means that Werther was not necessarily Oster, it was information of the sort which Oster, more than any other of the primary sources, would be most likely to have access to. It is important to note here that Roessler positively identified Gisevius and Goerdeler as two of his four primary sources, and gave sufficient indications to identify Oster as the most probable third source (Boelitz was the fourth). So while it would be wrong to identify Werther as Oster, we do know that Oster was a primary Roessler source
86 'His other sources are thought' Tarrant, *The Red Orchestra*, p.160; and Puenter, *Guerre Secrète en pays neutre*, pp.106, 254fn; and *The Rote Kapelle*, by the CIA, University Publications of America, 1979, pp.165 and 193
87 'I seem to detect' Malcolm Muggeridge, *Observer*, 8 January 1967, mentioned in Tittenhofer, 'The Rote Drei', op. cit.
87 'the Czechs' In mid-1939, thanks to an introduction made by Swiss intelligence, Rudolf Roessler also began to provide the Czech intelligence officer Karel Sedláček with a flow of high-level military reports which arrived almost weekly from Germany. Sedláček sent these back to his boss František Morávec in London, who passed them on to MI6, where they were referred to as 'Captain X's flimsies' after the tissue paper which was normally used to make carbon copies of his reports, as they were typed
87 'three of the main players' Max Waibel, Hans Hausamann and Bernhard Mayr von Baldegg

11: Halina
88 'Rain showers' Information from Mark Beswick, Archive Information Officer, Met Office National Meteorological Archive
89 'looked a decent' Telephone interview with Halina's daughter Marysia, 8 August 2017
90 'We will spare' From Helmuth Groscurth diaries, 9 Sept 1939, quoted in Höhne, *Canaris*, p.363
90 'completely shattered' Ulrich von Hassell, *Ulrich von Hassell Diaries*, entry 11 Oct 1939, p.49
90 'How terrible!' Ibid., quoting from Oscar Reile, *Geheim Ostfront*, Munich, 1963, p.310
90 'If there is any' Erika Canaris's letter to Donovan, 15 November 1945
90 'a cashbox' The quote is from Lahousen in Höhne, *Canaris*, p.362
91 'Humanity will not forget' Sylvie Young interview with Halina Szymańska's daughter Marysia, 17 October 2016, and Garlinski, *The Swiss Corridor*, p.87
91 'That afternoon Szymański' Höhne, *Canaris*, p.362

92 'with only Polish documents' Garlinski, *The Swiss Corridor*, p.88
92 'train arrived at' Josef Garlinski, who interviewed Halina Szymańska for his book *The Swiss Corridor*, claims that the train from Berlin took them to Düsseldorf, and the rest of the journey to Basel was by car. This seems unlikely however, since Düsseldorf is more than 400 kilometres from Basel. A more likely final destination for their train journey would have been Freiburg (52 kilometres from Basel) or Stuttgart (175 kilometres)
92 'They were met' Ibid.
92 'she was formally recruited' By head of Polish intelligence Colonel Tadeusz Wasilewski and General Kasimierz Sosnkowski, the commander of the Union of Armed Struggle (the ZWZ)
92 'She was known' TNA KV 2/281, and http://niepoprawni.pl/blog/rafal-brzeski/dyskretna-laczniczka-canarisa
93 'I don't suppose' Colvin, *Admiral Canaris*, p.91
93 'When he spoke' Ibid.
93 'The admiral never' Ibid., pp.91–2
93 'Canaris knew' Bassett, *Hitler's Spy Chief*, p.181
93 'a very wise' TNA KV 2/173
93 'a very attractive' Jeffery, *MI6*, p.380
94 'In February 1940' Gisevius moved permanently to Zürich as the German vice-consul in mid-1940
94 'A man of towering' Laqueur & Breitman, *Breaking the Silence*, p.168
94 'first and foremost' Jeffery, *MI6*, p.381
94 'Many of these' Ibid., p.381

12: *Sitzkrieg*

96 'This war implies' Erwin Lahousen describing Canaris's view of his aims (adapted slightly to account for poor translation and the historical context), 30 November 1945, at the Nuremberg War Crimes Trials http://avalon.law.yale.edu/imt/11–30–45.asp The original is: 'On its political motives or aims, I was not informed. I can only reiterate the thoughts and considerations which I, since I was one of Canaris's most intimate confidants, knew well. His inner attitude, which influenced and moulded not only my own actions but also those of the other men whom I mentioned, can be described as follows: We did not succeed in preventing this war of aggression. The war implies the end of Germany and of ourselves, a misfortune and a catastrophe of very great extent. However, a misfortune even greater than this catastrophe would be a triumph of this system. To prevent this by all possible means was the ultimate aim and purpose of our struggle. The sense of what I have just said was often expressed by Canaris among the group of which I am speaking.'
96 'He was whipping' Halder diaries, London, 1998. Mentioned in Garlinski, *The Swiss Corridor*, p.179, and Bassett, *Hitler's Spy Chief*, p.179
96 'An anti-Nazi general' Kurt von Hammerstein
97 'the advance of Bolshevism' Ritter, *The German Resistance*, p.140
97 'Why die for Danzig?' The title of an article written by the French socialist politician Marcel Déat in the Paris newspaper *L'Oeuvre* on 4 May 1939
97 'London and Paris watched' Jodl's evidence, The International Military Tribunal, Nuremberg, Vol. XV, 4 June 1946, p.350
97 'It would be idle' *Final Report by the Right Honourable Sir Nevile Henderson GCMG on the circumstances leading to the termination of his mission to Berlin September 20 1939*, HMSO
99 'one of his adjutants' Colonel Rudolf Schmundt, Wehrmacht adjutant to Hitler, quoted in Fest, *Plotting Hitler's Death*, pp.119–20
99 'When they protested … question them' Shirer, *The Rise and Fall of the Third Reich*, p.640; Fest, *Plotting Hitler's Death*, p.120

99 'fundamental changes' 14 Oct 1939 entry in *Private War Journal of Generaloberst Franz Halder*, 1950, Vol. II, p.30, http://cgsc.contentdm.oclc.org/cdm/singleitem/collection/p4013coll8/id/3971/rec/1

99 'unalterable' Mueller, *Canaris*, p.172

100 'a new band of plotters' These included Klaus, the elder brother of the theologian Dietrich Bonhoeffer, Hans von Dohnanyi, Justus Delbrück and Baron Guttenberg

100 'In an attempt' Klemperer, *German Resistance Against Hitler*, p.155

100 'for weeks on end' From Helmuth Groscurth (private) diaries, entry 1 Nov 1939, p.222, quoted in Mueller, *Canaris*, p.174 and p.313 fn 31

100 'promised to have them ready' It was expected that the explosives would be supplied by Lahousen's Abteilung II, which had an explosive laboratory at Quenzgut in Brandenburg: Mueller, *Canaris*, p.174

101 'Lahousen, you know' CIA memo of 17 December 1945 – German Intelligence Service (WWII), Vol. 2_0007 report by Major General Lahousen

101 'The coup planning' Ritter, *The German Resistance*, p.148

101 'chalky white' Groscurth diaries, entry 5 Nov 1939, quoted in Fest, *Plotting Hitler's Death*, p.127

101 'It is not possible' Von Brauchitsch to Groscurth in Orbach, *The Plots Against Hitler*, p.91

102 'I myself won't' Gisevius, *To the Bitter End*, p.389, and Fest, *Plotting Hitler's Death*, p.129

102 'the forces we were' Groscurth diaries, p.225, in Fest, *Plotting Hitler's Death*, p.128

102 'Then let the Admiral' Ibid.

102 'The entire edifice' Especially Witzleben and Leeb, ibid.

102 'I had to do it' Hellmut G. Haasis (trans. William Odom), *Bombing Hitler: The Story of the Man Who Almost Assassinated the Führer*, Skyhorse Publishing Co., Incorporated

103 'to the Isartorplatz' Gestapo Interrogation Report (November 1939) Bundesarchiv Koblenz, signatur R 22/310

103 'Security around' Fest, *Plotting Hitler's Death*, p.129

103 'Oster … had formed' Gisevius, *To the Bitter End*, pp.421–5

104 'There is no turning' Höhne, *Canaris*, pp.401, 642fn 287, from an interrogation of Maria Leidig by Dr H. Krausnick and Pr H. Deutsch (IfZ, ZS 2125)

104 'One may say' Orbach, *The Plots Against Hitler*, p.93

104 'It cannot be a coincidence' I am indebted to Peter Kamber for this information, and to Philip Cole for his translation of Kamber's notes, which are based in part on *Der Verschwörer: General Oster und die Militäropposition* (The Conspirator. General Oster and the Military Opposition), Graf von Thun-Hohenstein, Berlin, 1982, pp.154ff, 169, 187, 191 and 193 – see Kamber's notes on the Viking Line in his book *Geheime Agentin*, Basis Druck, 2010, pp.147–53

105 'was also using his' Mueller, *Canaris*, p.140

105 'one of the generals' General Walther von Reichenau

105 '[Canaris] has given up' *Ulrich von Hassell Diaries*, entry 5 Dec 1939, p.62

105 'The old man' Mueller, *Canaris*, p.174

105 'Countess Elena Alexandra Theotokis' Elena Theotokis, whose Greek name was Elena-Alessandra Teotochi, was also known by her English friends as Ellen Alexandra. She had been married to a German called Kohn, who had been German military attaché in Madrid. I am much indebted to Bruce Dennis for this information

105 'Canaris had first met the countess' TNA GFM 33/2393 – For the full story see Mogens Pelt, *Tobacco, Arms and Politics*, Museum Tusculanum Press, pp.133 et seq. I am indebted to Philip Cole for his translation of these papers

105 'A very clever' TNA KV 2/173

105 'MI6 records show' TNA HW 5/23

106 'He planted trusted' Waller, *The Unseen War in Europe*, p.91

106 'Not long after' TNA KV 2/173

106 'a member of the Budapest Abwehr station' Kurt Fechner
106 'separate peace feelers' Through the Swedish businessman and amateur diplomat Johan Birger Essen Dahlerus
106 'This *Schweinerei*' Bassett, *Hitler's Spy Chief*, p.177, quoting an interview with Canaris's secretary Inge Haag on 26 March 2004
108 'He gave instructions' TNA KV 2/282
108 'it had been "played"' Hastings, *The Secret War*, p.48

13: Warnings and Premonitions

109 'Thümmel had managed' *Het Koninkrijk der Nederlanden in de Tweede Wereldoorlog – Deel 2 – Neutraal* pp.89–90. With thanks to Mike van der Heijden
109 'sort of aerial torpedo' Amort & Jedicka, *The Canaris File*, p.59
109 'Thümmel's intelligence' Fest, *Plotting Hitler's Death*, p.141
111 'Documents which have come to light' See Chapter 9, and notes in Riebling, *Church of Spies*, pp.93–8
112 'You should not' Ritter, *The German Resistance*, pp.164–5
112 'a Benedictine monk' Damasus Zähringer. Other SD spies in the Vatican at the time were Gabriel Ascher, a Jewish convert, and Father Joachim Birkner, who worked in the Vatican Secret Archives. See Riebling, *Church of Spies*, p.106
112 'The German seminarists' Ibid., p.93
112 'a British traveller and amateur diplomat' Lonsdale Bryans; 'a former German chancellor' Josef Wirth; 'Ulrich von Hassell's son-in-law' Detalmo Pirzio-Biroli
112 'led to nothing' Ritter, *The German Resistance*, pp.158 et seq.
113 'avoid any hint' Fest, *Plotting Hitler's Death*, p.138 – quoting Hassell diaries, entry 21 Dec 1941, p.150
113 'the young Turks' problem' TNA KV 2/173
114 'a few women' Educated women married to male members: Freya von Moltke, Margrit von Trotha, Marion and Irene Yorck von Wartenburg, and Rosemarie Reichwein
114 'Freiburg Circle' Led by Professors Constantin von Dietze, Adolf Lampe and Gerhard Ritter
114 'One right-wing group' Led by Ulrich von Hassel and Johannes Popitz
114 'a series of papers' These were 'The Aim' (1941), 'The problem of unemployment' (7 pages, 1 December 1940), 'Money plays no part' (63 pages, June 1941), a historical retrospect (no title, 61 pages, probably spring 1944), 'Practical measures for the re-organisation of Europe' (probably spring 1939), 'State aid to art after the war' (3 pages, 29 August 1943), 'Thoughts of a condemned man on Germany's future' (42 pages, 8 September 1944) and 'Our ideal' (40 pages, 1 November 1944)
115 'Madeleine reported all this' Navarre, *Le Service de renseignements*, p.59
116 'The build-up continues' Amort & Jedicka, *The Canaris File*, p.67
116 'Main … attack to be' Morávec, *Master of Spies*, p.175
116 'A54 is an agent' Ibid.
116 'supplied [Max Waibel]' Special Report no. 43, 17 Dec 1942. See Braunschweig, *Secret Channel to Berlin*, p.405 fn 17, and Rossé, *Guerre Secrète en Suisse*, p.53
116 'Two weeks later' Riebling, *Church of Spies*, p.98 fn 21
116 'Sometime in early April' *Intelligence Co-Operation Between Poland and Great Britain During World War II: The Report of the Anglo-Polish Historical Committee*: Vol. 1 (Government Official History Series), p.144
117 'a Swedish diplomat' Erik Boheman
117 'the Swedish military attaché in Berlin' Colonel Curt Juhlin-Dannfelt
117 'frightfully snubbed' Most secret dispatch from Stockholm of 5/9/44, TNA FO 371/43503
117 'Returning to Stockholm' Ibid.
117 'On 6 April' Ibid.

117 'In the days' Schaub, *Call Your First Witness*, p.201

118 'they were circulated' Jeffery, *MI6*, p.399

118 'the Belgian minister to the Holy See' Father Hubert Noots

118 'From His Excellency' Bassett, *Hitler's Spy Chief*, p.191

119 'On that same day' Schaub, *Call Your First Witness*, p.201; and Gatard, *La Source MAD*, p.110

119 'Delivery of the' Morávec, *Master of Spies*, p.175, and Amort & Jedicka, *The Canaris File*, p.77

119 'Tomorrow morning at dawn' https://sites.google.com/site/oorloginlimburg/home–1/invasion/invasionnl

119 'the senior officer on duty' Major Jacobus van der Plassche

14: Felix and Sealion

121 'They are lucky' Colvin, *Admiral Canaris*, p.118

121 'He [Canaris] had the same' Ibid. (Colvin speaking to Richard Protze after the war)

121 'Churchill walked over' Ibid., p.119

122 'shrunk to fewer' Höhne, *Canaris*, p.422 and p.644 fn 424

122 'One group in the Kreisau Circle' Led by Fritz-Dietlof ('Fritzi') von der Schulenburg and Dr Eugen Gerstenmaier. See Fest, *Plotting Hitler's Death*, p.144

122 'Two Wehrmacht officers in Paris' Major Hans-Alexander von Voss and Captain Ulrich-Wilhelm Schwerin von Schwanenfeld

122 'One of these would-be assassins' Von Schwanenfeld

123 'In the conclusion of' Eltscher, *Traitors or Patriots?*, p.265

123 'next kill' Young, *The 'X' Documents*, p.43

123 'the gravest' Kirkpatrick, *The Inner Circle*, p.194

124 'encouraged by Franco's' Papeleux, *L'Amiral Canaris*, p.82

124 'Gibraltar Español' Ibid., p.86

124 'He hinted' Ibid., p.83

125 'intense preparation' Jeffery, *MI6*, p.399

125 'reported to London' Garlinski, *The Swiss Corridor*, p.97, p.201 fn (Halina Szymańska, interview with author)

125 'a diplomat at the US embassy in Bern' Donald Heath

126 'I am water shy' Shirer, *The Rise and Fall of the Third Reich*, p.757, quoting Shulman, *Defeat in the West*, New York, 1948, p.50

126 'The area Tunbridge' Colvin, *Admiral Canaris*, pp.121–2

126 'it would [now]' TNA CAB 66/9/44, Churchill's Memorandum to the Chief of the Imperial General Staff, 10 July 1940

126 'our attention must' Kershaw, *Hitler 1936–45*, p.305

126 'messages from Paul Thümmel' Piekalkiewicz, *Secret Agents, Spies and Saboteurs*, p.143

127 'one of these reports' Jeffery, *MI6*, p.399, and ibid., p.143

127 'postcards from different European cities' The cities were Cologne, Rome and Madrid: Gatard, *La Source MAD*, p.116

127 'Sea Lion had been' Schaub, *Call Your First Witness*, p.205

127 'chiefly to weather' Jeffery, *MI6*, pp.400–1

127 'Under the alias' Höhne, *Canaris*, p.425

127 'a leading Brandenburg Regiment expert' Hans-Jochen Rudloff

127 'Franco's government, whose ministers' Especially minister of air Juan Vigón and foreign minister Juan Luis Beigbeder

128 'Canaris privately admitted' OSS – SSU – CIG EARLY CIA DOCUMENTS VOL. 2_0001. pdf; and Gatard, *La Source MAD*, p.117

128 'The Admiral asks you' Mueller, *Canaris*, p.195

128 'According to a post-war' SS Group Chief Dr Walter Huppenkothen, mentioning General Munoz Grande. See Colvin, *Admiral Canaris*, p.132; 'The double life of Admiral Canaris',

The International Journal of Intelligence and Counterintelligence, 1996, Vol. 9, part 3, p.279

128 'divulged military secrets' Ibid.

128 'he decreed that' Payne, *Franco and Hitler*, p.85

128 'Spain does not' Papeleux, *L'Amiral Canaris*, p.82

128 'Canaris advised Franco's' Liddell Hart, *The Other Side of the Hill*, p.84

128 'On one occasion' 'The Spanish Government and the Axis: Notes of a Conversation Between the Fuehrer and the Spanish Minister of the Interior Serrano Süner in the Presence of the Reich's Foreign Minister in Berlin on September 17, 1940', DEPARTMENT OF STATE, Publication 2483, EUROPEAN SERIES 8, 1946 (http://www.ibiblio.org/pha/policy/1940/1940-08-08a.html)

129 'My vote is that' Mueller, *Canaris*, p.191

129 'Tell Franco' Bassett, *Hitler's Spy Chief*, p.21, quoting Werner Emil Hart, deposition 23 June 1953, and Bassett, *Hitler's Spy Chief*, p.197

129 'fiasco' Schmidt, *Hitler's Interpreter*, p.191

129 'Hitler's adjutant' Major Gerhard Engel

129 'F. [the Führer]' Engel, *At the Heart of the Reich*, p.98

129 'During a discussion' Ciano, *Ciano's Diplomatic Papers*, p.402

130 'Franco's overwhelming instinct' Franco's behaviour has often been qualified as '*hábil prudencia*'; Paul Preston, 'Franco and Hitler: The Myth of Hendaye 1940', *Contemporary European History*, I, 1 (1992), pp.1–16

130 'persuade [the Spanish]' Bassett, *Hitler's Spy Chief*, p.201, quoting David Stafford, *Churchill and Secret Service*, London, 1997, p.202

130 'breaking the code' TNA KV 3/3. The first of these decrypted message read: 'The Chief [Canaris] … with 4 officers and 3 drivers arriving at the Hague in armoured cars on 20 May'

131 'taken to the home' Bassett, *Hitler's Spy Chief*, p.233

131 'Popov records' Popov, *Spy Counter-Spy*, p.62

131 'Whether or not' Deacon, *A History of the British Secret Service*, p.282

15: The Red Three

132 'At a little before' TNA KV 2/1612/1

132 'La Taupinière' The French word for a molehill, which seems appropriate given 'Sonja's' profession. The chalet is on the Col de Jaman, midway between Caux and Les Avants

132 'perched at the end' Details taken from Werner, *Sonya's Report*, pp.187 et seq.

132 'the old Moscow Ballroom and Music School' The building had been converted to wartime use as the coding and transmission centre for the GRU. The description comes from http://www.untergrund-blättle.ch/gesellschaft/deckname_sonja_das_geheime_leben_der_agentin_ruth_werner.html (translation by Philip Cole)

133 'the penthouse flat' The building in which Radó lived has neither a front door nor a plaque showing its number – 113. Although this was Radó's registered private address, his personal letters and personal visitors came to the front door of 2, rue Gustave Moynier, in the next street. The fact that he collected his letters at 2, rue Gustave Moynier enabled Radó to use that as the registered address for his business, Geopress. By this means he was able to make use of two addresses for the same property, one of which he used for private matters and the other for his business

134 'rank of major general' https://www.cia.gov/library/center-for-the-study-of-intelligence/kent-csi/vol12i3/html/v12i3a05p_0001.htm

134 'Mikhail (Micha) and Janina (Nina)' Michael was by Ursula's husband, Rudolf Hamburger, and Janina by Johannes Patra (codename 'Ernst'), her GRU officer in Japanese-occupied Manchuria at the end of 1934. See TNA KV 6/41; Werner, *Sonya's Report*, and Green, *A Political Family*. See also Ursula Kuczynski's Swiss Permis de Séjour of 1940. Montreux Municipal Archives. With thanks to Andrew Stallybrass

134 'aged two' TNA KV 6/41

134 'chalet called La Taupinière' The chalet, which has changed very little in the intervening years, is still rented accommodation but has now been incorporated into the village of Caux. The address is 'La Taupinière', 63, chemin de Cerniaz, 1824 Caux. With thanks to Andrew Stallybrass of Caux for finding this information

134 'washing line' Email from Andrew Stallybrass in Caux, 10 Nov 2017

135 'villa on Berlin's Schlachtensee' Werner, *Sonya's Report*, p.3

135 'In the 1930s' Biographical database supplied by Peter Kamber (translation by Philip Cole)

135 '25 September 1938' Ursula Kuczynski's Swiss Permis de Séjour of 1940. Montreux Municipal Archives. With thanks to Andrew Stallybrass

135 'mid-October 1939' Len Beurton's Swiss Permis de Séjour of 1940 indicates that he arrived in Switzerland on 11 October 1939. Montreux Municipal Archives. With thanks to Andrew Stallybrass of Montreux

136 'retrain the two Englishmen' Foote, *Handbook for Spies*, p.38

136 'In December 1939' Radó, *Sous le Pseudonyme Dora*, p.116, Radó indicates a visit from Sonja in December 1939. See also Werner, *Sonya's Report*, p.214

136 'pool her finances with him' TNA KV 2/1648/1

136 'for personal reasons' Foote finally revealed that he had a girlfriend in the UK. See Werner, *Sonya's Report*, p.208

137 'frequent changes' Ibid., p.222

137 'The marriage took place' Ibid., p.221

137 'The date was chosen' Ibid.

137 'tried to tell' TNA KV 2/1611 2, and ibid., p.224

137 'neither could understand' TNA KV 6/41, and ibid. cdxvi 'Leon Beurton … Spain and France' Furthermore Beurton, having been part of the International Brigades, would not have been allowed in Spain

138 'in February 1941' TNA KV 6/41

138 'In early 1941' Tittenhofer, 'The Rote Drei', op. cit.

139 'not particularly brave' TNA KV 3/349 Report on the *Rote Kapelle*

139 'at least four of the agents' These were: 1. Radó to Puenter (who had his own independent ring), to Swiss intelligence, and through Neyrac to Chojnaski. 2. Foote, through Bohny to Sedláček and through Chamberlain and Abramson to MI6 3. Radó, through Duebendorfer, to Schneider, to Roessler (who ran his own independent ring), to Swiss intelligence, MI6 and to Sedláček 4. Radó, through Grimm to Chojnaski

139 'Foote described him as' TNA KV 3/349

139 'accused him of embezzling' Between 1941 and 1943 it is estimated that Radó spent SFR 300,000 on espionage – see TNA KV 2/1647/1

139 'Radó claimed sixty' TNA KV 2/1611/1

139 'for his own private purposes' TNA KV 2/1648

139 'in time, Moscow' TNA KV 2/1647/3

139 'gaining a reputation' Arsenovic, *Genève appelle Moscou*, p.29

139 'bought a chalet' TNA KV 2/1647/3

139 'withdrew from the Dora ring' TNA KV 6/41

139 'broke off all contact' TNA KV 2/1611/2

139 'he sold the' Ibid.

140 'useful intelligence information' TNA KV 6/641

140 'one of Sándor Radó's' TNA KV 6/641, and Werner, *Sonya's Report*, p.245: L.T. Wang was married to a Dutch woman and was close to General von Falkenhausen, the German commander in Belgium and former military adviser to Chiang Kai-shek. Von Falkenhausen visited Wang in Geneva

140 'After a year' TNA KV 6/641

140 'On arrival he immediately' Ibid.

140 'in touch with' Ibid.

140 'Espionage on behalf' Ibid.

140 'issuing Beurton with' Ibid.

141 'In the spring' TNA KV 2/1626: Secret memorandum dated 10 Feb 1949 following a journalist's conversation with Otto Puenter

141 'Christian Schneider' Radó wrote later that he only became aware of the existence of Taylor (Schneider) in the summer of 1942. See Radó, *Sous le Pseudonyme Dora*, pp.142 and 192

141 'Sándor Radó never reported' The timing of this approach is confirmed in Puenter, *Guerre Secrète en pays neutre*, p.127, in which he recollects Radó, in May 1941, asking him to check out Roessler. This is denied by Radó in his book

142 'On the face of it' Peter Kamber, letter to the author (translation by Philip Cole)

142 'Duebendorfer was also listed' See Read & Fisher, *Operation Lucy*, p.99; Rupert Allason's post-war interview with Andrew King – Allason email to author 24 July 2017; and Gannon, *Stealing Secrets, Telling Lies*, pp.170–1

142 'important intelligence [from' Radó, *Sous le Pseudonyme Dora*, p.210

143 'a prominent Swiss communist' Pierre Nicole

143 'The Abwehr's penetration' TNA KV 2/1741 SIS minute of 22 September 1949

143 'an estimated thirty' TNA KV 2/1626: Secret memorandum dated 10 Feb 1949 following a journalist's conversation with Otto Puenter

144 '12 April' Radó, *Sous le Pseudonyme Dora*, p.140. It is significant that in January 1942 the British 'military attaché' in Bern sent London a coded message with information provided by 'a Swiss Intelligence Officer' of the German order of battle at that time. Its format follows precisely the style of this message sent by Foote, lending weight to the suggestion that the information from the Tirpitzufer provided to Dora was also shared with, and probably manipulated by, British and Swiss intelligence. The relevant part of this message, which is dated January 5 1942, reads: '1. Following is German order of battle as given to a Source A by a Swiss IO ... Dated January 2; 2. Russia,180 divisions (about 100 in the front areas, 80 in reserve) all much under strength in men and material; Denmark and Norway, 8–10; France, Holland and Belgium, maximum 40; Libya, 7–8; Yugoslavia, 4–5; Bulgaria, 4–5; Greece, 6; Germany 30 ...' TNA FO 371/30893

16: Belgrade and Barbarossa

145 'It informed London' Morávec, *Master of Spies*, p.191

145 'Bulgaria has allowed' Amort & Jedicka, *The Canaris File*, p.103

146 'managed to steal' Höhne, *Canaris*, p.444

146 'militarily and as a' Shirer, *The Rise and Fall of the Third Reich*, p.824. The order to postpone Barbarossa was in an underlined passage, in the top-secret OKW notes of the 27 March meeting at the Chancellery

146 'The delay cost' Carl Ritter, German Foreign Office liaison officer with the Army High Command. See Bassett, *Hitler's Spy Chief*, p.213, quoting from D.C. Poole, 'Light on Nazi Foreign Policy', *Foreign Affairs* XXV, October 1946

146 'a Luftwaffe captain' Otto John; 'a German prince' Gottfried Hohenlohe-Langenburg, an old Canaris family friend; 'a Swiss diplomat and historian' Carl Burckhardt

147 'The coup d'état' Gatard, *La Source MAD*, p.134

147 'Senior Yugoslav officers' Colvin, *Admiral Canaris*, p.136

147 'containing documents which' Morávec, *Master of Spies*, p.191, and Amort & Jedicka, *The Canaris File*, p.104

147 'forty-eight hours' Gatard, *La Source MAD*, p.134

147 'Menzies sent an urgent message' Jeffery, *MI6*, p.415. Although Jeffery suggests the source here is Ultra, there seems a strong likelihood that it was the message from 'our faithful friend Franz-Josef', which Schellenberg later found, only partially destroyed, in the UK Embassy in Belgrade. 'Franz-Josef' was of course later identified as Hans Oster

147 'Inform Yugoslav general staff' Jeffery, *MI6*, p.415

147 'I shall never forget' Gisevius, *To the Bitter End*, p.441

148 'the origin of this information' Amort & Jedicka, *The Canaris File*, pp.120–1

148 'passed it on' Ibid.

148 'No, we won't attack Turkey' Colvin, *Admiral Canaris*, p.138

148 'a message warning' Morávec, *Master of Spies*, p.188

148 'The first proof' Waller, *The Unseen War in Europe*, p.93

149 'To start with' Ibid., p.204; Riebling, *Church of Spies*, pp.176, 292 fn 15, quoting among others Leiber, transcript, 9 April 1966, and Muller's transcript 24 March 1966, HDP, III, 1/7 and 31 August 1955, IfZ, ZS 659/1, 41

149 'the Germans were seeking' Waller, *The Unseen War in Europe*, p.195

149 'would be launched in' Piekalkiewicz, *Secret Agents, Spies and Saboteurs*, p.143

149 'convinced hostilities' Jeffery, *MI6*, p.381

150 'heated discussions' Ritter, *The German Resistance*, p.213. Evidence of Jodl at the Nuremberg trials – see Nuremberg 1949 Vol. 15, p.339

150 'If because of his' Ritter, *The German Resistance*, p.213 (written answer from Halder to Ritter)

150 'shot immediately' Hoffmann, *The History of the German Resistance*, p.263

150 'Everyone's hair' Entry of 4 May 1941 in *Ulrich von Hassell Diaries*, p.124

151 'He had a personality' Margarethe von Oven from *Courageous Hearts: Women and the Anti-Hitler Plot of 1944*, Dorothee von Medding, trans Michael Balfour and Volker Berghahn, Berghahn Books, 1997, pp.60–1, quoted in Orbach, *The Plots Against Hitler*, p.118

151 'In my life' Gersdorff, *Tuer Hitler*, p.117

151 'One has to resort' Orbach, *The Plots Against Hitler*, p.131, quoting from Horst Mühleisen, *Patrioten im Widerstand: Carl-Hans Graf von Hardenbergs Erlebnisbericht*, from *Vierteljahrshefte für Zeitgeschichte* 14 no. 3 (Jan 1993), pp.449–50

152 'the largest and most' Fest, *Plotting Hitler's Death*, p.175

152 'If we don't convince' Gersdorff, *Tuer Hitler*, pp.126–7

152 'We'll know how to' Ibid.

152 'Let it be noted' Fest, *Plotting Hitler's Death*, pp.176–7

152 'Goerdeler, Beck, Oster and others' Including Johannes Popitz

153 'a bunch of hopeless' Entry of 15 June 1941 in *Ulrich von Hassell Diaries*, p.130

153 'He even refused' Waller, *The Unseen War in Europe*, pp.191 et seq.

153 'received full details' Braunschweig, *Secret Channel to Berlin*, p.405 fn 17

153 'On 30 April, Hitler' Shirer, *The Rise and Fall of the Third Reich*, p.830

153 'At the end of May' Gatard, *La Source MAD*, p.136

153 '22 April' Radó, *Sous le Pseudonyme Dora*, p.140

154 'two further reports' Garlinski, *The Swiss Corridor*, pp.61 and 64; Radó, *Sous le Pseudonyme Dora*, pp.141 and 192; and Foote, *Handbook for Spies*, p.81

154 '6 June' Garlinski, *The Swiss Corridor*, p.60, and Radó, *Sous le Pseudonyme Dora*, p.138 (note the date difference between these sources)

154 'a US-decrypted telegram' Laqueur & Breitman, *Breaking the Silence*, p.102

154 '17 June' Radó, *Sous le Pseudonyme Dora*, p.141

154 'When Marshal Semyon Timoshenko' Waller, *The Unseen War in Europe*, p.207

155 'We have a' Braithwaite, *Moscow 1941*, p.58, quoting S. Stepashin (ed.), *Organy Gosudarstvenni Bezopasnosti SSSR Vol 1, Nakanune*, Moscow, 1995, pp.286–96

155 'Sparrows chirped' Ibid.

155 'heard the news' Evidence of Halina's daughter Marysia

155 'To the Director' Garlinski, *The Swiss Corridor*, p.64

17: General Winter

158 '*2 July*' Ibid., p.66
158 'On 23 August' Ibid.
158 '*6 September*' Höhne, *Codeword Direktor*, p.61 (from Flicke papers)
159 'twice a week' TNA KV 2/1648/1
159 'Helene Radó pitched in' TNA KV 2/1647/3
159 'the astonishing rate' TNA KV 2/1611/2
159 'Margrit Bolli, alias "Rosy"' Also 'Rosie' or 'Rosa'
160 'with her work' TNA KV 21612/1
160 'one-bedroomed flat' TNA KV 2/1404
160 'German listening stations' Garlinski, *The Swiss Corridor*, p.68
160 '*Radó for Director*' Höhne, *Codeword Direktor*, p.61 (from Flicke papers)
160 '*27 October*' Radó, *Sous le Pseudonyme Dora*, p.157
161 'on support from' Jeffery, *MI6*, p.381
161 '*29 October*' Radó, *Sous le Pseudonyme Dora*, p.156
161 'If we do not' Orbach, *The Plots Against Hitler*, p.127, quoting Bodo Scheurig, *Henning von Tresckow: Ein Preusse gegen Hitler*, Berlin, Propyläen, 1987, p.130, and Alexander Stahlberg, *Die Verdammte Pflicht: Erinnerungen 1932–1945*, Berlin, Ullstein, 1994, p.222
163 'This war … is irrevocably' Orbach, *The Plots Against Hitler*, p.128
163 'Poland was nothing' Colonel Helmuth Stieff
163 'A senior officer' Fest, *Plotting Hitler's Death*, p.179. The incident took place in Kovno, now Kaunas, 90 kilometres west of Vilnius, between 25 and 29 June 1941
163 '6,500 Jews' An eyewitness report written by an Abwehr office on this atrocity was sent to Lahousen. It can be found at https://forum.axishistory.com//viewtopic.php?t=62301. Also Gersdorff, *Tuer Hitler*, pp.138–40, and Schlabrendorff, *The Secret War Against Hitler*, p.175 (Schlabrendorff speaks about 5,000 Jews)
163 'by a Wehrmacht officer' Heinrich von Lehndorff-Steinort
164 'the Himmler-appointed civilian commissioner' Wilhelm Kube
164 'SS units slaughtered' TNA KV 2/173
164 '*The [Abwehr] is up against*' Amort & Jedicka, *The Canaris File*, p.114
164 'now conceded that' Ritter, *The German Resistance*, p.231
164 'a new draft constitution' Ibid.
164 'with Canaris's agreement' Höhne, *Canaris*, p.477
165 'the president of the General Motors Overseas Corporation' James Mooney
165 'an approach was made' *Canaris*, p.477
165 'a Jewish Abwehr agent in Stockholm and his female bridge partner' Edgar Klaus and Alexandra Kollontai
165 'the head of army personnel' Colonel Gustav von Ziehlberg
165 'prepared to do anything' Hoffmann, *The History of the German Resistance*, p.269
165 'prepared a shadow government' TNA FO 371/30893, 1942 Germany File No. 10, papers 10–1076: Report from the Polish Ambassador to the Holy See of 16 December

18: The Great God of Prague

167 'René's last reports' Amort & Jedicka, *The Canaris File*, p.127
168 'We are going to' Ibid.
168 'Traitor X' Ibid., p.146
168 'One of the radio operators' Jindřich Klečka
168 'but the other' Antonín Němeček
169 'Two were senior RSHA figures' Karl Frank and Hans-Ulrich Geschke
170 'I will not hide' Brissaud, *Canaris: chef de l'espionnage*, pp.356–7 (Schellenberg interview with Brissaud after the war)
171 'You can never tell' Höhne, *Canaris*, p.468, quoting from Gert Buchheit, *Der Deutsche Geheimdienst*, Munich, 1966, p.84

171 'some kind of Catholic mystic' Abshagen, *Canaris*, pp.16–17
172 'We walked through' The narrator is MI6 Agent Desmond Bristow, Bristow & Bristow, *Un Juego de Topos*, Ed. B. Barcelona (España), 1993, pp.98 et seq. With thanks to Alfonso Esquadra (translation by Prof Gareth Williams)
173 'one of his Balkan experts' Colonel Otto Wagner
173 'We ought to open' Höhne, *Canaris*, p.469, from Gert Buchheit, *Der Deutsche Geheimdienst*, Munich, 1966, p.85
173 'It was about this time' Bassett, *Hitler's Spy Chief*, p.230, quoting a private information
173 'Canaris himself' Popov, *Spy Counterspy*, p.62, and Bassett, *Hitler's Spy Chief*, p.22
174 'There, at a meeting' Amort & Jedicka, *The Canaris File*, p.141
174 'A bit like a lovers' tiff' Bassett, *Hitler's Spy Chief*, p.231, quoting a source in British Intelligence
175 'The assassination would not' Bassett, *Hitler's Spy Chief*, p.235
176 'This signal was shown to' According to some sources, Czech president in exile Benes also saw the signal. One source claims that he asked for the views of the local resistance to be respected. Another indicates that he ordered that no reply should be sent. See Callum Macdonald, 'The Assassination of Reinhard Heydrich', Birlinn, 2007, pp.188–90, quoting from Stanislas F. Berton, 'Who Ordered the Assassination of Reinhard Heydrich and Why?', unpublished
176 'the head of Czech Intelligence in London' František Morávec
176 'I learned after' Bassett, *Hitler's Spy Chief*, p.263
176 'Lahousen had warned' Gatard, *La Source MAD*, p.128
177 'a senior SD officer in the Paris Gestapo' Helmut Knocken
177 'On 17 September 1942' We can identify the precise date from Bletchley decrypts which identify that the only two evenings Canaris was in Paris in this month was 17/18 September (see TNA KV 3/3)
177 'Well, *Langer*' Höhne, *Canaris*, p.475, and Abshagen, *Canaris*, p.196
177 'Canaris told Lahousen' TNA KV 2/173

19: Rebound

180 'two of his resistance colleagues' Johannes Popitz and Ulrich von Hassell
180 'be able to obtain' Ritter, *The German Resistance*, p.216
180 'then we spoke of' Dalton, *Second World War Diary*, p.275, entry for 26 August 1941
180 'absolute silence' TNA PREM 4/100/8 (Churchill to Eden, December 1940 and September 1941)
181 'Phrases such as' Ritter, *The German Resistance*, p.218
181 'five-day visit to Stockholm' Nylander, *The German Resistance Movement and England*, op. cit., p.20 https://www.wallenberg.com/arkiv/sites/default/files/files/Arkivet/Bocker/german_resistance_movement_and_england.pdf
181 'to get a preliminary' Ibid., p.28
181 'I … tried to make' Ibid., p.29
181 'he declared that' Ritter, *The German Resistance*, p.233
181 'the Swedish military attaché in Berlin' Colonel Curt Juhlin-Dannfelt
182 'enabling Canaris to' Ibid.
182 'formally nominated' Entry of 28 March 1942 in *Ulrich von Hassell Diaries*, p.160
182 'the technical centre' Anonymous, Munzinger Archives, 'ME-O: (Oster) 8.12.1962, 1128, Hans Oster (former German general)'. (See Tittenhofer, 'The Rote Drei', op. cit.)
182 'He once described' Gisevius, *To the Bitter End*, p.424
183 'The so-called' Abshagen, *Canaris*, p.122
183 'The Abwehr organization' Anonymous, Munzinger Archives, 'ME-O: (Oster) 8.12.1962, 1128, Hans Oster (former German general)'. (See Tittenhofer, 'The Rote Drei', op. cit.)
183 'particularly powerful' Fest, *Plotting Hitler's Death*, p.191
183 'two co-conspirators' Rudolf-Christoph von Gersdorff and Fabian von Schlabrendorff

183 'They finally settled' Fest, *Plotting Hitler's Death*, p.191, and Gersdorff, *Tuer Hitler*, pp.167–70
183 'a bit like a biro' Mortimer, *The SBS in World War II*, p.54
183 'met Dietrich Bonhoeffer in Stockholm' Dr Hans Schönfeld was also present
184 'satisfied that it is not' Fest, *Plotting Hitler's Death*, p.208
184 'an American journalist in Berlin' Ludwig 'Louis' Lochner, head of the Berlin Associated Press Bureau
184 'in an awkward position' Fest, *Plotting Hitler's Death*, p.210, and Klemperer, *German Resistance Against Hitler*, pp.233–4
184 'coded message' Tarrant, *The Red Orchestra*, p.49–50, and Puenter, *Guerre Secrète en pays neutre*, p.133
185 'significantly reduced' Timothy P. Mulligan, 'Spies, Ciphers and "Zitadelle": Intelligence and the Battle of Kursk, 1943', *Journal of Contemporary History*, Vol. 22 (1987), pp.235–60, p.241 – quoting F.H. Hinsley, *British Intelligence in the Second World War: Its Influence on Strategy and Operations*, Vol. 2, pp.616–27, 658–66, Vol. 3, pp.477–87; and Janus Piekalkiewicz, *Unternehmen Zitadelle*, Bergisch Gladbach, 1983, pp.63–8, 75, 91, 17
185 'an exceptional agent' 'Knopf', Agent 594 – probably Isidore Koppelmann
185 'Other couriers' Theodore and Elisabeth Strünck, Eduard Schulte and the half-American, half-German Dr Eduard Waetjen
185 'a disgruntled Swiss employee' Named Fuerst
186 'wastepaper basket' TNA KV 2/1329/2
186 'Waibel was removed' Ibid.
186 '5,500 clandestine messages' Tittenhofer, 'The Rote Drei', op. cit.
186 'Almost every offensive' Garlinski, *The Swiss Corridor*, p.78, quoting from an interview with General Halder in an article in *Der Spiegel*, 16.01.1967
186 'within twenty-four hours' Dulles, *The Craft of Intelligence*, p.105. In *Sous le Pseudonyme Dora*, p.217, Radó says it took three to six days
186 'by secure Abwehr channels' In *Sous le Pseudonyme Dora*, pp.222–3, Radó says that the information was passed by telephone to the Abwehr station in Milan
187 'From here ... concourse' Peter Kamber, '"Die Macht der Gesinnung" und "das romantische Ich": Rudolf Roessler und der deutsche Widerstand 1939 – 1944', in Exil: Forschung, Erkenntnisse, Ergebnisse 31 (2011) 1, S. 87–105 [Über den anonym arbeitenden Journalisten Roessler (1897–1958)], p.91 (translation by Philip Cole); and Radó, *Sous le Pseudonyme Dora*, p.223
187 'a diplomatic pouch' Tittenhofer, 'The Rote Drei', op. cit.
187 'For very urgent' Ibid.
187 'By the late spring' NL Hans Bernd Gisevius/4.6.3 *Persönliche Aufzeichnungen über einige Erlebnisse, die ich im Zusammenhang mit der Person des Oberstdivisionär (Brigadier) Masson gehabt habe (verf. von Hans Bernd Gisevius, 5.2.1945), MS 15 S*, – Archiv für Zeitgeschichte, Zürich; with thanks to Peter Kamber (translation by Philip Cole)
187 'started sending agents' Garlinski, *The Swiss Corridor*, p.141

20: Codes and Contacts
188 'Sometime in mid-September' Claude Arnould's account of this was given during his final illness in 1974. According to his recollection the event took place in August, but there is no record from the Bletchley decrypts of the Abwehr administrative net that Canaris was in Paris in August. We know he was there from 16 to 19 September 1942 (TNA KV 3/3, p.16), and I have therefore placed this event during that period
188 'a most unusual' Testimony of Claude Arnould, written before his death, giving an account of his two meetings with Admiral Canaris; typed document sent to Professeur Michel Bergès on 17 March 1982 by Claude Arnould's daughter, Marie-Thérèse Raphanaud-Arnould

188 'recounted by Arnould' Ibid., and Ordioni, *La fracture*, pp.237 et seq

189 'in the early winter' Höhne, *Canaris*, pp.481 et seq.

189 'in the process of' Ibid., p.489, quoting Franz Josef Furtwängler, *Männer die ich sah und kannte*, Hamburg, 1951, p.211

190 'carpet layers' Fest, *Plotting Hitler's Death*, p.218, quoting Eberhard Zeller, *Geist der Freiheit*, Taschenbuchausg., 1956, pp.246–7

190 'Kill him' Ibid., p.244

190 'The point is no longer' Ibid., p.217, quoting from Joachim Kramarz, *Stauffenberg: The Architect of the Famous July 20th Conspiracy to Assassinate Hitler*, New York, 1967, p.113

190 'not a day to lose' Ibid., p.192, quoting from Count Romedio Galeazzo von Thun-Hohenstein, *Der Verschwörer: General Oster und die Militäropposition*, Cologne and Berlin, 1969, p.224

191 'On 17 July 1942' Laqueur & Breitman, *Breaking the Silence*, p.14, and Ritter, *The German Resistance*, p.218

191 'leading Jewish institutions' Ibid., p.120

191 'In early October 1942' Orbach, *The Plots Against Hitler*, p.195, quoting Axel von dem Bussche, ed. Gevinon von Medem, *Eid und Schuld*, Mainz, Hase & Koehler, 1994, p.138

191 'to die in battle' Fest, *Plotting Hitler's Death*, p.224

191 'describing the executions' Gatard, *La Source MAD*, p.166

192 '*8 October*' Tittenhofer, 'The Rote Drei', op. cit., p.3

192 '*21 October*' TNA KV 2/1611/3, Rote Drei W/T traffic (translation by Philip Cole)

192 '*Early November*' Radó, *Sous le Pseudonyme Dora*, p.237

193 '*19 December*' TNA KV 2/1611/3: Rote Drei W/T traffic (translation by Philip Cole)

193 '*22 December*' TNA KV 2/1611/3: Rote Drei W/T traffic (translation by Philip Cole)

194 '*The Statistical Handbook*' TNA KV 2/1611/1

195 'More likely, the investigators' Foote, *Handbook for Spies*, pp.126–7

21: Of Spies and Spy Chiefs

197 'Dulles's first act' Srodes, *Allen Dulles*, p.229

197 'bringing to my door' Von Hassell & MacRae, *Alliance of Enemies*, p.136, and Srodes, *Allen Dulles*, p.227

198 'the price of intelligence' Rossé, *Guerre Secrète en Suisse*, p.158

198 'It has been requested' Mark Murphy, 'The Exploits of Agent 110', CIA (https://www.cia.gov/library/center-for-the-study-of-intelligence/kent-csi/vol37no1/html/v37i1a05p_0001.htm) quoting from OSS/Director's Files: Telegram 8/19, WJD to Dulles, 29 April 1943

198 'a source with high-level contacts' Fritz Kolbe, alias 'George Wood'

198 'at weekly meetings' Braunschweig, *Secret Channel to Berlin*, p.205

198 'used some words' Speech given by Stalin on 19 October 1942, published in *Pravda*, TNA FO 371/30922/C11013

199 'one of his agents' Peter Kleist

199 'Among the key' Bassett, *Hitler's Spy Chief*, p.254

200 'You are a good' Ritter, *The German Resistance*, p.211, quoting a personal conversation with Jacob Wallenberg

200 'in order to ensure' Quoted in Bassett, *Hitler's Spy Chief*, p.256

201 'submitted for security clearance' Ibid., p.23

201 'Philby absolutely forbade' Trevor-Roper, *The Secret World*, pp.45–6, 106–7

201 'his handler at the Soviet embassy' Ivan Chichayev, alias 'Vadim'

201 'I want no action' Knightley, *Philby*, pp.105–6

201 'He hoped ... that' Bassett, *Hitler's Spy Chief*, p.257, quoting private information

201 'for fear of offending Russia' Deacon, *A History of the British Secret Service*, p.282

201 'would certainly not have' Winterbotham, *Secret and Personal*, p.162

201 'a splendid lunch' Winterbotham, *The Ultra Secret*, p.126
201 'a senior MI6 colleague' Frederic Winterbotham
201 'a close colleague' Karl Abshagen
202 'threw off his' Abshagen, *Canaris*, p.216
202 'General Mason MacFarlane' Colvin, *Admiral Canaris*, p.158
202 'an OSS officer visiting Cairo' Colonel Ulius Amoss
202 'Canaris would like' Mueller, *Canaris*, pp.220–1, and Cave Brown, *The Last Hero*, p.292
202 'a blanket prohibition' Ibid.
202 'an Abwehr officer who claimed' F. Justus von Einem
202 'Donovan, his British' Höhne, *Canaris*, p.486, quoting a letter from F. Justus von Einem of 29 December 1967. In 1984, however, Höhne said that there was no unequivocal proof that Canaris, Donovan and Menzies actually met, according to Klemperer, *German Resistance Against Hitler*, pp.396–7 fn 3

22: Mistake, Misjudgement, Misfire

203 'It was probably' There are other interpretations of this story in Arsenovic, *Genève appelle Moscou*, pp.127–30, and Radó, *Sous le Pseudonyme Dora*, pp.201–5
203 'paying daily visits' Accoce & Quet, *La guerre a été gagnée en Suisse*, p.128
203 'scanned the airwaves' Christian Rossé, *Les échanges de l'ombre*, thèse de Sciences Humaines, Université de Neufchatel et Université de Technologie de Belfort-Montbéliard, 30 September 2013, p.212
204 'On 9 November' Garlinski, *The Swiss Corridor*, p.134, and Bourgeois, *La véritable histoire de l'Orchestre Rouge*, p.228
204 'It was not long' Foote, *Handbook for Spies*, p.125
205 'Hans Peters, whose' TNA KV 2/1621/1
205 'an uncoded message' Garlinski, *The Swiss Corridor*, p.147
205 'chaos and revolution' Petersen, *From Hitler's Doorstep*, p.30, and OSS Archives, RG226, Natinal Archives, Washington DC
205 'the secretary general of the World Council of Churches' Dr Willem Visser t'Hooft
205 'It appears that' Tel. 314, ibid., pp.30–1
206 'At about the same time' Ritter, *The German Resistance*, p.263
206 'Peace can come' Beschloss, *The Conquerors*, pp.13–14, and Lamb, *The Ghosts of Peace*, p.222
207 'at the last minute' The formula was recorded, and according to Eisenhower (in *Crusade in Europe*) was mentioned in the American Joint Chiefs of Staff minutes of 7 January 1943: Colvin, *Admiral Canaris*, p.163, and Lamb, *The Ghosts of Peace*, p.222 and fn, quoting TNA PREM 3/476/9
207 'I think unconditional' Frank Roberts, as reported by Richard Lamb, *The Ghosts of Peace*, pp.222–3
207 'Perfect!' Ibid.
207 'Hear! Hear!' Ibid.
207 'One senior official' William Cavendish-Bentinck to Alexander Cadogan, recounted by Cavendish-Bentinck to Richard Lamb, *The Ghosts of Peace*, p.223
208 'total slavery' Dulles, *Germany's Underground*, p.132
208 'Our generals will not' Colvin, *Admiral Canaris*, p.163 (reported by Lahousen in an interview with Colvin after the war)
208 'by revealing to' Adams, *Historical Dictionary of German Intelligence*, p.141
208 'This caused panic' Dulles, *Germany's Underground*, p.131
208 'Prussian field marshals' Gersdorff, *Tuer Hitler*, p.188 (Gersdorff's conversation with Manstein)
209 'Dulles entertained' Garlinski, *The Swiss Corridor*, p.131. Maximilian Egon Hohenlohe report on meeting with Dulles, Berlin 30 April 1943. Documents of Department VI of the RSHA, in Edwards & Dunne, *A Study of a Master Spy*, pp.29–33

210 'a very special' TNA KV 4/83

210 'Canaris had once again' Fritz Hesse report of 19 February, TNA GFM 33/1087
      (translation by Philip Cole)

210 'a tetchy atmosphere' Klemperer, *German Resistance Against Hitler*, p.341; Fest, *Plotting
      Hitler's Death*, p.164

210 'Goerdeler should be' Hoffmann, *The History of the German Resistance*, p.367

211 'It's time to act' Bassett, *Hitler's Spy Chief*, p.264

211 'Have your people' German Intelligence Service (WWII), Vol. 2_0007.pdf, Report by
      Major General Lahousen, 17 December 1945

211 'It would be good' Bassett, *Hitler's Spy Chief*, p.264 (Reinhard Spitzy describing Canaris to
      Pr. Deutsch)

211 'You will be judged' Ibid.

212 'to a friend' Major General Helmuth Stieff

212 'I waited until' Ibid., p.238

213 'After gently' Ibid.

213 'Almost immediately' Ibid., p.180

213 'In the event' Ibid., pp.183–4

214 'Entitled "The Aim"' Ritter, *The German Resistance*, p.239

23: The Worm Turns

215 'the morning of 5 March' Braunschweig, *Secret Channel to Berlin*, photo opposite p.234

216 'ward off any danger' Ibid., p.195

216 'The balance [of power]' Ibid.

216 'and a colleague' Captain Paul Meyer-Schwertenbach

217 'a Swiss spy captured in Stuttgart' Ernst Mörgeli

217 'A German Operation' Braunschweig, *Secret Channel to Berlin*, p.224. Viking's
      informant's warning came from his German liaison person at the staff of the German
      Armed Forces High Command, and therefore must have been, directly or indirectly, from
      Oster

218 'a senior judge' Manfred Roeder; 'an SS officer' Franz Xaver Sonderegger

218 'Abwehr agents' The operation, which Canaris was aware of, was codenamed
      'Unternehmen Sieben' (Operation U–7). See Artist report of 7 October 1943, TNA HW
      19/325; Orbach, *The Plots Against Hitler*, pp.151–8, and Mueller, *Canaris*, pp.226–8

218 'conspiratorial vacuum' Gisevius, *Valkyrie*, p.106

218 'general manager' Schlabrendorff, *The Secret War Against Hitler*, p.246

219 'a medium-level plotter' Colonel Friedrich 'Fritz' Jäger

219 'I have been warned' *Ulrich von Hassell Diaries*, entry 20 Apr 1943, p.195

219 'How is it possible' Rothfels, *The German Opposition to Hitler*, p.86

219 'informing Madeleine' Gatard, *La Source MAD*, p.176

220 'Only now his' Orbach, *The Plots Against Hitler*, p.142, quoting from Peter M. Kaiser, *Mut
      zum Bekenntnis*, Lukas Verlag, 2010, pp.463, 465–6

220 'one general complained' General Edgar Röhricht

220 'scourge of God' Fest, *Plotting Hitler's Death*, p.213

220 'had to be persuaded' Ibid.

220 '*My Dear General*' Wheeler-Bennett, *The Nemesis of Power*, pp.567–9

221 'It proposed a detailed new' Ritter, *The German Resistance*, pp.221–2, and Nylander, *The
      German Resistance Movement and England*, op. cit., p.35 (https://www.wallenberg.com/
      arkiv/sites/default/files/files/Arkivet/Bocker/german_resistance_movement_and_
      england.pdf)

221 'commenting … "one of Canaris's"' Minute from Warner to Nichols, 30 May 1943, TNA
      FO 1093/287

221 'There have recently' Ibid.

221 'Eden responded' Rothfels, *The German Opposition to Hitler*, p.136

222 'Kittyhawk fighter bombers' Probably from No. 3 Squadron of the Royal Australian Air Force
222 'Radó warned Moscow Centre' Mulligan, 'Spies, Cyphers and "Zitadelle"', op. cit., p.241
222 'John Cairncross' Ibid., and Gannon, Stealing Secrets, Telling Lies, p.165
223 'I was convinced' Bassett, Hitler's Spy Chief, p.254, quoting Rüdiger von Manstein & Theodor Fuchs, Manstein: Soldat im 20 Jahrhundert Militärisch-politische Nachlese, Munich, 1981
224 'use it as a channel' Mulligan, 'Spies, Cyphers and "Zitadelle"', op. cit., p.238
224 'an attack on the Kursk salient' Ibid., p.241
224 'To the Director' Garlinski, The Swiss Corridor, p.139
224 'Our information about' Mulligan, 'Spies, Cyphers and "Zitadelle"', op. cit., p.243
224 'From Radó' Ibid., p.239
225 'The Russians have anticipated' Mungo, Manstein, p.363, quoting a handwritten note by Reinhard Gehlen dated 4 July 1943

24: The End of Dora
227 'Heinz Pannwitz' Höhne, Codeword Direktor, p.230
227 'a security scare' Hamel was arrested and spent some days in jail for political activity totally unconnected with his work for the Rote Drei – TNA KV 2/1625
227 'in May had moved' TNA KV 2/1611/2. The move was finished on 24 May 1943
227 'a Franco-German Jewish journalist' Ewald Zweig
227 '"Laura" and "Lorenz"' Their real names were Charles and Elsa Martin. See Foote, Handbook for Spies, pp.113 et seq., and Radó, Sous le Pseudonyme Dora, pp.359–60
228 'Schellenberg knew' TNA KV 2/1611/2
228 'revealed the lie' TNA KV 2/1611/2
228 'Director to Dora' Tittenhofer, 'The Rote Drei', op. cit., and Flicke analysis TNA KV 2/1611/2 (translation by Philip Cole)
229 'On 8 July … address too' TNA KV 2/1611/2
229 'Dear Sissy' Tittenhofer, 'The Rote Drei', op. cit.
230 'Gisevius met' NL Hans Bernd Gisevius/4.6.3 Persönliche Aufzeichnungen über einige Erlebnisse, die ich im Zusammenhang mit der Person des Oberstdivisionär (-Brigadier) Masson gehabt habe (verf. von Hans Bernd Gisevius, 5.2.1945), MS 15 S, – Archiv für Zeitgeschichte, Zürich; with thanks to Peter Kamber (translation by Philip Cole)
230 'On 10 September' Garlinski, The Swiss Corridor, p.153, and Arsenovic, Genève appelle Moscou, p.142
230 'a very strong radio signal' Rossé, Les échanges de l'ombre, op. cit., p.211
231 'Bolli reported' TNA KV 2/1612/1, and Garlinski, The Swiss Corridor, p.154
231 'probably be in danger' TNA KV 2/1404, Tittenhofer, 'The Rote Drei', op. cit., and TNA KV 2/1611/2
231 'They rushed to' TNA KV 2/1612/1, Arsenovic, Genève appelle Moscou, p.164
231 'As Radó approached' TNA KV 2/1612/2
231 'Edouard has been' Arsenovic, Genève appelle Moscou, p.166
232 'Schellenberg arrived' Garlinski, The Swiss Corridor, p.156
232 'long circuitous routes' TNA KV 2/1612/1
232 'He reached out' TNA KV/2/1611/2; TNA KV 2/1647/3; Foote, Handbook for Spies, pp.131–2
232 'You must do' TNA KV 2/1611/2 (translation by Philip Cole)
233 'You can and must' TNA KV 2/1627 (translation by Philip Cole)
233 'an ex-Swiss army wireless' TNA KV 2/1212/1
233 'Later the Swiss' TNA KV 2/1647/3, KV 2/161/2, KV 2/1611/2, KV 2/1616/2; Arsenovic, Genève appelle Moscou, p.161
233 'Moscow Centre kept on trying' TNA KV 2/1611/2
233 'accepted that he must' Garlinski, The Swiss Corridor, p.153

234 'a single-roomed attic' Ibid., p.163
234 'a small chalet' TNA KV 2/1647/3; Radó, *Sous le Pseudonyme Dora*, pp.393–5; TNA FO 371/48006
234 'all his relatives' TNA KV 2/1649 Intercepted letter to a friend in 1945; and Radó, *Sous le Pseudonyme Dora*, p.399
234 'only the lightest' Garlinski, *The Swiss Corridor*, p.173

25: Enter Stauffenberg

235 'a secret meeting' Under the direction of General Walter Warlimont
235 'You gentlemen know' TNA KV 2/173
235 'no confidence' Ibid.
235 'It was clear' Ibid.
235 'the head of the Abwehr station in Rome' Major Otto Helferich
236 'General Amè is ready' TNA KV 3/3
236 'The previous meeting' Holt, *The Deceivers*, p.123
236 'It was a brilliant' Information from Mark Beswick, Archive Information Officer, Met Office National Meteorological Archive, 4 Sep 2017
236 'Canaris presented him' TNA KV 2/173 p.99
236 'Be careful' TNA KV 2/173
236 'Thank you Amè' Brissaud, *Canaris: chef de l'espionnage*, p.415
236 'Afterwards the party' TNA KV 2/173
237 'Heartiest congratulation' Brissaud, *Canaris: chef de l'espionnage*, p.415
237 'Take my advice' Ibid.
237 'urging his friend' Holt, *The Deceivers*, p.123; Höhne, *Canaris*, p.531; Riebling, *Church of Spies*, p.176
237 'He loved Germany' *Canaris: chef de l'espionnage*, p.415
237 'not portend any' Bassett, *Hitler's Spy Chief*, p.275, quoting ADSS 7.439 and 458 (Vatican archives)
237 'is no need' Lamb, *The Ghosts of Peace*, p.224. For the full minute see TNA PREM 4/100/8
238 'I am sure' Ibid.
238 'Otto Skorzeny' TNA KV 23/3
238 'the old man in peace' Bassett, *Hitler's Spy Chief*, p.278, quoting *Memoiren*, Walter Schellenberg, Cologne, 1956
238 'The head of the local Abwehr station' Hans Meissner
238 'take care that' TNA KV 3/3
239 '*My Dear Field Marshal*' Wheeler-Bennett, *The Nemesis of Power*, pp.570–4
239 'interesting information' Ritter, *The German Resistance*, p.223
240 'a highly secret exchange', Nylander, *The German Resistance Movement and England*, op. cit., pp.36 et seq., and Bennett, *Churchill's Man of Mystery*, pp.236–7
242 'Anyone could' Ritter, *The German Resistance*, p.242
242 'His glowing eyes' Orbach, *The Plots Against Hitler*, p.162, quoting Eberhard Zeller, *Oberst Claus Graf Stauffenberg: Ein Lebensbild*, Schöningh, Paderborn, 1994, pp.14–15
244 'a piece of lint' Gisevius, *Valkyrie*, p.133
244 'a duty' Eltscher, *Traitors or Patriots?*, p.300
245 'It's time for me' Orbach, *The Plots Against Hitler*, p.180; Hoffmann, *Stauffenberg*, p.183
245 'The army alone' Ibid., p.302
245 'It is too late' Gisevius, *Valkyrie*, pp.135–6
245 'the High Priest' Eltscher, *Traitors or Patriots?*, p.301
245 'The Anti-Christ' Manvell and Fraenkel, *The Men Who Tried to Kill Hitler*, p.228

26: Valkyrie and Tehran

246 'internal disturbances' Hoffmann, *The History of the German Resistance*, p.302
246 'Hitler himself had' Fest, *Plotting Hitler's Death*, p.219
247 '"Swallow" and "Seagull"' Orbach, *The Plots Against Hitler*, p.198
247 'Every Friday evening' Hoffmann, *Stauffenberg*, p.199
247 'to keep open' Schlabrendorff, *The Secret War Against Hitler*, p.186
248 'Under no circumstances' Hoffmann, *Stauffenberg*, p.198
248 'always came down' Fest, *Plotting Hitler's Death*, p.220
248 'recorded the approach' Ibid., p.221
249 'the first' Major General Helmuth Stieff
249 'the second' Colonel Joachim Miechssner
249 'was put in touch' By Fritz-Dietlof von der Schulenberg
249 'a mass execution' See Chapter 20
249 'The plan was' Fest, *Plotting Hitler's Death*, pp.224–5, and Hoffmann, *The History of the German Resistance*, pp.325–8
249 'The sunny late-autumn' Fest, *Plotting Hitler's Death*, p.224, quoting Eberhard Zeller, *Geist der Freiheit*, p.334
250 'The two men assigned' Major Joachim Kuhn and Lieutenant Albrecht von Hagen
250 'a friend of Hans Oster's' Lieutenant Colonel Werner Schrader
250 'A cranky' Manvell and Fraenkel, *The Men Who Tried to Kill Hitler*, p.77, and Hoffmann, *The History of the German Resistance*, p.366
251 'had to work hard' Ritter, *The German Resistance*, pp.270 et seq.
253 'Now the fate of Europe' Beevor, *The Second World War*, p.513
253 'Germany is to be' Churchill letter from Downing Street, 15 January 1944, Lamb, *The Ghosts of Peace*, p.227

27: Disappointment, Disruption, Desperation

255 'very well read' Cave Brown, *The Last Hero*, p.360
256 'Now all is lost' Klemperer, *German Resistance Against Hitler*, p.331, quoting from Balfour & Frisby, *Helmuth von Moltke*, p.273
256 'an OSS agent in Istanbul' Archibald Coleman (codename 'Snapdragon')
257 'on my own responsibility' Cave Brown, *The Last Hero*, p.363, letter Alexander Kirk to Richard Tindall – 10 January 1944, Plan Herman File OSSDF
258 'Vermehren applied' TNA KV 3/3, 22 September 1943
259 'colleagues had remarked on' Höhne, *Canaris*, p.551
260 'Allied intelligence policy' Cave Brown, *The Last Hero*, p.408, and Waller, *The Unseen War in Europe*, pp.237–8, referring to how Abwehr agents' defections would undermine Canaris and put the Double-Cross system at risk
260 'Lahousen was sent' TNA KV 2/173
261 'He got straight to' Orbach, *The Plots Against Hitler*, p.203, quoting a 1998 interview with Ewald-Heinrich von Kleist-Schmenzin
261 'You have to do it' Ibid.
262 'That swine' Peter Yorck von Wartenburg; Gersdorff, *Tuer Hitler*, p.198
262 'the field marshal's adjutant' Eberhard von Breitenbuch
262 'You only do' Hoffmann, *The History of the German Resistance*, p.336

28: The Tip of the Spear

263 'a courier' Eduard Waetjen
263 'They are anxious' Petersen, *From Hitler's Doorstep*, p.263, and OSS Archives, RG226, National Archives, Washington DC
263 'Group prepared' Ibid.
264 'some Nazi generals' Ibid., p.289

264 'assassination was certain' Ritter, *The German Resistance*, p.221, and Nylander, *The German Resistance Movement and England*, op. cit., p.35 (https://www.wallenberg.com/arkiv/sites/default/files/files/Arkivet/Bocker/german_resistance_movement_and_england.pdf)

264 'They would have to' Ritter, *The German Resistance*, p.272

265 'his jailer' Lieutenant Colonel Albrecht Focke

265 'Admiral Canaris will be' Höhne, *Canaris*, p.557, and p.657 fn 9, quoting a letter dated 21 March 1944 from the Naval Personnel Department OKM to HQ Baltic Command, Canaris Personal File

265 'one of Canaris's Swedish friends' Baron Vladimir Kaulbars

265 'the Admiral's removal' Höhne, *Canaris*, p.561, quoting Kaltenbrunner report to Bormann of 29 September 1944, in *Spiegelbild einer Verschwöhrung*, p.425

265 'get a message through' Cave Brown, *Bodyguard of Lies*, p.595. Gerald Philip George Keun DSO, alias 'l'Amiral' ('Ami'), was the other part, with Claude Arnould, alias 'Colonel Ollivier' ('Col'), of 'Amicol', the MI6 French resistant network Jade-Amicol

266 'also the headquarters' Ibid.

266 'Canaris seemed' Ibid., p.599

266 'the mother superior' Henriette Frédé, known as Mère Jean

266 'simple but wholesome meal' Cave Brown, *Bodyguard of Lies*, p.599

266 '*Finis Germaniae*' Ibid., and testimony of Claude Arnould, written before his death, giving an account of his two meetings with Canaris; typed document sent to Professeur Michel Bergès on 17 March 1982 by Arnould's daughter, Marie-Thérèse Raphanaud-Arnould

267 'two old Abwehr colleagues' Colonel Wessel Freytag-Loringhoven and Lieutenant Colonel Werner Schrader

267 'a mutual friend' Lieutenant Heinrich Ahasverus Graf von Lehndorff-Steinort

267 'The attempt must' Ritter, *The German Resistance*, p.275, and Schlabrendorff, *The Secret War Against Hitler*, p.277

268 'The most terrible thing' Hoffmann, *Stauffenberg*, p.243

268 'It is quite clear' Ibid., p.237

268 'Finally a general staff officer' Fest, *Plotting Hitler's Death*, p.237

268 'always came down on the right side' Ibid., p.220

268 'in a daze' Ibid., p.238

268 'flew to the Berghof' Hoffmann, *Stauffenberg*, p.253

268 'yet another newly-recruited assassin' Major General Helmuth Stieff

268 'all the stuff' Hoffmann, *Stauffenberg*, p.253

269 '*Germans!*' Orbach, *The Plots Against Hitler*, p.199

269 'nineteen names' Hoffmann, *The History of the German Resistance*, pp.367–9

270 'Stauffenberg's cousin' Caesar von Hofacker

270 'the leaders of the Solf Circle' Including Nikolaus von Halem, Dr Herbert Mumm von Schwarzenstein and Otto Kiep

270 'an army colonel' Wilhelm Staehle

271 'an Abwehr officer' Ludwig Gehre

271 'It's time now' Hoffmann, *Stauffenberg*, p.243

271 'He did not say' Peter Kamber email to the author, 7 Dec 2017

271 'Hitler's overthrow is not' *Gisevius/Masson* – EN Archiv für Zeitgeschichte NL, Hans Bernd Gisevius/4.6.3 *Personal account of some of my experiences in connection with Brigadier Masson (written by Hans Bernd Gisevius, 5.2.1945), MS 15 pp.Date: 1945*. With thanks to Peter Kamber (translation by Philip Cole)

271 'Good God' Hoffmann, *Stauffenberg*, p.254

272 'disappear as quickly' Fest, *Plotting Hitler's Death*, p.252

272 'a friend's country estate' Baron Kraft von Palombini

272 'a naval officer' Lieutenant Commander Alfred Kranzfelder

29: Thursday, 20 July 1944

273 'an officer in Potsdam' Lieutenant Colonel von der Lancken

274 'a staff officer' Major General Helmuth Stieff

275 'These connected three' SHAEF Psychological Warfare Division Interrogation of eyewitness Karbinsky, 24 March 1945. TNA MSS.154/3/PW/1. With thanks to Bruce Dennis

275 'Facilities in the outer' Hoffmann, *Stauffenberg*, Appendix XI

275 'two senior officers' General Walther Buhle and Lieutenant General Henning von Thadden

276 'a messenger' Staff Sergeant Werner Vögel

277 'the classic image' Ibid., p.266, quoting the words of General Walter Warlimont from an interview

277 'Colonel Count Stauffenberg' Allen W. Dulles Papers, Call no. MC019, Public Policy Papers, Department of Rare Books and Special Collections, Princeton University Library, Box 33, Folder 19, Attempt on Adolf Hitler's life of 20 July 1944, courtesy of Bruce Dennis

277 'A communications officer' Sergeant Major Arthur Adam

277 'one of Hitler's briefers' Colonel Heinz Brandt

278 'In a flash' Jones, *Countdown to Valkyrie*, p.192

278 'The man in charge' Sergeant Kobe

278 'The colonel is not permitted' SHAEF Psychological Warfare Division Interrogation of eyewitness Karbinsky, 24 March 1945, TNA MSS.154/3/PW/1. With thanks to Bruce Dennis

278 'one of the Führer's adjutants' Leonhard von Möllendorff

279 'another conspirator' Quartermaster General Eduard Wagner

279 'tall pillars of' Information from Mark Beswick, Archive Information Officer, Met Office National Meteorological Archive, 27 Sep 2017

279 'Partially paralysed' Allen W. Dulles Papers, Call no. MC019, Public Policy Papers, Department of Rare Books and Special Collections, Princeton University Library – Box 33, Folder 19 – Attempt on Adolf Hitler's life of 20 July 1944

279 'I almost laughed' Junge, *Until the Final Hour*, p.130

280 'After a moment of panic' Jones, *Countdown to Valkyrie*, pp.197–9; Hoffmann, *Stauffenberg*, pp.267–9; and Hoffmann, *The History of the German Resistance*, which details the various testimonies on the timing

280 'two of his colleagues' Mertz von Quirnheim and General Friedrich Thiele

280 'What I will never forget' Ewald Heinrich von Kleist-Schmenzin in Orbach, *The Plots Against Hitler*, p.210

281 'at about five o'clock that afternoon' When he was visited by army judge advocate Karl Sack

281 'According to one version' Höhne, *Canaris*, pp.567–8

281 'For the Führer!' Jones, *Countdown to Valkyrie*, p.232

282 'And now, gentlemen' Hoffmann, *The History of the German Resistance*, p.503

282 'In the name of' Ibid., p.507

283 '*Es lebe das heilige Deutschland*' Jones, *Countdown to Valkyrie*, p.235

283 'One version relates' Hoffmann, *Stauffenberg*, p.353 fn 86

30: Calvary

284 'In a totally calm' Schlabrendorff, *The Secret War Against Hitler*, pp.294–5

284 'Just as God' It seems clear from the German here that von Tresckow is referring to the relevant passage in the Lord's prayer, and I have altered the quoted English translation accordingly

285 'My fellow countrymen!' https://www.theguardian.com/theguardian/1944/jul/21/fromthearchive and https://www.youtube.com/watch?v=LpCwuCzud-E

285 'Providence has decided' Fest, *Plotting Hitler's Death*, p.284, quoting Carl Buchheit, *Der Deutsche Geheimdienst*, Munich, 1966, p.445

285 'narrowly able to slip away' Ritter, *The German Resistance*, pp.288–91, for the facts that follow

285 'an old World War I comrade' Major Ludwig Ehrhardt

286 'with the help of friends' Kurt Schatter, a councillor from Chemnitz, and the ex-lord mayor of Freital, Gustave Klimpel

286 'a junior clerk' Bruno Labedzki

286 'the home of a friend' Hermann Lehman

286 'the pastor of the German Confessional Church' Johannes Lilje

286 'A German pastor' Minister Desert

287 'two friends' Baron Vladimir Kaulbars and his nephew Erwin Delbrück

287 'one of Canaris's ex-colleagues' SS Hauptsturmführer Baron von Völkersam

287 'Somehow I thought' Walter Schellenberg, *The Labyrinth: Memoirs*, p.357

288 'You can have us' *Von Schlabrendorff Diaries*, p.298

289 'They looked like' Kardorff, *Diary of a Nightmare*, p.134

289 'Since National Socialism' Letter to sons (in German), van Roon, G., ed., Berlin, Siedler Verlag, p.6

290 'I still hold today' Höhne, *Canaris*, p.578, quoting a handwritten statement by Canaris found in Kaltenbrunner Reports pp.409–10

290 'His driver' Kurt Kerstenhahn

291 'His last letter' Rothfels, *The German Opposition to Hitler*, p.152

291 'always came down on' Fest, *Plotting Hitler's Death*, p.220

292 'The little admiral took' Höhne, *Canaris*, p.596, quoting Fischer disposition *Die Welt* 1 October 1955

292 'On the morning of' Mark Devine, *Bonhoeffer Speaks Today*, Nashville, Broadman & Holman, 2005, pp.36–7

293 'I die for my' John H. Waller, 'The Double Life of Admiral Canaris', *International Journal of Intelligence and Counterintelligence*, 1996, Vol. 9, part 3, p.287, and Abshagen, *Canaris*, p.255

31: Epilogue

296 'sated, indolent' Chamberlain to Ida, 30 December 1939, quoted in Maurice Cowling, *The Impact of Hitler: British Politics and British Policy 1933–1940*, Cambridge University Press, 2005, p.355

298 'The other principal' TNA PREM 4/100/8

299 'they had never shown' Fest, *Plotting Hitler's Death*, p.336, and Rothfels, *The German Opposition to Hitler*, p.137

299 'A post-war CIA' CIA-RDP78-03362A002500070002-3: The General Intelligence Service and the War

299 'Inefficient, intriguing' All these quotes come from Cave Brown, *The Last Hero*, pp.128–9

300 'Personally, I am not' Memorandum from Churchill to Cadogan, 25 April 1944, TNA FO 371/39024, quoted in Pauline Elkes's thesis 'The Political Warfare Executive: A re-evaluation based upon the intelligence work of the German section', Degree of Doctor of Philosophy, History Department, Sheffield University, May 1996, p.138; with thanks to Peter Dixon for alerting me to this

301 'I do not' Edmund Burke speech, 22 March 1775

32: After Lives

303 'That's one we forgot' Nuremberg trials, 30 November 1945, from Gilbert, *Nuremberg Diary*

304 'when Erich Fellgiebel phoned' Gisevius, *To the Bitter End*, p.544

304 'Alexander Foote slipped over' TNA KV 2/1647/3, Foote, *Handbook for Spies*, p.145

305 'supported by Novikov' TNA KV 2/1647/3

305 'means would be found' Ibid.

305 'only scratched' Arsenovic, *Genève appelle Moscou*, p.253

306 'still displaying suicidal tendencies' TNA KV 2/1649

306 'the man who appears' Ibid.

306 'something to do' Ibid.

306 'we do not wish' TNA KV 2/1647/2

306 'wrote to London' TNA KV 2/1649

306 'of considerable interest' Ibid.

306 'London wrote complaining' TNA KV 2/1647/2, and KV 2/1649

307 'interesting and important' TNA KV 2/1647/1

307 'was finally sent' TNA KV 2/1647/2

307 'a good deal more' Ibid.

307 'at 0200 on 30 July 1945' TNA KV 2/1649/2

308 'My first six weeks' Foote, *Handbook for Spies*, p.180

308 'Rachel Duebendorfer' With thanks to Bernd-Rainer Barth for access to his article 'Goulag et Ordre du Drapeau rouge pour une résistante communiste allemande, Rachel Dübendorfer' of April 2014

308 'on 20 April 1945' There is some evidence that he might have been shot a week later on 27 April, Amort & Jedicka, *The Canaris File*, p.155

309 'a charitable organisation' 'Committee for the Aid of Survivors of the German Resistance', see Allen Dulles Papers, MC019 Box 3, Folders 1 and 2, with thanks to Bruce Dennis for alerting me to these papers. And MC019 Box 57 Folder 10, which includes a letter of thanks for the food parcels from Olbricht's widow, Eva

310 'Dietrich has gone' *Come Before Winter*, documentary directed by Kevin Ekvall, USA, January 2017, 1:02:44

Afterword: Cock-up or Conspiracy?

312 'to a friend' Hans Peters

312 'An interdepartmental group' Balfour & Frisby, *Helmuth von Moltke*, p.135

312 'Oster managed' Gisevius, *To the Bitter End*, p.423

Index